Neoplatonism in Late Antiquity

Neoplatonism in Late Antiquity

Dmitri Nikulin

UNIVERSITY PRESS

Oxford University Press is a department of the University of Oxford. It furthers
the University's objective of excellence in research, scholarship, and education
by publishing worldwide. Oxford is a registered trade mark of Oxford University
Press in the UK and certain other countries.

Published in the United States of America by Oxford University Press
198 Madison Avenue, New York, NY 10016, United States of America.

© Oxford University Press 2019

All rights reserved. No part of this publication may be reproduced, stored in
a retrieval system, or transmitted, in any form or by any means, without the
prior permission in writing of Oxford University Press, or as expressly permitted
by law, by license, or under terms agreed with the appropriate reproduction
rights organization. Inquiries concerning reproduction outside the scope of the
above should be sent to the Rights Department, Oxford University Press, at the
address above.

You must not circulate this work in any other form
and you must impose this same condition on any acquirer.

CIP data is on file at the Library of Congress
ISBN 978-0-19-066236-3

9 8 7 6 5 4 3 2 1

Printed by Sheridan Books, Inc., United States of America

For Elena

CONTENTS

Preface ix
Permissions xv
Acknowledgments xvii

PART I **Plotinus**

1. **The One and the Many** 3
2. **Number and Being** 14
3. **Eternity and Time** 33
4. **Unity and Individuation of the Soul** 54
5. **Memory and Recollection** 72
6. **Intelligible Matter** 90

PART II **Proclus**

7. **The Many and the One** 119
8. **Imagination and Mathematics** 129
9. **Beauty, Truth, and Being** 147
10. **The System of Physics** 158
11. **Matter and Evil** 177

Appendix: Indivisible Lines in Ancient Philosophy and Mathematics 205

Bibliography and Abbreviations 231
Index Locorum 251
Index 271

PREFACE

Until relatively recently, Neoplatonic studies were considered a venerable yet somewhat marginal and rather specialized kind of scholarship. Everyone knew of Plotinus, Iamblichus, Proclus, and Damascius, yet few ever engaged in a close reading and discussion of their work. Today, this attitude has changed irrevocably due to the exceptional contemporary scholarship, the publication of primary texts, and their exemplary translations with excellent historical and philosophical commentaries. As a result, we now have a much better understanding of the complexity, richness, and originality of late ancient thought. Perhaps our own time is to an extent congenial with that of late antiquity, with its multicultural aspirations within crumbling imperial policies, one predominant language of communication and thought, and the extension of philosophical topics and debates to areas not previously considered worthy of the intent philosophical gaze.

The current explosion of interest in Neoplatonism might also mean that we are ready to overcome a set of biased attitudes toward late ancient philosophy, exemplified in at least two modern beliefs: the idea of progress, which includes progress in philosophy, and the *sola scriptura* approach to the interpretation of texts. The first view presupposes a movement toward a progressive and rationally justifiable end, such as the realization of an even greater freedom in speech, thinking, and action. On this account, the telos of philosophy might be considered achievable in and by the increasing reflexivity and self-transparency of thought, which becomes self-aware by means of the opposition of modern to ancient philosophical practices. This position is best exemplified in Romantic readings of the history of philosophy, in which antiquity is represented primarily by classical Greek thought.

The very term "Neoplatonism," then, is a misnomer and a modern invention, as are the "Presocratics." In an attempt to make sense of a complex, refined, and sophisticated tradition, modern interpretations of the history of philosophy as a progressive universal enterprise take late ancient philosophy to be only an intermediate, even if a necessary, step toward the achievement of modern philosophy. Thus, in his *Grundriss der Geschichte der Philosophie für den akademischen Unterricht*, Wilhelm Gottlieb Tennemann gives a sketch of the entire history of philosophy for students, one that stretches from Thales to Hegel.[1] Tenneman uses the term "Neoplatonism" in the title of the section "Enthusiastic Philosophy of the Alexandrian Neoplatonists" (Schwärmerische Philosophie der Alexandrinische Neuplatoniker), dedicated to the discussion of Plotinus, Porphyry, Iamblichus, Proclus, and other "exalted" thinkers of the "new Platonism." The uplifting Romantic account of the "new Platonism" suggests that its followers became engaged in the "cognition of the Absolute and the inner unification with it" and did so in a lively, if "more enthusiastic than rational way." Tennemann is, in turn, referring to the 1782 book by Christoph Meiners, *Beytrag zur Geschichte der Denkart der ersten Jahrhunderte nach Christi Geburt, in einigen Betrachtungen über die Neu-Platonische Philosophie*, where the term "Neo-Platonic philosophy" (Neu-Platonische Philosophie) is used in the introduction, in which Plotinus, Porphyry, Iamblichus, and Proclus are called the "new Platonists."[2] For many years after, the Romantically inspired understanding of Neoplatonism as a mystic, ecstatic, and somewhat outlandish philosophy becomes associated with the entire tradition of late ancient thought.

The *sola scriptura* attitude, in turn, is closely connected with the progressive view of the history of philosophy, in that modern thought is held to be original in addressing the most pressing contemporary issues—and yet, at the same time, perennial and hence reverting to its source or origin, which it sees as lying in classical Greek thought. The extant writings of Plato and Aristotle become, then, the philosophical scripture, which need to be rethought and reinterpreted in a specifically modern and progressive way, apart from the muddling and dubious tradition of their transmission, appropriation, and commentaries, which flourish from Porphyry and Iamblichus to Proclus and Simplicius.

This book is a philosophical investigation of various aspects of Neoplatonic thought, in which each chapter is a revised and updated version of a paper published in recent years. The discussion revolves around topics in henology (the one and many), ontology (the constitution of being and intellect in their relation to the one, eternity, and temporality), science (the concept and ontological status of numbers, geometrical objects, indivisible lines, and their role in the constitution and cognition of the world), psychology (individuation of the soul and the role of imagination within the structure of cognitive faculties), matter, otherness, non-being (intelligible and bodily matter), and ethics (the question of evil). So, while the one and many, as well as being and matter, in their various disguises and appearances are among the main themes

---

[1] Wilhelm Gottlieb Tennemann, *Grundriss der Geschichte der Philosophie für den akademischen Unterricht*, 3rd ed. (Leipzig: Johann Ambrosius Barth, 1820), §§ 200–21; pp. 156–72.

[2] Christoph Meiners, *Beytrag zur Geschichte der Denkart der ersten Jahrhunderte nach Christi Geburt, in einigen Betrachtungen über die Neu-Platonische Philosophie* (Leipzig: Weidmanns Erben und Reich, 1782), pp. 8–9.

of this volume, it also stresses the importance and centrality of natural philosophy and mathematics in Neoplatonism—in Plotinus, who stands at its beginning, and in Proclus, who stands at its apex. In its entirety, the book proceeds more in the sense of Plotinus' *Enneads*, which contain a productive cosmos of mutually connected yet independent debates, rather than Proclus' systematic and unified *Theologia Platonica*, which provides a systematic deduction of the extant categories from a single source and principle.

The trajectory of the book begins with an exploration of Plotinus' thought, moving from the one and the many to matter in Chapters 1 through 6, then epistrophically reverts to the same set of topics in Proclus in Chapters 7 through 11, and ends with a study of the concept of indivisible lines, which can then be properly understood in light of the previous discussion.

The opening chapter studies the relation of the one to the many in Plotinus, which is fundamental for his entire philosophy. By establishing a system of axiomatic claims about the one, I intend to demonstrate that both the one and otherness are constitutive of three different representations of the many, which are the ideal numbers, the intellect, and matter. Otherness, then, inevitably appears as dual and ambiguous, as the rationally conceivable principle of negativity but also as pure indefiniteness, in which respect it is similar to matter.

In the treatise *On Numbers* (*Enn.* VI.6 [34]), as well as in *Ennead* V.5 (32).4–5, Plotinus considers the place and the ontological status of number within being and thinking, taking number to be a mediation between the original unity of the one and the multiplicity of the infinite and making an important distinction between essential and quantitative number. Yet he does not explicitly address the question of the constitution of number, leaving the problem without a definitive answer. In Chapter 2, I attempt to reconstruct the constitution, derivation, and construction of number in its various representations, doing so with reference to the hints and arguments provided in the texts of the *Enneads*.

Chapter 3 discusses the notion of eternity in *Ennead* III.7 (45), where, against the Pythagorean interpretation of eternity as intelligible substance, Plotinus argues that it primarily characterizes being as the intellect, which is the paradigm of all things. The intellect is marked by simplicity, which, however, presupposes a differentiation between the thinkable and thinking. But the intellect is also life, which is the life of thinking that turns toward the one, the source of the intellect—of its being, thinking, and life. This allows the intellect to think its objects as determinate, in an act that surpasses discursive thought, thus defying and suspending temporality. Against the Pythagoreans, then, eternity is the everlasting non-discursive and self-identical life of the intellect.

Chapter 4 shows that the understanding of the soul in the *Enneads* is marked by Plotinus' attempt to establish a Platonic account of the soul, which he does in constant polemics against other theories. On the one hand, such an account takes into consideration the exegetic and hermeneutic tasks of reading and interpreting Plato. Yet on the other hand, it also establishes the soul as both uniting and separating and hence as mediating between the intelligible and the sensible. In his psychology, Plotinus provides explanations for the unity of the soul and for its individuation, which he understands from the perspective of the synthetic unity of the one and the many. Against the material and formal accounts, I argue that it is the *logos* that is the source and principle of both unity and individuation of the soul in Plotinus.

Chapter 5 establishes the role of memory and recollection in their mutual relation in Plotinus. This requires a careful reading of the relevant texts in Plato and Aristotle and also a meticulous reconstruction of the arguments of *Enneads* IV.3 (27), IV.4 (28), and IV.6 (41). Memory for Plotinus is not the Platonic storage of images or imprints coming from the sensible or the intelligible. Rather, memory is a power of imagination used by the soul for the reconstruction and reproduction of the currently absent, which the soul performs starting with the initial sensible impact that becomes the occasion to form a particular memory. Recollection, on the contrary, takes the form of a rational discursive rethinking that reproduces the soul's experience of the intelligible objects. Recollection, then, is constituted by a triple motion of the descent, staying, and return of the soul to the intelligible.

The concept of matter is in many ways central to Plotinus, who portrays it as negativity, indefiniteness, and unlimitedness, as a deficiency that has nothing of itself and hence cannot be affected. However, in *Ennead* II.4 (12) he also famously introduces the notion of intelligible matter. In Chapter 6, I argue, first, that the notion of intelligible matter plays an important role not only in Plotinus' earlier treatises but also throughout the entire corpus of his works; second, that bodily matter and intelligible matter are necessarily related as different yet inseparable; and third, that intelligible matter is not only represented by the indefinite dyad and constitutes the primary indefiniteness of the thinking of the intellect, but is also connected with the imagination and thus with geometrical objects.

In response to Plotinus' treatment of the one and the many, Chapter 7 is devoted to the discussion of the same problem in the opening sections of Proclus' *Theologia Platonica* II.1–3. Beginning the deduction of his grand philosophical synthesis with only two elements in reference to the first two hypotheses of Plato's *Parmenides*, Proclus demonstrates that both the one and the many are necessary for the generation of the plurality of henadic, intelligible, psychic, and physical phenomena. While the many is dependent on the one and the one is not dependent on anything, the interaction between the one and the many is essential for the constitution of being. Through a number of precise and subtle arguments, Proclus further establishes the structure of participation as defined by the triad of the unparticipated-participated-participating, which is then applied to the clarification of a number of difficulties and implicit presuppositions in the text.

In Chapter 8, I consider the role of the imagination as it appears in Proclus' commentary on Euclid, where mathematical or geometrical objects are taken to mediate, both ontologically and cognitively, between thinkable and physical things. With the former, mathematical things share the permanence and consistency of their properties; with the latter, they share divisibility and the possibility of being multiplied. Hence, a geometrical figure exists simultaneously on four different levels: as a noetic concept in the intellect; as a logical definition, or *logos*, in discursive reasoning; as an imaginary perfect figure in the imagination; and as a physical imitation or representation in sense-perception. Imagination, then, can be equated with the intelligible or geometrical matter that constitutes the medium in which a geometrical object can be constructed, represented, and studied.

Chapter 9 discusses Proclus' concepts of truth and beauty in mathematics, science, and ontology. He accepts both Plato's claim in the *Philebus* that the good is present in the thinkable in beauty, truth, and symmetry, as well as Aristotle's assertion that beauty is exemplified in mathematics through order, symmetry, and definiteness. Proclus then demonstrates that, in mathematical objects, beauty transpires in four ways: in the beautiful shape of a sensible reproduction of a geometrical figure; in the beauty of the perfect geometrical figure existing in the intelligible matter of the imagination; in the mathematical object's definition, with all its properties becoming explicit in constructions and demonstrations by discursive reasoning; and in the beauty of the form in the intellect. On this account, science brings the knowledge, beauty, and goodness of its objects to completion within the unity of the intellect.

Chapter 10 considers the structure of Proclus' rarely discussed—yet important—*Elements of Physics* and its original contribution to the understanding of physics in antiquity. As I argue, the purpose of the treatise is not only a systematic arrangement of the arguments scattered throughout Aristotle's works on natural philosophy using the structure of Euclid's *Elements* as a model. Proclus also aims to develop a universal theory of motion or physical change that establishes the first principles as definitions, formulates and demonstrates a number of mutually related propositions about natural objects, and culminates in establishing the existence and properties of the prime mover. Unlike modern physics, which presupposes the applicability of mathematics to physics, Proclus shows that, in the study of natural phenomena, the *more geometrico* way can be a systematic rational science arranged by means of logic, rather than mathematics.

The problem of evil, one of the central ethical and ontological problems in Neoplatonism, is discussed in Chapter 11. In *Ennead* I.8 (51), Plotinus presents matter as utter deficiency, as the absence, lack, or privation of the good, and thus as radical evil. In *De malorum subsistentia*, Proclus explicitly responds to Plotinus and argues that evil does not exist since non-being does not exist. This means that evil is not opposite to the good, because the good has no opposite, and opposites belong to the same genus. Therefore, in its elusive and indefinite nature, evil should be characterized by the rethought and redefined concepts of privation, subcontrariety, and *parypostasis*. In its inescapable deficiency, then, evil is the privation and subcontrary of the good that exists parypostatically; that is, as elusively present in its absence as the misplacement of being and the displacement of the good.

The book concludes with a discussion of a text from the Corpus Aristotelicum, *On Indivisible Lines*, which presents a number of arguments that intend to demonstrate that a geometrical object cannot be built up of indivisible elements. I argue that the treatise's polemic primarily targets the Academic debate and makes sense only if one takes into consideration the implicit Platonic ontology of mathematical objects, in which the indivisible line is the principle and the form, and not an element, of the continuous. The underlying mathematical ontology, which is implicitly rejected by the author of the treatise, finds its way into Iamblichus' *De communi mathematica scientia* and Proclus' *Commentary on Euclid*, where geometrical entities are considered to be intermediate between the intelligible and physical objects and constituted by the principles of the one and the many. In this way, the Appendix brings together several central themes of the book, such as one and many, same and other, unity and divisibility.

PERMISSIONS

The individual chapters and the Appendix originally appeared in the following publications:

Chapter 1, "The One and the Many," as "The One and the Many in Plotinus," *Hermes* 126 (1998), pp. 326–40, published by Franz Steiner Verlag GmbH.

Chapter 2, "Number and Being," as "Foundations of Arithmetic in Plotinus: *Enn.* VI.6 (34) on the Structure and the Constitution of Number," *Méthexis* 11 (1998), pp. 85–102, published by Brill.

Chapter 3, "Eternity and Time," as "Plotinus on Eternity," in *Le Timée de Platon. Contributions à l'histoire de sa reception* (Paris: Éditions de l'Institut Supérieur de Philosophie/Leuven: Éditions Peeters, 2000), pp. 15–39, published by Peeters Publishers.

Chapter 4, "Unity and Individuation of the Soul," as "Unity and Individuation of the Soul in Plotinus," in *Studi sull'anima in Plotino* (Naples: Bibliopolis, 2005), pp. 275–304, published by Istituto per il Lessico Intellettuale Europeo e Storia delle Idee del Consiglio Nazionale delle Ricerche (ILIESI-CNR).

Chapter 5, "Memory and Recollection," as "Memory and Recollection in Plotinus," *Archiv für Geschichte der Philosophie* 96 (2014), pp. 183–201, published by De Gruyter.

Chapter 6, "Intelligible Matter," as "Intelligible Matter in Plotinus," *Dionysius* 16 (1998), pp. 85–113, published by Dalhousie University Press.

Chapter 7, "The Many and the One," as "The One and the Many in the Structure of Being in Proclus' *Theologia Platonica* II 1–3," *Diotima* 28 (2000), pp. 77–87, published by Ekdosis Hellēnikēs Hetaireias Philosophikōn Meletōn.

Chapter 8, "Imagination and Mathematics," as "Imagination and Mathematics in Proclus," *Ancient Philosophy* 28 (2008), pp. 153–72, published by Mathesis Publications.

Chapter 9, "Beauty, Truth, and Being," as "Commentary on M. Martin's 'Why Beauty Is Truth in All We Know: Aesthetics and Mimesis in the Neoplatonic Science," *Proceedings of the Boston Area Colloquium in Ancient Philosophy* 25 (2009), pp. 93–105, published by Brill.

Chapter 10, "The System of Physics," as "Physica More Geometrico Demonstrata: Natural Philosophy in Proclus and Aristotle," *Proceedings of the Boston Area Colloquium in Ancient Philosophy* 18:1 (2003), pp. 183–209, published by Brill.

Chapter 11, "Matter and Evil," as "Proclus on Evil," *Proceedings of the Boston Area Colloquium in Ancient Philosophy* 31:1 (2016), pp. 119–46, 156–8, published by Brill.

Appendix, "Indivisible Lines in Ancient Philosophy and Mathematics," as "Indivisible Lines and Plato's Mathematical Ontology," in *Platons Hermeneutik und Prinzipiendenken im Licht der Dialoge und der antiken Tradition* (Hildesheim: Georg Olms, 2012), pp. 291–326, published by Georg Olms Verlag AG.

I want to thank all the publishers for granting permission to reproduce the texts in this book.

ACKNOWLEDGMENTS

I want to express my gratitude for most helpful and thoughtful comments on various parts of the text to Alexander Altonji, Cinzia Arruzza, Werner Beierwaltes, Alain Bernard, Vladimir Bibikhin, Marcelo Boeri, Ulrike Bruchmüller, David Burrell, Annick Charles-Saget, Martha Detlefsen, John Dillon, Eyjólfur Kjalar Emilsson, Michael Frede, Jeremy Gauger, Stephen Gersh, Gary Gurtler, Jens Halfwassen, Philippe Hoffmann, Christoph Horn, Justin Humphreys, Hans Joachim Krämer, Duane Lacey, Joseph Lemelin, Alain Lernoud, Gregory MacIsaac, Claudia Maggi, Jean-Marc Narbonne, Elena Nikulina, Dominic O'Meara, Alvin Plantinga, Gretchen Reydams-Schils, Yuriy Shichalin, Suzanne Stern-Gillet, Thomas Szlezák, Emilio Vicuña, Alejandro Vigo, Bernard Vitrac, and Samuel Yelton.

Neoplatonism in Late Antiquity

PART I

Plotinus

1

The One and the Many

1.1 The One

The starting point of Plotinus' thought is not being but the one, "the marvel of the one, which is not being" (θαῦμα τοῦ ἕν, ὃ μὴ ὄν ἐστιν, *Enn.* VI.9 [9].5.30). The one defines both Plotinus' philosophy and life as an attempt to grasp this one and to escape "in solitude to the solitary" (*Enn.* VI.9.11.51), driven by the desire to become one.

Plotinus accepts the following statements about the one as implicit axioms that underlie all the other considerations in the *Enneads*:

α. There is a principle (ἀρχή, αἰτία, πηγή or ῥίζα, *Enn.* VI.9.9.1–2) of the whole, of everything that is. This principle is the good and the origin of everything, and nothing is better or greater than it (cf. *Enn.* VI.8 [39].8.9).[1]

β. Everything that is perfect necessarily *produces* or *gives* (πάντα δὲ ὅσα ἤδη τέλεια γεννᾷ, *Enn.* V.1 [10].6.38).

γ. That which gives is better than that which is given (*Enn.* VI.7 [38].17.5).

δ. A unified *simple* whole is better and more perfect than that which is complex, compound, and composite; it takes precedence over all the parts as distinctions and differences that afterward can be discerned in it.

These four axioms underlie and determine the entirety of Plotinus' philosophy. First of all, they entail that (1) there is only one (μόνον, *Enn.* V.1.7.20) principle, *the* principle, the one. Evidently, if there were two of them, they

---

[1] See Georg Siegmann, *Plotins Philosophie des Guten: eine Interpretation von Enneade VI 7* (Würzburg: Königshausen & Neumann, 1990), p. 142; and Eyjólfur Kjalar Emilsson, *Plotinus* (London: Routledge, 2017), pp. 70–82.

would have formed a complex system, which, according to δ, is not as good as a unique single principle. Therefore, as principles, they could not represent the good. The good and the one are thus identical. The one good or good one is one-good. It is the most important constitutive element in Plotinus, absolutely one and the same, so that the good as *different* from or *not identical* with the one can in fact only be discerned in a secondary way.

This one-good (2) has not come to be (μηδὲ γέγονε, *Enn.* VI.8.7.35–6) since otherwise, according to δ, there would be something better; that is, not perfect and not one. This "not-coming-to-being" of the one means that it is beyond all temporal characteristics or duration of any kind, abides in a supertemporal realm, and gives or produces the monadic "now" of eternity and then time and temporal duration (cf. *Enn.* III.7 [45].3.36; see Chapter 3).

It means (3) that the one produces *eternally*, not in a certain fixed moment or moments of time, but also not in each moment of time, because it is not in time at all. The one (4) is utterly simple (*Enn.* V.4 [7].1.5) and without parts. For if there were several parts in it, then only one of them, according to α, γ, and (1) would be the best and hence, according to β, would generate the other parts. Moreover, only the one is absolutely simple: it is αὐτό or "itself," simple and indissoluble, and without any addition. Therefore, (5) everything else is complex; that is, is itself *and* something else:

> It [the one] is something which has its place high above everything, this which alone is free in truth, because it is not enslaved to itself, but is only itself and really itself, while every other thing is itself and something else [τῶν ἄλλων ἕκαστον αὐτὸ καὶ ἄλλο]. (*Enn.* VI.8.21.30–3)

In particular, it means that, in each and every "αὐτό," in every substance, the essence differs from its existence. The only and unique exception is the one "itself," where no such distinction can be made. In this sense, the one identical to itself as "αὐτό" is *not* being (οὐδὲ τὸ ὄν, *Enn.* VI.9.2.47; cf. VI.9.3.37–8).[2]

At this point, we come to Plato's *Parmenides*, which is central for the understanding of Plotinus' discussion of the one. In Plato, the one found in the first hypothesis (*Parm.* 137C–142B), considered beyond any otherness or many, can neither be grasped by sensation nor imagination nor thought, and so it cannot even exist. As such, it is different from the one taken together with the many, the one-many of the second hypothesis (*Parm.* 144B–157B) that can be considered being, is being itself, and is first to be thought. Following Plato, Plotinus identifies the one with the one (ἕν) of the first hypothesis of the

---

[2] Plotinus keeps referring to the famous passage in Plato: "the good itself is not essence but transcends essence [ἐπέκεινα τῆς οὐσίας] in dignity and power" (*Rep.* 509B; cf. *Enn.* VI.8.9.28, VI.9.11.42, et al.). For Plotinus, "there is nothing above" (μηδέν ἐστι τὸ ὑπερκείμενον, *Enn.* VI.7.22.20–1), which is in obvious opposition to the Aristotelian ὑποκείμενον as the underlying *substratum*. In this sense, ὑπερκείμενον is a "superstratum," the source of being that precedes being.

Parmenides, the intellect with the one-many (ἓν πολλά) of the second hypothesis, and the soul with the one *and* many (ἓν καὶ πολλά) of the third hypothesis (*Parm.* 157B–159B).

Hence, if that which is logically after the one is one being, it should somehow contain the very form of multiplicity or participate in the many. This means that although the intellect as being is one (the one-being), it is not altogether simple, but contains a (finite, according to Plotinus and most of the Neoplatonists) number of forms of things. Therefore, ἕν is not identical with ὄν in the intellect, but ἕν-ὄν is the first multiplicity in the form of otherness or duality (*Enn.* VI.2.17.25). This implies (6) that the one above being is different from the intellect. The one is neither the intellect nor thinking (*Enn.* V.4.2.3–5). Not only does the one not think, but it is itself not thinkable. In a sense, paradoxically, it is not even thinkable that the one or the good is not thinkable, because the very concept of "not being thinkable" is thinkable. Thinking is striving toward completeness, yet the one does not think: it neither has need of being completed nor is it in need of anything (*Enn.* V.3 [49].10.46–7) and is neither incomplete nor deficient.

Therefore, (7) the one is not knowable in its essence. As not different from its existence, the one's essence can be represented to us only negatively, as not-essence (of anything else) or as above essence. Hence, the one (8) is before all things (πρὸ τούτων, *Enn.* VI.9.5.38; cf. VI.9.11.35) since it precedes being, just as being precedes and is separate from becoming.

Consequently, (9) the one is radically different from all that is, not only from the intellect and being, but also from becoming, from distinction into positive and negative, and so forth—from everything that can be thought, imagined, or sensibly apprehended, spoken of, or predicated. But since the one or the good is the first, the cause of bringing forth all the other things, the one is in a sense all these things and yet absolutely different from them (*Enn.* VI.8.21.24, VI.9.3.40).[3] For this reason, (10) we have to conclude that, after all, it is very difficult to speak about the one, which means that we must make recourse to a metaphorical or negative way of saying the unsayable.

1.2 Paradoxes of the One

Any discussion of the one therefore appears paradoxical: on the one hand, it seems to be impossible to speak about it in terms of the usual logical distinctions, including that between subject and predicates, since the one is above and before any definition through logos (οὐ λελογισμένον, cf. *Enn.*

---

[3] See John Bussanich, "Plotinus' Metaphysics of the One," in *The Cambridge Companion to Plotinus*, ed. Lloyd P. Gerson (Cambridge: Cambridge University Press, 1996), pp. 38–65.

VI.8.14.30). The one is not a particular subject: nothing can be predicated of it since it is prior to predicates (*Enn.* III.8 [30].10.28–31; cf. V.3.13.1, V.5 [32].6.24, VI.8.8.6). On the other hand, it is not the case that we simply cannot speak about the one at all or express it in any way: we are *unable not to speak* about the one as we are unable not to strive toward the good. The entire theoretical life of the philosopher is determined, according to Plotinus, by this crucial inability not to search for the one, not to be led by a sort of an "appeal" or "call" from the one.

It is then important to distinguish between "speaking about the one" ("knowledge about") and "speaking the one" ("knowledge of").[4] "Speaking the one" does not follow logical laws—namely, the law of non-contradiction—since the one is not really predicable and does not have an opposite. "Speaking the one" is therefore inevitably paradoxical. Thus, "not predicable" is itself a self-negating non-predicable predication. In other words, any contradictory propositions are false in "speaking the one." At the same time, each of such propositions can be true in "speaking about the one."

An example of such propositions is (a) the one is one; (b) the one is not one. Proposition (a) has already been discussed in (1), and yet the one itself is beyond oneness, and, therefore, (b) the one is not one. *Each* of (a) and (b) is true in "speaking about the one," but since they contradict each other, they cannot *both* be true. Another example is (c) the one is "itself" (αὐτό); (d) the one is not "itself" (*Enn.* VI.8.9.35–50). Proposition (c) has also already been discussed in (5), and (d) holds because the one, as the most self-sufficient (αὐταρκέστατον, *Enn.* V.4.1.12), is prior to any possible identification that requires the distinction of identified and the indentifiable, whereas the distinction should precede any identification (namely, identification to itself).[5] Therefore, the one is prior to any distinction. For this reason, it cannot be identity or sameness but rather is the source of identity beyond all identity and therefore cannot be considered even as non-identical before the act of identification.

But how can we think and speak about that which is neither speakable nor thinkable? Plotinus finds an appropriate language in the *via negativa*, even if Parmenides in Plato's *Sophist* warns us against the dangers of reasoning about the non-existent (*Soph.* 236E–237B). Plotinus keeps repeating that every way of "speaking about the one" (not "speaking the one") is inadequate. For this reason, it is only appropriate to understand the one negatively: it is neither intellect, nor discursive reasoning, nor substance, nor relation, nor λόγος of any kind, nor form, nor limit (*Enn.* VI.7.17.15–6). It is not even the good for itself,

---

[4] "We do indeed say something about [λέγομεν μέν τι περὶ αὐτοῦ], but we certainly do not speak it [οὐ μὴν αὐτὸ λέγομεν], and we have neither knowledge nor thought of it" (*Enn.* V.3.14.1–3). See Lloyd P. Gerson, *Plotinus* (London: Routledge, 1994), pp. 15–6.

[5] Another example is the one is beyond active actuality (ἐπέκεινα ἐνεργείας, *Enn.* VI.7.17.10; cf. VI.8.20.14), but also is primal actuality (ἐνέργεια) itself (*Enn.* VI.8.20.9–27).

but only for the other (*Enn.* VI.7.41.28–9). Therefore, the one is not the ground of and for itself, is not sub-stantia, ἀνυπόθετον (cf. Plato, *Rep.* 510B7). The one determines everything but is not itself determined by what it determines. Only when negativity reflexively applies to itself can it give way to that which is beyond definition. The one is "other than all the things which come after it" (πάντων ἕτερον τῶν μετ' αὐτό, *Enn.* V.4.1.6), a non-other, non-striving toward anything other than itself, a non-striving even to itself (because it is already there).

The congenial way of thinking about the one, then, is by negating the negation, *negatio negationis*, which plays a prominent role in Neoplatonism. The one itself, strictly speaking, is not, but for being it is impossible not to be (οὐκ ἔστι μὴ εἶναι, *Enn.* VI.7.12.18; cf. VI.5 [23].1.23–4). In a sense, the inability not to speak or not to think about the one is a modal rendering of the structure of the double negation in the form of "not possible not to." At the same time, the double negation does not pertain to the one itself because, as the first and the best (*Enn.* VI.8.10.26), it is not being and yet equally not non-being. Rather, the one "is" beyond being and above non-being. Therefore, the *negatio negationis* can only refer to and represent the one bound to multiplicity in the intellect as one-being. This is why the double negation appears in the expression of the freedom of thought as the action of the intellect, which "could be said to have freedom and anything in its power, when it does not have it in its power *not to act*" (οὐκ ἔχων ἐπ' αὐτῷ τὸ μὴ ποιεῖν, *Enn.* VI.8.4.5–7).

Thus, although the one is the first and prior to the many, it is nevertheless not the first *for us* by way of thinking, for the first thinkable is one-many as that which is after the one.[6] We have to begin with something *other*: namely, with that which is not the one itself, but is totally different from it. This primary otherness cannot be taken as just pure otherness or difference from everything else, for otherwise nothing—the first otherness itself—can neither be nor be thought. Therefore, the first otherness should be other than pure negativity, yet through the double negation it should come to the other of the otherness as something positive; namely, as the same.[7] So the first point of departure for us is not the absolute unity of the one but the dual unity of sameness–otherness. Together, the sameness (ταὐτόν) and the otherness (θάτερον) are two constitutive principles of being and intellect (*Enn.* III.7.3.8–11) and can be further equated with the one (ἕν, ταὐτόν) and the otherness, multiplicity as duality (ἀόριστος δυάς, θάτερον, πολλά) of the Platonic tradition. The otherness (the dyad) is inseparable from the sameness, and both constitute the entire sphere of the intellect as one-many.

---

[6] "πολλὰ δεῖ τοῦτο τὸ ἓν εἶναι ὂν μετὰ τὸ πάντῃ ἕν" (*Enn.* VI.7.8.17–8).

[7] For this reason, the same and the other in Plato's *Sophist* (254D–255E) are mutually inseparable within five categories that are applicable, according to Plotinus, to the noetic world (cf. *Enn.* VI.2 [43].8.25–49).

The many appears to be similar to non-being as privation of being, as non-existence. As pure multiplicity, πολλά, it can hardly be expressed, conceived, or defined: unlike the one itself, it is not superabundant or beyond being but rather "beneath" being. The favorite image of Plotinus, the one as the sun, as the source of light, suggests that the multiplicity itself is a kind of darkness devoid of light. The many, then, should be considered as multiplicity shaped by the two principles of oneness (sameness) and of the dyad (otherness), taken by the Pythagoreans as the active limiting principle (ὁρίζον) and as the passive limited one (ὁριστὸν καὶ ὁριζόμενον).[8]

1.3 The Many

It is possible to distinguish three ways in which the many transpires in Plotinus.

1.3.1 NUMBERS

First, it appears in the ideal numerical structure, in numbers. Notably, in the sphere of intellect-being the principles of oneness (ἕν) and of otherness (ἀόριστος δυάς) are not themselves numbers, but generative principles of numbers. Some Pythagoreans further distinguished ἕν as an ideal principle from μονάς as a numerical unit.[9] The two principles of ἕν and ἀόριστος δυάς act in that which comes after the one and are themselves formed by the primary otherness that is the other to the one. At the same time, the principle of the dyad stands not for a particular other but otherness as such; that is, the principle of difference. The two principles constitute being as bound multiplicity or the one-being of the second *Parmenides* hypothesis. Even the structure of *negatio negationis* can be understood only from otherness, which is reflexive, insofar as—always pointing toward something other—it primarily points at and is applied to itself as the other.

The two constitutive principles are principles only in a secondary way, for, as established in (1), the one is the sole and unique principle (*Enn.* VI.6 [34].3.3–10). The two principles generate numbers, in which the oneness (ἕν) posits a unit (the aspect of sameness or definiteness in numbers) and the dyad (δυάς) generates the passage from one to another (the aspect of otherness or indefiniteness in numbers), thus enabling the formation of the numbers (*Enn.* V.1.5.6–9).

---

[8] See, for example, Kallikratidos in Holger Thesleff, *The Pythagorean Texts of the Hellenistic Period* (Åbo: Åbo Akademi, 1965), p. 103.11. Cf. Plutarch, *De Is. et Os.* 75, p. 381F; [Iamblichus], *Theolog. Arithm.* 7.19, 9.6; Pythagoras in Thesleff, *The Pythagorean Texts*, p. 154.24; Anonymus Alexandri in ibid., pp. 234.18–20.

[9] Anonymus Photii in Thesleff, *The Pythagorean Texts*, p. 237.17.

The consideration of numbers is a matter of great importance in the late Academy (as we know from Aristotle's account in books M and N of *Metaphysics*), as well as in Neopythagoreanism and Neoplatonism. Plotinus himself clearly distinguishes between ἕν and ἀόριστος δυάς as the principles of numbers, numbers themselves, and multitude (εἴτε πλῆθος εἴτε δυάς, *Enn.* V.1.6.6). Furthermore, he makes a distinction between ideal numbers, which are forms, and quantitative or arithmetic numbers, by means of which we usually count (*Enn.* VI.6.16). It is not immediately clear whether these ideal numbers form a finite set (namely, ten: the decad is the completion of numbers, as it is held, for instance, by Anatolius in Περὶ δεκάδος) or not. Since, according to Plotinus, the number of forms is finite, and it is likely that the forms should be construed under the pattern of ideal numbers, the number of the ideal numbers should be finite (see Chapter 2).

1.3.2 THE INTELLECT

Second, the many is present in the structure of the intellect (νοῦς), which is the first energy, real activity, and perfect actuality without any detriment or diminishing (*Enn.* VI.7.13). In this respect, the intellect differs from the one, which is the engendering overwhelming potency (δύναμις τῶν πάντων, *Enn.* III.8.10.1, IV.8 [6].6.11, V.1.7.10, V.4.1.36, VI.7.32.31, VI.8.20.37, VI.9.6.7–8), infinitely great in power, and, as such, inconceivable.[10] Unlike the one, the intellect is fundamentally dual, constituted by ἕν/δυάς as abundance (ὑπερβολή) and deficiency (ἔλλειψις), other and same (ἕτερον καὶ ταὐτόν, *Enn.* V.3.15.40), and a *sui generis* motion without change. As the other invariably returning to the same, the intellect is fundamentally reflexive (πρὸς αὐτὸν πᾶς, *Enn.* VI.8.17.27). Therefore, in turning to itself it can contemplate that which is in itself and is itself, but also turn to that which is before itself (*Enn.* VI.9.3.33–4). And although νοῦς does not really think or understand the one that is above being and understanding (5), the intellect inevitably strives toward the absolute unity without ever really gaining it. Therefore, the intellect necessarily conceives something other; namely, that unity that is present as one among many (*Enn.* V.3.10.51–2, V.3.11.1–16). The many of the intellect appears to be *in* (ἐν), *around* (περί), *after* (μετά), and *toward* (πρός) the one (*Enn.* VI.5.4.17–20, VI.5.6.1–4). In doing so, νοῦς thinks itself as the other; that is, as not itself but one as the one-many of being (cf. *Enn.* III.8.6–7; Plato, *Phil.* 14C).

For this reason, the intellect is double (διπλοῦς), while only the one is simple (ἁπλοῦς). It is both thinking as activity and the noetic cosmos of thinkable actuality. The distinction between thought (νόησις or νοοῦν)

---

[10] See Gwenaëlle Aubry, *Dieu sans la puissance: Dunamis et Energeia chez Aristotle et chez Plotin* (Paris: Vrin, 2006), pp. 216–22.

and the thinkable (νοητόν, νοητά, or νοούμενον) as κόσμος νοητός, a self-contained system of forms, is well established in Plotinus (*Enn.* II.4 [12].4.8, III.3 [48].5.17–8, III.8.11.36, IV.7 [2].10.35, IV.8.3.8, V.8 [31].1.1, V.9 [5].9.7, VI.9.5.14). But the intellect is not two complementary opposing parts, but a complex unity, a first real synthesis (σύνθεσις) of the inseparable duality of oneness and otherness, a unity in diversity (*Enn.* V.4.2.9–12, VI.9.2.29–45).[11] The image that Plotinus uses to illustrate this structure is that of an army or a chorus (*Enn.* VI.9.1.4–5) where the whole is constituted by each of its elements yet is not reducible to any of them. The intellect is represented as both oneness and multiplicity, as simultaneously divisible and indivisible (ἀδιάκριτον καὶ αὖ διακεκριμένον, *Enn.* VI.9.5.16). It is a complete system (in this sense it is indivisible) of the entirety of distinct forms (and in this sense is divisible). It is one ordered unity (ἓν συντεταγμένος, *Enn.* VI.8.17.14), a kind of a multicolored sphere, all parts of which are mutually transparent and reflect each other (*Enn.* VI.7.15.25).

This unity in diversity of the intellect corresponds to the Platonic structure of the communication of forms as κοινωνία (cf. *Soph.* 254B–C; *Rep.* 476A), in which each εἶδος is connected with every other one, yet each one is unique. This interpenetrating, mutually inclusive communication of the νοητά in the noetic cosmos, distinct without separation, is the paradigm for the physical cosmos, where, however, all things are mutually exclusive because of the greater presence of matter as otherness.

But why does the one generate two principles of ἕν/δυάς or produce the intellect, which is a trace (ἴχνος) of the one (*Enn.* VI.7.17.39)? This is a most difficult problem in Plotinus and in Neoplatonism in general.[12] For, on the one hand, the one as the good inevitably produces or gives (β); but, on the other hand, this very act of begetting is a sort of "radiation" (περίλαμψις) or "effluence" from the one (*Enn.* V.1.6.28; V.2.1.8; V.3.15.6). It is difficult to provide a rational account of how the one produces the first otherness since this first not-one should be, on the one hand, different from the one, yet, on the other hand, the first not-one should not be different from the one because it is also different from itself as the very basis for all distinctions. Plotinus argues that that which comes from the one cannot be the same as the one, for otherwise the one would not have been the unique one; if not the same, then it cannot be better than the one, which is the good and, hence, more deficient. The more deficient is not one, but aspires to the one, being produced and kept in being by the one, which means that the produced is one-many (*Enn.* V.3.15.7–11).

---

[11] See Eyjólfur Kjalar Emilsson, *Plotinus on Intellect* (Oxford: Oxford University Press, 2007), pp. 141–4.

[12] See Heinz Robert Schlette, *Das Eine und das Andere: Studien zur Problematik des Negativen in der Metaphysik Plotins* (Munich: Hueber, 1966), pp. 62–87; and Thomas Alexander Szlezák, *Platon und Aristoteles in der Nuslehre Plotins* (Basel: Schwabe, 1979), p. 108.

The intellect is thus the first other for the one, but also, vice versa, the one is the first and absolute other for the intellect, remaining absolutely different beyond difference, itself by itself (αὐτὸ πρὸς αὐτὸ μένει, *Enn.* V.3.10.50–1). That is to say, the one is the absolute difference or otherness to everything else, and thus the sameness of ἕν is an image of the one, but the otherness of δυάς is also an image of the one, the unique principle and source of being as one-many.

The ascension to the one (ἀναγωγὴ ἐφ᾽ ἕν; ἀναγωγὴ εἰς ἕν, *Enn.* III.8.10.20, V.5.4.1) thus goes by the negation of negation from dispersion and division to unity. Yet this "henological reduction"[13] is a movement in reverse to that from thesis through the negativity of antithesis to synthesis. On the contrary, in Plotinus, the ascension from the intellect to the one is the dissolution of the composite synthetic unity in duality of the one-many, which is production of the one, not of the intellect itself, to the simplest non-dual thesis or, rather, unthesis.

1.3.3 MATTER

Finally, the third way in which the many appears in Plotinus is matter. In the Platonic tradition, matter is conceived as that which has nothing of its own: it neither is nor possesses form or actuality (see also Chapter 6). It is neither a subject of predicates (for it cannot receive predicates), nor anything definite. It is not body, since body is matter defined by form. Matter "is" non-being or nothingness (*Enn.* III.6.7.3–5; cf. Porphyry, *Sent.* 20 [Lamberz]). Matter is that which is not, never was, and never will be, only a receptacle of form and being (cf. Plato, *Tim.* 49A–51B). It is only a possibility of being. Therefore, although matter is the most distant from the one and is absolute privation of light (goodness and being), paradoxically, matter appears to be the closest to the one. Indeed, first, both appear as pure potentiality and, second, both cannot be found in the sphere of being. Nevertheless, matter cannot be identical with the one. For, first, the one is the overwhelming power or potentiality to produce being, a unique source of everything, an absolute richness and fullness, while the many as matter is lack of being, an absolute poverty and emptiness (*Enn.* VI.7.27.11–2). For this reason, the many does not come from the many; that is, it does not generate itself. Hence, matter as the many does not come from itself, but from the one (*Enn.* V.3.16.12–3). And second, the one is other to being, "before" or "beyond" being, while matter is "after" or "beneath" being.

That is why, in an attempt to avoid the conclusion that matter as potentiality and non-being (μὴ εἶναι) is not different from the one, Plotinus has to say that matter is evil, deficiency (ἔλλειψις, *Enn.* I.8 [51].5.5), or absolute

---

[13] See Jens Halfwassen, *Der Aufstief zum Einen: Untersuchungen zu Platon und Plotin* (Stuttgart: Teubner, 1992), p. 53.

otherness, different from the otherness as principle, as ἀόριστος δυάς (see Chapter 11). Matter as pure otherness is therefore different from itself yet, at the same time, is not different from itself since there is nothing in matter from which it might be different. However, matter does not return to itself through the double negation because pure otherness is not anything definite, is not a principle, but nothing. Unlike the one, matter is not "not non-being" but always remains non-being.

Matter as mere otherness is not a particular evil but the privation of goodness, insofar as the one as the good is the best, self-sufficient, and in no need of anything (*Enn.* VI.7.23.6–8). At this point, we encounter a paradox: as absolute otherness, matter has to be other and different not only from any particular thing but also from itself as otherness. Plotinus has to ascribe to matter a certain negative potency, different from mere indifference, from the lack of striving toward the good and being (*Enn.* I.8.14.35–6). This negative, although not zero, potentiality in matter is not that which is capable of bringing forth or producing anything. On the contrary, it is a privation of any productive potency, inexhaustible simply because there is nothing to be exhausted. Since matter is in its absence "behind" all being, this very striving in matter cannot be real but is exerted as if in a dream (*Enn.* VI.7.28.11) by a kind of phantasmagoric and inappropriate reasoning (cf. Plato, *Tim.* 52B2).

Unlike in ideal numbers or in the intellect, there is no structure in matter—only lack of any organization, which is translated into the infinite divisibility of the continuum in which everything divisible is always further infinitely divisible. Yet, in its elusive nature that cannot really be caught in reasoning, matter as pure otherness appears to be present in everything to which the many is present in some way. This means that matter is present even in being as intelligible matter (ὕλη νοητή), which is mentioned already by Aristotle (*Met.* 1036a9–12; 1037a4–5) and is discussed at length by Plotinus (*Enn.* II.4.3–5)—as the dyad that is produced by the one and as the principle of otherness that, together with the ἕν as the principle of sameness, generates the entire noetic realm of forms. Paradoxically, physical matter and intelligible matter, then, are one and the same matter (as negativity), yet at the same time they also oppose each other since intelligible matter is the principle of multiplicity in forms. Once again, we encounter the fundamental duality of otherness that always refers to or points at something else. In the case of matter, otherness appears, on the one hand, as pure privation of anything definite, as a possibility of the embodiment of form. But, on the other hand, it appears as the principle of multiplicity, as the intelligible matter.

The infinite, then, also appears in different ways: the one is the infinite in its creative potency that cannot be extinguished or diminished. Matter, however, is a different kind of the infinite in which nothing can be discerned: it is τὸ ἄπειρον, a limitless indefiniteness (*Enn.* II.4.15). And the infinite is bound in the intellect: when it turns and strives toward its source and origin, which is the one that has no limit (ὅρον οὐκ ἔχοντος, *Enn.* VI.7.17.15–6), the intellect becomes the defined one-many (*Enn.* VI.7.14.11–2).

Thus, the many as present in three different ways in Plotinus is itself dual: it is privation, pure negativity, and otherness—but also the otherness as the principle of duality and multiplicity. Otherness (ἑτερότης) itself has the structure of the limiting ἕν—the indefinite δυάς. Only the one is above otherness of the intellect (ὑπὲρ νοῦν, *Enn.* VI.9.8.25) since it is before and beyond being and any distinctions, while everything else comes from it and participates in various ways in the many through otherness.

2

Number and Being

In the treatise "On Numbers" (Περὶ ἀριθμῶν, *Enn*. VI.6 [34]), Plotinus discusses the place and ontological status of number in the whole structure of being and thinking, in which number mediates between the original unity of the one and the multiplicity of the infinite.[1] He dedicates *Ennead* V.5.4–5, part of the immediately preceding treatise chronologically, to the consideration of the one in its relation to number, outlining the main problems about the structure of number. In *Ennead* VI.6, however, we do not find a discussion of the constitution of number, which remains explicitly unresolved in both *Ennead* V.5 and VI.6, where Plotinus leaves it without a definitive answer. In what follows, I attempt to reconstruct the constitution, derivation, and construction of number in Plotinus in its various forms on the basis of various of Plotinus' texts.[2]

2.1 The Ontology of Numbers

Plotinus distinguishes between essential or substantial number (ὁ οὐσιώδης ἀριθμός) and quantitative or monadic number (μοναδικός, τοῦ ποσοῦ, *Enn*. V.5.4.16–20, VI.6.9.34–5, VI.6.16.25–6).[3] The latter is the image (εἴδωλον)

---

[1] For an in-depth discussion of Plotinus' theory of number, see Christoph Horn, *Plotin über Sein, Zahl und Einheit: eine Studie zu den systematischen Grundlagen der Enneaden* (Stuttgart: Teubner, 1995), p. 149.; Bernard Collette-Dučić, *Plotin et l'ordonnancement de l'être: Étude sur les fondements et les limites de la "détermination"* (Paris: Vrin, 2007), pp. 128–58; and Svetla Slaveva-Griffin, *Plotinus on Number* (Oxford: Oxford University Press, 2009), pp. 95–107.

[2] *Ennead* VI.6.10.13 *et passim*. Plotinus himself uses the term ἀριθμητική only rarely (in *Enn*. VI.3 [44].16.20–1, I.3 [20].6.3, III.1 [48].3.26), when referring to the science of numbers within the Pythagorean distinction of sciences.

[3] See the commentary *ad loc*. in Plotinus, *Die Schriften 30–38 der chronologischen Reihenfolge*, vol. 3 of *Plotins Schriften*, ed. Rudolf Beutler and Willy Theiler (Hamburg: Meiner, 1964), pp. 450–1; *Plotino sui numeri: Enneade VI 6 [34]*, trans. and ed. Claudia Maggi (Naples: Università degli Studi Suor Orsola Benincasa, 2009), pp. 218–20; *Ennead V.5: That the Intelligibles Are Not External to the Intellect, and on the Good*, trans. and ed. Lloyd P. Gerson (Las Vegas: Parmenides, 2013), pp. 126–8; and Claudia Maggi,

of the former through participation (μετοχή, *Enn.* V.5.4.3; μετάληψις, *Enn.* V.5.5.11–2). The quantitative number is that by which things are numbered and counted. The essential number always provides existence (ὁ τὸ εἶναι ἀεὶ παρέχων, *Enn.* V.5.4.18). In the act of numbering, the quantitative number constitutes quantity in the numbered as the realization or actualization of the essential number.[4]

Essential number is contemplated primarily in or "over" (ἐπιθεωρούμενος) the forms—εἴδη (*Enn.* VI.6.9.35–6). In order to find the place of the essential number as the ordering principle within being, Plotinus distinguishes being (ἡ οὐσία, τὸ εἶναι, *Enn.* V.5.5.22) into being proper (ὄν) and beings (ὄντα); that is, being as one and as many (see Chapter 1). This distinction, however, is not a real one because being is a synthetic unity of ἕν-ὄν or ἕν-πολλά, which transpires in the unity of one and many within the νοῦς (ὁμοῦ ἐν ἑνὶ πάντα, *Enn.* VI.6.7.4).[5] Plotinus speaks about the structure of the intellect (νοῦς) as the unified duality of thinking (νόησις) that thinks itself as things thought (νοητά, *Enn.* V.1.4.30–4, V.9.7.6–18)—but also as the triad of being, intellect, and life (*Enn.* VI.6.8.15–22, VI.6.9.27–31, VI.6.15.2–3, VI.6.18.31–3, III.9 [13].6.1–9).[6] The difficulty here is how to understand the being–beings distinction. At a certain point, in the early *Ennead* IV.8 [6], Plotinus even calls the intellect one *and* many (εἷς καὶ πολλοί, *Enn.* IV.8.3.10), which he otherwise reserves for the characterization of the soul (see Chapter 4).[7] In the case of the νόησις–νοητά division, the former might be taken as the ὄν and the latter as the ὄντα. But being (ὄν) is already a multiplicity bound into a unity, the ἕν-ὄν

Sinfonia matematica: Aporie e soluzioni in Platone, Aristotele, Plotino, Giamblico (Casoria: Loffredo, 2010), pp. 93–104. The term οὐσιώδης is neither used by Plato nor by Aristotle: see the commentary *ad loc.* in Plotinus, *Traité sur les nombres: Ennéade VI, 6 [34]*, ed. Janine Bertier and Luc Brisson (Paris: J. Vrin, 1980), pp. 179–81, 199. See also Syrianus, *In Met.* 186.30–6. On the basis of *Ennead* VI.6.9.35–7, Horn further distinguishes between "epitheoretical" (existing due to the activity of our thinking) and accidental numbers (Horn, *Plotin über Sein, Zahl und Einheit*, pp. 201–20).

[4] The distinction between these two types of number is similar to that between ideal (essential) and mathematical (quantitative) numbers, or εἰδητικοὶ ἀριθμοί and μαθηματικοὶ ἀριθμοί, discussed by Plato in the Academy: see Aristotle, *Met.* 1088b34–5, 1090b32–3. See also John Cleary, *Aristotle and Mathematics: Aporetic Method in Cosmology and Metaphysics* (Leiden: Brill, 1995), pp. 346–65; and Dmitri Nikulin, "Plato: *Testimonia et fragmenta*," in *The Other Plato*, ed. Dmitri Nikulin (Albany: SUNY Press, 2012), pp. 25–8.

[5] Cf. Anaxagoras (DK 59 B1) and Plato, *Parm.* 143A, 144D–E. See also Michael Wagner, "Realism and the Foundations of Science in Plotinus," *Ancient Philosophy* 5 (1985), pp. 269–92, esp. 280–5; and Halfwassen, *Der Aufstief zum Einen*, pp. 56–7.

[6] The terms "life" and "living being" refer back to Plato, *Tim.* 30B–31B, 39E, and *Soph.* 248E–249A. See Pierre Hadot, *Être, vie, pensée chez Plotin et avant Plotin* (Geneva: Foundation Hardt, 1960), pp. 105–41, and the commentary to Plotinus, *Traité sur les nombres*, pp. 166–7.

[7] See Plotinus, *Ennead IV.8: On the Descent of the Soul into Bodies*, trans. and ed. Barrie Fleet (Las Vegas: Parmenides, 2012), pp. 116–8.

of the second hypothesis in the *Parmenides*.[8] In the triad of being, intellect, and life as the living being, however, life stands for the cosmos of the forms in and through which the intellect realizes its being, in which the intellect thinks itself as the νοητά. Yet since every object of thought (νοητόν) is an instance of being, life as the living being should be identical with the ὄντα. But if beings (ὄντα) stand for multiplicity within the νόησις, they should be identical either with the intellect as thinking or with being, insofar as νόησις is being as first produced by and after the one.

Comparing, then, the ὄν–ὄντα and the ὄν–νοῦς–ζῷον partition schemes, one might argue that the ὄντα are represented as νοῦς in the activity and actuality of thinking that thinks itself (νόησις considered as the actuality of the νοῦς, *Enn.* V.4.2.3–4). In this case, the νοῦς would split into the numerical multiplicity in and of the ζῷον (*Enn.* III.9.1.1–37; Plato, *Tim.* 30C-D; cf. 39E). Plotinus seems to be aware of the difficulty of establishing a connection between ontological accounts based on double or triple distinctions. The dyad of the opposite principles is mainly used by Plato, whereas the triad of the principles in which one might be considered as mediating between the other two is employed by Aristotle. But Plotinus himself does not explicitly resolve the aporia, although in *Ennead* VI.6.9.29–31 he introduces the distinction among four terms (ὄν–ὄντα–νοῦς–ζῷον) that might provide a further hint toward resolving the problem of reconciling the two- and the three-term ontological accounts.

Plotinus formulates four hypotheses regarding the possible relation of numbers and forms (εἴδη): number can be considered as existing either after, together with, or independent of the forms. In the last case, number may be in turn conceived either before or after the forms (*Enn.* VI.6.4). Plotinus opts for the primacy of the (essential) number as constitutive, and thus ontologically before, the forms, as already present in the intellect and in the living being because "being came into existence from the one, as that one was one, being must also in this way be number; this is why the forms are called henads and numbers" (*Enn.* VI.6.9.32–5).[9] If we stage a thought experiment in which we produce something, we have to know beforehand precisely how many things are to be made. For this reason, number has to precede beings (cf. *Enn.* VI.6.9.14–24). As the structuring principle of being that itself is already structured by the one, number is inseparable from being split by thinking (νόησις) according to

---

[8] See Christoph Horn, "Der Platonische *Parmenides* und die Möglichkeit seiner prinzipientheoretischen Interpretation," *Antike und Abendland: Beiträge zum Verständnis der Griechen und Römer und ihres Nachlebens* 41 (1995), pp. 99–113.

[9] Cf. *Enn.* VI.6.15.29–30: "τὸ δὲ ὂν γενόμενον ἀριθμὸς συνάπτει τὰ ὄντα πρὸς αὑτό." See Jean Pépin, "Platonisme et antiplatonisme dans le traité de Plotin (VI.6 [34])," *Phronesis* 24:2 (1979), pp. 199–200. Proclus disagrees with Plotinus' positing "τὸ πρώτιστον ὂν πρὸ τῶν ἀριθμῶν" (*Theol. Plat.* I 50.18–9).

the essential number into the united multiplicity of life, which is the "living being," the collection of forms, the noetic cosmos of the intelligible objects (νοητά). At this point, Plotinus changes the order of being–life–intellect found in *Ennead* III.9 [13].1 to being–intellect–life in *Ennead* VI.6 [34].8. This has been noticed by Proclus, who resolves the difficulty by considering life as implied in two different intellects: the higher and the lower.[10]

Against the reconciliatory attempt of Proclus, I think, however, that the order of being–intellect–life should be preserved. Specifically, within the one-being, the unity, which is the image of the one, becomes the ontological precondition for the possibility of being (ὄν) because being cannot be thought as not one. Furthermore, being is itself the ontological precondition for the possibility of thinking (νόησις). In order to be able think at all, the activity of thinking has to *be*. No wonder, then, that in *Ennead* VI.6.15.16 number is characterized as νοῦ ἐνέργεια. Thinking, then, is the precondition of the possibility of life. Life as the cosmos of beings or the intelligible objects (νοητά) has to presuppose thinking that thinks itself in and as these particular forms. In other words, even before something can be thought as a noetic object (νοητόν), there should be an act of thinking (νόησις). Before the act of thinking there should simply *be* something, the ὄν. Before being there should be unity. Without unity, being is impossible (οὐδὲν γὰρ ὄν, ὃ μὴ ἕν, *Enn.* VI.6.13.50–1). The order of being–life–intellect, then, may be preserved only in the sense that life mediates being and thinking; that is, thinking as one-being is realized in the plurality of the objects of thought, which is the living being.

The relation between the various representations of being is therefore established in the following way: unity relates to being as the (essential) number to beings, or unity relates to the (essential) number as being to beings.[11] Essential number is then *in* (ἐν) being, *with* (μετά) being, and *before* (πρό) the beings that have their foundation, source, root, and principle (βάσις, πηγή, ῥίζα, ἀρχή) in the essential number, while the principle of being is the one as the source of being, transcendent to being.[12] The essential number that exists in and with being becomes fully developed and expressed in all of its powers only at the level of life (*Enn.* VI.6.15.8–18, VI.6.16.48).[13]

---

[10] Proclus, *In Tim.* I 427.6–20.

[11] *Enn.* VI.6.9.29; VI.6.9.39–40. Cf. Plotinus, *Traité sur les nombres*, pp. 74, 186; and Pépin, "Platonisme et antiplatonisme," pp. 179–208.

[12] *Enn.* VI.6.9.35–9. For the "metaphysics of prepositions," see *Enn.* VI.6.18.17–9; Proclus, *Theol. Plat.* II 60.22–61.9 and the commentary *ad loc.* in Proclus, *Théologie platonicienne: Livre II*, trans. and ed. H. D. Saffrey and L. G. Westerink (Paris: Les Belles Lettres, 1974), p. 117; Simplicius, *In Phys.* 10.35–11.3.

[13] According to Krämer, the intellect in Plotinus is the (essential) number thinking itself ("sichselbstdenkende Zahl"). See Hans Joachim Krämer, *Der Ursprung der Geistmetaphysik: Untersuchungen zur Geschichte des Platonismus zwischen Platon und Plotin* (Amsterdam: Schippers, 1964), p. 304.

Plotinus begins the discussion of number by implicitly accepting the following fundamental postulates: first, the producing unconditioned unity of the one is prior and superior to the indefinite unlimitedness of non-being. And second, the one-being is ontologically situated between the one and the unlimited privation of unity and being. This allows Plotinus to come up with a number of contradictory unmediated opposites in which the first element displays more unity and is thus ontologically and axiologically prior to the second one that exemplifies multiplicity and is destitute of productive power. The opposites are, then, ἕν, ἀληθῶς ἕν, τὸ μὴ μετοχῇ ἕν, καθαρῶς ἕν, ὄντως ἕν, οὐ κατ᾿ ἄλλο ἕν, αὐτό, τὸ ἔνδον, ἔχει ἑαυτό, καλόν—and τὰ ἄλλα ἕν, πολλὰ ὄντα μετοχῇ ἑνὸς ἕν, οὐ τὸ καθαρῶς ἕν, ἄλλο, ἀπόστασις τοῦ ἑνός, τὸ ἔξω, ἀπολλύμενον, αἰσχρόν, ἄκοσμον, ὕλη, ἄπειρα (*Enn.* V.5.4.1–19, VI.6.1.10–29; cf. Aristotle, *Met.* 986a21–6).

2.2 The Constitution of Being

The problem of the constitution of numbers in Plotinus is closely related to that of the constitution of being as thinking. Since number as constitutive of being mediates between unity and multiplicity, number should itself be brought forth by unity and multiplicity. Plotinus does not give an explanation of how this happens but instead provides a number of indications and a henological-ontological system within which the problem of the constitution of number can be addressed.

In *Ennead* V.5.4.20–38, by looking at the difficulties implied in the concept of the essential number, Plotinus suggests that the following be postulated:

(a) The one is the principle of number and being, the "bare one" (ἓν ψιλόν, *Enn.* VI.6.11.19) before being.
(b) The essential number is ontologically prior to and causes the existence of the quantitative number by participation.
(c) There are two principles that constitute essential numbers, the monad (μονάς) and the dyad (δυάς), the former being the principle of sameness, the latter the principle of otherness.[14]
(d) In number units can be distinguished.

First of all, for the sake of clarity, I need to lay out a number of terminological distinctions. In what follows, the one (ἕν) refers to the one as the unique principle of being, the monad (μονάς) refers to the one as the first principle in being, and the henad (ἑνάς) or unit refers to the unity within number.

---

[14] Cf. Alexander, *In Met.* 56.5–33.

Plotinus himself does not make a strict distinction among these terms, using them rather loosely and interchangeably.[15]

The postulate (c) raises the question about the ontological status of the two principles of number and the way these principles are constituted. The monad is the first and simplest undifferentiated unity of being when being is produced by the one (*Enn.* III.8.9.1–5). Such a unity is not different from being (ὄν), which itself is not different from the as yet still indeterminate thinking (νόησις). But the one being is, however, already the one-being, ἓν ὄν, and as such already presupposes the multiplicity that first appears as a simple dyad. The dyad and the monad, then, constitute the two principles of number and being within being.[16]

But how is the dyad constituted? First of all, the essential dyad cannot be considered a collection of two units because before the dyad there is no multiplicity or duality. Therefore, the dyad should be taken as one. The dyad may be taken as not the monad, but as the other to it. But where does this other come from? How does the ἓν ὄν become πολλὰ ὄντα? The logical and ontological (not temporal) sequence of acts that engender the dyad may be considered in the following way: when being is brought forward by the one, there is nothing else in and as being besides the as of yet undifferentiated being itself that is nothing else but the monad, the ideal principle of number. Plotinus argues that, logically, the monad may be said to be before being because "one" may be predicated of being and of each of the beings or the noetic forms (*Enn.* VI.6.5.36–8). At the same time, since in the ἓν ὄν each of the two terms, ἕν and ὄν, may in turn be considered as the subject and the other as the predicate, it may also be said that "being" is predicated of the one monad (contrary to Aristotle, *Cat.* 2a11–4).

Every act of thinking, however, is the thinking of something. Hence, being, which at first is nothing else but thinking (νόησις), strives to grasp that which has produced it; namely, the one that, as beyond being, cannot be properly thought. In order to conceive the νόησις as capable of thinking itself as complete and completed, we need to assume a kind of movement of and within

---

[15] As, for instance, at *Enn.* VI.6.4.4, VI.6.5.6, VI.6.5.37–8, VI.6.9.33, VI.6.10.3–4, VI.6.10.19 (τὸ ἓν τὸ κατὰ τὴν μονάδα), VI.6.11.16–24, and VI.6.12.1 (τὸ ἓν καὶ τὴν μονάδα). Cf. Plato, *Phil.* 15A; and "καὶ γὰρ εἰ παρὰ Πλάτωνι ἑνάδες εἴρηνται ἐν Φιλήβῳ, οὐ παρὰ τὸ ἓν ἐλέχθησαν, ἀλλὰ παρὰ τὴν ἑνάδα, ἥτις ἐστὶ μονὰς μετοχῇ τοῦ ἑνός" (Theon, *Expos. rer. math.* 21.14–6). See also Syrianus, *In Met.* 183.24–5; and Proclus, *In Parm.* 880.22–5. Anonymus Photii ascribes to the Pythagoreans the usage of μονάς for the description of the intelligible and ἕν for numbers: see Thesleff, *The Pythagorean texts*, p. 237. Cf. Iamblichus, *In Nicom. arithm.* 11.1–26. I follow Iamblichus, for whom ἕν refers to the one productive of being, whereas μονάς refers to the produced (being; μονὰς ἐκ τοῦ ἑνός [Iamblichus, *De myst.* 262.3–5]). Cf. Plotinus, *Traité sur les nombres*, pp. 170, 174–5; and Gottlob Frege, *Die Grundlagen der Arithemetik: eine logisch mathematische Untersuchung über den Begriff der Zahl* (Hamburg: Meiner, 1986), p. 44.

[16] Cf. "ἓν ὄν, ἀλλ' οὐκ ὄν, εἶτα ἕν" (*Enn.* VI.6.13.52–3); Plato, *Parm.* 142D, 143A, 144D-E; and Pépin, "Platonisme et antiplatonisme," pp. 203–4.

being as thinking, in which the νοῦς returns to itself and thus defines itself in the act of self-thinking, which is opposed to the initial indefinite thinking without the objects of thought (νοητά). In Plotinus' words, the perfect unity of the monad and that of the one is kept standing absolutely still in fear of departing from this unity. Even the slightest departure already brings forward the other and thus the two (*Enn.* V.5.4.8–10). But the movement away from the unity of the one in being is not proper to the monad but appears only in the "falling away" (ἀπόστασις, *Enn.* VI.6.1.2) from that unity. Such a movement is directed toward its end, which is the thinking that thinks itself in the forms of itself as the intelligible objects.

The primary movement and the otherness appear thus inseparable and constitutive of the dyad, whereas rest and sameness characterize the monad.[17] This first movement, then, is pure otherness (ἑτερότης) that forever separates (κεχωρίσθαι) the νοῦς from the one (*Enn.* V.1.6.53; cf. VI.4 [22].11.9–10). The fundamental principle that Plotinus implies here is that "everything seeks not another but itself" (ἕκαστον γὰρ οὐκ ἄλλο, ἀλλ᾽ αὐτὸ ζητεῖ, *Enn.* VI.6.1.10–1). The pure otherness or bare negativity is therefore nothing else but the essential (ideal) dyad that enables the thinking to return to itself in the sameness of self-thinking through the otherness of multitude of the intelligible objects. The one simple undifferentiated thinking (νόησις) "sees" or thinks itself as one in and as the object of thought (*Enn.* V.4.2.4–7) and thus not as one but as thinking *and* thought.[18] One as thinking and thought turns out to be triple: as that which thinks, as that which is thought, and as the act of thinking itself—or the knower, the known, and the knowledge (ὁμοῦ ὁ ἐπιστήμων, τὸ ἐπιστητόν, ἡ ἐπιστήμη, *Enn.* VI.6.15.19–20).

In this way, the dyad as the pure otherness makes being of the initial thinking (νόησις) leave its state of sameness and unreflective identity. When νόησις necessarily misses the only object worth thinking or seeing (the postulate [a]), the source of thinking and being—namely, the one—then thinking can only turn to itself and think itself since, at that point, there is nothing else to be thought. But the thinking is itself *not other* to itself, οὐκ ἄλλο. The "not other" is nothing else but one, or the monad in being. But the act of constituting the one-monad itself requires the *other*, which is the dyad. The otherness, represented in the form of the indefinite dyad, ἀόριστος δυάς, is

---

[17] Cf. Aristotle, *Met.* 1004b29: "στάσις τοῦ ἑνὸς κίνησις δὲ τοῦ πλήθους"; see also *Met.* 988a14–5, 992b7–8, 1066a7–16, 1084a35, 1091b13–6; Willy Theiler, "Einheit und unbegrenzte Zweiheit von Plato bis Plotin," in *Isonomia: Studien zur Gleichheitsvorstellung im Griechischen Denken*, ed. Jürgen Mau and Ernst Günther Schmidt (Berlin: Akademie, 1964), pp. 106–7; and John M. Rist, "The Problem of 'Otherness' in the *Enneads*," in *Le Néoplatonisme*, ed. Pierre Maxime Schuhl and Pierre Hadot (Paris: Éditions du Centre national de la recherché scientifique, 1971), pp. 77–87.

[18] See John Bussanich, *The One and Its Relation to Intellect in Plotinus* (Leiden: Brill, 1988), pp. 10–4.

then the principle of indefiniteness. This indefinite, however, is not the pure ἀπειρία that by itself is absolutely indefinite (there is neither "it" nor "self" in it) and may be considered as embracing the opposites without mediation, to be both moving and at rest, big and small, μέγα καὶ σμικρόν (*Enn.* VI.6.3.29; the postulate [c]).[19]

Therefore, the constitution of being necessarily has to presuppose *two* principles in being, the one-monad and the dyad, and not one only (the postulate [c]; *Enn.* V.4.2.7–9).[20] The second principle, that of the otherness, the dyad, may be considered posterior to the monad.[21] Yet, at the same time, the dyad may be also considered prior to the monad because the sameness of the monad is first realized as the negation of the otherness, as not-other, οὐκ ἄλλο (*Enn.* VI.6.13.9–11). The dyad itself is thus τὸ ἄλλο and τὸ ἕτερον, or is merely an indefinite other, τὸ ἄλλο. But when the monad comes forth, the dyad is thought of as the other, τὸ ἕτερον, to the monad. In this sense, the monad is both prior and posterior to the dyad, although in different respects.[22]

Constitution of the dyad as the otherness (ἑτερότης) that separates being from its origin presupposes, then, not only the duality of same and other, of rest and movement, but also implies a more complicated structure of the triplicity of coming out, turning back, and staying in unity (*Enn.* VI.6.3.7–9).[23] In *Ennead* V.1, Plotinus argues that in and by returning to the one, the being-intellect "sees" or thinks, and this "seeing" (ὅρασις) is the intellect itself (*Enn.* V.1.7.5–6). The initial act of seeing can be compared to the yet unlimited and indefinite (ἀόριστος) thinking, as if thinking "unintelligently" (ἀνοήτως, *Enn.* VI.7.16.14). Such a thinking does not yet think itself unless it thinks in definite forms (νοητά). As if in movement, thinking comes out toward the one, then returns back to itself without having really left itself, and stays

---

[19] Cf. Aristotle, *Met.* 987b26, 1089a35–6, 1091a3–5; *Phys.* 203a15–6; and Sextus Empiricus, *Adv. Math.* X 261, 274–6. Otherness in the intelligible is also present as intelligible matter, ὕλη νοητή (*Enn.* II.4; see Chapter 6).

[20] Cf. Philip Merlan, "Aristotle, *Met.* A.6, 987b20–25 and Plotinus, *Enn.* V 4, 2, 8–9," *Phronesis* 9:1 (1964), pp. 45–7; and Szlezák, *Platon und Aristoteles in der Nuslehre Plotins*, p. 58. In *Enn.* V.1.5.13–9, Plotinus argues that number determines the structure of the intellect and is constituted by the monad and the dyad; the dyad is indefinite (ἀόριστος) and a kind of substrate (ὑποκείμενον). Numenius deduced the soul from the monad and the dyad; cf. Xenocrates, *Darstellung der Lehre und Sammlung der Fragmente*, ed. Richard Heinze (Leipzig: Teubner, 1892), fr. 60 = Xenocrates, *Frammenti*, ed. Isnardi Parente (Naples: Bibliopolis, 1982), pp. 165–87; *Enn.* VI.6.16.45; and Aristotle, *De an.* 404b27–8.

[21] *Enn.* V.5.4.24–5; cf. πλῆθος ἑνὸς ὕστερον, *Enn.* III.8.9.3–4. Cf. also Aristotle, *Met.* 1083b23–5.

[22] Cf. Aristotle, *Met.* 1084b29–30.

[23] The order of procession–staying–return is different from that of Proclus' πρόοδος-μονή-ἐπιστροφή (*In Tim.* I 87.28–30, 211.28–212.1, 274.25–30, II 215. 22–4, III 18.1–2; *In Remp.* I 88.11–6, 140.2). Perhaps it is not by chance that the structure of *Enn.* VI.6. is itself triadic: two chapters in the beginning and two chapters at the end are dedicated to the consideration of number and infinity (*Enn.* VI.6.2–3, VI.6.17–8), while the middle chapters (*Enn.* VI.6.4–16) discuss the constitution of number and its relation to the being of intellect. The very structure of the treatise appears to imitate the original infinity of the one, the multiple unity of ἕν-πολλά of the being-intellect, and the unlimited dyad.

in the fullness in itself as both the same and the other, thus acquiring limit, boundary, and form (ὅρος, πέρας, εἶδος, *Enn.* VI.7.16.14–24, VI.7.17.14–21). One can also understand this (again, ontological and logical, and not temporal) process of unfolding the unity of being into the unified "multicolored" multiplicity within the same being, now unfolded according to the essential number. Such a multiplicity is present as beings (ὄντα) in thinking (νόησις) that thinks itself as the forms or objects of thought (νοητά). This process, then, may be represented in four terms: namely, of the initial simple unity of being; the unfolding of the multiplicity of beings; the intellect moving in itself; and, finally, the synthetic unity of life (ζωή), of the living being of the noetic cosmos.[24]

Since otherness is constitutive of the intellect itself, it is present in the most fundamental acts of intellection; namely, in making distinctions between two different things. The very act of counting may then be considered as the simplest and originative act of distinguishing the primary units, which are equal in all respects except for being different numerically (as distinguished within the essential number). These non-discursive and non-logical (οὐ λόγοις) acts of establishing distinctions are called ἐπιβολαί by Plotinus.[25] The acts that establish the primary form of the otherness as dyad, or movement within the intellect, are constituted as an elementary pointing at the other, the recognition of the other as "this is this, and this is this" (τόδε τόδε, τόδε τόδε, *Enn.* VI.3.18.13). The otherness-dyad establishes the other in the τόδε τόδε, which, in order to be understood as the other to each other, requires sameness in an act of double negation, as the other of the other, so that the thinking of the intellect does not need to go into infinity. Two primary principles, then, suffice for thinking and being.

---

[24] "τὸ μὲν ὂν ἀριθμὸς ἡνωμένος, τὰ δὲ ὄντα ἐξεληλιγμένος ἀριθμός, νοῦς δὲ ἀριθμὸς ἐν ἑαυτῷ κινούμενος, τὸ δὲ ζῷον ἀριθμὸς περιέχων" (*Enn.* VI.6.9.29–31).

[25] The term ἐπιβολή is of Stoic and Epicurean origin. Plotinus argues that, in order to think a particular object—for instance, a horse—one has to already be in the position to use the concept of the "one." When Plotinus asks whether the monad precedes being and number precedes beings in thinking, in an intuitive act of the intellect or also in reality (τῇ ἐπινοίᾳ καὶ τῇ ἐπιβολῇ ἢ καὶ τῇ ὑποστάσει, *Enn.* VI.6.9.13–4), he uses three terms, the first of which—ἐπίνοια—is a term of Plato which is not found in Aristotle; ἐπιβολή is used by the Stoics and the Epicureans and is absent in Plato and Aristotle; and ὑπόστασις is used only by Aristotle and is absent in Plato. See Plotinus, *Traité sur les nombres*, pp. 197, 200–1. I am grateful to Marcelo Boeri for pointing out that, in the Stoics, the concept of ἐπιβολή is used primarily as an anticipatory concept ap. Stobaeus II 87.18, the definition of the ἐπιβολή as an impulse that anticipates ὁρμή, while in the sense of immediate mental presentation, ἐπιβολή is rather used by Epicurus in Diogenes Laertius, *Vitae phil.* X 31. Cf. Andrei Cornea, "*Athroa epibolē*: On an Epicurean Formula in Plotinus' Work," in *Plotinus and Epicurus: Matter, Perception, Pleasure*, ed. Angela Longo and Daniela Patrizia Taormina (Cambridge: Cambridge University Press, 2016), pp. 177–88.

2.3 The Two and the Henad

Let us now turn to the question of how the essential or ideal numbers are constituted. The monad and the dyad are not yet numbers, but the ideal principles of numbers. The first essential number as mentioned by Plotinus is number two (*Enn.* VI.6.5.4).[26] As such, it is different from the indefinite dyad, ἀόριστος δυάς, which is not a number but the principle of indefiniteness. Together with Plato, the dyad may be considered as great-and-small, μέγα καὶ μικρόν, πολλὰ καὶ ὀλίγα, or ὑπεροχὴ καὶ ἔλλειψις, which are not two different opposed principles but one, "more or less" (*Enn.* VI.3.28.10–1, VI.4.2.30–1). The dyad makes essential number go beyond the stable identity of the monad, which, however, is prevented from moving into unlimitedness by the limiting power of the monad. Due to the presence of the dyad, being becomes other than it is, which originates two as essential number.

One could consider the production of two as the first number by first constituting a henad and then either increasing (doubling) it or dividing it.[27] However, Plotinus denies that the number two can be arrived at either by an addition (union, σύνοδος) or division (splitting, σχίσις). Otherwise, the number would have been reduced to merely a relation, τὸ πρὸς τι or σχέσις, but relation is the relation of something that is already there: in this case, of being that is divided or split according to the form of number.[28] Bringing together two units will not produce the number two because it should already be there for the two units to be thought, predicated, and to exist as two. Moreover, the dyad (ἡ δυάς) as the principle and the two as the first essential number (τὰ δύο) are not in relation as entities of equal ontological status (*Enn.* VI.6.14.15–9). By its presence (παρουσία), the dyad determines the two as the first number, so that both are connected by participation.

Rejecting the hypothesis that makes number posterior to forms, Plotinus argues that one can establish the logical and ontological priority of being one from the analysis of predication (see Chapter 3). If we say "one man," the "one" that is one in being, the monad, is already predicated of human being (*Enn.* VI.6.5.29–34). The same argument comes up in the second hypothesis of Plato's *Parmenides* (144B–157B): being can only be one-being, ἓν ὄν. And although being is one, it nevertheless always already involves the form of pure duality in the primary unity of two components, of ἓν ὄν, since being presupposes that it is one, and one, if thought and predicated, is in being. Since the essential

---

[26] Cf. Alexander, *In Met.* 56.32; Simplicius, *In Phys.* 454.28 (πρῶτος δὲ ἀριθμὸς ἡ δυάς).

[27] Cf. Porphyry as quoted by Simplicius, *In Phys.* 454.9–16. See also Plato, *Phaedo* 96E–97B (does the number two come from the addition of two units or from the division of one unit?); Aristotle, *Met.* 1081b14–5; *Phys.* 206b3–16; and Plotinus, *Traité sur les nombres*, p. 184.

[28] The double and the half, τὸ διπλάσιον καὶ τὸ ἥμισυ, as an example of relation, σχέσις, *Enn.* VI.1.6.3–4. Cf. Aristotle, *Met.* 1020b26–7.

number, according to Plotinus, is *in* being (*Enn.* VI.6.15.24) and defines the structure of being in its unified duality of ἓν ὄν, the very form of the number two is thereby established as the synthetic one-being. Still, since being is unity (of thinking-νόησις) in multiplicity (of the thought-νοητά), the one as monad should be prior to being that in the monad is only "falsely or spuriously one." Plotinus thus argues: "And if the one is like an element of a compound (ὡς στοιχεῖον δὲ συνθέτου), there must be beforehand a one which is one in itself, that it may be compounded with another; then, if it is compounded with another which has become one through it, it will make that other spuriously [ψευδῶς] one, by making it two" (*Enn.* VI.6.5.43–6).

Hence, the constitution of the first essential number—two—suggests that being is constituted by the monad and the dyad and is structured according to the number two. This means that the unit within the number—the henad—should be posterior to the number. In its very form, the number is prior to its units that may only be distinguished after it has been constituted (the postulate [d]).[29] Each henad of the two and the number two itself are one (that is, participate in the monad) yet differently: the unity of the henad is similar to that of a house that is one in virtue of its continuity (τὸ συνεχὲς . . . ἕν), even if the henad is not continuous but discrete: its unity is that of one subject. The unity of the number two may be compared to that of an army that is one substantially or quantitatively (*Enn.* V.5.4.29–33). In other words, strictly speaking, the number neither consists of the henads nor is it counted by them, although when the henads are distinguished within a number, the number may be said to comprise the henads. For this reason, Plotinus disagrees with Aristotle that the henad may be regarded as the matter of number (Aristotle, *Met.* 1084b5–6). Rather, the matter of the essential number is the multiplicity of the dyad, bound by the form of the monad.

In order to be able to properly discuss the structure of number, we should first distinguish the constitutive element of number. The difficulty that arises here is that number, as Plotinus argues, is prior to thinking that thinks itself in particular forms and that is thus already structured according to the number.[30] This difficulty may be resolved by accepting a unity in number, the henad, as one by participation in the monad or through the presence of the monad (παρουσίᾳ, *Enn.* VI.6.5.49, VI.6.14.27–8, VI.6.41–2).[31] This distinction

---

[29] According to Aristotle, for Plato, two is also prior to its units: Aristotle, *Met.* 1084b36–7; cf. 1085a6–7.

[30] Cf. Dominic O'Meara, *Structures hiérarchiques dans la penseé de Plotin: étude historique et interprétative* (Leiden: Brill, 1975), pp. 79–82.

[31] On the one as the principle of numbers, see Cleary, *Aristotle and Mathematics*, pp. 365–77. As Cleary argues (p. 369), Aristotle is somewhat ambiguous (*Met.* 1052b14–20; cf. 1088a6–8: "οὐκ ἔστι τὸ ἓν ἀριθμός . . . ἀλλ' ἀρχὴ [τοῦ ἀριθμοῦ] καὶ τὸ μέτρον καὶ τὸ ἕν") on whether the essence of the unity is being indivisible (Aquinas, Cleary) or being the first measure of a number (Ross).

resolves a seeming paradox and explains how and why the one is both prior and posterior to the dyad and to the number two: the one is prior to the dyad as the one and as monad, and the one is posterior to the dyad as henad (*Enn.* V.5.4.11, V.5.4.24).

The one and the monad should precede the henad, since there are many henads that participate in one monad that is common (κοινόν) to the henads and itself participates in the one (cf. *Enn.* VI.6.11.6–7, VI.6.5.31). As transcendent to being, the one cannot be equal to other unities or units (to the monad and the henads), so as to be one of them or with them (τοῖς ἄλλοις δὲ οὐκ ἴσον, ἵνα σὺν αὐτοῖς, *Enn.* V.5.4.14–5). The multiplicity of the henads (πλῆθος ἑνάδων) can be proven by a *reductio ad absurdum* (*Enn.* VI.6.11.10–33). If there is only one monad, it should be joined or associated with the one being, ἓν ὄν, either (1) as being (ὄν) or (2) as one (ἕν). The (1) is impossible because (1.1) either the units that are distinguished in number are the same only in name but are not at the same ontological level (οὐ συνταχθήσονται) and, therefore, are only equivocally (ὁμωνύμως) said to be henads, which means that there are no units in number at all. Or, (1.2) number would consist of unlike units (ἐξ ἀνομοίων μονάδων), which Plotinus implicitly rejects because any distinction between the henads is impossible. If the henads were all different, there would need to be an additional explanation of how the first principles of the monad and the dyad constitute this difference. And if henads were all identical, there would be a non-identity represented in them as multitude. Yet there are many henads within each essential number. Such a multitude differs, however, from the multitude of the one-many of the νοῦς, where all the intelligible objects (νοητά) are different as various forms. Henads, to the contrary, form a set of equals that are intrinsically indiscernible for Plotinus because the distinction is extrinsic to them and is brought by the essential number as setting a definite number of the henads. If the henads of the essential number two are exactly the same and equal, how can it be that there are two henads, and how can they be numerically different? The only explanation is to assume the number two as the very form that allows for the duality of the henads, for otherwise it could not even be said that there are two henads. Different henads may be thought, then, not as consequential but rather as coexistential. In other words, henads, unlike the forms, do not have individuality. Their very distinction comes from what defines them as a set, as this particular number of henads. But, furthermore, (2) is also impossible because, in order to be one that *is*, the monad needs to be a unique one and not another one—in particular, not a henad. Therefore, the primary duality of the ἓν ὄν is sufficient for generating all the numbers and forms within being. However, it should be stressed that although the henad is not individualized, it is not divisible because the henad is defined solely by the essential number as the principle of individuation of the henad. For if the henad were divisible, it would have defined another number. Hence, if one henad of two henads of the number two would have been divided into two henads, there would have been three henads, which means that they would have referred to the number three and not to the number two.

2.4 The Constitution of Essential Numbers

Now that the first number, two, and the henad are deduced, we may turn to the other essential numbers in Plotinus as they are produced by the monad and the dyad.[32] Since otherness is always there in being, in the form of ἓν ὄν or ἓν πολλά, and the dyad as otherness is present in and as movement,[33] Plotinus finds an original way of describing the deduction of the essential numbers by means of their kinematic production, or by intelligible movement. If the nature of being is ἓν ὄν or ἓν πολλά, it

> generates in a kind of succession [ἐφεξῆς], or rather has generated, or does not stand still at one thing of those which it has generated, but makes a kind of continuous one, when it draws [a line] [περιγράψασα] and stops more quickly in its outgoing [στᾶσα θᾶττον ἐν τῇ προόδῳ] it generates the lesser numbers, but when it moves further [εἰς πλέον δὲ κινηθεῖσα], not in other things but in its very own movements, it brings the greater numbers into existence; and so it would fit [ἐφαρμόσαι] the particular multitudes [τὰ πλήθη] and each particular being to the particular numbers, knowing that, if each particular being was not fitted to each particular number, it could not exist at all or would get away and be something else by becoming innumerable and irrational [ἀνάριθμον καὶ ἄλογον]. (*Enn.* VI.6.11.24–33)[34]

The main steps in Plotinus' deduction of essential numbers are thus the following: (1) essential number results from a "stop" (or consecutive stops) of and within the intelligible movement. These "stops," pauses, interruptions, or ruptures do not form a temporal succession, for time appears only with the soul (*Enn.* III.7.11). Therefore, the stops can only establish a logical sequence, although not yet really a series in the proper sense, which is characteristic of the quantitative numbers. Hence, (2) all the numbers are *already* there, already having been moved. Plotinus finds it more appropriate to describe the essential numbers, even if produced by movement, not temporally—for this

---

[32] *Enn.* V.5.5.2–4. Cf. Iamblichus, *De comm. math. sci.* 18.3–4: "ἐκ δὲ τῆς συνθέσεως τοῦ ἑνὸς καὶ τῆς τοῦ πλήθους αἰτίας ὕλης ὑφίσταται μὲν ὁ ἀριθμός."

[33] Otherness as the intelligible matter is the first movement. See *Enn.* II.4.5.28–30.

[34] Cf. *Enn.* V.5.4.8–10. The closest passage in Plato might be *Phil.* 24D, although Plato does not speak about the kinematic generation of either arithmetic or geometrical entities.

movement is not temporal—but rather in quasi-spatial terms.³⁵ (3) The nontemporal kinematic production of the numbers is then presented by Plotinus as the multiplication of being (ὄν) into beings (ὄντα), when the being is split (σχίζεται) according to the potencies of the essential number, which, as the first and true number, is the principle and the source of the existence of beings (*Enn.* VI.6.15.29–35).³⁶ Things, then, may be numbered only because of the existence of the essential numbers that are the ontological precondition for numbering and are not simply an abstraction from the things numbered.

Most importantly, (4) the kinematic production of geometrical entities, later used by Proclus (see Chapter 8),³⁷ is already present in Plotinus and is possible because of the similar though ontologically precedent kinematic generation of numbers. This production, known and exemplified in drawing geometrical figures that are ontologically intermediate between the sphere of the discrete, of essential numbers and forms—and the sphere of the continuous, the physical entities and bodies, is extended by Plotinus to essential numbers (cf. *Enn.* VI.7.13.9; Plato, *Phil.* 16C-D). The "expansion" (ἐπέκτασις) of number is then the paradigmatic example for the extension or prolongation of the continuous into the distance (εἰς τὸ πόρρω). "So there is a quantum [ποσόν] when the unit [τὸ ἕν, as the henad] moves forward, as also when the point [τὸ σημεῖον] does" (*Enn.* VI.3.12.9–13).³⁸ In this way, one proceeds from one essential number to another.

Finally, (5) in the very description of the constitution of essential numbers, one can easily recognize the πρόοδος–ἐπιστροφή–μονή sequence, which Plotinus used in the description of the constitution of the dyad.³⁹ Namely, the original movement constitutes the moment of πρόοδος. The stop in movement, as the beginning of turning to itself as a definite number, corresponds to the ἐπιστροφή. And the "recognition" of a particular quantitative determination of a number, in which all of its retrospectively discernible "parts" or henads are gathered into a unity of being this number (τὰ πάντα μέρη πρὸς ἕν, *Enn.* VI.6.1.19–20), embodies the μονή moment of the kinematic constitution of numbers.

---

³⁵ Cf. Plotinus' explanation of the ubiquity of the one: it is everywhere "because there is nowhere where it is not" (πανταχοῦ· οὐ γάρ ἐστιν ὅπου οὔ, *Enn.* III.9 [13].4.1–2).

³⁶ "ἀρχὴ οὖν καὶ πηγὴ ὑποστάσεως τοῖς οὖσιν ὁ ἀριθμὸς ὁ πρῶτος καὶ ἀληθής" (*Enn.* VI.6.15.34–5, in reference to Plato, *Phaedr.* 245C).

³⁷ Proclus describes drawing a line by the uniform movement or "flowing" (τῷ ῥύσιν) of a point: see Proclus, *In Eucl.* 185.8–15; cf. 51.21.

³⁸ The difference between a henad and a point is that the point is the unit that has position, which means that the point exists in the continuous, where otherness is present not as the ἀόριστος δυάς but as matter. Cf.: "ἡ γὰρ στιγμὴ μονάς ἐστι θέσιν ἔχουσα" (Aristotle, *De an.* 409a6); "ἡ γὰρ μονὰς στιγμὴ ἄθετός ἐστιν" (Aristotle, *Met.* 1084b26); "ἡ μὲν ἄθετος μονὰς ἡ δὲ θετὸς στιγμή" (ibid., 1016b30–1; cf. 1016b24–6); "μονάδα προσλαβοῦσαν θέσιν" (Proclus, *In Eucl.* 95.22).

³⁹ Cf. Proclus. *Elem. theol.* §§ 31–9, 34.28–42.7.

In *Metaphysics* M 6 (1080a15–b4), Aristotle discusses three hypotheses (which he eventually rejects) of the possible relation between the units within the numbers: a unit may be either (1) incompatible with another unit (ἀσύμβλητος) within any number, or (2) compatible with any other unit, or (3) compatible with the unit(s) within this particular number but incompatible with the units within any other number (see Appendix).

Plotinus poses similar questions (which, however, he leaves without an explicit answer) about the constitution of numbers: How are two units of the dyad different? How is the dyad one? Are the two units equal within the dyad (*Enn.* V.5.4.27–9)?

First of all, what is the relation of henads to the number? Is the essential number a multitude consisting of indivisible henads, and is it defined by them, as it comes in Theon's definition of number as a collection of units (ἀριθμός ἐστι σύστημα μονάδων; Theon, *Expos. rer. math.* 18.3)? The answer has to be no, just as in the case with the number two. As Plotinus explains, the essential number does *not* consist of henads but rather precedes them as a unity, as a chorus or an army may be said to precede their parts. This can be clearly seen from the way the numbers are constituted kinematically. Each number should be considered, then, not as a set or a collection of henads. Rather, each number is the successor of the previous essential number, by performing another step within the intelligible movement. It makes no sense to try to determine the "length" of each step nor to even ask if they are all of equal "length" because the unit of length is not yet established, so that every new movement brings forth another number by simply presenting it as different from the previous one. Since every subsequent number differs from the preceding by one unit or henad, every step constitutes a difference of one henad. And since the steps are discrete, the henads are also discrete and indivisible. Divisibility in the essential number exists only as its divisibility into a particular multitude of its units-henads and not as the divisibility of its constituents.

Essential number is thus determined as an ordinal and not a cardinal number. In other words, essential number is determined by and from the order of its kinematic production, defined recurrently, from the previous number plus one more step. A similar procedure might have been meant in the Academy by Plato, for whom, as Aristotle explains (*Met.* 1080a30–5), quantitative or mathematical numbers are constituted as counted: $1 + 1 = 2$, $2 + 1 = 3$, and so forth, while the essential or ideal numbers are simply presented as 1, then 2, then 3, and so forth. Essential numbers are constituted as the structured wholes that do not consist of units. The units or the henads may be discerned, then, in all the essential numbers—as in the number two—only in a secondary way. Since the number three is kinematically constituted after the number two, in which two henads can be discerned, one can consider there to be three henads in number three. In number four, constituted after the number three, one can discern four henads, and so forth.

However, it should be noted that, first, the kinematic production is not itself a temporal process; second, the logical sequence that establishes the set of essential numbers exists only within the discursive dianoetic thinking absent in the νοῦς; and third, the notion of succession presupposes number as its very precondition. Therefore, we cannot properly say that the essential numbers are established in the succession of one after another. Rather, they *already* exist or have been generated as coexisting and constituting one single set of numbers that determines the entire multiplicity of beings-ὄντα (cf. *Enn.* VI.6.10.1–4) and subsequently defines the structure of the intelligible objects-νοητά. Hence, as having been already produced, the essential numbers (and the henads in them) may be considered not as following each other but as coexisting.

But are the henads in the essential numbers mutually comparable, or are they all different within one number and within different numbers? Since the henads are separated from each other by a "unit of movement," which is discrete and of no length, then, by way of their constitution and distinction, they are not different but are all equal. Yet what is the principle of individuation of the henads? As in the case of the essential number two, all the henads within any essential number are all alike, to the extent that they have no individuality. The principle of individuation, then, can only be the number itself as a whole that precedes particular henads. In other words, seven henads are all exactly alike, but they are distinguishable only because of the essential number "seven," which is a precondition for the possibility of discerning exactly seven henads, all of which are different as seven henads, yet all of them are alike as henads. Essential number can only establish numerical distinction between the henads, but there is no specific distinction between them. This means that the henads are all comparable with each other within one number. But are they also comparable with the henads of another essential number, for example, in numbers five and ten (*Enn.* V.5.4.33–5)? Plotinus does not provide a clear answer to this question in the text. In fact, the henads within different numbers may be considered both comparable and incomparable although in different senses. The henads may be said to be mutually comparable: first, insofar as they are all distinguishable in the same way from the essential number as the form of a particular multitude of henads, and, second, insofar as a henad may be considered as constituted by another step in the kinematic production of numbers. But to the extent that the henads are constituted not one by one but as a particular multitude within which they coexist as a system of henads (of the number seven, eight, etc.), they may be considered different in different numbers and thus incomparable because each number defines a different multitude of the henads.

Finally, is the total number of the essential numbers limited or not? Plotinus often uses ten as an example (in *Enn.* VI.6, δέκα/ δεκάς is mentioned forty-five times),[40] but again, he gives no clear indication of whether the number of numbers is limited by a particular number. However, if we take into consideration what has been said about the constitution of essential number in Plotinus, it is possible to argue that such a number has to be limited. For, first, the essential number cannot go into infinity but has to stop because number as a unified multiplicity of units is itself both limiting and limited. The infinite number, therefore, cannot exist. The number is unlimited only in the sense that it is not measured but is itself the measure for being.[41] The infinite "struggles" with the number (τὸ γὰρ ἄπειρον μάχεται τῷ ἀριθμῷ, *Enn.* VI.6.17.3). And second, since number defines and measures the multitude of the forms, and the number of forms is limited, the number of essential numbers cannot be unlimited. For the infinite may define the finite only as the actual infinity of the power of the one (as δύναμις τῶν πάντων, *Enn.* III.8.10.1, V.4.1.36) and not as a potentially infinite, even if numerable, as the potentially infinite series of natural numbers because the potentially infinite is ontologically posterior to the limit, by which being is first established and introduced.

2.5 The Constitution of Quantitative Numbers

Let us now turn to the question of how the quantitative numbers are constituted. Since beings (ὄντα) are generated and organized according to the essential numbers, and things are determined by the forms through participation, things are organized and separated according to number (μετὰ ἀριθμῶν ἡ γένεσις ἑκάστοις, *Enn.* VI.6.15.35–6). The quantitative numbers are also organized according to the pattern of the essential numbers as their paradigm. The quantitative numbers are numbering (ἀριθμοῦντες), insofar as they are applicable to things that are in constant change, even though the numbering number cannot properly grasp the sheer becoming that always escapes any definition and limitation. The essential numbers, on the contrary, are numbered (ἀριθμητοί), insofar as they are already existing and exempt from any change. The essential numbers are numbered in the sense that they are not the ultimate measure but are themselves measured through the transcendent measure of the one which alone is not measured by anything (μέτρον γὰρ αὐτὸ καὶ οὐ μετρούμενον, *Enn.* V.5.4.13–4).[42] The one is thus the measure of measure that

---

[40] Cf. Aristotle, *Phys.* 206b32–3; *Met.* 1073a19–21, 1084a12, 24–5.

[41] *Enn.* VI.6.2, VI.6.17–18.6., esp. VI.6.18.5–6. Cf. Plato, *Parm.* 144A; Aristotle, *Met.* 1083b36–1084a7; *Phys.* 203b23–4.

[42] In his distinction between essential and quantitative number, Plotinus probably has in mind Aristotle's distinction between numbered and numbering number, in his definition of time as the numbered and not the numbering number: "ἀριθμός ἐστι διχῶς (καὶ γὰρ τὸ ἀριθμούμενον καὶ τὸ ἀριθμητὸν ἀριθμὸν λέγομεν, καὶ ᾧ ἀριθμοῦμεν), ὁ δὴ χρόνος ἐστὶν τὸ ἀριθμούμενον καὶ οὐχ ᾧ ἀριθμοῦμεν" (Aristotle, *Phys.* 219b5–9).

provides the unity for measure, both for the monad that imitates the one and for the henad that participates in the monad. The one itself, however, is absolutely transcendent to being and incommensurable with anything else.

As was argued, the essential numbers may be considered as coexisting.[43] The quantitative number exists by participation in the essential number. The essential number, as already numbered, is then the pure actuality of number, fully unfolded as number in the living being or the intelligible cosmos. The actuality in being and thinking precedes the potentiality, which is the general principle in Aristotle (πρότερον ἐνέργεια δυνάμεώς ἐστιν, Met. 1049b5) and which is valid for Plotinus for and in being and the existent but not for the one that, as the infinite πάντων δύναμις, is never actual or actualized. Therefore, the purely quantitative numbering number (καθαρῶς ποσόν, Enn. VI.6.16.18) should have an admixture of potentiality. The quantitative number, even if it may be considered as (potentially) existing before the act of counting, has yet to be fully actualized in the very act of numbering, ἐνεργεῖς ποσόν (Enn. VI.6.16.51).[44] Therefore, as numbering, the quantitative number may be presented in the form of 1 + 1 + 1, and so on. For this reason, the quantitative number may be located within the discursive logical process and thus grasped by διάνοια.

One can consider the quantitative henads as the units of the quantitative number constituted by the participation in the essential henad, which itself participates in the monad. But do the quantitative henads constitute the quantitative number? Or are they discerned in it only once the quantitative number is already there, as in the case of the essential numbers? Even if taken as counted, as produced by the consecutive addition of quantitative henads, the quantitative or mathematical number is still not really generated by the act of counting. For it does already exist potentially as a unity—for instance, as the number of the people in a chorus of ten—even if not yet actually counted. The quantitative number is only actualized as definite for and within discursive thinking through the number of the added quantitative henads (cf. Enn. VI.6.16.28–37). In other words, the quantitative number as numbering exists in the discursive dianoetic activity of counting. For we do not yet know the number of people in the chorus until it is actually numbered as counted, before which it is present only potentially and not yet "ordered together into one" number (μὴ συντεταγμένοις, Enn. VI.6.16.34; cf. VI.6.13.20). In this sense, the quantitative number precedes its henads, but only as a potential number and not an actual number, as is the case with the essential number.

---

[43] Enn. VI.6.15.37–42. Cf. Éliane Amado, "À propos des nombres nombrés et des nombres nombrants chez Plotin," Revue Philosophique de la France et de l'Étranger 143 (1953), pp. 423–5; Plotinus, Die Schriften 30–38 der chronologischen Reihenfolge, p. 456; and Traité sur les nombres, p. 187.

[44] According to Schwyzer, Plotinus is the first to use the verb ἐνεργεῖν as transitive. See Hans-Rudolf Schwyzer, s.v. "Plotinos," in RE 21:1, pp. 471–591.

Thus, the problem of the constitution of number can be addressed only by taking into consideration the implicit distinctions that are central in Plotinus, such as those between the related participating and the unrelated participated one, and between essential and quantitative number within the structure of the one-many as represented in being, intellect, and life.

3

Eternity and Time

A number of significant studies of the concept of time and eternity in Plotinus have been published over the course of decades.[1] In what follows, I will mostly discuss the nature of eternity and attempt to demonstrate that the concept of eternity is indispensable for Plotinus' account of being and intellect. Even before Augustine, Plotinus begins his "On Eternity and Time" (Περὶ αἰῶνος καὶ χρόνου, *Enn.* III.7 [45]) with a puzzle: when we are not questioning what eternity and time are, they seem clear, but, when asking about them, we run into difficulties (*Enn.* III.7.1.3–9).[2] The discussion opens by establishing eternity and time as distinctly different and opposed to each other (ἕτερον), as characterizing two essentially different realms—that which always is and

---

[1] Hans Jonas, "Plotin über Zeit und Ewigzeit," in *Politische Ordnung und menschliche Existenz: Festgabe für Eric Voegelin*, ed. Alois Dempf and Hannah Arendt (Munich: C. H. Beck, 1962), pp. 295–319; Werner Beierwaltes, *Plotin über Ewigkeit und Zeit* (Frankfurt am Main: Klostermann, 1967); André-Jean Festugière, "Le sens philosophique du mot aiôn," in *Etudes de philosophie grecque* (Paris: Vrin, 1972); Karen Gloy, "Die Struktur der Zeit in Plotins Zeittheorie," *Archiv für Geschichte der Philosophie* 71:3 (1989), pp. 303–26; Andrew Smith, "Eternity and Time," in *The Cambridge Companion to Plotinus*, pp. 196–216; Richard Sorabji, *Time, Creation, and the Continuum: Theories in Antiquity and the Early Middle Ages* (London: Duckworth, 1983), pp. 112–4; Steven K. Strange, "Plotinus on the Nature of Eternity and Time," in *Aristotle in Late Antiquity* ed. Lawrence P. Schrenk (Washington, DC: Catholic University of America Press, 1994), pp. 22–53; Peter Manchester, *The Syntax of Time: The Phenomenology of Time in Greek Physics and Speculative Logic from Iamblichus to Anaximander* (Leiden: Brill, 2005), pp. 55–86; Michael F. Wagner, *The Enigmatic Reality of Time: Aristotle, Plotinus, and Today* (Leiden: Brill, 2008), pp. 275–363; and Filip Karfík, "Le temps et l' âme chez Plotin: à propos des *Énneades* VI 5 [23] 11; IV 4 [28] 15–16; III 7 [45] 11," *Elenchos* 33 (2012), pp. 227–57.

[2] Cf. Augustine, *Conf.* XI.13; and Proclus, *In Tim.* III, 8.22–4: "But what is eternity and what is time imitating it in a moving fashion, this is most difficult to understand and convincingly interpret." On the later Neoplatonic discussions of time and eternity, see W. O'Neill, "Time and Eternity in Proclus," *Phronesis* 7:2 (1962), pp. 161–5; Samuel Sambursky and Schlomo Pines, *The Concept of Time in Late Neoplatonism: Texts with Translation, Introduction and Notes* (Jerusalem: Israel Academy of Sciences and Humanities, 1971); Philippe Hoffmann, "Jamblique exégète du pythagoricien Archytas: trois originaliités d'une doctrine du temps," *Les études philosophiques* 3 (1980), pp. 307–23; and Dirk Baltzly, "Introduction to Book 4," in Proclus, *Commentary on Plato's Timaeus*, trans. and ed. Dirk Baltzly (Cambridge: Cambridge University Press, 2016), vol. 5, pp. 3–11.

that which comes to be (*Enn.* III.7.1.1–3). Ontologically, the sphere of being precedes that of becoming, while the consideration of the eternal precedes that of the temporal, as the paradigm that is antecedent to its image (*Enn.* III.7.1.18–20).[3]

In doing so, Plotinus draws on the preceding history of the debate, beginning with Plato, who famously refers to, but does not much elaborate on, the topic of eternity in the *Timaeus* (37C–38C). Here, Plato briefly makes three important points about eternity: that eternity is the paradigm for time, which is the moving image of eternity; that eternity represents the living being of the νοῦς; and that eternity abides in the one. For Plotinus, being has its origin in the one, which alone is without beginning and allows for being to be constituted as the unity of one-many (see Chapter 1), which, however, is discussed by Plato not in the *Timaeus*, but in the *Parmenides*. The ontology of the *Timaeus* is that of the demiurgical νοῦς, while the ontology of the *Parmenides* is that of the one-many. For this reason, *Ennead* III.7 may be considered not only as an explicit commentary on the *Timaeus* (to which *Enn.* III.7 makes at least fifteen references), but also as an implicit commentary on the *Parmenides*. Moreover, Plato's *Sophist* also appears to play a key role in Plotinus' understanding of eternity, which means that his discussion is an integrative exegesis of Plato's insights that are dispersed throughout various dialogues.

Although critical of Aristotle's theory of time (*Enn.* III.7.9.1–84), Plotinus comes much closer to the systematic Aristotelian way of exposition and argumentation in his method of investigation.[4] Plotinus abandons the narrative story-telling or the μῦθος-exposition of the *Timaeus* in favor of a more speculative account (with an exception of the story about the origin of time in his invocation of the Muses at *Enn.* III.7.11.4–44). In addition, he follows the pattern of critique established by Aristotle and used up to this day, first presenting and criticizing the extant views and theories, but proceeding as a philosopher rather than as a doxographer (*Enn.* III.7.7–10, III.7.10.11–2; cf. I.4 [46].1–2, VI.1 [42].1–30). In order to be able to establish his own account

---

[3] Paradigm and image should be in a certain proportion to each other (Plato, *Tim.* 31B–32C; *Rep.* 509D–511E). Among various proportions, one of the most significant is the "golden cut." A point divides an interval in the proportion of the "golden cut" if the ratio of the smaller part to the bigger part of the interval is equal to the ratio of the larger part to the whole of the interval. If we assume the length of the interval to be one unit, then the exact value of the "golden cut" is ($\sqrt{5}$ − 1) / 2 or approximately 0.618. It might be worth noting that Plotinus dedicates the first part of the treatise "On Eternity and Time" to eternity (*Enn.* III.7.1.1 to III.7.7.7, a total of 235 lines) and the second part to the consideration of time (*Enn.* III.7.7.8 to III.7.13.69, a total of 382 lines; 617 lines in the entire treatise). The relation of the length of the two parts is 382 / 617 (approximately 0.619), or exactly the "golden cut." I do not assign any special meaning to this fact, nor does it seem that Plotinus, unlike some of his followers (e.g., Porphyry, who numerically ordered his teacher's treatises into six *Enneads*), deliberately paid attention to the "magic of numbers." Yet, the fact itself appears to be interesting.

[4] On Plotinus' method in *Ennead* III.7, see Szlezák, *Platon und Aristoteles in der Nuslehre Plotins*; and Strange, "Plotinus on the Nature of Eternity and Time," p. 23.

of eternity, Plotinus has to clear the way by showing first what eternity *is not* (*Enn.* III.7.10.9). In doing so, he mostly draws on Pythagorean arguments that, however, he eventually rejects. Yet, despite this rejection, Plotinus arrives at a concept of eternity that is still a Pythagorean one but that also incorporates Plato's insights about eternity.

3.1 Three Arguments on Eternity and Their Rejection by Plotinus

The main thesis that Plotinus critically examines is that of the Pythagoreans; namely, that eternity is the intelligible essence or substance itself (νοητὴ αὐτὴ οὐσία, *Enn.* III.7.2.2; cf. Aristotle, *Phys.* 218b1). There are three arguments in support of the Pythagorean thesis, which are eventually rejected by Plotinus.

3.1.1 THE ARGUMENT FROM THE MOST "DIGNIFIED" ENTITY

The premises of the argument are (a) we conceive eternity (αἰών) as the most dignified or majestic thing. It is (b) the intelligible nature (νοητὴ φύσις)—the ever-thinking intellect—that is considered the most dignified (σεμνότατόν τι). And (c), there is nothing else that might be thought as equally dignified because the one, the source of all thinking, is not itself thinkable, so that nothing can be predicated of it (τοῦ δ'ἐπέκεινα οὐδὲ τοῦτο κατηγορητέον, *Enn.* III.7.2.7–8; cf. *Enn.* III.8.10.31), and so, the one cannot be said to be the most dignified thing. Therefore, eternity and the intelligible nature should be identical (*Enn.* III.7.2.5–9; cf. III.7.5.18). But, argues Plotinus, if the two are considered dignified or majestic, this does not yet make them identical because it may be that this highest dignity is present in one of them coming from the other (παρὰ τοῦ ἑτέρου, *Enn.* III.7.2.15–7). If this is the case, "dignity" is then only a predicate, not even the essential one, that does not characterize eternity and cannot be its definition. Moreover, such a predicate may be transmitted to one subject by the other, in which case the latter appears to be the cause of the former. However, one cannot make conclusions about the identity of both subjects from the identity of an accidental predicate such as "dignity."

3.1.2 THE ARGUMENT FROM INCLUSIVENESS (*ENN.* III.7.2.9–10)

Eternity and the intelligible cosmos are (a) both inclusive (περιεκτικά), and (b) both contain or embrace the same things or objects; therefore, they should be identical. But, objects Plotinus, "inclusiveness" (περιοχή) should be taken here in two different senses since, in the intelligible cosmos, it is present "in the way in which [a whole includes] its parts [ὡς μερῶν], but eternity includes the whole all at once [ὁμοῦ τὸ ὅλον], not as a part, but in the sense that all things which are of such a kind as to be eternal are so by conforming to it [κατ' αὐτόν]" (*Enn.* III.7.2.17–9).

It should be noted that Plotinus does not reject the very notions of "dignified" and "inclusiveness" that he himself uses earlier in his critique describing the goodness of the intellect (*Enn.* II.9 [33].4.29–31). Yet the content of the terms and the way they are used is nonetheless rethought by Plotinus. The term περιεκτικός relates to Plato's "living being" (*Tim.* 39E), which Plotinus interprets in his exegesis as the intelligible cosmos of archetypes or the collection of all thinkable forms, the objects of thinking (*Enn.* III.9.1; cf. V.9.9.4, VI.6.17.36).

In the intellect, however, thinking is to be distinguished from thought, not as actually separated but as representing two aspects of the same reality. One and the same intellect appears as a unity in multiplicity, in which thinking thinks itself in and through the objects of thought and every such object is connected with every other one. Such a structure of a unity in multiplicity, one-many (ἕν-πολλά), is familiar from Plato's *Parmenides* (144E) and is realized there through the communication (κοινωνία) of the intelligible forms, where each form is independent while at the same time actually—not potentially—reflecting and containing all the other forms (Plato, *Soph.* 254B–C; *Rep.* 476A). In the intelligible realm, κόσμος νοητός, every constituent εἶδος or νοητόν expresses every other one and is both individual and universal. Κοινωνία, then, is the principle of the organization of the intelligible sphere in which that which is "really a whole has not been put together out of its parts, but has produced its parts itself, in order that it may truly be a whole [πᾶν] in this way too" (*Enn.* III.7.4.8–11).

If we take into account this unique structure of the intelligible unity, we may provide a critique of Plotinus' second counterargument. In particular, the "parts" of the intelligible, mentioned by Plotinus, are in constant uninterrupted communication with each other and therefore are such that, although each one is an individual part, it is a part that fully expresses every other part and is itself expressed by them. In this way, one single part reflects the whole entirely and without detriment. The multiplicity of the intelligible, then, does not seem to differ from that of eternity, which, in Plotinus' own description, is also multiple (ἐκ πολλῶν, *Enn.* III.7.5.22–5). Eternity does not consist of parts added to each other, but its "parts" coexist in a unity where each "part" is different from every other one through eternity's infinite power or potency (διὰ δύναμιν ἄπειρον, *Enn.* III.7.5.23). Eternity has many different "faces," as it were, which are different only virtually, as potential infinities, characterizing one single complete whole. But if there is no difference between the multiplicity within the noetic realm and within eternity, then Plotinus' objection might be beside the point. For both appear as a unity of virtually different entities where each one fully expresses the others.

3.1.2.1 Eternal and Sempiternal, Participation and Predication

But it might be further answered to this objection to Plotinus' objection to the second argument that there still can be traced a subtle and important difference hinted at by Plotinus but not elaborated in detail. Namely, if the structure of the intelligible is established according to the principle of κοινωνία, then every intelligible "part" participates in the whole in the same way and to the same extent, so that this equal participation may be taken as one of the main characteristics of the intelligible world. Yet one cannot say that there are parts in the eternal because it has to be thought as existing all together, ὁμοῦ πάντα (cf. Aristotle, *Met.* 1069b21). In other words, every eternal "thing" is different not in the way of *participation* but in the way of *predication*. "But when we *say* that one set of things [the intelligible objects] lies in the other [τὰ ἕτερα ἐν θατέρῳ]—in eternity—and when we *predicate* [κατηγορῶμεν] eternal existence of the intelligible realities . . . we again say that eternity is something different [ἄλλο], but are saying that it is connected with it [περί, with the intelligible cosmos], or is in it [ἐν], or is present to it [παρεῖναι]" (*Enn.* III.7.2.10–5, emphasis added; cf. III.7.13.68–9).

Eternity and the intelligible are then not identical but different, although they are still intimately connected. On the one hand, in terms of the S–P relation, we can say that S (the intellect, as intelligible objects, νοητά) is P (eternal) by way of *participation*. The intellect is eternal as expressed by way of participation in one of its νοητά, namely, in the "eternal." The intellect participates in the eternal as that which, when produced by the one, is always there not changing and as not capable of not existing. On the other hand, S (eternity) is P (intelligible) by way of *predication*: eternity is *said* to variously express the intelligible cosmos (περί, ἐν, and παρά). Correspondingly, there are two different types of inclusiveness: through participation and through predication.

There are further indications that the participation–predication distinction is important for Plotinus in his discussion and critique of the previous thinkers. Simplifying somewhat, one might say that the language of participation (μέθεξις) is more typical of Plato (*Parm.* 132C–D; *Rep.* 585B–C), whereas that of predication is more often used by Aristotle, in particular, in his φύσει/ λόγῳ distinction.[5] Plotinus distinguishes between two kinds of eternity: namely, between the eternal (τὸ αἰώνιον), which corresponds to eternity proper (αἰών)—and the everlasting (τὸ ἀίδιον), which corresponds to everlastingness or sempiternity (ἀιδιότης, *Enn.* III.7.2.25–9, III.7.3.1–4; τὸ ἀεί, *Enn.* II.1 [40].1.10–2). Plato uses the terms "αἰών" and "αἰώνιος" four times in *Timaeus* 37D–38C, and "ἀίδιον" and its derivatives five times in *Timaeus*

---

[5] Cf. Xavier Zubiri, *On Essence* (Washington, DC: Catholic University of America Press, 1980), p. 41.

29A–40B (at 37D, "ἀίδιον" refers to the eternal living being) without making a clear distinction between them.[6]

I would think, however, that the αἰώνιον–ἀίδιον distinction is important to the extent that it corresponds to the participation–predication one. Otherwise, it is difficult to explain why we should not say that eternity is eternal (αἰώνιον). And eternity is not eternal for Plotinus because the "eternal is that which *participates* in eternity" (*Enn.* III.7.2.25–6; emphasis added), whereas something is only predicated or *said* to be sempiternal (ἀίδιον, *Enn.* III.7.2.29). One can thus say that "eternal" expresses the idea of participation, whereas "sempiternal" expresses that of predication (cf. *Enn.* III.7.2.34–6).[7] When Plotinus comes to the characterization of eternity, he says: "everlastingness would be the corresponding condition of the substrate, existing from it and with it, and eternity the substrate with the corresponding condition appearing in it" (*Enn.* III.7.5.12–8).[8] In other words, eternity itself participates in the "substrate," being or intellect, while everlastingness or sempiternity as a "condition" (κατά στασις) is predicated about that substrate.[9]

But what is the distinction between participation and predication? First, participation is an ontological characteristic that describes the way a thing *is* and *why* it is so; that is, participation exhibits the ground and cause from which this particular thing obtains its properties. Thus, if A participates in B, the participation shows both the origin of A and establishes a causal relation between

---

[6] Leonard Brandwood, *A Word Index to Plato* (Leeds: W. S. Maney and Son, 1976); cf. Friedrich Ast, vol. 1 of *Lexicon Platonicum* (Leipzig: Libraria Weidmaniana, 1835). Apart from the *Timaeus*, the terms are rarely used in the rest of Plato's corpus. If we do not take into account the inauthentic "Axiochus" and "Definitiones," "ἀίδιον" occurs only in Plato's *Phil.* 66A, *Phaedo* 106D, and *Rep.* 611B, whereas "αἰών"/ "αἰώνιος" occurs in *Gorg.* 448C, *Prot.* 345C, *Rep.* 363D, and *Legg.* 701C, 904A. Hans Jonas has argued that both concepts appear as synonyms in Plotinus and are discerned only for reasons of style; see Jonas, "Plotin über Zeit und Ewigzeit," p. 297. On the everlastingness of the cosmos in Plato, see James Wilberding, introduction to Plotinus, *Plotinus' Cosmology: A Study of Ennead II.1 (40): Text, Translation and Commentary* (Oxford: Oxford University Press, 2006), pp. 20–1.

[7] It seems that Plotinus tends also to oppose αἰών-ἀιδιότης in terms of counterpoising seeing (contemplation) to speaking (saying), or εἶδος to λόγος. The eternal as participating in eternity is *contemplated* (θεώμενος), eternity itself is *said* (λέγει) about the god (θεῷ), that is, about the intellect (*Enn.* III.7.5.9–19). That the αἰών / ἀιδιότης is introduced by Plotinus on purpose for a subtle tuning of the concept of eternity finds oblique support in the fact that, except at III.7, Plotinus always uses the term "ἀίδιον" for "eternal" (in the *Enn.* VI.1–3 it is not used at all) and that, in the whole corpus of the *Enneads*, "αἰώνιος" is used only at *Enn*ead III.7. See J. H. Sleeman and Gilbert Pollet, eds., *Lexicon Plotinianum* (Leiden: Brill, 1980), cols. 46–9. Cf. Syrianus' distinction between eternity (αἰών) as the dyad of eternal being (τὸ ἀεὶ εἶναι) that unites the "always" (ἀεί) and being (ὄν), in which the multiplicity of the intelligibles is united—and the eternal (τὸ αἰώνιον) as participating in eternity, ap. Proclus, *In Tim.* III, 15.11–16.1. See Sara Klitenic Wear, *The Teachings of Syrianus on Plato's Timaeus and Parmenides* (Leiden: Brill, 2011), pp. 154–6.

[8] "ἀιδιότης δὲ ἡ τοιαύτη κατάστασις τοῦ ὑποκειμένου ἐξ αὐτοῦ οὖσα καὶ ἐν αὐτῷ, αἰὼν δὲ τὸ ὑπο κείμενον μετὰ τῆς τοιαύτης καταστάσεως ἐμφαινομένης" (*Enn.* III.7.5.15–8).

[9] A similar view is defended by Andrew Smith ("Eternity and Time," pp. 202–3), who argues that everlastingness should be taken simply as the manifestation ("corresponding condition") of eternity (as "substrate").

A and B, between the participating image and the participated paradigm (*Enn.* V.3.15.22). The concept of participation is mostly used to establish a causal ordered relation between a thing in becoming and its noetic paradigm. This understanding of participation is found later in Boethius' *Quomodo substantiae*.[10] Plotinus himself often speaks of a thing participating in being (μετέχει τὸ μῖγμα τοῦ εἶναι, *Enn.* II.4.7.7; cf. VI.8.14.3–4). In the *Sophist*, Plato uses the concept of participation (μέθεξις) when characterizing the relation of the five *genera* of the noetic realm to each other (*Soph.* 256B, 259A). Following Plato, I extend here the use of the term "participation" also to the description of the relation between the intelligible objects themselves. In this case, the relation has to be double because, on the one hand, it describes the participation of the νοητά in one another according to the principle of communication-κοινωνία. Participation, then, characterizes the self-causation of being: when being already *is*, it is self-sufficient. But, on the other hand, being as the intellect-νοῦς has its origin and source in the one, and hence being may also be said to participate in the one. Predication, on the contrary, belongs to logical and epistemological description: it is *said* that A is such and such; that is, A has a number of predicates, essential or accidental. At the same time, the way of predication is not supposed to give an account of why A has exactly these and not other predicates. It is not by chance that Aristotle, who thinks in terms of predication, tends to ignore the problem of the origin of being or thinking, which for him is the reality (cf. *Met.* 1072b18–30) that is given and cannot be further questioned as to why it is such as it is.

Second, the concept of participation allows for a multiplicity of substances or subjects: a number of different things, $A_1, A_2, \ldots A_n, \ldots$ may participate in one and the same B at the same time. Predication, on the contrary, presupposes only one subject to which this set of predicates refers. There may be different subjects with coinciding predicates, yet the subjects themselves never coincide for either there can be another predicate A_{n+1} not yet mentioned or thought, or a particular subject, A_p, may itself be considered a predicate. Correspondingly, the problem of individuation will be addressed differently from the point of view of either participation or predication (although this is a different topic going beyond the scope of the current discussion).

Third, participation may be considered even without taking into account the participating because participation is the causation exercised by the participated. Predication, to the contrary, implies the impossibility of the predicates' existence separately and without their subject, or, as the old scholastic principle runs, no predicate can exist without a subject.

---

[10] "Quod est participare aliquo potest, sed ipsum esse nullo modo aliquo participat. Fit enim participatio cum aliquid iam est; est autem aliquid, cum esse susceperit" (Boethius, *The Theological Tractates*, trans. H. F. Stewart, E. K. Rand, and S. J. Tester [Cambridge, MA: Harvard University Press, 1973; 1st publ. 1918], p. 40).

And, fourth, a predicate may be indifferently ascribed to a subject of any kind, either physical or intelligible. Participation may also be ascribed to both physical and intelligible objects, yet here we need to make a further distinction. In particular, in Platonic terms, a physical thing may participate in an intelligible thing (or in a form), which is the reason why that physical thing may be called such and such (big, small, etc.). One kind of participation is then similar to predication; namely, when the exclusive participation allows for different physical things to participate in one and the same form (and also to have the same predicate) but makes them disconnected and mutually exclusive since one physical thing cannot exist in the place and function of another. Yet the other kind of participation is dissimilar to predication; namely, the inclusive participation of the intelligible objects-νοητά, which allows for their mutual communication and participation in one another. The entirety of the intelligible cosmos is constituted through such participation, where each object is independent and every one is in every other one without detriment (ἐκεῖ δ' ἕκαστον τὸ ὅλον καὶ οὐκ ἔχει τὸ μᾶλλον, *Enn.* VI.3.20.42). It is this inclusive participation that constitutes the structure of the one-many, which exists only in the noetic.

Taking into account these four distinctions between participation and predication, we may establish the relation between the intellect and eternity in a more distinct way. As Plotinus implies in his refutation of the first two arguments about eternity, the relation is not that of identity because the intellect *is not* eternity. Yet one can *say* or *predicate* that the intellect is sempiternal. However, the intellect cannot be said to be eternal because the eternal is that which participates in eternity. In the intellect, the intelligible objects participate in each other and thus form one single whole of the noetic cosmos, and, furthermore, the intellect itself in its multiple unity participates in the one that alone is beyond multiplicity (*Enn.* V.4.1.5). For this reason, the intellect is not eternal by way of participation but is sempiternal by way of predication. Eternity itself is not eternal since it does not participate in itself. This once again implies that eternity is not identical with the intellect. Eternity *is not* the intellect but is intelligible through participation in the intellect. What, then, is eternity in relation to the intellect? Plotinus' answer is that eternity is the *life* (ζωή) of the intellect, which will be discussed in what follows.

3.1.3 THE ARGUMENT FROM REST

The third argument of the "ancients" suggests that just as it is commonly supposed that time is associated with movement, eternity should be associated with rest (στάσις, *Enn.* III.7.2.20–36). Plotinus objects that this claim may be taken it two different ways: either (a) that eternity *is* rest, and so rest and eternity are identical, or (b) that eternity is rest as connected with or belonging to the being and substance (περὶ τὴν οὐσίαν) of the intellect. Plotinus rejects

(a) on the ground that rest is not eternal because it is not necessary for rest to participate in eternity. Therefore, rest is only *predicated* of eternity (*Enn.* III.7.2.24–5). But (b) is impossible as well since eternity cannot simply be rest belonging to the intellect, for there one should also recognize and include other *genera* that are excluded from eternity (*Enn.* III.7.2.29–31). In the reference to the other *genera* (γένη), Plotinus reaches a crucial point in his critique because they obviously refer to the five μέγιστα γένη of Plato's *Sophist*, those of being (οὐσία), rest, movement, sameness, and otherness (*Soph.* 254D–257B; cf. esp. *Enn.* VI.2 [43].7–8).[11] It should be noted that *Ennead* III.7 immediately follows the voluminous *Ennead* VI.1–3 [42–4] "On the Kinds of Being," in which Plotinus dedicates much of his effort to the discussion of the five *genera*. Therefore, the true relation of eternity and the intellect is a more complex one, and the categorical apparatus for such a description should not only include the distinction of participation and predication, but also other concepts, in particular those of life and rest.

3.2 The Intellect

3.2.1 THE STRUCTURE OF THE INTELLECT

The discussion of eternity so far has turned around the intellect. The five categories of the *Sophist* are already applied by Plotinus to the analysis of νοῦς in *Ennead* V.1. The main features of the intellect in Plotinus that are relevant to the discussion of eternity (cf. *Enn.* V.1.4.16–35) are the following: (1) the intellect is one, but, due to the intellect's intrinsic multiplicity—its being one-many—it is possible to distinguish thinking from thought as the thinking that thinks itself as the intelligible objects. The intellect, therefore, is not absolutely simple (*Enn.* VI.7.13.1) but is inescapably dual; it is both the activity of thinking, νόησις or νοοῦν—and thought, the ordered cosmos of the intelligible objects, νοητά or νοούμενον (*Enn.* V.1.4.30–4).[12] (2) All the thinkable objects are without detriment, so that the intellect thinks everything that it has by being what it thinks, and there is nothing in νοῦς that it does not think.[13]

---

[11] Plotinus refers to μέγιστα γένη of the *Sophist* many times throughout the *Enneads* (III.7.3.9–11, V.1.4.35–6, V.3.15.40, VI.2.7.30, VI.7.39.4–6). See H-S *editio minor*, T.III, p. 359; and Denis O'Brien, *Plotinus on the Origin of Matter: An Exercise in the Interpretation of the* Enneads (Naples: Bibliopolis, 1991), pp. 24–5.

[12] The structure of the intellect appears to be more complex, involving both double and triple structures, because, in every act of identification, A = B (or even A = A), there are always three terms involved: two terms of the equation and the act of the identification itself. This structure is present even in an attempt of thinking the unthinkable. Namely, the one, the source and the principle of every identification, is αὐτὸς παρ' αὐτοῦ αὐτός, "himself as himself from himself" (*Enn.* VI.8.20.19), without being any particular subject.

[13] See H. J. Blumenthal, *Plotinus' Psychology: His Doctrines of the Embodied Soul* (The Hague: Martinus Nijhoff, 1971), pp. 100–11; Eric D. Perl, *Thinking Being: Introduction to Metaphysics*

That is, self-thinking of the intellect in the form of the intelligible objects seeks nothing (unlike the discursive thinking, διάνοια, of the soul), but rather already *has* everything in itself in the way that it constantly thinks what it has.

(3) The intellect is the paradigm and the archetype of everything that is, yet, at the same time, the intellect is itself caused by the one without being. (4) The intellect *is* being. The intellect may be defined as that which, once generated, always necessarily and properly *is* or exists. Only the νοῦς is and is incapable of not being. As being, it is not affected or is pure active actuality without any affection whatsoever. Therefore, the intellect can have no striving toward anything that only participates in being. This means that the intellect as being is the end (τέλος) of itself and has the end within itself as not different from itself. Therefore, the intellect is always *already* there, with itself and by itself as being, not searching but already having being, so that nothing can be added to it.[14] Being is then the end of striving, ἔφεσις, of all other things that struggle for being, as it were (*Enn.* III.7.4.17–31). However, the intellect is not altogether free from ambiguity because it itself strives, always missing, toward its beginning and principle, the one that is free of being and any τέλος.

(5) The communication between the intelligible objects within the intellect is established as the mentioned κοινωνία, where every object of thought keeps its individual identity as εἶδος yet at the same time is present to every other intelligible object and every other intelligible object is present to it (cf. *Enn.* V.8.4.6–11, VI.7.14.12; Plato, *Soph.* 256B, 257C–D). (6) Because the intellect is being, its *is* is always the same, so that the intellect is not related to any "will be" or "was": it always *is* and *always* is (cf. Plato, *Tim.* 37E–38B).[15] The intellect thus necessarily presupposes eternity as "always" (*Enn.* V.8.3.11).

Since (7) the intellect is essentially dual, there should be categories expressing this duality in unity. This means that the intellect "there" (ἐκεῖ) should be present not only through sameness, ταὐτότης, but also through otherness, ἑτερότης. Sameness in and of the intellect means that the intellect always *is*, and, as thinking that thinks itself in the form of νοητά, is always the *same*. Otherness within the intellect is represented as inherent multiplicity in three different ways: first, within the intellect itself, where being and thinking are the other of and to each other. Second, every intelligible object within the realm of thought is different and other to every other intelligible object. And, third, the intellect in its integrity of being as one-many is the other to its own

---

in the Classical Tradition (Leiden: Brill, 2014), pp. 107–14; and Damian Caluori, *Plotinus on the Soul* (Cambridge: Cambridge University Press, 2015), pp. 44–51.

[14] Since the intellect is already there in its entirety, no "will be" can be added to it, for otherwise the intellect would have "fallen from the seat of being" (τὸ ἔρρειν ἐκ τῆς τοῦ εἶναι ἕδρας, *Enn.* III.7.4. 21–2).

[15] As Plotinus puts it, the intellect is "τὸ "ἔστιν" ἀεί, καὶ οὐδαμοῦ τὸ μέλλον—ἔστι γὰρ καὶ τότε—οὐδὲ τὸ παρεληλυθός—οὐ γάρ τι ἐκεῖ παρελήλυθεν—ἀλλ' ἐνέστηκεν ἀεί" (*Enn.* V.1.4.22–4).

source, to the one that is beyond multiplicity and being. Hence, otherness not only "wakes the intellect to life" (*Enn.* VI.7.13.11–2), but "there is nothing of it that is not other" (οὐδέν ἐστιν αὐτοῦ, ὅ τι μὴ ἄλλο, *Enn.* VI.7.13.54–5) to it as the object of thought appropriated in and by thinking.

(8) And yet, in the *Sophist*, Plato introduces two more categories within the intelligible, those of rest and motion, arguing that they are irreducible to sameness and otherness because sameness and otherness are necessarily present in both rest and in motion since, otherwise, motion would have come to a stop and rest would have moved (*Soph.* 254E–255B). For this reason, rest and motion are both applicable to the intelligible and the physical realms. But Plotinus seeks to distinguish the two spheres in order to justify Plato's division in the *Timaeus* (37D–E) between the eternal that pertains to being and its imitation in the moving image of time. Therefore, on the one hand, Plotinus faces an exegetical task of making a concordance between the five categories-*genera* in the *Sophist* and those of the eternity/time distinction in the *Timaeus*. On the other hand, after having rejected the arguments of the "ancients," Plotinus needs to come up with his own systematic explanation of the relation of the intellect to eternity. And, for this purpose, the concepts of rest and movement appear to be indispensable.

Since the intellect is being, it is always the same and everything in it (all the intelligible objects) is at rest (πάντα ἑστῶτα, *Enn.* V.1.4.21). However—and this reasoning parallels Plato's argument in the *Sophist*—the intellect cannot be at rest only (cf. *Enn.* V.9.10.8–9). Why? Because one single act of thinking of one particular object of thought involves rest as being there, staying in and on the thought. But thinking is primarily an activity and therefore cannot stop at one particular νοητόν. This means that thinking is always present to each and every object of thought. This in turn means that there can be no thinking without some sort of movement. Therefore, the activity of thinking is represented through the category of movement (κίνησις), as thinking the other and going from one object of thought to another without really leaving or ever having left any of them. And the being of the intellect, both of thinking and of thought, is represented by rest (στάσις). Rest and movement are inseparably connected in the intelligible: movement is always stable, and rest is a stillness that is always in motion and, for this reason, does not bring change. As Plotinus himself puts it,

> there could not be thinking [in the intellect as both thinking and thought] without otherness, and also sameness. These then are primary, the intellect, being, otherness, sameness; but one must also include motion and rest. One must include movement if there is thought, and rest that it may think the same; and otherness, that there may be thinker and thought; or else, if you take away otherness, it will become one and keep silent; and the objects of thought, also, must have otherness in relation to each other. But

one must include sameness, because it is one with itself, and all have some common unity; and the distinctive quality (διαφορά) of each is otherness. (*Enn.* V.1.4.33–41; cf. VI.2.8.25–49)

Hence, one understands (or "sees") the multiple complex unity of the intellect differently by way of predication (λέγει). Namely, as subject or substrate the intellect is predicated or said to be substance, as life—movement, as absolutely unchanging—rest, and as one-many—the same and the other (*Enn.* III.7.3.7–11). We may thus say that the categories of sameness and otherness represent the dynamic structure that constitutes the intellect as intelligible, as thought, whereas the categories of rest and movement represent the νοῦς in its intellectual aspect, as the eternal activity of thinking.

3.2.2 MOTION IN THE INTELLECT

Since the category of motion in the intellect is important for the understanding of eternity, we need to say more about it. As pure activity and actuality of thinking, intellectual motion should be distinguished from physical motion, which is the activity of that which exists potentially and its actualization (cf. Aristotle, *Phys.* 201a10–202b29). Plotinus rejects the Aristotelian theory of motion, which is applicable only to physical things, in favor of the Platonic concept of movement in the *Sophist*. Plotinus explicitly criticizes the Aristotelian theory of motion in his discussion of previous theories of time, all of which take time as somehow connected with movement (*Enn.* III.7.9).[16] The movement that Plotinus has in mind is not a locomotion from one point to another but rather is an exemplification of sameness through otherness, a staying in motion, *status movendi*. The other (the object) that the intellect thinks is not different from the intellect itself since it resides within the same νοῦς, so that the intellectual movement appears to be a kind of circular motion that stays identical and moves on without ever really abandoning its state.

Because the intellect necessarily comprises being and thinking, movement and rest are always present in the intellect: the being of the intellect

> is that in which thinking [νόησις] comes to a stop, though thinking is a rest which has no beginning, and from which it starts, though thinking is a rest which never started: for movement does not begin from or end in movement. And the form at rest is the defining limit of the intellect, and the intellect is the movement of the form [ἔτι δὲ ἡ μὲν ἰδέα ἐν στάσει πέρας οὖσα νοῦ, ὁ δὲ νοῦς αὐτῆς ἡ κίνησις]. (*Enn.* VI.2.8.20-4)

---

[16] See a detailed discussion in Riccardo Chiaradonna, *Sostanza, movimento, analogia: Plotino critico di Aristotele* (Naples: Bibliopolis, 2002), pp. 147–225.

Movement should presuppose an end (τέλος), which in the case of the intellect is a noetic object as its limit at rest, ἐν στάσει πέρας. Rest, then, characterizes the entirety of the intelligible cosmos, ἰδέαι or νοητά, the realm of being (ὄν) and substance (οὐσία), whereas movement represents νοῦς in and as the intellectual activity of thinking (νόησις). And yet, movement and rest in the intellect are not and cannot be rigidly separated because the activity of thinking is always directed *to* and comes *from* the being of thought (εἰς ὅ, ἀφ' οὗ, *Enn.* VI.2.8.14). Movement does not belong to being and is neither "under" (ὑπό) nor "over" (ἐπί) being, but is *with* (μετά) being (*Enn.* VI.2.7.16–7). Since the intellect is unable to not be one in its multiplicity, as the "double one" (διπλοῦν ἕν, *Enn.* VI.2.7.24), all binary distinctions and oppositions within it are not real but belong only to our conception (ἐπίνοια) of the intellect.

Rest in the intellect expresses its perseverance in being that is the end (τέλος) for movement, the intellectual movement that does not bring change to being and which does not exist potentially in the first place, but makes being perfect and complete (τέλειον, *Enn.* VI.2.7.26). This perfection is the perfection of reflexivity since the intellect thinks itself in the form(s) of intelligible objects that are not actually different from the intellect, so that its intellectual activity is always directed to itself and thus always returns to itself. This self-thinking constitutes self-knowledge, always present in the intellect through the activity of the self-movement of νοῦς (αὐτοκίνησις, *Enn.* VI.2.18.8–9; cf. I.1 [53].13.3–5) that is incessantly "wandering" in itself, as it were (ἐν αὐτῷ πλανηθέντος, *Enn.* VI.7.13.30). In the fullness of its being, the intellect completes itself by returning to itself without really ever having left itself. But if the intellect were to be understood only in terms of identity and rest, it would have been inactive (ἀργεῖ) and without thought and would not even have existed (*Enn.* VI.7.13.39–57). Therefore, there is nothing in the intellect that is not at the same time the other. The intellect in its thinking is always present to all of its objects as if moving toward them all and *already* having moved, being them all.[17]

Yet two categories of motion and rest are not sufficient for characterizing the life of the intellect because, for Plotinus, there is also motion in the soul and in the world, although these kind of movements are distinct from each other. In particular, the life of the νοῦς remains in perfect stillness and quietude (ἡσυχία) and at rest (ἐν στάσει, *Enn.* III.7.11.14, III.7.11.45–6). The movement of the intellect is then participated and imitated by the movement of the soul, whose discursive thinking much more resembles linear motion from point to point. Since the soul is produced by the intellect, the relation of both kinds of

---

[17] The intellect "in its movement moves always in the same way and on one same and identical course, but still is not the same and one partial thing, but all things" (νοῦς τε κινούμενος κινεῖται μὲν ὡσαύτως καὶ κατὰ ταὐτὰ καὶ ὅμοια ἀεί, οὐ μέντοι ταὐτὸν καὶ ἕν τι ἐν μέρει, ἀλλὰ πάντα, *Enn.* VI.7.13.4–8).

movement is then that of the paradigm and image, just as time is a moving image imitating eternity (*Enn.* III.7.11.20, III.7.11.43–5, III.7.13.23–6).

In order to distinguish one kind of movement from the other we need to make use of the other pair of categories, that of sameness and otherness. It is only in the intellect that there is a proper balance of the same and the other in the inseparability of one-many, so that the life "there" is always equal to itself, possesses itself, and is present to itself without diminution. When the soul comes to be, it is already unable to hold the equilibrium of the same and the other that is now dissolved into the separate one *and* many, so that the life of the soul is not complete any more but is weakened in a succession (ἄλλην μετ' ἄλλην; ἐφεξῆς) or "spreading out" (διάστασις, *Enn.* III.7.11.36–7; III.7.11.41). In this state, thinking becomes inevitably discursive, unable to embrace and know itself in one single act, and thus always striving to apprehend the fullness of the life of the intellect that it cannot grasp (cf. Themistius, *In de an.* 109.18–21). In place of the eternity of the intellect there comes the time of the soul: "eternity belongs [περί] to the intellect and time to soul" (*Enn.* IV.4 [28].15.2–3; cf. III.7.11.1–44). Metaphorically, this unstable state of the soul can be described as dominated by an "unquiet power" (δύναμις οὐχ ἥσυχος) that tends to do what it should not and cannot do, of a "restlessly active nature (φύσεως πολυπράγμονος) which wanted to control itself and be on its own, and chose to seek for more than its present state" (*Enn.* III.7.11.15–21; cf. VI.3 [44].23.1–5).[18] Only at this point of the dissolution and separation of the one and the many does evil appear, which consists both in desire and in the inability to preserve the entirety of life, thinking, and being in and of the intellect (see Chapter 11).

3.2.3 LIFE

Using the above categories, we can say that the unity in plurality of the intellect is realized through the interaction of sameness and otherness in a kind of movement that remains ever at rest. Whereas, as was said, the good as such for Plotinus is the one (Chapter 1), the good for something is defined by the measure of its participation in the one. In particular, the good for the intellect is to be one (both to *be* one and to be *one*; τὸ ἀγαθὸν τὸ ἓν τὸ ἐν τῷ ὄντι), and the good for being is "its activity towards the good; but this is life; but this is movement" (τὸ ἀγαθὸν τούτῳ ἐνέργεια πρὸς τὸ ἀγαθόν· τοῦτο δὲ ἡ ζωὴ αὐτοῦ· τοῦτο δὲ ἡ κίνησις; *Enn.* VI.2.17.25–9). So, finally, we come in our

---

[18] On the connection between the restlessness of the soul and the "audacity" (τόλμα), "independence" (αὐτεξούσιον), and "striving" (ὄρεξις), see Jonas, "Plotin über Zeit und Ewigzeit," pp. 315–7; Strange, "Plotinus on the Nature of Eternity and Time," p. 48; and Peter Manchester, "Time and the Soul in Plotinus, III.7 [45], 11," *Dionysius* 2 (1978), pp. 101–36. Cf. Aristotle, *De an.* 433a9–10.

analysis to the concept of life (ζωή), which appears to be crucial for the understanding of eternity.

Life, as Plotinus says, is connected with movement. Life appears as the inherent principle of communication within the intellect (cf. Plutarch, *De an. procr. in Tim.* 1012d–f). As such, this "first life" (πρώτη ζωή) should be distinguished from both being and thinking. The life of the intellect may be considered as mediating between thinking (νόησις) and the objects of thought (νοητά). Because of life, communication is possible within the intellect for, in communication, thinking moves from one object to another without having moved, being always already at every object of thought, thinking them all at once. In this way, the life of the intellect is at rest (ἐν στάσει, *Enn.* III.7.11.45–6). Communication thus animates the νοῦς, balancing sameness and otherness within it. Due to the presence of otherness through the mediation of movement, the intellect brings its multitude into unity as constituted by sameness and rest. Because of the indissoluble unity of the one-many within the intellect, life as mediating in stable movement is proper to the intellect only. In the soul, this unity already becomes disrupted, so that the ψυχή only has life insofar as it participates in the νοῦς. In other words, the soul also moves and thinks, but, in its movement and thinking, the soul attempts to recollect its wholeness through the discursive motion of thinking as bringing together the parts of the puzzle of the νοητά.

Hence, life may be considered under one single genus in the intellect and soul, as movement (*Enn.* VI.2.7.4–5), even if it is differently exemplified in the two. Without movement or "journeying" there is no life and, consequently, no communication (κοινωνία), no thinking, and no cosmos of the noetic "living beings" in the intellect (πᾶσα δὲ διὰ ζωῆς ἡ πορεία καὶ διὰ ζώων πᾶσα, *Enn.* VI.7.13.44–5). Life as κίνησις is constituted by both sameness (insofar as it is in and of the unchanging being) and otherness (insofar as it moves on to different objects, always remaining where it is): "and there in the intelligible, through which [the movement goes,] the life is the same, but because it is always other, not the same" (ἐκεῖ ἡ μὲν ζωή, δι' ἧς, ἡ αὐτή, ὅτι δὲ ἀεὶ ἄλλη, οὐχ ἡ αὐτή, *Enn.* VI.7.13.46–7; cf. Plato, *Soph.* 255A–B). The connection of life with some kind of movement can also be seen in physical things, among which being alive means being capable of self-movement (cf. Aristotle, *De an.* 434a22–b9; *Phys.* 200b12–4).

If we turn to another Aristotelian distinction, that between being and being-something, or *existentia* and *essentia*, we may say that in the intellect—unlike in a physical thing, a stone for instance, for which "to be a stone" does not necessarily presuppose or imply "to be"—"to be intellect" already includes "to be." In other words, the intellect *is* always, or is eternal. Put otherwise, the intellect is not able not to be. It exists necessarily: it is insofar as it thinks, and it thinks insofar as it is. That the νοῦς constantly thinks itself in the forms of itself and that it is as if motion at rest means that the intellect is alive. One can say that, in a sense, the intellect is life because life cannot be separated from it, as the essence of the intellect cannot be separated from its existence. Life of the intellect expresses, then, the inseparability of being and being-intellect and their necessary connection without ignoring their distinction established by the movement at rest. This movement distinguishes the intellect into thinking and thought, always reflexively bringing the intellect to itself without interruption or deferral, in the "already" (ἤδη) of eternity.

The source, giver, or provider (χορηγός) of life for the intellect is the one that itself, however, does not have life, as it does not have being or thinking (see Chapter 1). Since soul imitates the intellect, and the soul's movement is an image of the movement of the intellect, the life of the soul, as an image of the life of the intellect, is weaker and dimmer in all its functions.[19] In the soul, being and being-soul are already not identical but yet are necessarily tied together. This means that the soul exists necessarily and is alive to the extent that it participates in the intellect. In this sense, we may say that the soul *has* life, while the intellect alone *is* life.

The understanding of life as a kind of κίνησις becomes possible under two main implicit presuppositions. First, life as the intellectual movement makes sense only within the system of the communicating νοητά in the νόησις. Life as intellectual movement can only be conceptualized from the understanding of the intellect as

> abiding life and a thought whose activity is not directed towards what is coming but what is here already, or rather "here already and always here already (ἤδη καὶ ἀεὶ ἤδη)," and the always present, and it is a thought thinking in itself and not outside. In its thinking, then, there is activity and motion, and in its thinking itself, substance and being. (*Enn.* VI.2.8.8–13)

And second, Plotinus' understanding of life is developed within the system of five Platonic *genera*, where the opposite principles of sameness and otherness are constitutive of every object, be it intelligible or physical. Life, on the contrary, is not opposite to rest but rather represents an immanent condition of the possibility of the eternal being of the intellect in communication with itself (cf. *Enn.* III.7.3.7–38). As a specific movement, life is not a movement from a not-yet-present state of being to its actualization. On the contrary, everything is *already* there in being as thinking, actualizing each other and itself through the other. An illustration here might be a child who lives in the not yet developed fullness of life, and, although not yet able to give an account (λόγος) of what she and her world are, already possesses the fullness of the not evolved life that is already present in her and only gradually passes away with time.[20]

---

[19] *Enn.* I.4.3.24–8, III.2.1.30–4, III.7.11.48–9, IV.7.9.7–9, VI.2.6.9–12, VI.3.7.21–2, VI.6.18.12–8.
[20] Cf. Hans-Georg Gadamer, "Concerning Empty and Ful-filled Time," *The Southern Journal of Philosophy* 8:4 (1970), pp. 341–53; esp. 349.

Thus, bringing together everything we have said about life, we may finally define life as incessant intellectual activity free of the restful movement "from," "around," and "to" being, as the movement of thinking that always thinks itself in and as the intelligible forms.

3.3 The Eternal

3.3.1 ETERNITY AND LIFE

Now that Plotinus finds a way to appropriate five Platonic *genera* and to inscribe them into the system of intellect, he can describe eternity in these terms that emerge from the consideration and the analysis of one single phenomenon. He finds such a phenomenon in the multiple unity of the intellect that is only possible under the presupposition of the communication of the νοητά brought in the unity of the νόησις, which is the intellectual life that, in Plato's terms, "remains or abides in one" (μένοντος αἰῶνος ἐν ἑνί, Plato, *Tim.* 37D).

One can say, then, that this life, (1) is *in* (ἐν) the one or unity of being and is *from* (ἐξ) it and *with* (σύν) it (*Enn.* III.7.4.2; cf. III.7.11.61–2, VI.9.9.14–6). However, the one-many of the intellect is itself *around* (περί) the one that alone is outside of multiplicity. But since the intellect is *from* (ἀπό) the one and is directed *toward* (πρός) the one, "in no way going out of it but always [ἀεί] abiding around [περί] it and in it and living according to [κατ'] it" (*Enn.* III.7.6.1–4), such also is the life of the intellect. As was said, life (2) is a movement of a specific kind: it is intellectual movement, κίνησις νοερά, which, unlike the movement of the soul which represents time, is without parts, and is thus present in its entirety, remaining as if in rest (*Enn.* III.7.11.50).[21]

This life is (3) always "selfsame" or self-identical (ὡσαύτως), remaining (4) the same in the same (μένοντος ἐν τῷ αὐτῷ, *Enn.* III.7.3.20–1). As such, intellectual life (5) is present in and through "compressing the otherness in the intelligible objects, and seeing the unceasingness and self-identity of their activity, and that it is never other and is not a thinking of life that goes from one thing to another" (*Enn.* III.7.3.12–5). This life of the intellect, then, (6) can only be without expansion, extension, or interval (ἀδιάστατος) because there is no sequence in it. In this respect, again, life as movement differs from rest because, unlike movement, rest does not presuppose either a dynamic unity or non-extension (*Enn.* III.7.2.32–4; cf. III.7.3.15, III.7.13.63).

From (1) and (6) it follows that, (7) there are no separate parts within life, and hence "not now this, and then again that, but all things at once [ἅμα τὰ

---

[21] Plotinus clearly makes a distinction between νοητός and νοερός, the intelligible as belonging to the sphere of the objects of thought and the intellectual as belonging to the thinking itself. The life of the intellect is thus intellectual and not intelligible.

πάντα], and not now some things and then again others," so that everything is all together in life (*Enn.* III.7.3.16–9, III.7.3.37, III.7.11.55, V.3.15.21–2; cf. Anaxagoras B1 DK). Such life represents (8) the partless completion (τέλος ἀμερές) of the intellect, due to which the intellect is always at its end, which is not different from itself. The intellect brings itself into a unity of thinking that thinks itself. Since such a completion, according to (6), is without extension, it is also similar to a point that is ever the same and that has not yet moved or flown to produce a line (*Enn.* III.7.3.19–20).

Since this life remains the same, it (9) only *is* (ἔστι μόνον), full without dissipation, it does not change and is not deficient in anything (οὐκ ἐνδεές, *Enn.* III.7.3.23, III.7.3.34–5, III.7.4.15, III.7.6.37). This eternal *is* (10), is not a substrate or substance (which corresponds to rest), but, as perfect activity, it "shines forth" (οἶον ἐκλάμπον) from it (*Enn.* III.7.3.24–5). This activity fully manifests being. It does not demonstrate but simply shows being as true. The truthfulness of being, then, is not a paradigm-image correspondence, but is simply being there as it is in the form of νοητά, every one of which simply is in its communication with the others and in this "simply-being" or "being-there" every intelligible object is what it is and as it is. It is what it is and is true because in the intellect there is no difference between being and being-something (*Enn.* III.7.4.12–5, III.7.6.12–4). This presentation of being in the activity of its life implies that, ontologically, being is never not-being. Epistemologically, it implies that being cannot be known as not-being because not-being is not anything that might be positively known or expressed and therefore cannot be known in principle or, modally, being cannot be otherwise than it is.

Since the life of the intellect is always there and does not change, it (11) always *already* (ἤδη) is there in its completion and is already eternal (ἤδη ἀίδιον, *Enn.* III.7.5.4, VI.6.18.4).[22] This "already," which is often taken as the essential characteristic of the intellect in Neoplatonism, expresses the pure actuality of the intellect, where there is nothing that could change into something else since everything is already present there as it is (*Enn.* II.5 [25].3.1–8). It also means that when we think or understand something discursively, we neither construct nor produce the object of thought by the act of thinking but rather discover that which is already there in the intellect.

From (7), (9), and (11) it follows that, (12) the life of the intellect can have no future or past, no "before" or "after," for it cannot acquire anything that it would not already have (*Enn.* IV.3.25.14–7). So it can neither become nor be otherwise than it is now. The "is" of being may mean that being always *is*, as existing—and that it *always* is, as gathered together and having no extension or duration that could bring about any intrinsic distinction. That is why being is without difference (ἀδιαφόρως, *Enn.* III.7.6.14). In order to represent being,

---

[22] Cf. *Enn.* III.7.3.26–8, I.5.2.12–3, VI.2.8.9–10, VI.7.1.48–57.

the life of the intellect should also always *be* and *always* be, fully in the present (ἐν τῷ παρόντι ἀεί)—again, without any extension, detriment, or change.[23]

The life that governs the communication within the intelligible cosmos, (13) displays the same structure of one-many for, although the life is without parts, it is constituted as multiplicity (ἐκ πολλῶν, *Enn*. III.7.5.22). Finally, (14) because the νοῦς is infinite in its δύναμις, life, too, is infinite as representing the infinite (τὸ ἄπειρον) of the intelligible objects in its power of unification and production, which includes the production of the image of time (*Enn*. III.7.5.23–4, III.7.11.54; cf. Plato, *Tim*. 37D, 38B–C).

3.3.2 ETERNITY

Now we can finally turn to eternity, which for Plotinus is partless in life and being (τῇ ζωῇ ἀμερὲς καὶ τῇ οὐσίᾳ, *Enn*. III.7.6.49–50; cf. Aristotle, *De caelo* 279a18–28). The life, as was argued, allows for the communication of the thought in the being of the intellect, bringing multiplicity into unity. In addition, the very notion of "always existing" or "eternal being," τὸ ἀεὶ ὄν, is already included in the notion of "existing" or "being," as a predicate analytically included in the subject (*Enn*. III.7.6.29–36).

Eternity, then, is the manifestation of the intellect as its life and can be described in terms of the same properties (1–14) that may be considered mutually convertible, so that any one of them might be arbitrarily chosen as essential.[24] Since the life of the νοῦς is complete in its entirety and is without extension, eternity is also simple and indivisible in its unity.

---

[23] *Enn*. III.7.3.20–3; cf. I.5.7.15–6. Plotinus does not take the eternal life of the "now" as *nunc stans*. The "now" in *Ennead* III.7 is rather a negative characteristic of the eternal (thus, it will become "nothing that it would not be now," *Enn*. III.7.3.28–9). Plotinus often uses "now" negatively as "not now" (οὐ νῦν, μὴ νῦν, *Enn*. III.7.3.17–8, III.7.3.17.30). Criticizing Aristotle's concept of time, he uses the "now" in the Aristotelian way, as standing for the limit within time at which "before" ends and "after" begins. The "now" thus primarily characterizes time and not eternity (*Enn*. III.7.9.65; cf. IV.3.13.21–2, VI.1.5.15–7, VI.3.19.22–4). The life as a stable movement is rather in "present" than in "now." The "now" is even once opposed to the eternity of ἀεί (*Enn*. IV.3.8.33–4). Quite often "now" does not have any special technical meaning in the *Enneads* (cf. *Lexicon Plotinianum*, cols. 715–6). The *nunc stans* of Augustine, Themistius (*In de an.* 110.5), and of the later scholastic tradition, as well as the "all at once" (*interminabilis vitae tota simul et perfecta possessio*) of Boethius (*De consol*. V.6) originate in Plotinus, but it would be misleading to present Plotinus himself as a propagator of the view of eternity as "standing now."

[24] Cf. *Enn*. III.7.5.19–23, I.5.7.24–30, IV.3.25.15, IV.4.1.12. A slightly different, shorter account of the properties of eternity represents it as life; activity of the intelligible; present all together; not deficient in any respect; without any extension; not admitting past and future and infinite. See Strange, "Plotinus on the Nature of Eternity and Time," p. 37; cf. Beierwaltes, *Plotin über Ewigkeit und Zeit*, pp. 43–9, against Armstrong, who argues that Plotinus' account of eternity in terms of life is inconsistent and brings more puzzles than answers. See A. H. Armstrong, "Eternity, Life and Movement in Plotinus' Account of Νοῦς," in *Le Néoplatonisme*, pp. 67–74.

Plotinus' account of eternity in many points follows Parmenides' characterization of being (B7–8 DK). An important distinction between the two approaches is that being for Parmenides is the primary and ultimate reality and is therefore ἀτέλεστον, without any further purpose beyond itself. But the same cannot be said about Plotinus' eternity, which, as life, represents the double τέλος or purpose of the intellect: on the one hand, since νοῦς always thinks itself, it is the end of itself, and, on the other hand, νοῦς aspires to think the unthinkable, the one as its unique origin.

Bringing together all the preceding properties and the already mentioned brief account of eternity in Plato's *Timaeus* 37D into one brief definition, one can say that eternity is "the life, always the same, of real being around the one" (ἡ περὶ τὸ ἓν τοῦ ὄντος ζωὴ ὡσαύτως, *Enn.* III.7.6.7–8). A more elaborate definition of eternity that brings together all its properties is that

> which was not and will not be, but *is* only, which has being which is static by not changing to the "will be," nor ever having changed, this is eternity. The life, then, which belongs to that which exists and is in being, all together and full, completely without extension or interval, is that which we are looking for, eternity. (*Enn.* III.7.3.34–8)[25]

Plotinus neither invents nor constructs the concept of eternity but rather describes that which we have already known and seen as if by touching it, by participating and sharing in it (μετεῖναι), by contemplating eternity in the intellect by the eternal in ourselves, seeing eternity as something close to ourselves, even though at times it is not so easy to give an account, λόγος, of what it is (*Enn.* III.7.5.11–2, III.7.7.3–5).

Against the Pythagoreans, Plotinus takes eternity to participate in the intelligible, to disclose the immanent activity of the intellect without being identical to it. Eternity is not being but the *life* of the intellect that allows for the uninterrupted communication of the intellect with itself (as self-thinking) as the other (as the intelligible objects). Eternity, then, is contemplated in the

---

[25] Cf. *Enn.* IV.4.15.7–10, VI.2.21.54–5, VI.5.11.16–7. There are also other definitions of eternity in *Enn.* III.7, formulated in terms of the life of the intellect. Thus, eternity can also be characterized as life "which is already endless because it is total and expends nothing of itself, since it has no past or future" (ζωὴν ἄπειρον ἤδη τῷ πᾶσαν εἶναι καὶ μηδὲν ἀναλίσκειν αὑτῆς τῷ μὴ παρεληλυθέναι μηδ' αὖ μέλλειν, *Enn.* III.7.5.26–7). Or eternity can be defined as "quiet life, all a single whole, already infinite, altogether without declination, resting in and directed towards the one" (τὴν ἀτρεμῆ ἐκείνην καὶ ὁμοῦ πᾶσαν καὶ ἄπειρον ἤδη ζωὴν καὶ ἀκλινῆ πάντη καὶ ἐν ἑνὶ καὶ πρὸς ἓν ἑστῶσαν, *Enn.* III.7.11.2–4; cf. III.7.4.37–43, III.7.6.37–8).

intelligible and is *from* and *with* its being as substance (ἐκ τῆς οὐσίας ... καὶ σὺν τῇ οὐσίᾳ, *Enn.* III.7.4.3–5).[26] As such, eternity as the life of the intellect does not disclose the source or the principle of being, which is the one. For this reason, the one cannot be said to be eternal but rather is (strictly speaking, is *not*) before, above, and beyond all being, life, and eternity.

---

[26] We might distinguish the time *of* something (as a life span) and time *for* something of which there is always a greater shortage the less time *of* (human life, for example) is left. For eternity, on the contrary, no such distinction as eternity *of* and eternity *for* is meaningful because both refer to the intellect, in which, due to the reflexive teleological structure of thinking, "of" and "for" coincide.

4

Unity and Individuation of the Soul

Plotinus' understanding of the soul, through all its transformations within the treatises of the *Enneads*, is marked by an attempt to establish, in constant polemics against other theories, a Platonic account of the soul. On the one hand, such an account has to take into consideration the exegetic and hermeneutic tasks of reading and interpreting Plato. On the other hand, it has to establish the soul as both uniting and separating, or mediating, between the intelligible and the sensible. In his psychology, Plotinus has to provide an explanation for both the unity of the soul, as well as its individuality and individuation. Since one of the starting points in his philosophy is the understanding of being as a synthetic unity of one and many, or sameness and otherness, which is represented as unity and diversity but with a particular stress on unity or oneness, the diversity *qua* individuality, which would also allow for uniqueness, becomes a rather difficult problem. In what follows, the discussion will focus on Plotinus' attempts, sometimes not explicitly present in arguments but rather only hinted at, to solve the problem of the individuation of the soul.

4.1 Soul

Before turning to the problem of individuation proper, let me first briefly recollect the main points of Plotinus' psychological doctrines, which to a great extent recall his critical school discussions of the contemporary psychological opinions, including those of the Stoics, the Pythagoreans, and the Peripatetics. One of Plotinus' main insights, also found in Plato's texts and in the tradition of their transmission and interpretation, is that, on the one hand, the soul is intimately connected with being, which is represented in and as the intellect (νοῦς). But, on the other hand, the soul is also tied to the not (yet) being of becoming, which is represented in and by the body.[1]

---

[1] Dominic O'Meara, *Plotinus: An Introduction to the* Enneads (Oxford: Oxford University Press, 1993), pp. 65–8.

That the soul is connected with the νοῦς and with being as a weaker representative of the unity of the one, and that it is more tightly bounded by multiplicity, which is still not excluded from being, is expressed by the reference to the soul as an independent entity, substance, οὐσία (*Enn.* IV.3 [27].2.9). As such, the soul is bodiless, ἀσώματον (*Enn.* IV.9 [8].4.25–6), and, within the division between the intelligible and the sensible (ἀισθητὴ καὶ νοητὴ φύσις), it primarily belongs to the intelligible (*Enn.* IV.2 [4].1.8–9). Plotinus energetically stresses that the soul belongs to the realm of real beings that do not cease to be: ἀπολεῖται οὐδὲν τῶν ὄντων (*Enn.* IV.3.5.5–6). And yet, the *conditio psychologica* of this kind of being is that it can be connected with the still greater plurality and dispersion within matter; that is, it can be embodied. This possibility of embodiment belongs to the essence of the soul. The soul can be associated with a body, although it does not need to be. Not being embodied sends the soul "into the depth" (*Enn.* IV.3.6.25): the soul's connection with the body is not necessary, but rather accidental (κατὰ συμβεβηκός). In other words, not every soul is the soul *of* something (ψυχή τινος), precisely because the soul is οὐσία and thus is independent (*Enn.* IV.3.2.8–10). And so, Plotinus' conception of soul is not the Aristotelian ἐντελέχεια that is the soul *of* a body. Nevertheless, the soul for Plotinus, as it is for Plato, is *intermediate* between the intelligible and the sensible:

> next to that altogether indivisible nature [the intellect-νοῦς] there is another essence [οὐσία] which follows upon it [ἐξῆς] and is from [ἀπό] it, having indivisibility from that other [intelligible] nature . . . established itself in the middle between the two, the indivisible and primary [being *qua* νοῦς] and the divisible within the bodies which is upon bodies. (*Enn.* IV.2.1.41–6)

The soul is thus the *middle*, both *dividing* and *separating* that which is otherwise opposite; namely, becoming and being, the bodily and the intelligible. The bodily is taken to be divisible and dispersible (μεριστὰ καὶ . . . σκεδαστά), its every part being less than the whole and present in a single place (and thus defined by that place). The intelligible entity, on the contrary, is indivisible and partless, not admitting of any extension, not even in its concept (ἀμερής τε καὶ ἀμέριστος, διάστημά τε οὐδὲν οὐδὲ δι' ἐπινοίας δεχομένη): it is not in any place and does not reside in any entity, either in part or as a whole, but is present in all beings at once (*Enn.* IV.2.1.12–9).

Hence, the soul is to be characterized by the opposite, but not mutually exclusive, terms of one and many, or one-*and*-many, indivisible and divisible (ἕν τε καὶ πολλὰ καὶ μεμερισμένον καὶ ἀμέριστον ψυχὴν εἶναι, *Enn.* IV.2.2.40–1). The soul, then, is not a substrate (ὑποκείμενον) but a unity of the opposites, which, however, differs from the unity of the one-many of the νοῦς in that the soul is more associated with multitude and dispersion. Plotinus appropriates the hypotheses of Plato's *Parmenides* for his own purposes, describing various orders of being as variously partaking in one and many. Only the one is simple, it "is" (strictly speaking, it is *not*) before everything else, radically different from and other than anything that comes after it (see Chapter 1). The primary "is" of being is best described, together with the Pythagoreans and Plato, as a synthetic unity of one and many. This being is the intellect (νοῦς), as thinking bound by thinking itself in its own forms, and as derived from the unity of the one and the otherness of the indefinite dyad (ἐκ τῆς ἀορίστου δυάδος καὶ τοῦ ἑνὸς τὰ εἴδη καὶ οἱ ἀριθμοί· τοῦτο γὰρ ὁ νοῦς, *Enn.* V.4.2.7–9; cf. Aristotle, *Met.* 987b20–3; see Chapter 2).

Adopting the one-many approach, Plotinus argues that the soul cannot be said to be just one because it participates in the divisible nature within bodies. Hence, the soul is "one *and* multitude" (μία καὶ πλῆθος, *Enn.* IV.9.2.24–8). The soul thus dispenses life to all the bodily parts in which it is, doing so by its "manifold oneness" (τῷ ... πολλῷ αὐτῆς ἑνὶ ζωὴν χορηγοῦσα τοῖς μέρεσι πᾶσι, *Enn.* IV.2.2.45–7; cf. Plato, *Tim.* 35A). The soul is one, being one everywhere (ἓν ... πανταχοῦ), including its various activities (ἐν τοῖς διαφόροις τῶν ἔργων, *Enn.* IV.3.3.25–6). At the same time, the soul participates in the many, particularly because each soul has a number of different faculties (such as λογική, ἄλογος, αἰσθητική, φυτική, θρεπτικόν, *Enn.* IV.3.3.29–31, IV.9.1.5, IV.9.1.20, IV.9.3.10–1, IV.9.3.23–8). Being one *and* many, the soul is then both divisible and indivisible (*Enn.* IV.2.1.62–6).

The one, beyond being, is "one only" (ἓν μόνον); the soul is "one and many" (ἓν καὶ πολλά); the forms, as exemplified in bodies, are "many and one" (πολλὰ καὶ ἕν); and bodies are "many only," πολλὰ μόνον (*Enn.* IV.2.2.52–5)—to which one might add that the intellect is ἕν-πολλά. Yet, we also find the description of the νοῦς as "one and many" (ἓν καὶ πολλά, *Enn.* IV.8.3.10–1). This might suggest a closeness of the soul to the intellect and further hint at the soul's intermediate position: being in a body, the soul is equally in the νοῦς, or rather *is* the νοῦς in its highest part. Thus dependent on the νοῦς, which is being per se, the soul is to be conceived within a certain order of being, τάξις, in which it is intermediate, μεταξύ, between being and becoming. The soul, then, is a mediator, a *sui generis* ambassador, a negotiator and an interpreter of the synthetic being of the intellect to and within becoming.

In the order of descent and the augmentation of multiplicity and divisibility, the soul comes down to its lowest part, which is nature (φύσις). Nature is productive and embraces a whole multiplicity of powers (δυνάμεις), the unfolding of which is similar to that of a seed, which also has many powers and, being one, produces the one and many of an individual organism (καὶ ἐξ ἑνὸς τούτου πολλὰ ἕν, *Enn.* IV.9.3.18; cf. V.7 [18].3.10–1). For Plotinus, the very first act of the production of being by the one is already an act of giving because the inextinguishable productive power cannot stay "as if it had drawn a line round itself in envy" (οὐκ ἔδει στῆσαι οἷον περιγράψαντα φθόνῳ, *Enn.*

IV.8.6.12–3). Giving the gift of being, therefore, is an act of generosity, all the way down down to the φύσις.

4.2 Unity

Already in the early treatise *Ennead* IV.9 [8] Plotinus comes up with the thesis that all souls are one. Not only is each soul one as the same (ταὐτόν), insofar as it is an οὐσία, a substance identical in its essence, but each soul, as οὐσία, has to be one as a representation or an individuation of one soul, of the universal soul that follows and depends upon one universal νοῦς. The thesis of the unity of all the individual souls is supported by a number of arguments. Thus, if this particular soul is one with that one—that is, if both are really one—it does not have to follow that this composite (of soul and body, τὸ συναμφότερον) has to coincide with that one in its perceptions and in its affections (πάθη). For the same in two different substances can be differently exemplified without thereby ceasing to be the same and without violating the principle of non-contradiction (as, for instance, being a human in motion and being a human at rest can occur in two different people). In order that an affection (πάθος) in a composite (τὸ συναμφότερον) of a soul-body, or in an embodied soul, might coincide with another πάθος, the two would need to occur in one and the same body (*Enn.* IV.9.2.1–10).

Furthermore, many perceptions within the body may not be immediately noticeable. Thus, a part can be affected without originating a sensible perception in the whole, and even the whole can be affected in its entirety (συμπάσχειν) without sensible perception (τύπωσιν . . . αἰσθητικήν). Obviously, the implicit presupposition here is that the (material) whole affects its part more than a part affects the whole (*Enn.* IV.9.2.20–33).

The unity of the souls might also be demonstrated by a closer examination of the co-affectionate states of the souls; that is, through universal sympathy. That all humans are naturally inclined to love others (εἰς τὸ φιλεῖν ἑλκομένους κατὰ φύσιν) suggests sharing of each other's affections (for instance, in feeling the other's pain by observing it). Such universal sympathy, however, is only possible if one assumes the initial unity of the souls (*Enn.* IV.9.3.1–4; cf. IV.3.8.2–3). Therefore, the arguments from affection (πάθος) and from co-affection or sympathy (συμπάθεια) support the view that all souls are one. In particular, this implies that each soul's being is not a separate individual substance or οὐσία, but rather a different case of the instantiation of one οὐσία-soul.

But if all souls are one, *how* (πῶς) are they one? Going through different possibilities of all the souls being one, Plotinus uses the diairetic method to establish various hypotheses: all souls are either all (essentially) one (μία αἱ πᾶσαι), or they are *from* one soul (ἀπὸ μιᾶς). In the latter case, the one soul is either divided, or it remains whole, still producing many from itself (εἰ ἀπὸ μιᾶς, μεριζομένης ταύτης ἢ μενούσης μὲν ὅλης, ποιούσης δὲ παρ' αὐτῆς οὐδὲν ἧττον πολλάς, *Enn.* IV.9.4.2–5).

Plotinus begins his discussion by reiterating the (Platonic) theses that, first, if there is many, there must be one prior to it, and, second, the many must come from this one (*Enn.* IV.9.4.7–8).

If the soul is neither an entelechy, nor a form in matter, nor a harmony, nor a material entity, but is rather an οὐσία, it must be, as was argued, one *and* many, and hence, as one universal soul, it must be one substance. But how does this universal soul exist in the multitude of other individual souls, each of which might be further associated with a body that is part of the body of the whole cosmos? The question of how many souls are one (discussed in *Enn.* IV.9.4) is closely connected with the question of how one soul as οὐσία is in the many (discussed in *Enn.* IV.9.5). In the latter case, the one soul is either present as one whole *in* (ἐν) all the individual souls, or the multitude of souls comes *from* (ἀπό) the one and whole soul, while this whole still remains what it is (πῶς οὖν οὐσία μία ἐν πολλαῖς; ἢ γὰρ ἡ μία ἐν πᾶσιν ὅλη, ἢ ἀπὸ ὅλης καὶ μιᾶς αἱ πολλαὶ ἐκείνης μενούσης, *Enn.* IV.9.5.1–3). Of the two models of the one soul's presence in the many, the "in" (ἐν) and the "from" (ἀπό), Plotinus chooses the "ἀπό" because an individual soul can be present in the becoming (that is, within the bodily), although not as an image (εἴδωλον) of the universal soul or αὐτοψυχή (*Enn.* V.9.13.4–7). For this reason, every soul, both the universal soul and the individual soul, is both one and many, in which case the many depends on and returns to the one in the soul, so that the soul both "gives itself to multiplicity and does not give itself" (ὡς μίαν δοῦσαν ἑαυτὴν εἰς πλῆθος καὶ οὐ δοῦσαν) because it can extend to all things that are not cut off from any one and is thus the same in many (τὸ αὐτὸ οὖν ἐν πολλοῖς, *Enn.* IV.9.5.4–7).

But how should this presence of one soul in many, which remains whole without detriment, be further described? The universal soul for Plotinus depends on ("looks at") the whole of the intellect (πρὸς τὸν ὅλον νοῦν ἰδεῖν), whereas individual souls depend on individual or partial intellects (*Enn.* IV.3.6.15–7), which are constituents of the whole of the universal intellect. Therefore, the soul in its entirety and the souls in their multiplicity reproduce the one-many structure of the intellect. Since every reproduction is an imitation and thus reinforces the many, the soul and the souls have to be both one *and* many. The universal soul, then, is one in that it remains the same οὐσία, but it is many in that it allows for a multiplicity of souls to come from (ἀπό) it. The individual souls are many, but they keep their unity of individuation. The souls thus "keep identity and difference; each soul remains one, and all are one together" (τὸ ταὐτὸν καὶ ἕτερον σῴζουσαι, μένει τε ἑκάστη ἓν καὶ ὁμοῦ ἓν πᾶσαι, *Enn.* IV.3.5.13–4). The question of the unity and multiplicity within the soul is further complicated in Plotinus by a teaching about the distinction between the universal soul, on the one hand, and the world soul, on the other. This teaching is not developed in detail, especially in the earlier treatises, but it is still distinctly traceable in Plotinus (cf. *Enn.* IV.2.2.10–1).[2] The universal soul, ψυχὴ (ἐκείνη, μία) is the soul as hypostasis, the one soul immediately coming after and depending on the one intellect, thus remaining in a τάξις κατὰ φύσιν (cf. *Enn.* II.9.1.15; II.9.7–8). The soul of the world (ἡ τοῦ παντός, τῆς ὅλης) depends on the one soul and is embodied in the whole of the physical cosmos. Blumenthal convincingly argues that, first, the universal soul should be distinguished from the world soul. One can certainly interpret *Ennead* IV.9.4.15–20 in this way, where Plotinus distinguishes between one soul before (πρό) the souls in bodies, from the one soul which comes from that one in the manifold cosmos (ἀφ' ἧς ἡ ἐν πολλοῖς μία). However, it should be noted that a clearer distinction between the two souls, the universal one and that of the world, comes in *Enned* IV.9.1.10–3 and IV.3.2.54–9, where the soul of the world, as a partial soul, is set apart from the universal soul (cf. *Enn.* IV.3.6.12). And, second, in Blumenthal's interpretation, in the relationship between an individual soul and the soul of the world, the former, which belongs to the plurality of partial souls, is not subordinate to the world soul, but rather the two are equal in their relation to the universal soul to the extent that they equally come from that universal soul. Plato's famous passage on the immortality of the soul (*Phaedr.* 245C–246A) allows for an ambiguous interpretation, insofar as the ψυχὴ πᾶσα of the initial statement of the thesis, ψυχὴ πᾶσα ἀθάνατος (245C), can be taken as either the "soul of the all"—that is, the world soul (as it was understood by Posidonius)—or as "every soul" (as it was understood by Harpocration, ap. Hermias, *In Plat. Phaedr.* 102.10–5). However, in *Ennead* IV.3.6.13, Plotinus famously calls the world soul "sister" (ἀδελφὴ ψυχή) of the individual ones, which implies that they exist at the same ontological level.

Why does Plotinus need the soul of the world in addition to the universal soul? In discussing the relation of the soul to the ensouled—that is, the soul as possibly embodied—he faces the problem of the production of the world. In Plato's myth it is the νοῦς that acts as the demiurge who creates the whole of the cosmos that is to be further governed by the world soul, which is equally produced by the νοῦς (*Tim.* 29D). Plotinus, however, delegates the task and function of creation of the world to the universal soul, which then makes the

---

[2] See H. J. Blumenthal, *Soul, World-Soul, and Individual Soul in Plotinus* (Paris: Centre national de la recherché scientifique, 1971), pp. 55–66; Wypkje Helleman-Elgersma, *Soul-Sisters: A Commentary on Enneads IV 3 [27], 1–8 of Plotinus* (Amsterdam: Rodopi, 1980), pp. 89–103; Eyjólfur Kjalar Emilsson, *Plotinus on Sense-Perception: A Philosophical Study* (Cambridge: Cambridge University Press, 1988), pp. 24–5; Filip Karfík, "Parts of the Soul in Plotinus," in *Partitioning the Soul: Debates from Plato to Leibniz*, ed. Klaus Corcilius and Dominik Perler (Berlin: De Gruyter, 2014), pp. 107–48, esp. 110–4; and Caluori, *Plotinus on the Soul*, pp. 37–68.

world soul govern the whole of the cosmos and of partial souls as its single parts (*Enn.* IV.3.6.20–3; cf. Plato, *Tim.* 34B–37C). On such a reading, the partial souls are not instantiations of the world soul, but rather are individuations of the universal soul. The question, then, is how such individuations become possible, and what is the principle of individuation in and of each partial soul.

4.3 Episteme

But how exactly is the one universal soul present in many souls, both "giving and not giving itself"? Since the one-many is primarily exemplified in and as the intellect, and since every soul, both the universal and the individual, depends, respectively, on either the universal or a partial νοῦς, then the one-many structure of being should also be reflected in every soul as one *and* many. A partial soul is one in its individuality, *and* there is a whole multiplicity of such souls. The universal soul is one as both unique and as primarily mediating between the intelligible and the sensible, *and* it is many as present in the multitude of the individual souls without losing its unity.

Plotinus takes the one-and-many character of the soul to come out of its dependence on the one intellect, which is itself one-many and is constituted by the communication (κοινωνία) of a plurality of the noetic constituents that it thinks. The being of the intellect is in the thinking of itself as not other than itself. And because the νοῦς always thinks itself as identical in the otherness of its objects that always *are*, the intellect always is its objects and always *is*; that is, the intellect is the same as being, νοῦς δὴ καὶ ὂν ταὐτόν (*Enn.* V.4.2.43–8).

In *Ennead* IV.8 [6], Plotinus establishes the relation between the whole multitude of individual souls that arise from the universal soul and the one soul, as that between the species (εἴδη) and one single genus (*Enn.* IV.8.3.10–3). Soon after that, in *Ennead.* IV.9 [8], however, he suggests a rather different model of the relation between the universal and particular souls; namely, that of the one-and-many in and of knowledge (ἐπιστήμη), in which the many is represented by the bulk of the objects of knowledge and contemplation, or "theorems." The (Aristotelian) genus–species model, in the end, might not be exclusive of the (Platonic) knowledge–theorem model because the former presupposes the concept of specific difference, whereas the latter presupposes the difference of the actually existing noetic constituents of the intellect as reflected in the discursive thinking of the soul that considers the potential deducibility of one entity from another. At the same time, each θεώρημα is identical with itself, and, therefore, each one has an individual οὐσία. But since every theorem can be deduced in principle from every other one that has been explicitly formulated and demonstrated, every θεώρημα is only virtually different from another one and thus might be properly characterized in terms of its specific difference.

The organizational principle in the objects of thought, interconnected without mixture and separation, is thus the unity-in-diversity of knowledge or science (ἐπιστήμη). "Knowledge is a whole," says Plotinus, "and its parts are such that the whole remains and the parts derive from it" (καὶ γὰρ ἡ ἐπιστήμη ὅλη, καὶ τὰ μέρη αὐτῆς ὡς μένειν τὴν ὅλην καὶ ἀπ' αὐτῆς τὰ μέρη, *Enn.* IV.9.5.7–9). Every constituent, every "part" of science is entwined into a system, in which the whole does not subordinate the part yet does not exist without its parts either. In this way, all the parts are present to the whole as if actual and all at once in the intelligible (ἐκεῖ . . . οἷον ἐνεργείᾳ ἅμα πάντα, *Enn.* IV.9.5.16–7), where every object of thinking does actually, and not potentially, contain every other one and thus "shines out" (φανὰ πάντα καὶ ἕκαστον, *Enn.* IV.9.5.27–8). In science as a system of knowledge, however, which is established and unraveled by the discursive thinking of and within the soul, and of which the best example is the mathematical geometrical theory (of Euclid), every part, every "theorem" can be actualized by the demonstration within discursive thinking. In the partiality of such thinking, every θεώρημα does potentially contain every other one (ἔχει δυνάμει καὶ τὰ πάντα), and all the theorems are made explicit in a succession or sequence (ἀκολουθία) by the mathematician, in an order and system. "The geometer in his analysis makes clear that the one [proposition] contains all the prior ones by means of which the analysis is made and the subsequent [propositions] [τὰ ἐφεξῆς] which are generated from it" (*Enn.* IV.9.5.22–6).

Therefore, the "how" of the relationship of individual souls, both to each other and to the universal soul, is defined by the one-many model of science and knowledge. Dependent in their multiplicity both on the one soul and their respective intellects, the souls reproduce the one science of many theorems. These actually coexist in the noetic communication-κοινωνία as a potential actualizability of the theorems by way of their successive deduction from one another, within the partiality of the discursive logical thinking in every soul.

The geometrical ἐπιστήμη model fits within Plotinus' henological agenda of explaining *how* the souls are many. What it does not explain, however, is *why* the souls are not only multiple but also individualized, and what the principle of their individuation is. Unlike the intellect(s), the souls are exposed to a much greater multiplicity and partiality, particularly in the possibility of being connected with materiality in bodies. Individuation becomes a rather difficult problem within the one-many approach. For this reason, Plotinus returns to the discussion of the problem of individuation and of the principle of individuation several times in his writings.

Plotinus needs to provide an explanation for the unity and plurality of both one universal soul and the derived souls, both the world soul and the partial individual ones, especially in their relation to the bodily. First of all, as was already mentioned, every soul is both divisible and indivisible, being intermediate between the indivisible intellect and the divisible physical entities.

In the early *Ennead* IV.2 [4], Plotinus argues that because of its middle position, the soul, being indivisible, becomes divisible in bodies; and, since bodies are divisible, so is the soul in them, being individually within each one and yet remaining whole in each body. Present in and to bodies (which, however, is not necessary), the (universal) soul is still one and is divisible in them without being affected; that is, giving itself wholly to each body, it nevertheless does not abandon its unity or its being-οὐσία (*Enn.* IV.2.1.29–62).

Being both divisible and indivisible is possible without the violation of the principle of non-contradiction because the soul is divisible and indivisible in different respects. The soul is divisible insofar as it is present in each and every part of the body with which it might be associated. But the soul is also indivisible in that it is present in all the parts of the body and is in each one as a whole (*Enn.* IV.2.1.64–6). In order to properly characterize this divisibility and indivisibility and the relation of parts and the whole within the soul, Plotinus turns to the model of ἐπιστήμη, understood as a Euclidean geometrical theory, which is mentioned not only in the early *Ennead* IV.9 [8] but also in his major work on psychology, *Ennead* IV.3–5 [27–9]. In *Ennead* IV.3.2.50–4, Plotinus argues that a part (μέρος) of a science as a division (μερισμός) of the whole (ὅλη) is the manifestation (ἐνέργεια) of that whole. Unlike the unity of the multiplicity of the κοινωνία within the intelligible cosmos of the νοητά, where each νοητόν actually represents every other one and the whole, every part of the geometrical ἐπιστήμη, which is a theorem (θεώρημα), only potentially contains others as deducible from it and thus interconnected. Each part is thus independent of the others, yet it also expresses the entire theory that is only differently represented in each theorem. This relation of the part to the whole, as that between a theorem and the whole theory, can be extended to the relation between each partial soul (including the world soul) and the universal soul: being of the same kind, the individual souls represent one soul. A "part" (μέρος) within a soul is different from a part of a body or of a geometrical figure, in which every part is further divisible and may be dissimilar to the whole in its form, as, for instance, the arm of a human body or the semicircle of a circle (cf. *Enn.* IV.3.2.10–24). All individual souls, then, are "parts" of the universal soul in so far as they have the same form (ὁμοειδεῖς, *Enn.* IV.3.2.58): namely, that of the one soul divided into many, which, however, is not divisible in itself—just as a theory is divided by and into its theorems without ceasing to be one whole.

4.4 Individuation

The Platonic henological one-(and)-many approach allows Plotinus to aptly explain the unity of souls (in *Enn.* IV.9 and elsewhere), as well as their multiplicity *qua* beings (τὸ πλῆθος ... τῶν ὄντων, *Enn.* IV.8.6.3–4). The number of souls for Plotinus is great but finite. Actual infinity is reserved for Plotinus only for the inextinguishable creative power of the one, which cannot be properly represented or known. For this reason, he accepts the Stoic theory of the finite number of the individual souls as embodied within the repeating world periods that are indefinite in number (*Enn.* V.7.3).

The numerical multiplicity alone (that of the numbers and of the units within a number) does not yet suffice, however, for an explanation of the *difference* between the souls. The individual is already not so easily accounted for in the Platonic theory, which works much better within the realm of the noetic and the mathematical, but not within the world of concrete instantiations and of individual differences (cf. Aristotle, *Met.* 999a1–23).

Since the souls can be embodied, or connected with the physical, the bodily, and the material, one inevitably faces a rather difficult problem of individuation.[3]

How can one account for concrete individual differences (καθέκαστα) between souls as individual (e.g., of two different people, cf. *Enn.* IV.3.5.1–5)? The question now is not just why the souls are many (the units within a number are many as well), but why are they all *different*? If each soul is considered an οὐσία of the same kind, a substance of the same essence, then what is the source or the principle of their individuation?

Plotinus discusses individuation a number of times in the *Enneads*, and yet it is not easy to establish a univocal theory behind the particular instances. The fundamental fact about the soul that does not immediately follow from its henological description in terms of ἓν καὶ πολλά is that the soul can be *in* body, that is, can be physically embodied. The soul for Plotinus, contrary to the Peripatetics, is not a form in and of the material organic body because, first, the soul does not need to be embodied, and, second, because the soul, as οὐσία, is "separable" (χωριστὸν ἡ ψυχή, *Enn.* IV.3.20.30) and is thus independent from the body. Hence, if a soul is individualized, it should be due either to body or to the soul itself. In other words, the principle of individuation should be either in matter or in form. Plotinus considers both possibilities when referring to τὸ ψυχαὶ εἶναι, "being souls," which, in the context of his discussion of the unity of all souls, is to be understood as "being souls all together," also allowing for "being individual souls," each one distinct from each of the others. Being an individual soul can be understood, then, either in accordance with the material component or "bodily mass" (κατὰ τοὺς ὄγκους), or with the form (κατὰ τὸ εἶδος, *Enn.* IV.9.4.9–15).

---

[3] See Pauliina Remes, *Plotinus on Self: The Philosophy of the "We"* (Cambridge: Cambridge University Press, 2007), pp. 59–91.

4.4.1 MATTER AS A POSSIBLE SOURCE OF INDIVIDUATION

If there exist forms of universals only, then a form cannot account for individual differences, such as snubness (Plotinus uses Aristotle's example, *Enn.* V.9.12.6). In this case, it is matter (ὕλη) that has to be responsible for such differences, due to which a universal form—say, that of the human—is always differently represented in each individual (cf. *Enn.* V.7.2.13–4). The differences (διαφοραί) might thus come from matter (παρὰ τῆς ὕλης). If, however, there might also be forms of individuals, and, if matter has nothing of its own that might serve as the principle of individuation of the form in matter, then matter can hardly be itself the principle of individuation. Perhaps only the already formed matter, embodied materiality, such as (concrete) place (τόπος) or "nature of places and waters and air" might affect a human as an already embodied soul (παρὰ φύσεως τόπων πολλὰ ἀπομάττεσθαι καὶ ὑδάτων καὶ ἀέρος, *Enn.* IV.3.7.22–4; cf. *Enn.* V.9.12.8–11).

In *Ennead* IV.9.2.1–12, Plotinus considers the possibility that the difference in the constitution of the composite (τὸ συναμφότερον) of soul and body might account for the difference in affections (πάθη) within individual souls. In order to account for the affections (πάθη) a soul undergoes at various moments, or the affections that different souls have at the same time (even those experiencing one and the same thing), one might consider these differences between souls resulting from the body with which each soul is associated. Two different souls, then, can have the same affection only if they had a joint body, which is apparently impossible. The explanation of the soul's individuation in terms of perception and affection as based on the difference of bodies, however, is not sufficient because the body is already formed and thus already individualized, so that the explanation of individuation is simply postponed and relegated to being individualized in a body.

Another possible way of understanding matter as responsible for individuation might come in the aforementioned passage from *Ennead* IV.4.5, where Plotinus discusses unity and multiplicity of the soul within a "geometrical" ἐπιστήμη, in which one and many interact as if in a seed (σπέρμα). In the seed, "a whole and the parts into which it naturally divides derive from it, and each part is a whole and the whole remains an undiminished whole, but matter divides it (ἡ δ' ὕλη ἐμέρισε) and all the parts are one" (*Enn.* IV.9.5.9–12). The nature (φύσις) of and within the soul is the lowest power or "part" of the soul, φυσικόν, responsible for life and growth, due to which an ensouled body is alive.[4] If it is the φύσις in body that organizes the body as a living physical organism, and if it is the φύσις that is at work in the seed, then the division of the φύσις by matter might mean that the φύσις is divided as a part that is *already* included within the whole of the physical

---

[4] Cf. Blumenthal, *Soul, World-Soul, and Individual Soul in Plotinus*, p. 63.

cosmic order. However, in the cosmic order and in the physical world, the relation between form and matter, in which matter has nothing of itself and thus cannot bring anything of itself, should hold for any of its constituents. Hence, it should also hold for φύσις. But φύσις itself is already formed, and, if it is divided by matter that is thus individualized in it, this must be due to the same principle of individuation as everything else. Therefore, the seed simile does not really help to explain the role of matter as a principle or possible source of individuation.

Thus, matter, because it is nothing, because it is not a substance, and because it neither has nor brings anything of its own (see Chapter 6), can hardly account for individuation. As Plotinus argues, a soul does not need to be embodied (at least, not at all times, cf. *Enn.* IV.3.12) and, hence, if the soul's individuation results from the material component, the unembodied souls would be exactly alike, as are the units in number—but this is not the case. If individuation implies some kind of distortion, it is difficult to account for it because distortion can neither come from the self-sufficient and unchanging form, nor from matter, which, as pure receptacle, has no power of its own. This might be the reason why, thinking about evil as distortion, as non-being and the utter lack of measure (ἄμετρον), Plotinus later revises, to some extent, his views on matter and ascribes to it its own nature opposite to that of form, as a power to corrupt and distort the form that is embodied in matter (*Enn.* I.8 [51].8; see Chapter 11).

4.4.2 FORM AS A POSSIBLE SOURCE OF INDIVIDUATION

Discussing the problem of the origin of individual difference (τὸ διάφορον), Plotinus points out that the diversity of the beautiful comes in many instantiations (τὸ διάφορον πολλαχοῦ καλόν). However, such multiplicity of the beautiful cannot be ascribed to matter, to which only ugliness can be attributed (τῷ αἴσχει μόνῳ ἀποδοτέον τὸ παρὰ τὴν ὕλην) as the privation of the beautiful. But if there are different exemplifications of the beautiful, the form (τὸ εἶδος) cannot be one (*Enn.* V.7.2.14–6). Does it mean that in each of the different instantiations of the same there is a different form, which is thus responsible for individuation?

An important presupposition in Plotinus' psychology is that the universal soul, as well as each individual soul, depend in their being ("look toward") on the one universal intellect and on the individual intellects, respectively (*Enn.* IV.3.6.15–7). The intellect (νοῦς) is always transcendent to the world, always remaining "up there" (ἀεὶ ἄνω), and can never be outside of its own intelligible cosmos of the νοητά. The intellect communicates with the things "here," with the material and composite, through the soul (ψυχή), which is intermediate between the intelligible and the sensible and has a share in both. The soul is thus never "cut off [from] the intellect" and is "disposed according to the form, which comes to it from the intellect, and gives to the things below it" (*Enn.* IV.3.12.3, IV.3.12.30–5).

Depending on and living off its close association with the intellect, the soul has to be closely associated with the intelligible form (εἶδος). In the early *Ennead* IV.8.3.12, Plotinus argues that an individual soul might be considered an εἶδος, which is a species of the genus of the one universal soul, although later he moves away from this explanation, preferring instead that of the theorem and "geometrical" science. The soul, however, is itself *not* a pure form, but rather makes the form *in* matter (although the soul itself is not a form in matter) once the soul becomes associated with a body (ἡ δὲ ψυχὴ τὸ εἶδος ποιεῖ ἐν τῇ ὕλῃ ἄλλη τοῦ εἴδους οὖσα, *Enn.* IV.3.20.38–9). With the soul, the form is present in the body in such a way that, when the body is divided, the form is divided, yet nevertheless remains a whole in each of the parts of the body (*Enn.* IV.2.1.34–8).

If, as was argued, the individuation of the soul cannot be explained by reference to matter, then individuation might have to do with some formal aspect. Thus, individual differences appear for Plotinus notably as those "in the character, and in the activities of discursive reason and as a result of the lives they have lived" (ἐν τοῖς ἤθεσι μάλιστα καὶ ἐν τοῖς τῆς διανοίας ἔργοις καὶ ἐκ τῶν προβεβιωμένων βίων, *Enn.* IV.3.8.7–9). The differences within the souls also account for their "destiny" (εἱμαρμένον, IV.3.13.21): an individual soul, subordinated to the universal soul, is sent into the world according to law (νόμῳ πέμπεται, *Enn.* IV.3.13.24), and the embodiment of the souls, their ascent and descent into the bodies, and thus into the world, is ordered by one λόγος of the universal soul (ὑφ' ἕνα λόγον, *Enn.* IV.3.12.17). The soul's disposition (διάθεσις) according to which a body is "prepared" for the soul's descent into it (*Enn.* IV.3.12.37–8), is an individual characteristic that distinguishes one soul from another and is equally formal, as is the soul's "character" (ἦθος), the activity of its discursive thinking (διάνοια), and even its previous lives (*Enn.* IV.3.8.5–9; cf. Plato, *Rep.* 619E–621B). Being predestined by law, already always inscribed within a particular eidetic structure, the soul still keeps the ability "to be itself as much as it wants to be" (αὐτή ἐστιν ὅσον θέλει, *Enn.* IV.3.8.40). All these features that differentiate one soul from another implicitly refer to a formal characteristic of "that which is active and actualized in each soul" (κατὰ δὲ τὸ ἐνεργῆσαν ἐν αὐτῇ ἑκάστῃ) and which accounts for individuation as actualization, as "fullness" (τὸ πλῆρες) and "completion" (τέλειον) in and of each soul (*Enn.* IV.3.8.12–7). But what exactly is this formal characteristic that might account for individuation?

The answer to the problem of individuation also appears to depend on the solution of the problem of the existence of the forms of individuals, which might yield the answer to the question of whether or not there are forms of individual souls. An individual soul for Plotinus is *not* an image of the universal soul. An individual soul is not a form in matter either, particularly because not every soul has to be embodied, at least not at a given time. Every soul is a form. But is this the form of a universal, in which case the form of an individual soul would not be different from that of the universal soul—or is it the form of a single individual soul? And if it is an individual form, then how does such a form relate to the form of the universal soul? Would it be a relation of a particular intelligible (νοητόν) to the whole of the noetic cosmos of the νοητά?

Throughout his writings, Plotinus provides different answers to the question of whether or not there are forms of individuals. In the early *Ennead* V.9 [5], he denies the existence of forms of individuals, rejecting the form of "this human," Socrates, in favor of that of the human (ἄνθρωπος, *Enn.* V.9.12.3–4). Later, however, Plotinus gives the opposite answer to this question, dedicating the entire *Ennead* V.7 to establishing the thesis of the existence of forms of individuals. Here, he already argues for accepting the form of Socrates, of the soul of Socrates (ψυχὴ Σωκράτους), as universal, as Αὐτοσωκράτης: everybody has a noetic or formal beginning (ἀρχή) in the intelligible because everyone has access to the intelligible (ἀναγωγὴ ἐπὶ τὸ νοητόν, *Enn.* V.7.1.1–5). Blumenthal convincingly argues that, despite a number of exegetic attempts to reconcile the two opposite positions, Plotinus does not have a consistent view about the forms of individuals.[5] This suggests once again that, within the henological approach, it is difficult to explain individual differences. In the last instance, Plotinus does not have a convincing argument that it is the form that accounts for individual differences and individuation.

But, again, if it is not matter, then it should be either the form, or something *of* the form, which is responsible for individuation, for differences (διαφοραί) in and between souls. First of all, a particular soul is not an image of the universal soul: the two are not related as εἴδωλον and εἶδος (*Enn.* V.9.13.5). Each individual soul, as was argued, relates to the universal soul as a theorem (θεώρημα) relates to the whole of a science (ἐπιστήμη). What, then, constitutes the difference between the individual souls, and what, precisely, is this difference? In *Ennead* V.9, Plotinus mentions, without further elaboration, that one soul differs from another "in honor" or "dignity" (τιμιότητι δὲ ἄλλην ἄλλης διαφέρειν, *Enn.* V.9.13.6; τιμιότης is a *hapax* in Plotinus, although he uses the words of the same root, most notably the adjective τίμιος, very frequently). If an individual soul is *not* an image of the universal soul, then the difference in "dignity" appears to suggest that such difference does not exist as directly caused by a difference in and between the forms (εἴδη), but, equally, for the reasons stated earlier, it is also not a difference caused by matter.

In Aristotle, the concept of difference (διαφορά) appears as the *specific* difference, which, together with the genus, constitutes the definition (λόγος)

---

[5] Blumenthal, *Plotinus' Psychology*, pp. 112–33, esp. 121–9; for the discussion of various interpretations of the two positions in Plotinus, see pp. 129–32.

(Aristotle, *Top.* 103b15–6, 143a22–4) and is a quality (Aristotle, *Top.* 144a19–22). However, speaking about the soul, Plotinus uses the concept of difference not as a specific, but rather as an individual difference, as the one that characterizes the distinction between individual souls and not as that defining the soul as a genus. The individual as particular is then marked off by this distinctive difference or by a number of them.

4.5 Logos

In order to understand difference and its connection with individuation, we need to look further at the way the form is represented and differentiated in the soul. In addition to the forms as intelligibles (νοητά) and forms *in* matter, Plotinus also accepts the "rational principles" or λόγοι as intermediate between the two.[6] Plotinus understands λόγος as responsible for differences in general; for instance, in color (*Enn.* V.9.12.9–10). As we have seen, the major characteristic of the soul in Plotinus is its intermediate position: the soul depends on the intellect and "follows" it (ἐφεξῆς, *Enn.* IV.3.5.9). As such, the soul is ontologically situated "between" the intelligible and the sensible in that it both separates and unites them, reflecting the noetic and representing it in the physical. And, in its highest "part" (the "self"), the soul coincides with a νοῦς. For this reason, the souls are the λόγοι of their respective intellects (λόγοι νῶν, *Enn.* IV.3.5.9–10).

Λόγος is thus a representation or representative of the intelligible in the greater multiplicity of, and in, the soul.[7] As a soul, each λόγος is unfolded further than its corresponding νοῦς, as if going from brevity to multiplicity (οἷον πολὺ ἐξ ὀλίγου γενόμεναι, *Enn.* IV.3.5.10–1). Λόγος presupposes distinctions and parts. Respectively, the thinking of the soul (διάνοια) is discursive and "logical." It is a thinking of its objects (λόγοι) as partial, yet potentially related and referring to each other—as theorems are in a geometrical theory—which again suggests that the ἐπιστήμη metaphor is a particularly appropriate one for the explanation of the plurality of individual souls.

Multiplicity is further present in the soul in that the one universal soul represents one single λόγος of the intellect (λόγος εἷς τοῦ νοῦ), from which come partial immaterial λόγοι (λόγοι μερικοὶ καὶ ἄυλοι, *Enn.* IV.3.5.17–8). Every λόγος is thus many and manifold (πᾶς λόγος πολὺς καὶ ποικίλος, *Enn.* IV.3.8.18), for every λόγος is a simplex within the psychological structure of the one-and-many of the soul that represents the noetic cosmos of one-many. One could say that λόγος is the translation of one-many into one-*and*-many.

---

[6] See Emilsson, *Plotinus on Sense-Perception*, pp. 120–1.
[7] Cf. Michel Fattal, *Platon et Plotin: Relation, logos, intuition* (Paris: L'Harmattan, 2013), pp. 43–81.

Each soul, therefore, "remains one and all are together" (μένει τε ἑκάστη ἓν καὶ ὁμοῦ ἓν πᾶσαι, *Enn.* IV.3.5.14), which is a reflection of the unity of the noetic cosmos within greater plurality. For this reason, the structure (σύνταγμα) in which the souls are present is manifold and complex (ποικίλον), as is every λόγος, potentially related to other λόγοι, which can be rendered explicitly by a theory. Hence, all the souls form a system (σύνταξις) in which they are not cut off from each other and thus constitute a diversified unity in which plurality as separation is greater than that within the intelligible of the νοῦς (*Enn.* IV.3.8.17-22). This structure of the souls *qua* system of λόγοι is an imitation of the κόσμος νοητός, described by Plato as a "living being" (ζῷον; see Chapter 2). The whole σύνταγμα or σύνταξις of the souls, then, is a representation of the noetic "living being" of the λόγος, or the "organism of the soul" (ζῷον ψυχικόν), which is similar to that of the intellect although bound by a greater plurality in which many forms are present (ζῷον ψυχικὸν πολλὰς μορφὰς ἔχον, *Enn.* IV.3.8.19).

This leads Plotinus to assert that each soul has *all* of the forming principles. Each soul already has all the λόγοι (as "forms" or μορφαί of something), not only of those individuals in whom the soul might reside in turn, but all the λόγοι of the world (*Enn.* V.7.1.7-12, V.7.3.21-2). In this sense, "all souls are all things" (πάντα πᾶσαι, *Enn.* IV.3.8.13). Even in matter, the λόγοι are hidden yet are contained in their entirety (*Enn.* V.7.2.16-7). The number of the different λόγοι in the universal soul, as well as in each individual one, is therefore infinite. However, this infinity does not need to be actual: rather, it is potential infinity since the number of individuals in the world is finite, at each time and in each period, while the world periods repeat indefinitely (*Enn.* V.7.3.13-23). Such potential infinity of the λόγοι in each soul appears to reflect the infinite in the νοῦς since λόγος is a discursive reflection of εἶδος, and ψυχή is a reflection of the νοῦς. But the infinite (τὸ ἄπειρον) of the νοῦς need not be considered actual either: in fact, there is a certain, definite number of the νοητά (*Enn.* IV.3.8.22). Being members of an organized whole of the noetic cosmos, reproduced as the σύνταγμα of the souls, the forms as νοητά are definite in number, and hence such are also the souls. Indeed, being form implies being numerically one because being of the non-composite is being one; that is, being *this* (form) (ἕκαστον [scil. τῶν νοητῶν] ἓν ἀριθμῷ εἶναι· οὕτω γὰρ τὸ τόδε, *Enn.* IV.3.8.24). The infinite of the νοῦς, then, is the infinity of the power or potentiality of production (of the λόγοι) and of potential divisibility and not being divided into the actual infinity of its constituents (ἢ τῇ δυνάμει τὸ ἄπειρον, ὅτι ἡ δύναμις ἄπειρος, οὐχ ὡς μερισθησομένης εἰς ἄπειρον, *Enn.* IV.3.8.36-7).[8]

---

[8] Cf. Blumenthal, *Plotinus' Psychology*, pp. 117-9.

4.6 Logical Difference

We may now return to the question of how the distinctions between the souls are constituted. Discussing the differences between individuals, Plotinus argues that although each soul (potentially) contains all λόγοι, one and the same λόγος cannot be responsible for all differences, but rather only for particular, individual, "special" differences (ἰδικαῖς [*hapax* in Plotinus] διαφοραῖς, *Enn.* V.7.1.18–21). Although *Enn.* V.7 supports the existence of the forms of individuals, which is denied elsewhere in the *Enneads*, it is *not* the form, but rather its discursive realization and formative implementation in the soul as λόγος that is responsible for individual difference(s) (δεῖ τὴν διάφορον ποίησιν ἐκ διαφόρων λόγων, *Enn.* V.7.1.23). The number of different individuals equals that of the different λόγοι, so that there have to be differences among different individuals even if they resemble each other.

Individual difference is better understood in a simile of production of similar yet different things by an artisan:

> For, as the craftsman [ὁ τεχνίτης], even if he is producing things which do not differ from each other [ἀδιάφορα], must apprehend the sameness by means of a *logical difference*, according to which he will make the thing another by bringing some difference to its sameness [τὸ ταὐτὸν διαφορᾷ λαμβάνειν λογικῇ, καθ' ἣν ἄλλο ποιήσει προσφέρων διάφορόν τι τῷ αὐτῷ], so in nature [ἐν τῇ φύσει], where the other does not come to be by discursive reasoning [μὴ λογισμῷ] but only by λόγοι [λόγοις μόνον], the difference must be linked with the form [συνεζεῦχθαι δεῖ τῷ εἴδει τὸ διάφορον], but we are unable to grasp the difference. (*Enn.* V.7.3.7–13, emphasis added)

The sameness in a thing is thus captured through a "logical" difference, which represents the same of the form (εἶδος) both to and within the otherness and multiplicity of the discursive and the bodily. The difference (διαφορά) between two things or individuals, even those that are seemingly identical but are at least perceived as *numerically* different, is the difference created not by the discursive reasoning (λογισμός) but by the λόγος in a thing as the representation of an εἶδος, down to the lowest part of the soul, the nature (φύσις) that produces individual organisms. Hence, the difference between individuals is the *logical* difference, διαφορὰ λογική, the difference of, by, and through the λόγος. Therefore, the individual differences (διαφοραί) between particular souls are neither those of the form nor of matter, but are the differences brought in by the λόγος as intermediate and mediating between the intelligible forms and the sensible forms in matter.

It is thus not the form but its representation of and in λόγος that is responsible for individual difference. The forms stand in an uninterrupted communication with other forms within the intelligible cosmos of one-many. The λόγοι, however, represent the forms within the plurality of one-*and*-many, where each λόγος potentially, and not actually, is discursively connected with all other λόγοι, which are interconnected and mutually deducible as the theorems in a science (ἐπιστήμη). The differences between individuals, therefore, should be characterized as *logical* differences that might be thought of as intermediate between formal and material differences, or as formally represented within the greater plurality of the soul. Λόγος is the principle of individuation.

The answer to the much debated question of whether there are forms of individuals or only those of universals, in the end, might not be that important for the account of individuation. Indeed, the difference would consist in explaining the implementation of either this particular λόγος or a set of λόγοι: if there are forms of particulars, then each form generates a λόγος responsible for individual differences. And if there is a universal form, then a whole multiplicity of various λόγοι, which account for καθέκαστα, are already established within such form. The result, however, will be the same in both cases; namely, the production of individual differences (διαφοραί) through a λόγος that is potentially related to all other λόγοι.

Thus, despite a number of instances in which Plotinus refers to individuation without much elaboration and despite his hesitance to accept the forms of individuals, we may conclude that it is the λόγος as representing an intelligible form (εἶδος) in and as the soul that is the source and principle of individuation. Individuation between souls should be thought of, then, as neither material nor formal, but as *logical* difference.

5

Memory and Recollection

Until recently, the question of memory was not considered a central one in Neoplatonic studies. However, the situation has changed as we have seen a renewed interest in the topic of memory in Plotinus in the publications of Luc Brisson, Cristina D'Ancona, Richard King, and Daniela Taormina, who have reestablished the importance of memory for Plotinus' psychology.[1] Memory is mentioned many times in Plotinus' writings, but two texts are especially important: a long digression on memory in *Ennead* IV.3 [27].25–IV.4 [28].12 and the later "On Sense Perception and Memory," *Ennead* IV.6 [41]. Despite the abundance of relevant texts, the exact function of memory in Plotinus needs a careful reconstruction. The reason for this is that, first, he makes a number of different, sometimes seemingly contradictory, claims about memory. Second, the connection between memory and recollection in Plotinus is not at all evident and should be established on the basis of a careful reading of his texts. And, third, while in his discussion of memory Plotinus draws on the whole preexisting tradition, he critically uses and often rethinks Platonic, Aristotelian, and Stoic concepts to achieve his own synthetic understanding of the topic. Hence, in order to appreciate Plotinus' originality, we need to turn briefly to Plato's and Aristotle's treatment of memory and recollection, which forms the basis for Plotinus' own tradition and innovative reflection.

---

[1] Luc Brisson, "La place de la mémoire dans la psychologie plotinienne," in *Études Platoniciennes III: L'âme amphibie—Études sur l'âme selon Plotin* (Paris: Les Belles Lettres, 2006), pp. 13–72; Cristina D'Ancona, "Plotino: memoria di eventi e anamnesis di intelligibili," in *Tracce nella mente: Teorie della memoria da Platone ai moderni*, ed. Maria Michela Sassi (Pisa: Edizioni della Normale, 2007), pp. 67–98; R. A. H. King, *Aristotle and Plotinus on Memory* (Berlin: De Gruyter, 2009); and Daniela P. Taormina, "Dalla potenzialità all'attualità: Un' introduzione al problema della memoria in Plotino," in *Plato, Aristotle, or Both?: Dialogues Between Platonism and Aristotelianism in Antiquity*" ed. Thomas Bénatouïl, Emanuele Maffi, and Franco Trabattoni (Hildesheim: George Olms, 2011), pp. 139–59.

5.1 Recollection and Memory in Plato

How do we know *that* we know something? And *when* do we know that we know and what we know? If I just learned something, I need to know *that* I have learned it and *how* I have learned it. And, if I learned it some time ago, I need to know that and how I had done it. In either case, I need to retain—to remember and recollect—the knowledge of the subject matter, the fact that what I know constitutes knowledge, and the way in which (at least in outline) I got this knowledge, either by myself or as taught by someone else.

These questions appear to be at the very heart of epistemology and are addressed by Plato, who was the first to explicitly stress the importance of memory and recollection for gaining knowledge. At this point, I only need to mention that the paradox of recognizing that we have now found what we did not know before, and therefore could not have even known what we were looking for, is resolved by Socrates' famous suggestion in the *Meno* that we can only know what we somehow *already* know. In its Platonic expression, then, recollection (ἀνάμνησις) is coming to the realization of what we have already known (Plato, *Meno* 80D–E). For this reason, learning (μάθησις) is knowing, and knowing is recollection as coming to understand what one has known before but has somehow forgotten (Plato, *Meno* 81C–E; *Phaedo* 73C). Therefore, learning *is* recollection: μάθησις is ἀνάμνησις (Plato, *Meno* 72E). Μάθησις for Plato is knowledge only of those things that cannot be otherwise, which means that what one learns or comes to know is the forms, the intelligible, the non-empirical (Plato, *Rep.* 524B–534B). The sensible can be an occasion, or trigger, of the knowledge of the forms and thus of recollection, but it cannot be known as such.[2]

To know is to recollect, restore, and recognize that which is already ours, that which is and has always been our own (Plato, *Phaedo* 75E). But such things can be only noetic—and not empirical—because only forms for Plato are (self-)identical and do not change their properties over time. In this respect, learning as recollection is analytic because we do not produce or invent new knowledge but only discover that which is already true before and

---

[2] For a discussion of recollection in the *Meno* and the relationship between knowledge and learning, which implies the question of the relationship between the non-empirical and empirical knowledge, as well as between the forms and the sensible, see David Sedley and Alex Long, introduction to Plato, *Meno and Phaedo*, trans. and ed. David Sedley and Alex Long (Cambridge: Cambridge University Press, 2011), p. xvii; and Julius Moravcsik, "Learning as Recollection," in *Plato's Meno in Focus*, ed. Jane M. Dayx (New York: Routledge, 1994), pp. 112–28. Dominic Scott argues for a more radical position, where the sensible constitutes a realm of its own detached from that of the forms. See Dominic Scott, *Plato's Meno* (Cambridge: Cambridge University Press, 2006), pp. 85–128. For Vlastos, Plato's doctrine of recollection "carries not only the implication that non-empirical knowledge can exist but also, unfortunately, that empirical knowledge cannot exist" (Gregory Vlastos, "*Anamnesis* in the *Meno*," in *Plato's Meno in Focus*, p. 103).

independently of the act of discovery. For this reason, learning about empirical things and their properties cannot count as knowledge but only as opinion (δόξα).

The existence of ἀνάμνησις is demonstrated by Socrates in the famous mathematical example when, by asking appropriate questions, he motivates a slave boy to solve the problem of doubling the area of a square by his own means and thus "recollect" what the boy has apparently already known before (Plato, *Meno* 82B–85B). In order to explain the very possibility of recollection, Plato needs to assume that each individual soul had already preexisted before it was embodied in its current form—and is therefore immortal—and thus had already learned and known everything that it now "discovers" through acts of ἀνάμνησις (Plato, *Meno* 70C–D; *Phaedo* 81A).

But how does recollection relate to memory? Although Plato is the first to introduce and use the concept of ἀνάμνησις as recollection in philosophy, the term μνήμη as memory is attested well before him. Plato mentions memory together with other qualities, such as ready wit, sharpness, diligence, sagacity, and the like, as indispensable for learning well and quickly and for eventually becoming wise (Plato, *Rep.* 486D, 490C, 503C, 535C). Although we can hardly find an unambiguous and consistent "theory" of memory in Plato, memory is important for him because it is closely associated with wisdom. This connection becomes clear in the famous critique of writing in the *Phaedrus* (274C–277A). While memory for Plato preserves its objects intact and alive, writing serves only as a reminder (ὑπόμνησις) that in fact makes us forgetful of being. Writing makes us forgetful because it makes us reliant on external, rigidly fixed signs incapable of defending themselves and always repeating the same story. So, if memory can be thought of as a kind of writing, it should be considered as writing on the soul, rather than on physical material. The image of memory as a writing tablet (δέλτος) of the mind onto which the events of the past are written appears already in the *Prometheus Bound* (788–9) attributed to Aeschylus. In the *Theaetetus*, when discussing right opinion, Socrates famously suggests that we have a gift from Mnemosyne, a kind of a wax tablet (κήρινον ἐκμαγεῖον, Plato, *Theaet.* 191C) where all sorts of marks, imprints, impressions, stamps, or images (σημεῖον, τύπος, ἀποτύπωμα, σφραγίς, εἴδωλον) both of sense perceptions and thoughts are inscribed and preserved. Such images can be considered as being similar to images of signet rings (Plato, *Theaet.* 191C–E; cf. 192A–194D). Socrates also compares memory to an aviary where birds of different kinds are kept once caught (Plato, *Theaet.* 197C–198A). Memory thus can be taken as a *power* or capacity of storing and preserving certain impressions, both mental and sensible. Yet the questions of how the wax tablet and aviary similes are connected and how exactly memory is related to recollection are never explicitly addressed by Plato. They thus remain unanswered.

5.2 Aristotle on Memory and Recollection

Aristotle takes on exactly these questions in his short treatise Περὶ μνήμης καὶ ἀναμνήσεως ("On Memory and Recollection"), which can be read as a critical response to Plato's discussion of memory and recollection.[3] Without going into a detailed discussion of the main points of Aristotle's argument, let me summarize the account of the treatise since it was known by Plotinus and clearly affected his thinking about memory. Most importantly, memory for Aristotle requires imagination, and imagination is a faculty that produces images (φαντάσματα, *De an.* 427b14–428a5; cf. 431a14–7, 432a8–14). Memory, too, is always accompanied by an image (*De mem.* 450a12–3). The exact nature of these images—namely, whether they are pictorial or should be taken as causal antecedents of the experience of memory—is still contested among scholars who find support in Aristotle's text for both conjectures.[4] Thus, on the one hand, in line with Plato's suggestion in the *Theaetetus, Phaedrus*, and *Philebus*, Aristotle speaks about images as a sort of picture (ζωγράφημα) or as traces of signet rings (*De mem.* 450a29–32). Yet, on the other hand, he also mentions motions (κινήσεις), which are similar to a succession or order of steps in a mathematical proof (*De mem.* 452a1–3) or a process of recollecting a name, melody, or saying (*De mem.* 453a28–9). The latter often come almost effortlessly, and evidently are not accompanied by a pictorial image.

For Aristotle, however, memory is not itself a faculty, such as are sense perception (αἴσθησις) or imagination (φαντασία). Nor is memory a judgment (ὑπόληψις), which means that memory does not provide knowledge. Rather, memory is a *state* (ἕξις) or *having* of images that correspond to previous knowledge, judgments, or sense perceptions, once time has elapsed (*De mem.* 449b24–5). Ἕξις is not an actual activity nor is it a pure potentiality but rather an acquired capacity of exercising or actualizing something that once has been experienced—in the case of memory, it is actualized through a memory image.[5]

When it comes to recollection, Aristotle wants to establish both a connection and a distinction between it and memory, which is not evident in Plato. In the *Analytics*, Aristotle explicitly criticizes the *Meno*'s thesis that learning is recollection on the grounds that a singular thing—this particular

---

[3] See Helen S. Lang, "On Memory: Aristotle's Corrections of Plato," *Journal of the History of Philosophy* 18:4 (1980), pp. 379–93.
[4] See Richard Sorabji, *Aristotle on Memory* (Chicago: University of Chicago Press, 2006), pp. ix–xvi, 2–8; Julia Annas, "Aristotle on Memory and the Self," in *Essays on Aristotle's* De Anima, ed. Martha C. Nussbaum and Amélie Oksenberg Rorty (Oxford: Oxford University Press, 1992), p. 305; and David Bloch, *Aristotle on Memory and Recollection: Text, Translation, Interpretation, and Reception in Western Scholasticism* (Leiden: Brill, 2007), pp. 64–70.
[5] Cf. Aristotle, *MM* 1184b15–7.

triangle—cannot be known before the act of learning and experience (*An. priora* 67a21–5; *An. post.* 71a29–30). In Aristotle's account, recollection is the recovery of those acts of knowledge and sense perception that originally led to a state of memory (*De mem.* 451b1). Recollection, then, is an *inquiry* or search (ζήτησις) for an image that would allow for such a recovery (*De mem.* 453a15). Yet, in order to be successful, such an inquiry should be organized. This means that recollection should presuppose an orderly method, which is usually called an association of ideas or images. Such a method presupposes that images are arranged in an order (τάξις) of moves (κινήσεις) that lead to recollection, in which one chooses a beginning (ἀρχή), a successor (τὸ ἐφεξῆς), and often a middle (τὸ μέσον), as well as the way of forming associations by similarity, opposition, or neighboring (*De mem.* 451b10–452a3, 452a17). Because recollection is well-ordered and self-directed reasoning (συλλογισμός, *De mem.* 453a10), it bears a striking structural similarity to logical syllogism (cf. *An. priora* 24b18–20; *Top.* 100a25–7). Thus, memory for Aristotle is a state or having of an image, which comes as a *sui generis* conclusion to an argument or syllogism. As such, memory is non-propositional and is similar to scenic memory. Recollection, on the contrary, is a process, an active mediation, a kind of discursive motion through a series of steps in an argument, proof, or syllogism. Recollection is thus propositional and is similar to narrative memory. Memory one can *have*; to recollection one should *come*. In this way, memory and recollection in Aristotle are both opposed to and complement each other in keeping and retrieving instances of sense perception and knowledge.

5.3 Memory in Plotinus

In order to establish the role of memory and recollection in Plotinus, we need to turn to his account of thinking and perception, on the one hand, and the position of the soul as mediating between the thinkable and the perceptible, on the other. To be sure, the soul appears in different ways in Plotinus' order of the existent: as a hypostasis, which is the soul abiding in the intelligible realm and characterized primarily by thinking; as the world-soul, which animates the whole cosmos and of which the "higher" part is engaged in thinking while the vegetative soul is immanent to the world; and as an individual human soul that becomes embodied and "descends" into the world during the lifetime and returns to the intelligible after death.[6] The soul is the rational principle (λόγος) of all things and is the last rational principle in the order of the intelligibles, yet it is the first in the order of the sensibles (*Enn.* IV.6.3.5–8). Being intermediate between the intelligible and the sensible, the soul thus both separates and

---

[6] See Emilsson, *Plotinus on Sense-Perception*, pp. 23–5.

unites the two realms; memory plays an important role in such mediation (see Chapter 4).

Before explaining what memory as a power or capacity is, Plotinus needs first to situate memory within the order of being with reference to the hypostases, which explains his digression into ontology. And, second, he needs to clear the ground for his own interpretation by providing a critique of the existing accounts of memory (primarily, in the Stoics), which explains his initial negative approach of telling us what memory is not.

Plotinus begins by observing that memory plays no role in the constitution of well-being or happiness because well-being is an active state (διάθεσις) and does not consist in the memory or anticipation of well-being (*Enn.* I.5 [36].1.3–5). This is why well-being, which consists in the atemporal abiding in intelligible eternity (see Chapter 3), does not increase with time.[7] For this reason, even if memory can be that of the best, it itself is *not* the best (οὐκ ἄριστον, *Enn.* IV.4.4.1–10). Indeed, a memory of virtue does not increase virtue and a memory of pleasure is not itself pleasure the way it was experienced (*Enn.* I.5.8.1–11). And if the human soul is itself divided into the "higher" (or "better") and "lower" (or "worse") soul, the one abiding in the intelligible and the other immersed into the sensible, then the lower soul should aspire to the activities of the higher soul, yet the higher soul should be happy to forget what it received from the lower soul. It is therefore better to be separated from human memory altogether because—and here Plotinus refers to Plato (*Phaedr.* 249C–D)—it is better to be detached from human concerns (*Enn.* IV.3.32.6–18).

Memory, then, might be taken as a sign of our finitude and temporality, which we can and need to overcome by ascending to being in thinking the intelligible. However, being for Plotinus is timeless or eternal, which means that it exists all together and outside any succession. This is why it is difficult for discursive thinking to grasp being in a single act of thought: eternity is the eternity of the intellect and being (and of well-being since it is the life of real being, *Enn.* I.5.7.20–2), and time is the time of the soul (*Enn.* III.7.1–6). Yet memory is *of* the past, of things past (τῶν γὰρ γεγενημένων καὶ παρεληλυθόντων ἡ μνήμη, *Enn.* IV.4.6.2–3). Because memory refers to the past and presupposes distinctions and a succession of events, it needs time. Therefore, first, there is *no* memory in the intellect that thinks itself outside of time by thinking intelligible objects (*Enn.* IV.4.1.12–4, IV.4.2.1–8, IV.4.15.2). The intellect has no memory: it does not *need* memory since it has nothing to remember, for it already *has* and thereby knows everything. Second, memory is only the memory in and of the soul.

---

[7] See Alessandro Linguiti, "Plotinus and Epicurus on Pleasure and Happiness," in *Plotinus and Epicurus*, pp. 189–98.

For this reason, the soul as a hypostasis does not have memory either, for it stays in close contact with the intellect. Memory might be attributed to the soul of the all, yet one need not do so since its activity of producing and maintaining the cosmos is not conscious or reflective. Celestial bodies that are considered alive and ensouled do not have memory because they either keep moving always in the same way or maintain their same location. In addition, the soul of the all and the celestial souls do not reason discursively or investigate since they already have knowledge and thus do not need to learn. They do not need calculations (λογισμοί), logical deductions (συλλογισμοί), or discursive reasoning (διανοήσεις), which they might need to remember (*Enn.* IV.4.6.8–23, IV.4.15.7, IV.4.30.1–2).[8] It is thus primarily our individual human soul that has memory.

5.4 Images, Imprints, and Impressions

In order to establish Plotinus' account of memory, we might begin with a negative interpretation of memory, with what it is not. Since memory belongs to the soul and the soul spans the sensible and the thinkable and thus has to relate both to sense perception and thinking, we need to briefly turn to the role of sense perception and thinking in the functioning of memory. From early on, already in the second treatise of the *Enneads* (IV.7 [2]), Plotinus comes up with a critique of the Stoic theory of the corporeality of the soul. According to the Stoic teaching, which was well known in Plotinus' time and is reported in Sextus Empiricus and Proclus, sense perceptions are "imprints" (τύποι) similar to the bodily imprints of a seal on wax.[9] Against the Stoics, Plotinus argues that accepting the soul as corporeal would mean making sense perceptions similar to seal impressions left on wax from signet rings (οἷον ἐν κηρῷ ἐνσημανθεῖσαι ἀπὸ δακτυλίων σφραγῖδες, *Enn.* IV.7.6.39–40).[10] In IV.4.13.13, Plotinus speaks about the impression of nature (φύσεως τύπου), thereby placing τύπος within the physical. Now, if the soul is corporeal, its perceptions should themselves be bodily images. This, however, cannot be the case because, if such images were imprinted onto the soul as something liquid, they would have soon disappeared, and, if as something solid, then each new imprint would obliterate the previous one. In either case, memory (μνήμη) or remembering (μνημονεύειν) would be impossible (*Enn.* IV.7.6.37–49). Therefore, if memory is at

---

[8] Brisson, "La place de la mémoire," pp. 13–27.
[9] For Sextus Empiricus' discussion, see SVF I 484 (Cleanthes). For Proclus' discussion, see SVF II 343 (Chrysippus).
[10] See Katerina Ierodiakonou, "The Stoics and the Skeptics on Memory," in *Tracce nella mente*, pp. 47–65.

all possible as the remembrance of events of the past separated in time, then the soul cannot be corporeal.

An important consequence of this critique is Plotinus' explicit rejection of Plato's understanding of memory in the *Theaetetus* as a *sui generis* collection of imprints, stamps, or inscriptions onto writing tablets (οἷον γὰρ ἐν πίναξιν ἢ δέλτοις γεγραμμένων γραμμάτων, *Enn.* IV.6.3.75). For if imprints or impressions (τύποι) remained, we would not need to examine them (σκοπεῖν) in order to make a series of associations, nor could we even forget them because they would have always been there, and therefore we would not need repetition or exercise to improve memory (*Enn.* IV.6.3.27–9). This account is quite remarkable in that Plotinus rarely criticizes Plato explicitly: usually, if he has to disagree with Plato, he does it by providing a reconciliatory interpretation of Plato's view that fits within his own system of thought.

Therefore, if sense perceptions are not impressions (τυπώσεις) or seal stamps (ἐνσφραγίσεις), then no impression (τύπος) can remain in the soul in the form of retention (κατοχή) of what we have perceived or learned before, which would be kept in the soul as a mental object or image ready to be taken out when needed (*Enn.* IV.6.1.1–3, IV.6.3.56–7).[11] Memory is thus *not* a collection of images or mental pictures imprinted on, or kept in, the soul (μνήμας οὐ τύπους ἐναποσφραγιζομένους οὐδὲ τὰς φαντασίας ὡς ἐν κηρῷ τυπώσεις, *Enn.* III.6 [26].3.28–30). Plotinus' rejection of the image theory of memory is thus perfectly in line with his critique of the Stoics.

Yet, there is a considerable difficulty in Plotinus' interpretation of images for, on the one hand, he rejects ready-made τύποι—images, imprints, or impressions—at any level of sensible, psychological, or mental activity. This means that (i) sense perceptions are *not* images or impressions, (ii) memories are *not* images or retentions (οὐ . . . τύποι, *Enn.* IV.4.4.16–7), and (iii) knowledge of the intelligibles (τῶν . . . νοητῶν ἡ γνῶσις) is *without* images (ἀτύπωτος, *Enn.* IV.6.2.18–9).

On the other hand, in the *Enneads,* we find claims that appear to directly contradict these three assertions. It might mean that Plotinus is straightforwardly inconsistent. This, however, does not seem likely since he is usually a careful thinker who only occasionally is carried away by the beauty of noetic vision and by the anticipation of ineffable beyond being. Or it may be the case that in his discussion of memory and image, which mostly occurs in later treatises, Plotinus forgets what he has said before. This, as we know from Plato's critique of writing in the *Phaedrus,* is almost inevitable for anyone who writes, so this is a possible yet not very interesting explanation. Finally, Plotinus might use the term "image" in different ways in different treatises,

---

[11] See Emilsson, *Plotinus on Intellect*, pp. 127–9.

depending on a particular problem he is addressing, and thus there will be no real contradiction. This is probably the most fruitful approach.

Thus, contrary to the preceding assertion, Plotinus suggests (i′) that sense perceptions *are* impressions: sense perception sees something (a human being) and gives the *impression* to discursive reason (ἔδωκε τὸν τύπον τῇ διανοίᾳ, *Enn.* V.3.3.1–2). Moreover, Plotinus also argues (although he uses a different term) that sense perception apprehends only an *image* of a thing and *not* the thing itself (τοῦ πράγματος εἴδωλόν ἐστι καὶ οὐκ αὐτὸ τὸ πρᾶγμα, *Enn.* V.5.1.17–9). That is, similarly to Kant, the thing itself is not accessible to sense perception; yet, *contra* Kant, the thing itself is thinkable for Plotinus. A way out of the apparent contradiction here is to assume, as Plotinus does in the *Ennead* IV.6, that these sensible images are not of the seal stamp kind but are actively formed by the soul when it turns to the sensible and uses sense perception.

In opposition to the claim that memory does not keep a retention of a perceived thing, in *Ennead* IV.3.29.24, Plotinus says (ii′) that memory *is* retention or κατοχή, which seems to contradict his own assertion in IV.6.1.3 that memories *are not* retentions. A possible solution to this problem has been suggested by Taormina, who argued that, in this passage, Plotinus uses the term "retention" in a different meaning; namely, as standing for Aristotle's "state" or ἕξις in the *De memoria*. Her conclusion is further supported by Porphyry's assertion that memory for Aristotle is the retention of an image (κατοχὴν φαντάσματος).[12] A simpler solution here could be that, strictly speaking, in *Ennead* IV.3.29.24 Plotinus speaks about "the memory *and* the retention of the object [τὴν μνήμην καὶ κατοχήν]" without identifying them. In this way, memories, once again, are not assimilated to retentions as memorable imprints that are preserved and produced on demand.

Finally (iii′), in a late treatise, Plotinus seems to ascribe images also to the intellect when arguing that the soul observes images as if coming to it from the intellect (ἐκ τοῦ νοῦ . . . τύπους, *Enn.* V.3.2.9–10).[13] Again, in order to avoid contradiction, we might presuppose that Plotinus uses "image" in this passage in a different meaning; namely, not as a bodily wax-like imprint—but as a way of producing a mental representation and appropriation of a form by the soul's discursive thinking, which can never think an intelligible object at once in its entirety but only ever partially. Therefore, in each of the three cases, Plotinus is using the term "image" differently from the way he uses it when speaking about memory.

---

[12] Taormina, "Dalla potenzialità all'attualità," pp. 142–9. The passage from Porphyry may be found in *Porphyrii Philosophi Fragmenta*, ed. Andrew Smith (Stuttgart: Teubner, 1994), fr. 255F, ap. Stobaeus III.25.1.

[13] Cf. Marco Ninci, "Un Problema Plotiniano: L'identità con l'uno e l'alterità da lui," *Giornale Critico Della Filosofia Italiana* 21:3 (2001), pp. 484–5.

5.5 Memory, Power, and Imagination

But if memory does not accept and store images or retentions, what is it, then? Memory for Plotinus is a *power* or *capacity* (δύναμις) that the soul uses in order to reproduce what it currently does not have (*Enn.* IV.3.28.16–21, IV.6.3.70–1). The soul itself can be thought of as a power, as a capacity to perform various perceptive, mental, and cognitive tasks. For Plotinus, the soul's sizelessness (ἀμέγεθες) clearly indicates that it is a power (*Enn.* IV.6.3.70–1). Taking memory to be a δύναμις solves several problems for Plotinus. Because memory is a power of and within the soul, memory belongs to the soul only and not to the composite of the soul and body (*Enn.* IV.3.26) since body is a hindrance (ἐμπόδιον) to memory and causes forgetfulness (*Enn.* IV.3.26.50–4). In addition, because memory is a power, it is therefore not an affection (πάθος) since, first, an image *is* an affection (*Enn.* IV.6.3.47–8) and memory does not operate with images; and second, being affected is opposite to being capable of doing something (*Enn.* IV.6.2.2–3). Metaphorically speaking, memory as power is a "preparation for the readiness" (παρασκευὴ πρὸς τὸ ἕτοιμον, *Enn.* IV.6.3.58), for the activity of recalling and restoring a previous experience. Memory is a "strength" (ἰσχύς, *Enn.* IV.6.3.55) that allows the soul to actualize and bring to life what it has once thought or perceived.

Hence, memories exist not because they are somehow put away or stashed for a later use when an occasion arises, for they are not objects or retentions that could be stored in a safe place. Rather, the soul awakens the power of memory in order to have what it does not have (ὃ μὴ ἔχει ἔχειν, *Enn.* III.6.2.44). The seemingly paradoxical "having what it does not have" means that, since memory is a power and does not accept images or hold retentions, it actively *forms* or makes them (ποιεῖ, *Enn.* IV.6.3.17). It is thus the image-making power (τὸ φανταστικόν, *Enn.* IV.3.30.7) that is the seat of the faculty of memory in the soul.

It is here, in the imagination (ἡ φαντασία), that sense perception terminates (λήγει).[14] Once the seen (τὸ ὅραμα) is no longer there, it is reproduced and is thus present as imagined in and by the memory. Because memory for Plotinus is inextricably associated with imagination, the perceived (αἴσθημα) is remembered as a φάντασμα, a product of the image-making power or imagination (*Enn.* IV.3.29.22–32). This is Plotinus' way of appropriating Aristotle's claim (which Plotinus does in his own way and for his own purposes, without paying much attention to the context of Aristotle's discussion) that memory is always accompanied by a φάντασμα (Aristotle, *De mem.* 450a12–3). In Plotinus' interpretation, φάντασμα is not an image but a dynamic reproduction

---

[14] See the discussion of memory and φαντασία (as representation) in King, *Aristotle and Plotinus on Memory*, pp. 170–8.

of the perceived and thus is not a Platonic imprint onto wax in the soul but a reconstruction by the power of imagination that starts from the initial sensible impact, which becomes the occasion for the soul to form a memory.[15] It is thus through memory that the soul can refer to the absent, to the things that it currently does not experience or does not have (λέγει περὶ ὧν οὐκ ἔχει, *Enn.* IV.6.2.1–2). Among all the faculties of the soul, it is the imagination that can speak about the absent and that sometimes invents the non-existent.

5.6 Double Memory

So far, Plotinus has mostly discussed the memory that relates to sense perception. But does the soul also remember its thoughts? And if so, how? Since the soul for Plotinus occupies the middle position in the order of the existent (ἐν μέσῳ, *Enn.* IV.6.3.10), it therefore mediates between thinking and sense perception, partaking in both. And, even within the soul itself Plotinus, as was said, distinguishes the "higher" or "better" soul (*Enn.* IV.3.32.6–7), which is "undescended" and remains in touch with the intellect. Since imagination is located in the soul, it, too, is intermediate between (μεταξύ) thinking and sense perception (*Enn.* IV.4.13.13) and as such makes the soul into a kind of *mirror* (οἷον ἐν κατόπτρῳ) that reflects both the being of the thought and the becoming of the perceived (*Enn.* IV.3.30.10).[16]

In Plotinus' ordered structure of the existent, an object of thinking (νόημα or νοητόν), on the one hand, is thought by the intellect (νοῦς) and is further represented in discursive thinking (διάνοια) in an argument or verbal expression as a λόγος or διανόημα. The νοῦς and the διάνοια both know the intelligible, but while the former thinks it in a singular act, the latter conceives it in a logical or verbal sequence (*Enn.* V.6.2.7–16). The dianoetic object can be also reflected as an imaginary representation or φάντασμα in the imagination (φαντασία, or image-making power, τὸ φανταστικόν) capable of (or

---

[15] Memory is also one of the crucial components in rhetoric, where it is closely connected with the imagination: for Longinus, memory is the preservation of the products of imagination (σωτηρία φαντασιῶν, *Ars rhet.* 314.21 Spengel). In his discussion of memory in the *Ennead* IV. 6, Plotinus directly responds to Longinus' *On Memory*. See Cassius Longinus, *Fragments: Art rhétorique*, ed. Michel Patillon and Luc Brisson (Paris: Les Belles Lettres, 2001), frs. 125–7; and Kalligas' comprehensive commentary to Plotinus, Ἐννεάς Τετάρτη, ed. Pavlos Kalligas (Athens: Kentron Ereunes tes Hellenikes kai Latinikes Grammateias, 2009), p. 544. In Roman rhetoric, memory is trained to produce images of the things to be remembered, which are then arranged and put into imaginary places, from which they can be retrieved. Cf. Cicero, *De ora.* II.86.353; [Cicero], *Rh. ad Her.* III.23.38–9; and Quintilian, *De in. ora.* XI.2.21, 29–30.

[16] Similarly, Proclus takes imagination to play the role of a mirror onto which the soul projects the rational principles of geometrical figures in order to study them (Proclus, *In Eucl.* 141.2–13). See Dmitri Nikulin, *Matter, Imagination, and Geometry: Ontology, Natural Philosophy, and Mathematics in Plotinus, Proclus, and Descartes* (Burlington, VT: Ashgate, 2002), pp. 175–9.

"disposed" to) such representations. However, an object of sensation (αἴσθημα or αἰσθητόν) is equally reflected in the imagination. Being in the middle and using imagination, the soul is thus capable of remembering the thinkable and the sensible. As Plotinus puts it, "remembering is either thinking or imagining; and the imagination is in the soul not by possession, but as it sees, so it is disposed" (τὸ μνημονεύειν ἢ νοεῖν ἢ φαντάζεσθαι, ἡ δὲ φαντασία αὐτῇ οὐ τῷ ἔχειν, ἀλλ' οἷα ὁρᾷ, καὶ [οἷα] διάκειται, *Enn.* IV.4.3.6-8). In either case, the imaginary reflection is not a passive act of copying the sensible or the thinkable—but an active (re)production, a reconstruction of an imaginary representation.

But how does the soul represent and remember the thinkable? Plotinus argues that, as with the memory of the sensible, remembering a thought is equally impossible without imagination and the φάντασμα it produces. Indeed, since memory does not operate with images but produces imaginary representations, we need to presuppose that a partless intelligible object (νόημα) is not presented and preserved as a kind of image. Rather, it is translated into and unfolded as the dianoetic, logical, or verbal expression, which is then reflected in a φάντασμα of the imagination. Therefore, what we think and have thought—and we think discursively or "logically" par excellence—becomes reflected in the imagination as a φάντασμα and is then remembered as such (*Enn.* IV.3.30.5-11; cf. V.3.2.2-14).

Plotinus ascribes memory to both the higher and the lower soul, which should mean that there are two different image-making powers (δύο τὰ φανταστικά, *Enn.* IV.3.31.2).[17] But how, then, would these two interact? Plotinus' answer is that when the two souls are in agreement (συμφωνῇ), then the "better" one dominates, and its image-making power provides its φάντασμα for both souls. When, however, the two are in disagreement (διαφωνία), the φάντασμα of the lower soul becomes manifest by itself, yet we still do not notice the duality of the souls because the higher soul still overrides the lower one (*Enn.* IV.3.31.9-16).

In the *De memoria*, Aristotle observes that one cannot really remember without at the same time knowing that one remembers (*De mem.* 452b26-7) because the remembered is actually and actively had in memory, which thus cannot miss the fact that it remembers. Remembering, therefore, presupposes the awareness of remembering. But for Plotinus we become aware of the remembered thought only when it becomes "seen" and reflected—and in this way becomes reflective—in the imagination (*Enn.* IV.3.30.11-6). Imagination, therefore, becomes a "mirror" that can reflect thought in memory. This mirror is situated "between" the intelligible and the sensible, which is why imagination

---

[17] See Elena Gritti, "La φαντασία plotiniana tra illuminazione intellettiva e impassibilità dell'anima," in *Studi sull'anima in Plotino*, ed. Riccardo Chiaradonna (Naples: Bibliopolis, 2005), pp. 251-74.

is capable of actively representing both the thinkable νοητά (which are first discursively unfolded into λόγοι) and the αἰσθητά. Because it is turned toward both being and becoming, imagination thereby "is a stroke of an irrational from outside" (πληγὴ ἀλόγου ἔξωθεν, *Enn.* I.8.15.18). This "irrationality" of the imagination becomes manifest in that it inevitably portrays partless νοητά as partial φαντάσματα. An important problem that arises here, one that Plotinus does not explicitly address, is whether the imaginary reconstructions are true to that which they are reconstructing. Plotinus implicitly assumes that the veracity of such reconstruction, even if it remains incomplete and affected by irrationality, is secured by the imagination being inscribed into the ontological order of the existent. Hence, we can and do remember our thoughts as reflected in the imagination, which is thus a kind of double-sided mirror that can replicate, reproduce, and represent both thinkable and sensible objects, which then can become objects of memory.

5.7 Anamnesis and Its Discontents

Therefore, rather than being two distinct memories, one of the sensible and the other of the thinkable, memory is double. In either case, the remembered is not an image or retention transmitted to memory for storing but is reflectively constructed in and by the imagination in the form of an imaginary representation or φάντασμα. This leaves open the question of ἀνάμνησις in Plotinus. Is recollection different from memory, as it is in both Plato and Aristotle? And what is its relation to the memory of the intelligibles? There is no consensus among scholars about the meaning and role of ἀνάμνησις in Plotinus. In Warren's interpretation, memory in Plotinus falls into unconscious (that is, habit and disposition) and conscious memory, and the latter is either the memory proper (which, in turn, is of two kinds: of sensible objects [αἰσθητά] and of discursive thoughts [διανοήσεις]) or recollection (ἀνάμνησις). Recollection, then, is "the highest kind of cognitive experience short of the direct apprehension of νοητά."[18] For Blumenthal, on the contrary, intellectual intuition does replace the ἀνάμνησις.[19] McCumber has further argued that recollection in Plotinus is the memory of intelligibles, which consists "in their successive actualisation within the soul."[20] Brisson, however, takes ἀνάμνησις to belong not to memory but rather to characterize the state of the undescended soul.[21] D'Ancona, too,

---

[18] Edward W. Warren, "Memory in Plotinus," *Classical Quarterly* 15:2 (1965), p. 257. According to Warren, Plotinus "regards all intellectual knowledge which is not a direct intuition of *Nous* to be the result of recollection" (ibid., p. 256).

[19] See Blumenthal, *Plotinus' Psychology*, pp. 96–7.

[20] John McCumber, "Anamnesis as Memory of Intelligibles in Plotinus," *Archiv für Geschichte der Philosophie* 60:2 (1978), p. 165.

[21] See Brisson, "La place de la mémoire," pp. 13–27, esp. 16.

recognizes the importance of recollection for the undescended soul but takes recollection to be the application of the soul's power to know the real beings, which are not impressed onto the soul but rather are known as the result of the cognitive process.[22] Finally, King argues that Plotinus speaks about the memory of thought in two ways: the memory of the noetic non-discursive thought and the memory of the dianoetic discursive thought. Correspondingly, we can have a recollection of a noetic thought but no memory of it, but we can have both a recollection and a memory of a discursive thought.[23]

Plotinus does not define ἀνάμνησις, so one needs to reconstruct its meaning from the ways it is used throughout the *Enneads*, where it occurs a dozen times, much less than μνήμη. Moreover, Plotinus does not make a clear distinction between μνήμη and ἀνάμνησις, nor does he see it as a problem. In the beginning of a long digression on memory, Plotinus mentions that "the ancients" (οἱ παλαιοί, by whom he means Plato and his followers) apply both terms closely if not synonymously when describing the situation of a newly descended soul (*Enn.* IV.3.25.32–3).

For Plotinus, there is no memory in the purely thinkable because there is no need for it: the νοῦς always thinks what it thinks—non-discursively, atemporally, and in the same way.[24] Therefore, if there is a memory or recollection of the intelligible, then it can be only that of the soul striving to recall what it has "seen" or known "there." As Plotinus has argued, we can remember what we thought. And yet, strictly speaking, "our" thoughts are not quite ours because *our* thoughts are elaborate logical explications or discursive unfoldings of the νοητά by and within the soul, which it then can remember. In this sense, one should distinguish "our" remembering from thinking, which is not "ours" but can be appropriated and remembered by us (τό τε μνημονεύειν παρὰ τὸ νοεῖν ἄλλο, *Enn.* IV.3.25.24).

But is the memory of a thought identical with recollection? Plotinus mentions "the other kind of memory" (ἕτερον εἶδος μνήμης, *Enn.* IV.3.25.33), which characterizes the soul when it "has just arrived here"—that is, has "descended" and became embodied. Does this "other kind of memory" stand for ἀνάμνησις? Textually, the "other kind of memory" comes right after the reference to μνήμη and ἀνάμνησις, where the two are not clearly distinguished. In addition, later in his discussion of memory, Plotinus also argues that it is the same power (δύναμις) that allows the descended soul to speak about the intelligibles here, and hence remember them, as well as to contemplate the intelligibles "there" (καὶ ἐνθάδε οὖσι τῷ αὐτῷ λέγειν, ὃ δύναμιν ἔχει τἀκεῖ θεωρεῖν, *Enn.* IV.4.5.7–8). This could mean that memory as the soul's power

---

[22] D'Ancona, "Plotino: memoria di eventi e anamnesis di intelligibili," pp. 67–98.
[23] See King, *Aristotle and Plotinus on Memory*, pp. 180–6.
[24] Cf. Sara Rappe, *Reading Neoplatonism: Non-Discursive Thinking in the Texts of Plotinus, Proclus, and Damascius* (Cambridge: Cambridge University Press, 2000), pp. 56–66.

to recreate—and thus to recollect—the remembered (in this case, the thought) can be considered one and the same both in memory and recollection. Yet this kind of remembering, if it is indeed to be associated with recollection, might still be different from memory the way it was described before because memory for Plotinus always uses imagination and imaginary representations, whereas it is not yet clear if ἀνάμνησις has anything to do with the imagination.

Rather, as it becomes clear from Plotinus' discussion throughout the *Enneads*, recollection is always associated with some kind of *motion*, progression or digression. Often, when speaking about recollection, Plotinus uses the verb "to come": the soul arrives or *comes* to recollection (εἰς ἀνάμνησιν . . . ἐλθοῦσιν, *Enn.* III.5 [50].1.34–5; cf. II.9.12.6–7, II.9.16.47, III.7.1.22–3; εἰς ἀναπόλησιν . . . ἐρχόμεθα, *Enn.* IV.6.3.59). Now, movement might mean (1) a cognitive movement of thinking, that of discursive reasoning. In *Ennead* IV.4.12, Plotinus aligns memory (μνήμη) with calculation (τὸ λογίζεσθαι, λογισμός), which both testify to the deficiency of the human condition in our "descended" state. Here, one needs to make an effort of remembering and recalling, through a number of logical steps and solutions to various aporias, in order to arrive at the knowledge of the real being. Plotinus also compares obtaining knowledge by "touching through a medium" to the work of memory and, even more so, to that of syllogism, where the conclusion is obtained by the motion of reasoning through the premises by excluding the middle term (ὕστερον τὸ διὰ μέσου ἅπτεσθαι ποιεῖ τὴν γνῶσιν, οἷον τῇ μνήμῃ καὶ ἔτι μᾶλλον συλλογισμῷ, *Enn.* IV.5 [29].4.44–5; cf. IV.4.5.5–8).[25] Once again, Plotinus draws a parallel between the motion of reasoning of the logical kind and the work of memory. As we remember, for Aristotle, recollection is precisely a sort of syllogistic reasoning that allows us to restore—and thus recollect—the truth of the thought (*De mem.* 453a10). For Plotinus, calculation and "syllogism" represent the motion of the soul's gathering or collecting the partiality of thoughts into the unity of understanding of the νοητά. But it still remains an open question whether the calculative logical reasoning is meant to be a helpful analogy of memory, in which case the two are synonymous—or whether the "syllogistic" thinking stands for the *other* kind of memory, for recollection, which then would differ from and complement the work of memory. The use of the μᾶλλον in IV.5.4.45 might suggest a distinction between memory and recollection. In addition, as Plotinus repeats twice, referring to the opening lines of Aristotle's *De memoria*, "the same people are not the best at thinking [διανοεῖσθαι] and at remembering [μνημονεύειν]" (*Enn.* IV.3.29.16–7, IV.6.3.63–6; Aristotle, *De mem.* 449b6–8),

---

[25] Plotinus' account of touch (ἡ ἁφή) in this discussion is altogether Aristotelian, which presupposes a mediation (μεταξύ, *Enn.* IV.5.4.22–5; Aristotle, *De an.* 422b34–424a10; cf. 419a30–1), rather than an unmediated coincidence of the touching (intellection) and the touched (the intelligibles), which characterizes the non-discursive thinking of the intellect in the later Neoplatonic tradition.

which might imply that discursive thought, if it indeed stands for recollection, complements memory. However, Plotinus does not elaborate on the topic of a possible difference between μνήμη and ἀνάμνησις and, in fact, evades using "ἀνάμνησις" in the context of the discussion of memory.

5.8 The Soul's Triple Movement

However, the movement of recollection might also refer (2) to the ontological situation of the soul in the order of the existent, to the soul's "fall" from the atemporal unity into the greater plurality of the temporal and to a life's journey down here with the subsequent return "there." This motion from the intelligible to the sensible and back to the intelligible is thus a triple movement of descent, staying, and return (see Chapter 11).

(2.1) *Descent.* When the soul leaves the intelligible and descends into this world, it still has some recollection of the intelligible but loses it with time (*Enn.* IV.4.4.14–8, IV.4.5.22–6). Because the soul falls into the world of plurality, the soul "cannot endure unity," which results in the acquisition of memory. Yet the soul's "memory (μνήμη) of what is in the intelligible world still holds it back from falling, but its memory of the things here below carries it down here; its memory of what is there keeps it there; and in general, it is and becomes what it remembers" (*Enn.* IV.4.3.1–6). However, since there is no memory in the intelligible, memory first originates in "heaven," when the soul has already left the "higher" world of the intelligible on its way down to the sensible (*Enn.* IV.4.5.11–3). Only then can the soul recover some of its memories, which were already there potentially (δυνάμει), although the actuality (ἐνέργεια) of the intelligibles made memory *invisible* (ἠφάνιζε, *Enn.* IV.4.4.14–8). Paradoxically, the light of the intelligible thus obscures and obliterates memory, so the soul needs to make an effort at restoring what it has seen and known without remembering it (*Enn.* IV.3.25.32).

This means that the memory of what the soul thought in and with the intellect can be discursively restored or remembered only *after* it was thought. This is what recollection is for Plotinus: the ἀνάμνησις is not a discovery of forms that are already there to be recovered by the soul. Rather, recollection is a *process* of the actualization of such objects by the power of memory, which is the same power the soul employs for remembering. For this reason, terminologically "recollection" and "memory" are not clearly distinguished in Plotinus.

(2.2) *Staying.* During its "sojourn" in this world, the soul is still capable of (rare) glimpses into the intelligible, which constitutes the second movement of its journey as accompanied by memory and recollection. It is when speaking about the soul staying in this world that Plotinus uses the term "ἀνάμνησις." Recollection is a reminder of the real beings, which are reflected in the sensible and can be recognized as such by the attentive soul. As recognition, recollection can occur in a double way: on the one hand, (2.2.1) the soul can recognize the νοητά in images of beauty. Thus, when we look at paintings, through a sensible imitation (μίμημα), we recognize that which is in our thought (ἐν νοήσει) and thus come to the recollection of the truth (*Enn.* II.9.16.43–7). In such a manner, from an image of beauty we can come to the recollection (εἰς ἀνάμνησιν) of the intelligible archetype (τὸ ἀρχέτυπον, *Enn.* III.5.1.32–6).[26] Even the worst can be a reminder of being: Plotinus concludes his discussion of the origin of evil by suggesting that, since evil appears out of necessity, it often becomes visible in beautiful fetters, so that the images of beauty serve as a reminder (εἰς ἀνάμνησιν) of the intellect (*Enn.* I.8.15.28). Yet, on the other hand, (2.2.2) the soul can also recall the intelligibles by a rational understanding of them, which it acquires through reasoning, by fitting what it has newly understood with what it has already known (*Enn.* V.3.2.11–4). These acts, then, are "recollections" (ἀναμνήσεις), and the intelligible objects become thinkable and recognizable in mutually connected and coherent discursive thoughts, as in logical or mathematical arguments that can be fit within a system.

(2.3) *Return*. Finally, recollection is exemplified in the third movement, that of the return of the soul to the intelligible. In a sense, recollection *is* such a return, which now finds its completion. Strictly speaking, this movement is double, too: (2.3.1) one aspect is experienced as the turning to the intelligible through the soul's thinking while it is embodied. This is Plato's ἀνάμνησις that can be considered the completion of the intellectual discursive endeavor of the soul's second movement or its "stay" in the world. It is here that the soul accomplishes the recollection of "the real beings" (τὰ ὄντως ὄντα, *Enn.* V.9.5.32; cf. Plato, *Phaedo* 72E). During its lifetime, the soul for Plotinus is fallen, bound by fetters, and it lives as if in a cave. And when the soul turns to the intelligible (ἐπιστραφεῖσα δὲ πρὸς νόησιν), from the temporal to the eternal, it does so in order to be freed and to ascend from recollection (ἐξ ἀναμνήσεως) to the contemplation of the real beings (*Enn.* IV.8.4.25–30, with reference to Plato, *Phaedr.* 249E; cf. *Enn.* III.7.1.20–4).

This epistrophic turn is *difficult* and requires a considerable effort on the way to the actualization of the knowledge of the intelligible. But even then only very few manage to "attain to recollection, [and] with difficulty recapitulate what they once saw" (*Enn.* II.9.12.6–7). But because the soul is in the middle, between the sensible and the intelligible, and is "buried" in the body, its vision of the intelligibles is still inevitably rather dim and faint (ἀμυδρότερον, *Enn.* IV.6.3.11–6). So, in order to achieve a full vision and recollection

---

[26] It is worth noting that, for Plotinus, there can be no recollection of the good (τὸ ἀγαθόν) as arousing the desire for the beautiful because the good is always there and was always there (*Enn.* V.5.12.11–4). Therefore, the good is not different from the one in that it is not only beyond being but also beyond beauty.

of the νοητά, the soul needs to overcome its current boundedness. Hence, the other aspect of the ἀνάμνησις as return (2.3.2) is experienced by the soul once it fully moves to the intelligible after having served its time as embodied. At this point, the lower soul connects with the higher soul and communicates to it its lifetime experiences. However, as Plotinus argues, the higher soul should be happy to forget (λήθην ἔχειν) what it received from the lower soul. For, being in touch with the intelligible, the higher soul strives to be detached, and thus forget, the everyday and the ordinary and thus leave all human concerns and memories (τῶν μνημονευμάτων, *Enn.* IV.3.32.9–18; cf. Plato, *Phaedr.* 249C8–D1). Indeed, what will one remember of this life in the intelligible? Plotinus' surmise is that one will not remember there any of the things that happened here for they do not matter there. Moreover, we will not even remember that we were engaged in philosophy, either the acts or the contents of philosophizing, or that we contemplated intelligible things while we were here (*Enn.* IV.4.1.1–11)! In other words, philosophy does not ultimately matter, and all our striving and effort for the recollection we exerted during our stay here is, in a sense, useless since it will be forgotten once we return there, to the place of our origin.

So, in the final movement of the return, when the soul unites with, and becomes again, the higher soul, it becomes forgetful (ἐπιλήσμονα, *Enn.* IV.3.32.17). Paradoxically, the ultimate moment of recollection is oblivion because, in the intelligible, the soul does not need either recollection or memory. In this sense, being amounts to the total forgetfulness of being. For when we ultimately recollect the intelligible, we lose memory and thus forget being.

Therefore, recollection in Plotinus is realized in the triple movement of descent–staying–return, when, through discursive, logical, and narrative means, the soul strives to restore and attain what it has non-discursively thought in the intelligible but has later forgotten. Yet, when the soul reaches back "there," it does not need memory any longer and once again forgets everything it had to remember, and the recollection becomes redundant and obsolete.

6

Intelligible Matter

Matter plays a central role and is ubiquitous in Plotinus' works. In what follows, I intend to establish three claims. First, the concept of intelligible matter, ὕλη νοητή, is a fundamental component not only in Plotinus' earlier writings but throughout his entire philosophy. Second, bodily matter and intelligible matter are necessarily related, being different yet at the same time inseparable. In other words, if thoroughly analyzed, the notion of matter inevitably entails the notion of intelligible matter. And third, intelligible matter is closely connected not only with the indefinite dyad but also with the imagination. I then trace implications and consequences of such a connection.

6.1 The Featureless Features of Matter

In depicting the main characteristics of matter as primarily the matter of physical bodies, Plotinus mostly follows Plato and to some extent Aristotle.[1] Plotinus depicts matter as (1) non-being (μὴ ὄν, *Enn.* II.5.5.9–13), darkness, and as absolutely different from form that represents being because matter is imagined as something formless (ἀνείδεόν τι φανταζομένη, *Enn.* II.5.4.12).[2] For this reason, matter can be rather vaguely represented as "a kind of unmeasuredness

---

[1] Following Plato, Plotinus describes matter as receptacle (ὑποδοχή) and nurse (τιθήνη, *Enn.* II.4.1.1, III.6.13.12) and also as space (χώρα) and seat (ἕδρα, *Enn.* III.6.13.19). Cf. Plato: matter is ὑποδοχή, τιθήνη (*Tim.* 49A), μήτηρ, πανδεχές (*Tim.* 51A), χώρα (*Tim.* 52A–D), and ἐκμαγεῖον (*Tim.* 50C). Following Aristotle, Plotinus also characterizes matter as substrate, ὑποκείμενον (*Enn.* II.4.1.1, II.4.11.22, III.6.7.1–2, III.6.10.8). Cf. Aristotle, *Phys.* 192a31. See also Schwyzer, s.v. "Plotinos," in *RE* 21:1, p. 568. According to Narbonne, the new features of matter introduced by Plotinus are impassibility and inalterability. See Jean-Marc Narbonne, *La métaphysique de Plotin* (Paris: J. Vrin, 1994), pp. 41–2. For my present purpose, the distinction of prime and proximate matter is not crucial. Cf. the discussion in O'Meara, *Structures hiérarchiques dans la pensée de Plotin*, p. 71.

[2] See the commentary to Plotinus, *Ennead II.5: On What Is Potentially and What Is Actually*, trans. and ed. Cinzia Arruzza (Las Vegas: Parmenides, 2015), pp. 149–62.

in relation to measure, and unlimitedness in relation to limit, and formlessness in relation to formative principle (εἰδοποιητικόν), and perpetual neediness in relation to the self-sufficient; always indefinite, nowhere stable, subject to every kind of affection, insatiate, complete poverty" (*Enn.* I.8.3.13–6). Strictly speaking, there is nothing in matter to be properly described—as such it is not describable. Hence, since matter is indeterminate, it cannot really be known. We conceive of matter only by a "spurious reasoning" (νόθῳ λογισμῷ, *Enn.* II.4.10.11; cf. II.4.12.33–4, III.6.13.46; Plato, *Tim.* 52B), as if in a dream.[3] The "knowledge" of matter is thus negative and can be achieved only negatively, by removing all form (ἀφαιρέσει, *Enn.* I.8.9.7; cf. VI.6.3.26–35).[4] This "knowledge" of matter is like seeing darkness (*Enn.* I.8.4.31): we see it not as anything positive and thus not by seeing but rather by a certain "unusual" kind of reasoning. Yet, if we remove or abstract all the "predicates" of matter, what is left is not a subject since matter is not anything definite but pure negativity.

Therefore, the negativity of the non-being of matter is (2) itself necessary and cannot be removed, abstracted, or taken away from the existent. In the late treatise "On What Are and Whence Come Evils" (*Enn.* I.8 [51]), Plotinus finds it appropriate to speak about the necessary existence (ὑπόστασις) of matter (*Enn.* I.8.15.1–3; cf. I.8.7.2–4). In this way, the mere negativity of matter may be rethought not only as a lack of all definiteness but rather as a negative potentiality that even stands for radical evil (*Enn.* I.8.5; see Chapter 11).[5] When Plotinus presents matter as privation in terms of negation (ἄρσις . . . ἡ στέρησις, *Enn.* II.4.13.22–3), he borrows Aristotle's terminology (*Phys.* 192a3–6), yet rethinks the concept of privation (*Enn.* II.4.14; cf. I.8.11.1–4).[6] As Narbonne has observed, privation in Aristotle is *nihil privativum*, which always stands in relation to something else (to being as form), to the extent that it is privation *of* something. However, Plotinus takes matter as a negativity capable of embodying and representing something definite, although matter itself is not

---

[3] Cf. Clemens Baeumker, *Das Problem der Materie in der griechischen Philosophie: eine historisch-kritische Untersuchung* (Frankfurt am Main: Minerva, 1963; orig. pub. 1890); and Leonard J. Eslick, "The Material Substrate in Plato," in *The Concept of Matter in Greek and Medieval Philosophy*, ed. Ernan McMullin (Notre Dame: University of Notre Dame Press, 1965), pp. 39–58.

[4] Cf. Aristotle, *Met.* 1029a11–26; and Simplicius, *In Phys.* 225.22–226.16. Cf. also Heinz Happ, *Hyle: Studien zum Aristotelischen Materie-Begriff* (Berlin: De Gruyter, 1971), pp. 661–7, 683, esp. 674–5: "Dieses 'Nicht-Denken' des Unbestimmten ist kein absolutes Nicht-Wesen, sondern die Seele tastet sich gleichsam zum Unbestimmten vor . . . Die Seele nimmt die Bestimmtheiten weg und denkt die übrigbleibende Unbestimmtheit auf dunkle Weise für sich, ja verschmilzt sogar wie bei der νόησις der Formen irgendwie mit ihrem Gegenstand."

[5] Cf. Hans-Rudolf Schwyzer, "Zu Plotins Deutung der sogenannten platonischen Materie," in *Zetesis: Festschrift E. de Stryker* (Antwerp: De Nederlandsche Boekhandel, 1973), pp. 266–80, esp. 277; John M. Rist, "Plotinus on Matter and Evil," *Phronesis* 6:2 (1961), pp. 154–66, esp. 160; Hubert Benz, *Materie und Wahrnehmung in der Philosophie Plotins* (Würzburg: Königshausen & Neumann, 1990), pp. 125, 147; and Narbonne, *La métaphysique de Plotin*, p. 125.

[6] See Paul Kalligas, *The Enneads of Plotinus: A Commentary* (Princeton: Princeton University Press, 2014), vol. 1, pp. 231, 321–3.

the source of embodiment or definiteness. Hence, contrary to Aristotle, matter for Plotinus should be considered as *nihil negativum*.[7]

Matter is thus (3) indefinite and unlimited (τὸ ἄπειρον, *Enn.* II.4.15.17, 33, II.4.16.9–10; cf. I.8.3.13, VI.6.3.3) and without measure (ἄμετρον, *Enn.* I.2 [19].2.20–1).[8] "Matter is indefinite and not yet stable by itself, and is carried about here and there into every form, and since it is altogether adaptable becomes many by being brought into everything and becoming everything" (*Enn.* II.4.11.40–2). For this reason, matter can be properly characterized only in negative terms: it is without quality (ἄποιος), is not body, has no size (or magnitude), is without quantity and shapeless (*Enn.* II.4.8.1–3, II.4.12.34–7; see Chapter 11).[9]

Since (4) matter has nothing of itself, everything is brought to it by form, for matter needs form and is pure receptivity (*Enn.* II.4.8.23–4, III.5.9.54–5, VI.5.8.15–22).[10] As such, it has "no resistance [τὸ ἀντικόπτον; cf. ἀντερεῖδον, *Enn.* III.6.7.30], since it has no activity, but is a shadow, waits passively to accept whatever that which acts upon it wishes" (*Enn.* III.6.18.29–31).

Matter (5) cannot be affected and therefore is unalterable (*Enn.* III.6.9.34–5, III.6.10.21–2). The question of whether matter has an origin or not has been the subject of much debate (see Chapter 11). Matter (6), then, cannot have any inner structure and thus cannot be destroyed (ἀνώλεθρον, *Enn.* IV.7.9.11; cf. III.6.8.11–2; Plato, *Tim.* 52A) since there is nothing in it to pass away. Matter may be said to endure or remain (μένει) what it already is, which is not as anything concrete or definite (*Enn.* III.6.11.18, III.6.19.14).

Finally, matter (7) is potentiality that never becomes actuality: it is always only an "announcement," a "promise" of being (ἐπαγγελλόμενον), but not being itself (*Enn.* II.5.5.4, III.6.7.21–3). In other words, matter is potentiality that is never actualized (*Enn.* II.5.4; cf. Aristotle, *Met.* 1045a23–4, 1045b18–9, 1088b1).[11] This potentiality is negative and not only privative. Moreover,

---

[7] Narbonne, *La métaphysique de Plotin*, pp. 43–9. The distinction between *nihil privativum* and *nihil negativum* appears in Baumgarten, who introduces the notion of being as derived from the fundamental concept of *nihil negativum* as absolute, simple, impossible, and irrepresentable (see Alexander Gottlieb Baumgarten, *Metaphysica* [Hildesheim: G. Olms, 1963; orig. pub. 1779], p. 3). The negation of nothing, which is *non-nihil*, originates something, *aliquid* (not yet definite or defined). Taken actually, it is a determined object or *ens*; as not determined, it is *non-ens*, or *nihil privativum*, which represents mere possibility.

[8] Emile Bréhier, *La philosophie de Plotin* (Paris: J. Vrin, 1982; orig. pub. 1928), p. 206.

[9] Cf. Simplicius, *In Phys.* 255.17–256.13.

[10] In contrast to matter, intellect is unreceptive (ἄδεκτον, *Enn.* III.6.6.20). See Jonathan Scott Lee, "The Doctrine of Reception According to the Capacity of the Recipient in *Ennead* VI. 4–5. III," *Dionysius* 3 (1979), pp. 79–97; and Michael F. Wagner, "Plotinus' Idealism and the Problem of Matter in *Enneads* VI. 4–5," *Dionysius* 10 (1986), pp. 57–83, esp. 64.

[11] See Narbonne, *La métaphysique de Plotin*, p. 8; and Kevin Corrigan, *Plotinus' Theory of Matter-Evil and the Question of Substance in Plato, Aristotle, and Alexander of Aphrodisias* (Leuven: Peeters, 1996), pp. 120–31.

as I will argue, on the one hand, it is not only bodily matter that is mere potentiality—this is also true of intelligible matter, which is potentially all intelligible objects. But, on the other hand, the negative potentiality of matter differs from the potentiality of the one.

6.2 Intelligible Matter

In *Ennead* II.4.2–5, Plotinus provides us an account of intelligible matter.[12] Yet the very notion of intelligible matter comes from Aristotle. Some philosophers maintain, says Plotinus, that "there is another, prior, kind [of matter] in the intelligible world [ἐν τοῖς νοητοῖς] which underlies the forms there and the incorporeal substances" (*Enn.* II.4.1.14–8). The notion of ὕλη νοητή appears three times in the *Metaphysics* (Aristotle, *Met.* 1035a9–1036a12, 1036b35–1037a5, 1045a33–6). In *Metaphysics* Z.11 (1036b35–1037a5) and *Metaphysics* H.6 (1045a33–4), Aristotle opposes sensible (bodily) matter to intelligible matter (ἔστι γὰρ ὕλη ἡ μὲν αἰσθητή ἡ δὲ νοητή, *Met.* 1037a4–5), and, in *Metaphysics* Z.10, he stresses the unknowability of matter as such (ἄγνωστος, *Met.* 1036a8–9) and refers to intelligible matter as present "in sensible things not *qua* sensible, as in the objects of mathematics" (νοητή δὲ [*scil.* ὕλη] ἡ ἐν τοῖς αἰσθητοῖς ὑπάρχουσα μὴ ᾗ αἰσθητά, οἷον τὰ μαθηματικά, *Met.* 1036a11–2). Yet, from Aristotle's three brief descriptions it is not immediately clear what the intelligible matter is. In his commentary on the *Metaphysics*, Alexander understands intelligible matter as the generic constituent in the definition of a geometrical figure ("plane figure" in: "circle is a plane figure" [Alexander, *In Met.* 562.21]), which can be taken as extension (διάστασις, Alexander, *In Met.* 510.2–5). This is also the understanding of Happ.[13] Rist, however, challenges this interpretation and agrees with Ross that intelligible matter is the generic element in both species and individuals and concludes that Plotinus appropriates the Aristotelian notion of intelligible matter that is found in the relation between genus and species and turns it into the relation between "the first effluence from the one [which is] the base of form and form itself."[14]

It is important to note that, in his examples, Aristotle refers to the geometrical figures as instantiating intelligible matter. In particular, intelligible matter appears to be associated with the following features: (α) irrationality (there is

---

[12] In the *Enneads*, II.4 appears under the title "On Matter"; the other title "On the Two Kinds of Matter" is found in Porphyry, *Vita Plotini* 4.45; 24.46. However, neither title originally appears in Plotinus but reflects the school's usage. Cf. Schwyzer, s.v. "Plotinos," in *RE* 21:1, p. 487.

[13] Happ, *Hyle*, p. 581, interprets ὕλη νοητή as "reine Ausdehnung," διάστασις or διάστημα.

[14] William David Ross, *Aristotle's Metaphysics* (Oxford: Clarendon Press, 1953), p. 199; see John M. Rist, "The Indefinite Dyad and Intelligible Matter in Plotinus," *Classical Quarterly* 12:1 (1962), pp. 99–107, esp. 106–7.

something in it which cannot or can hardly be apprehended), (β) mathematical (geometrical) objects, and (γ) certain extension. If, as I will argue, intelligible matter is also connected with imagination, then, although the Ross-Rist hypothesis still remains valid, the hypothesis of Alexander-Happ cannot be rejected either, to the extent that imagination might be considered as a *plenum* of geometrical figures (for instance, of a circle). Moreover, both accounts are not incompatible insofar as intelligible matter may be understood as the generic element of geometrical (mathematical) species as existing in the geometrical extension, in which case genus in the Ross-Rist hypothesis should be restricted mainly to geometrical objects. If this is the case, then Plotinus' interpretation, however original in many points, might not be as far from that of Aristotle as it may seem.

But why does Plotinus need the notion of intelligible matter at all? A plausible answer is that he just tries to incorporate the Aristotelian notion (never found in Plato) into his own philosophy. Plotinus discusses ὕλη νοητή mainly in the early *Ennead* II.4 [12]. In the treatises of the middle period, *Ennead* II.5 [25] and *Ennead* III.6 [26], there are a few occasional mentions of ὕλη νοητή, whereas the late *Ennead* I.8 [51] does not refer to intelligible matter at all. However, in the immediately preceding *Ennead* III.5.6.44, intelligible matter reappears as characterizing the distinction of δαίμονες as intermediate between gods and humans. Still, as I will attempt to demonstrate, the notion of intelligible matter is not likely to be introduced by Plotinus solely for the exegetic purpose of reconciling Platonic and Aristotelian views, but represents an important constituent in his philosophy.

What is the role of intelligible matter in the *Enneads*? In *Ennead* II.4.2.1–2, Plotinus outlines the program of investigation of intelligible matter: we have to find out (a) whether intelligible matter exists (εἰ ἔστι), (b) what it is (τίς οὖσα), and (c) how it exists (πῶς ἐστιν). All three points of the program of study should be mutually connected because the question of existence entails the question of essence, and the question of essence presupposes the discussion of existence as the way essence is expressed in being.

Plotinus presents several arguments in support of his view that intelligible matter is a necessary constituent of everything that is.

(a). Does intelligible matter exist (εἰ ἔστι)? It should exist, and (1) the *mimetic* argument (*Enn.* II.4.4.7–11) supports this claim. Namely, if there is intelligible order or cosmos "there," in the intelligible (κόσμος νοητός), and this bodily cosmos is an imitation (μίμημα) of the intelligible cosmos and the physical cosmos has matter, then there should be matter in the intelligible, too, as the paradigm for bodily matter. In addition, form cannot really be form without being imposed onto something different from it.

This brings us (2) to the argument from *substrate* or ὑποκείμενον. Intelligible matter should exist (*Enn.* II.4.4.2–7) because we assume that the forms (εἴδη) exist (cf. *Enn.* V.9.3). But if the forms exist, there should be something common to all of them, but also something individual, by which the forms differ from each other. This individual difference is every form's shape (μορφή); if there is shape, there should be that which is shaped as the forms. Therefore, there should be matter that receives this shape, and this is intelligible matter. From this point of view, intelligible matter is substrate, ὑποκείμενον (cf. Aristotle, *Phys.* 192a31; *Met.* 1024b8–9), of the forms. In other words, shape is a peculiar characteristic in and of the forms, the source of individuation, while intelligible matter is that which is *common* to all of them as the undifferentiated substrate of the intelligible, representing the aspect of *unity* of and within the forms.[15] However, although this substrate is *in* the intelligible, it is *not* being as such, for being is the synthetic unity that comes as the result of the turning of the not yet differentiated thinking of the intellect to its source, to the superabundant unity (which is not even really a unity) of the one.

(3) We can also establish the existence of intelligible matter by the argument from *parts* (*Enn.* II.4.4.11–20). "There," in the intelligible, everything is partless (ἀμερές), although, in a way, the forms still have parts. In bodies, parts can be separated and thus matter is "cut" (τμηθεῖσα, *Enn.* II.4.4.14). But in the intellect as one-many, every form is single and individual but at the same time actually contains all the other forms in their communication (see Chapter 1). Intelligible matter should then be understood as one single shapeless *plenum* in which many shapes (μορφαί) of the forms are embodied: "But if intelligible reality is at once many and partless, then the many existing in one are in matter which is that one, and they are its shapes; conceive this one as varied and of many shapes" (*Enn.* II.4.4.14–7). Intelligible matter is then an indefinite and undefined source of unity in the forms and, as such, is a potentiality of being.

(4) In addition, matter also appears as a "ladder." That which precedes hypostatically and ontologically can be considered hierarchically "higher," and thus the form of the "lower," which is then "matter" to that "higher" in a "ladder" of form and matter. Intelligible matter is closer to being (since it constitutes a moment *in* being), hence it should be in a "higher" position to the "lower" or bodily matter. This structure is commonly present in Plotinus: what is more potential is matter to what is more actual. The undefined and formless, then, should not be looked down on nor rejected because it makes itself available to that which is before it, as soul is disposed to the intellect and λόγος, the rational principle (*Enn.* II.4.3.1–5).[16] Likewise, soul may be considered as matter to the intellect (*Enn.* III.9.5, V.1.3.22–3; cf. V.8.3.9, VI.3.16.14–5). Therefore, "soul is matter to the first that makes it [the intellect] and is afterwards shaped

---

[15] Cf. A. H. Armstrong, *The Architecture of the Intelligible Universe in the Philosophy of Plotinus: An Analytical and Historical Study* (Cambridge: Cambridge University Press, 1940), pp. 67–8; Rist, "The Indefinite Dyad and Intelligible Matter in Plotinus," pp. 99–107, esp. 104–5.

[16] Cf. Kalligas, *The Enneads of Plotinus: A Commentary*, vol. 1, pp. 310–1.

and perfected" (*Enn.* V.9.4.10–2). At this point, it is important to note that intelligible matter may be associated not only with the intellect but also with soul. This will be crucial in the discussion of the relation between intelligible matter and imagination.

(b). Considering ὕλη νοητή as a shapeless unity that embraces many shapes brings us to the question of what intelligible matter is (τίς οὖσα). Plotinus argues (5) that intelligible matter should be thought of as the *indefinite dyad,* ἀόριστος δυάς. The indefinite dyad is the primary source and potentiality of multiplicity that, however, itself is not multiplicity (cf. Plato, *Phil.* 23C–D; Aristotle, *Met.* 987b20–988a1). The dyad stands for the not yet definite and not defined thinking, νόησις, that searches for, and attempts to think, its source, the one (*Enn.* III.8.11).[17] However, since the one is beyond being, any determination or representation is thus not thinkable, the indefinite thinking necessarily "misses" the one and can only grasp it as not one, as multiplicity and plurality. The not yet defined thinking thinks or "looks" at that which cannot be thought or "seen" and, in this respect, is similar to "seeing in the darkness" (cf. *Enn.* I.8.4.30–1). Missing its source and origin, such thinking as the indefinite dyad produces a whole multiplicity of the forms as inevitable yet necessary (mis)representations of the one. The intellect, then, becomes definite and self-defined as thinking the forms or intelligible objects that it itself has generated in the unrealizable attempt to go back to its source and origin.

In this way (which can only be a metaphorical description), the primary (intelligible) indefiniteness of "seeing"-thinking is informed by the multiplicity of the forms-νοητά. For this reason, intelligible matter is not different from the indefinite νόησις as a mere capacity of seeing (or rather, intention of seeing) that which cannot be seen.[18] Hence, the dyad represents the material aspect of the intellect and thus may be considered intelligible matter because it is indefinite before the act of turning back and "looking" at the one and the subsequent (not temporal, but logical and ontological) definition by the noetic forms (*Enn.* V.1.7, V.3.11, V.4.2). Therefore, the dyad is intelligible matter, which, however, may be considered as matter only when the noetic objects arise as being thought by the intellect that in this way becomes definite and defines itself. When the indefinite thinking as the dyad turns toward the one, it becomes defined both from the one and from the multitude of the forms

---

[17] [Iamblichus], *Theolog. arithm.* 7.15. See Armstrong, *The Architecture of the Intelligible Universe*, p. 66; Rist, "The Indefinite Dyad and Intelligible Matter in Plotinus," p. 104; and A. H. Armstrong, *The Cambridge History of the Later Greek and Early Medieval Philosophy* (Cambridge: Cambridge University Press, 1967), p. 241. According to Rist, Plotinus identifies Aristotelian intelligible matter with the Platonic indefinite dyad.

[18] See Rist, "The Indefinite Dyad and Intelligible Matter in Plotinus," pp. 100–2; and Theiler, "Einheit und unbegrenzte Zweiheit von Plato big Plotin," pp. 89–109.

as one-many.[19] The indefinite dyad thus should be associated with a thinking capacity of the not yet reflective thinking. This contemplative ability to stare at and into the complete darkness is then realized, as I will argue, in the irrationality of imagination.

Intelligible matter as the dyad is then also a substrate: the indefinite dyad is neither being nor non-being (while bodily matter "is" non-being) since it is different from the one that alone is beyond being. But intelligible matter is the necessary substrate that is prior to being for the forms as being thought by the intellect. The intellect is therefore the simplex of νόησις/ νοητά constituted as the unity of thinking that engenders, but is also in turn itself defined by, the objects of thought.[20]

Finally (6), intelligible matter should be considered as the *potentiality of being* as the first yet indefinite thinking after the one defined both by the one and by the forms, whereas matter in general (as bodily matter) is mere potentiality of any existent.

(c). The consideration of intelligible matter as dyad (as potentiality of multiplicity) in fact answers the last question of Plotinus: namely, (c) how does intelligible matter exist (πῶς ἐστιν)? For the way of introducing the dyad—as being closer to the one than anything else and as thus intimately related to the ultimate source of the all—presents intelligible matter as the potentiality of and for real beings, as the possibility of their subsistence and embodiment as the forms.

6.3 Matter and Imagination

An important aspect of intelligible matter that has not been analyzed so far is the affinity of intelligible matter with the imagination. In Plotinus, imagination or φαντασία (1) can be broadly construed as the ability to produce psychic images. In other words, a distinctive feature of imagination is that it is *creative*. Criticizing the Gnostics, Plotinus argues that the soul may create "through imagination [διὰ φαντασίας] and, still more, through rational thinking [τοῦ λογίζεσθαι]" (*Enn.* II.9.11.22–3). The notion of φαντασία is used in the *Enneads* rather broadly as an ability to represent things as mental or psychic images.[21] Yet imagination as a capacity of representation is not simply a passive reflecting

---

[19] Rist, "The Indefinite Dyad and Intelligible Matter in Plotinus," p. 103: "νοῦς sees the one as the Forms, but the intelligibility of those Forms is supplied by the one."

[20] See O'Meara, *Plotinus: An Introduction to the* Enneads, pp. 62–5.

[21] See Barrie Fleet, Ennead *III.6: On the Impassivity of the Bodiless* (Oxford: Oxford University Press, 1995), pp. 73, 266; Evanghelos Moutsopoulos, "Dynamic Structuralism in the Plotinian Theory of the Imaginary," *Diotima* 4 (1976), pp. 11–22; and Gerard Watson, *Phantasia in Classical Thought* (Galway: Galway University Press, 1988).

or mirroring because imagination forms its images not like impressions on wax that receives them. Imagination therefore should possess (or, rather, itself be) certain active potency, but potency of a peculiar kind, always distorting and misrepresenting its object.

(2) This brings us to a distinctive feature of the imagination, namely, its connection with the irrational, which comes in Plotinus' definition of the imagination: "Imagination is a stroke of something irrational from outside [φαντασία δὲ πληγὴ ἀλόγου ἔξωθεν]" (*Enn.* I.8.15.18).[22] Images of the imagination are thus represented as vague and unclear (ταῖς ἀμυδραῖς φαντασίαις, *Enn.* I.8.14.5) and are described by Plotinus by the same term that Plato uses to characterize matter (χαλεπὸν καὶ ἀμυδρὸν εἶδος, Plato, *Tim.* 49A).

Yet consideration of the imagination as only distortive entails a difficulty. Indeed, if all the images-φαντασίαι are necessarily unclear and distorted, how can the soul know any of its images for sure? Images of sense-perception might be vague, and yet, since they are judgments (κρίσεις), they should be already interpreted in the sense-perception.[23] But if the images of the imagination come from the soul and not from senses, then the distortion in the soul might be explained by the uncertainty of knowledge as opinion, δόξα. There should be, then, two different aspects of psychic (mental) representation in the soul, which implies Plotinus' briefly formulated distinction between two imaginations, the primary imagination understood as opinion (δόξα) and the secondary, "uncritisized, indeterminate, indistinct" (ἀνεπίκριτος) "mental picture" or "impression" (φαντασία, *Enn.* III.6.4.19–21).[24]

(3) In his analysis of sense-perception, Emilsson stresses the connection between sense-perception and imagination in Plotinus. Emilsson argues that the imagination is a *faculty* that is the terminating point of perceptions or φαντάσματα, "unextended entities" that arise in the soul as the result of sense-perception (cf. Aristotle, *De an.* 427b14–26; *Enn.* IV.3.29.23, IV.4.20.17). Imagination and perception, then, have to be connected, although they have different objects. As his conclusion, Emilsson raises the hypothesis that "there is no sharp distinction between sense-perception and representation [imagination]: sense-perception is directed towards the external, but it apprehends its object by means of a judgement that itself is simultaneously apprehended by the faculty of representation."[25] Although different, sense-perception and

---

[22] Another reading accepted by Henry-Schwyzer: imagination *is* itself a stroke (πληγή).

[23] See Emilsson, *Plotinus on Sense-Perception*, pp. 121–5.

[24] See Fleet, *On the Impassivity of the Bodiless*, pp. 124–6. See also Moutsopoulos, "Dynamic Structuralism," pp. 11–22; and Watson, *Phantasia in Classical Thought*.

[25] Emilsson, *Plotinus on Sense-Perception*, p. 109. "The most important function of phantasia is to be the 'locus' of these unextended entities that are involved in memory and reasoning, and it is clear that these entities are in some sense representations of things" (ibid.; cf. pp. 111, 121–5). See also Malcolm Schofield, "Aristotle on the Imagination," in *Aristotle on Mind and the Senses: Proceedings of the Seventh Symposium Aristotelicum*, ed. G. E. R. Lloyd and G. E. L. Owen (Cambridge: Cambridge University

imagination thus always meet in the act of perception. Their difference lies in that, unlike perception, the imagination does not have to do directly with physical objects. In creating its objects (φαντάσματα), the imagination begins with the sense-data as already interpreted and judged by senses and not with the physical objects themselves. The faculty of imagination therefore should be a faculty "higher" than that of the sense-perception; that is, closer to the dianoetic interpretative discursive reasoning of the soul.

Since the imagination represents its objects as pictorial (that is, as quasi-extended images), imagination appears to be close to the bodily (cf. *Enn.* IV.4 [28].17.11–4). Thus, when describing the exhortation of the higher part of the soul to the state of pure being and thinking, Plotinus takes it as the detachment not only from the bodily, but from the imagination as well (*Enn.* V.1.10.24–7). "He who wishes to see the intelligible nature will contemplate what is beyond the perceptible if he has no mental image [φαντασία] of the perceptible," says Plotinus (*Enn.* V.5.6.17–9). Yet imagination cannot be reduced to the bodily only since it has certain features in common with the intelligible that physical things do not have. Thus, for instance, imagination may represent something that is pictorial and yet a self-identical and unchanging image (e.g., the image of a circle; see Chapter 8). In addition, if it is the same intellect that thinks and thinks that it thinks or is self-reflective, then one might also say that when imagining, imagination is aware of imagining, similarly to thinking (cf. *Enn.* I.4.10.19–21, II.9.1.34–5).[26] Hence, on its "upper side," the imagination meets the discursive reasoning of διάνοια and is thus reflective, and, on its "lower side," it meets sense-perception (cf. *Enn.* V.3.3.5–6).

It is reasonable to assume, then, that the imagination occupies an intermediate position between the sensible (bodily) and the thinkable (discursive; see Chapter 8). Plotinus describes the imagination as positioned between the impression of nature (those images that imagination shares with sense-perception) and the thinking of intellect (φαντασία δὲ μεταξὺ φύσεως τύπου καὶ νοήσεως, *Enn.* IV.4.13.13; cf. II.9.11.22–3), which renders perfectly comprehensible his claim that "the imaging part [of the soul] has a sort of intelligence [φανταστικὸν οἷον νοερόν]" (*Enn.* IV.3.23.32).

Another argument in favor of situating imagination as an intermediate faculty may be recovered from *Ennead* VI.8.2, where, discussing our being

---

Press, 1978), pp. 99–140, esp. 101. Cf. Martha Nussbaum, *Aristotle's* De Motu Animalium: *Text with Translation, Commentary, and Interpretive Essays* (Princeton: Princeton University Press, 1978); and Michael Wedin, *Mind and Imagination in Aristotle* (New Haven: Yale University Press, 1988).

[26] See Edward W. Warren, "Imagination in Plotinus," *Classical Quarterly* 16:2 (1966), pp. 277–85, esp. 277–8; Emilsson, *Plotinus on Sense-Perception*, p. 108 ("There are passages where phantasia seems to cover all kinds of apprehension below the level of intellection"); and the commentary to Plotinus, *Plotinus on Eudaimonia: A Commentary on Ennead* I.4, trans. and ed. Kieran McGroarty (Oxford: Oxford University Press, 2006), p. 158.

compelled by desire and impulse, Plotinus says that imagination, linked here with the experiences of body, is compelling (ἀναγκάζουσα, *Enn.* VI.8.2.17), and the compelling force is primarily associated with the necessity of matter. Since freedom is determined by closeness to the one and thus emerges through ascension to the good (*Enn.* VI.8.4.4–41), it is the intellect that is mostly free. Now, the intellect is really free "when it does not have it in its power not to act by producing [the intelligible objects]" (οὐκ ἔχων ἐπ' αὐτῷ τὸ μὴ ποιεῖν, *Enn.* VI.8.4.6–7). However compelling it may seem, freedom consists in the voluntary act of pursuing the good (the best) and therefore in the free accepting of the necessity not to act (against the noetic representations of the good which are not different from the intellect). This "not able not to" is very much different from the simple necessity of the "not able" of matter.

But in the imagination there are traces not only of being compelled but also of freedom, insofar as it can voluntarily construct (imagine) its object. And yet this "freedom" of imagination differs both from the necessity of matter and from the freedom of the intellect while at the same time having a certain similarity with both of them. Imagination may also be considered free in that it can put its images together by free associations, connecting, disconnecting, and distorting them. Hence, in respect of the (relative) voluntary freedom of its operation, the imagination has certain features of the intellect as freely productive. The difference is that the intellect thinks without pictorial representations or images, which means that there is a fundamental ontological distinction between the intelligible and the imaginary (ἄνευ εἰδώλου ἡ διάνοια καὶ ὁ νοῦς νοεῖ καὶ ἄνευ φαντασίας ἡ νόησις, *Enn.* I.4.10.18–9). Imagination compels and is compelled in that it receives the shape of and for its images from something else—from physical bodies, on the one hand (head of a man, body of a horse in the image of centaur), and from the intelligibles, on the other (form of a circle as represented in the imagination). As for various "phantastic" images that can never be seen in (physical and intelligible) reality, the shape of their appearances nevertheless should come from the intelligible forms since everything that is shaped is finally determined by the measure of the participation of a thing in its form, and only bodily matter has no form whatsoever. Imagination, then, should have features of both the intellect and matter but also be different from both of them since it has certain traits that are alien to the intelligible and the bodily.

(4) Finally, imagination represents the *plenum* where psychic images are present as embodied and, in this sense, is associated with a quasi-spatial extension. As was said, intelligible matter is understood by Plotinus as the indefinite dyad, as not yet formed intellection that, in its attempt to grasp its origin, the one, (mis)represents it as a multiplicity of intelligible objects or forms. In this way, the one beyond being cannot be really thought—but it can be *imagined*. For this reason, when speaking about the one in *Ennead* VI.8.11, Plotinus finds it possible to make a kind of imaginary experiment. Thinking about the one,

we first assume a space and place [χώραν καὶ τόπον], a kind of vast emptiness [χάος], and then, when the space is already there we bring this nature into that place which has come to be or is in our imagination, and bringing it into this kind of place we inquire in this way as if into where from and how it came here, and as if it was a stranger we have asked about its [the one's] presence and, in a way, its substance, really just as if we thought that it had been thrown up from some depth or down from some height. (*Enn.* VI.8.11.15–22)

We may now draw some conclusions about the relation of the intelligible matter and the imagination. (a) The desperate yet inevitable attempt to think the unthinkable beginning of all being leads to the (mis)representation of the one as not-one but many forms. This constitutes the structure of being, insofar as the intelligible cosmos of the forms is produced by the intellect in its (re)turn to the one. But when we attempt to think the one we cannot think it otherwise than by putting it into an imaginary place. The imagination is connected both with non-being (the beyond-being) and being (thinking) and is thus cognitively and ontologically between existing and non-existing. All the things other than the one-good—primarily the intelligible objects—"are satisfied with themselves by their participation [μετουσία] in or imagination of the good" (*Enn.* VI.8.13.46–7). In other words, the imagination provides intelligible matter to the intelligible.

(b) We are able to think "about the one" (but not "to think the one"), then, only as located or abiding in a certain place that is not real (for it is not yet defined), but not altogether unreal either (for as the indefinite dyad it represents the as of yet not [self-] defined thinking of the intellect). Therefore, this can only be an *imaginary* place, an "as-if" place. This "as-ifness" becomes an important feature of intelligible matter.

(c) In this respect, the imagination has some similarity with χώρα, which is close to non-being, a mere possibility of embodiment not yet defined by the form (Plato, *Tim.* 52A–D). Yet the imaginary "space" is not a privative non-being or sheer nothingness but has some affinity with being, to the extent that it is present primarily not in physical or bodily things but in the intelligible objects.

Furthermore, (d) this "place" of the above-being (of the one) is itself non-existent but *imaginary*, while the "place" of things is "real." This imaginary "place" may be taken then (in fact, imagined) as quasi-spatial, especially since there is no distinct interpretation, in either Plotinus or in Plato, of space as geometrical; that is, as already measured. It is that place where images are imagined as extended while not really being extended. Space or spatiality cannot be taken as defining the distinction between the physical and mental in Plotinus because spatiality does not have a distinct essence.[27] It is a

---

[27] Contra Emilsson's claim that, in Plotinus, "spatiality is really the formal distinguishing feature; the sensible can be identified with spatial, the intelligible with non-spatial" (Emilsson, *Plotinus on Sense-Perception*, p. 18). This is more characteristic of Descartes. See Nikulin, *Matter, Imagination and Geometry*, pp. 12–9.

potentiality to accommodate and embody form, either as bodily or as imaginary. As Armstrong notes, Plotinus understands chaos "as the empty space or place which things occupy."[28] However, empty space is neither extension nor should it necessarily be extended, but the extended may be put into space as an empty receptacle. In addition, Alexander's interpretation of intelligible matter as extension-διάστασις suggests that there is a striking similarity between the imagination and intelligible matter.

As a cognitive faculty, (e) the imagination does its work between (dianoetic and noetic) thinking and sense-perception, which leads Plotinus to make an even further distinction between two φαντασίαι, the higher and the lower imagination, which parallels the distinction between intelligible and bodily matter.

And, finally, (f) the ability to keep its images as if in a certain place is connected with the faculty of memory as the capacity of retaining images.[29] Yet the apprehension of an image requires both discursive reasoning and memory, which supports Plotinus' claim that the imagination is at work in the operation of discursive reasoning (see Chapter 5).

This preliminary analysis of the four features of imagination—namely, creativity, inalienable irrationality, the intermediate position between the sensible and the thinkable, and its quasi-spatial character—has been undertaken in order to demonstrate the relation between intelligible matter and the imagination. Indeed, all these four features of the imagination can be equally traced in intelligible matter.

First, intelligible matter may be said to be creative in a way, insofar as in its striving toward the one it brings forth the (finite, according to Plotinus) multitude of forms. Yet the true source of creativity is the one. However, since the one is beyond being and all possible representation, and the dyad is the mere potentiality of being and as such is undefined, creativity should be ascribed primarily to the intellect as producing and thinking being, the intelligible cosmos of definite and defined forms. In this sense, the creativity of intelligible matter is imaginary or illusory. The same can be said about the imagination, which creates its objects only *as if* (οἷον) because it makes *as if* visible, in the form of an image, that which already *is* and is an object of thought. Intelligible matter thus can be considered creative, as a paradigm or a kind of form of bodily matter that, however, is never formed since it "is" non-being.

---

[28] A. H. Armstrong, note to Plotinus, *Enneads*, trans. A. H. Armstrong (Cambridge, MA: Harvard University Press, 1988), vol. 7, pp. 262–3. See Hesiod, *Theog.* 116; and Aristotle, *Phys.* 208b30–3.

[29] See John Dillon, "Plotinus and the Transcendental Imagination," in *Religious Imagination*, ed. James P. Mackey and John McIntyre (Edinburgh: Edinburgh University Press, 1986), pp. 55–64.

Second, irrationality can also to be found in intelligible matter since, as the primary indefinite potentiality, it is alogical before it becomes determined (although differently) by the one and the forms.

Third, intelligible matter is intermediary as well. Yet this intermediateness is itself double. For, on the one hand, intelligible matter is "between" the one and the forms (νοητά), but, on the other hand, it is also comes between being (forms) and non-being (bodily matter).

Fourth, intelligible matter as a "space"-χώρα is an empty, indefinite "place" for the embodiment of forms and geometrical figures. It should be noted that geometrical figures are closely connected with imagination. For Plotinus, geometrical objects are representations of the forms of geometrical objects. Hence, the geometrical figures belong to the intelligible (γεωμετρία δὲ νοητῶν οὖσα τακτέα ἐκεῖ, *Enn.* V.9.11.24–5). And since the intelligible objects are necessarily connected with intelligible matter, geometrical figures should be, too, and thus are also connected with the imagination. Hence, we see all the four features of intelligible matter and the imagination present in the geometrical figures. They may be considered (i) as produced in imagination by the act of contemplation, as in Plotinus' famous soliloquy of nature: "And my act of contemplation makes what it contemplates [τὸ θεωροῦν μου θεώρημα ποιεῖ], as the geometers draw their figures while they contemplate. But I do not draw, but as I contemplate, the lines which bound the bodies come to be as if they fell [from my contemplation]" (*Enn.* III.8.4.7–10; cf. Plato, *Tim.* 53C–55C). Yet (ii) geometrical objects have a share not only in the intelligible, to the extent that they represent indivisible form—but also in the irrational, to the extent that they also, being divisible (at least, in the imagination), represent otherness (*Enn.* IV.7.8.42–3; cf. VI.3.16.14–5). Furthermore, (iii) geometrical figures are intermediate, belonging both here and there, to the imaginable (of the soul) and to the intelligible (of the intellect, *Enn.* VI.3.16.20–3; cf. Plato, *Phil.* 16C–17A, 56A–57D; *Rep.* 525A–530D). Geometrical figures are objects of discursive analysis: "the knower in knowing [one part] brings in all the others by a kind of sequence [ἀκολουθίᾳ]; and the geometer in his analysis makes clear that the one proposition contains all the prior propositions by means of which the analysis is made and the subsequent propositions which are generated from it" (*Enn.* IV.9.5.22–6). On the one hand, geometrical objects are similar to intelligible ones since they all are mutually connected and interrelated (in this respect they represent the structure of the communication of the forms in the intelligible), but, on the other hand, they are presented and analyzed in consecutive steps, one after another (and in this respect they can only be understood as associated with intelligible matter that brings discursiveness to the world of geometrical objects). However, one could make an important distinction here, which can be implied from Plotinus' analysis but which is not made by him explicitly. Namely, the discursiveness of the steps of the *analysis* of geometrical objects is different from the discursiveness of the process of their *construction*. In the first case, geometrical figures are taken as whole, as already existing, while in the second case they are taken as being produced by a movement in the imagination as intelligible matter (see Chapter 8). This distinction shows both the close connection of geometrical objects with imagination and the intermediary position of the imagination between the pure intelligible and the bodily. Finally, (iv) although the geometrical figure is characterized primarily not by its size or magnitude but by its shape (μορφή) of a certain quality (circular, triangular, etc.), it still cannot be considered without and outside of extension or magnitude (*Enn*. VI.3.14.20–6). In other words, the geometrical figure should be related to quasi-spatial extension.

Imagination and intelligible matter thus share the same four constitutive features of creativity, irrationality, intermediateness, and quasi-spatiality. Imagination, then, is a kind of intelligible matter of the soul. This conclusion is supported by a passage where Plotinus speaks about imagination as matter to the soul that does not properly affect the soul: "In the soul the image [εἴδωλον] is imagination [φαντασία], while the nature of the soul is not of the nature of an image [οὐκ εἰδώλου]; and although the imagination[30] in many ways seems to lead the soul and take it wherever it wants to, the soul nevertheless uses the imagination as if it was matter or something like it [ἀνάλογον]" (*Enn*. III.6.15.16–9). Located between the intelligible and the bodily, imagination creates, receives, and embodies images exactly as intelligible matter does.

6.4 Two Matters, Two Imaginations

The intermediate position of the imagination secures its access both to the sensible and to the thinkable. At the same time, in *Ennead* IV.3.31.1–20, we find an important doctrine of two imaginations or image-making powers (δύο τὰ φανταστικά, *Enn*. IV.3.15.2) that belong to the higher and the lower soul. Does this mean that the two imaginations are separate and perform different functions, such that one φαντασία operates only in the intelligible, the other in the sensible? Plotinus argues that this cannot be the case, "for in this way there will be two living things with nothing at all in common with each other" (*Enn*. IV.3.31.6–8). This means that there would be two different and separate

---

[30] In Armstrong's translation, "the mental picture." Nevertheless, "imagination" in this sentence seems to be more appropriate, since, first, Plotinus has just said that in the soul image and imagination are the same, and, second, in the Greek text of this sentence the subject is missing (*Enn*. III.6.15.17–8). In Fleet's interpretation, the subject of the last sentence (lines 18–9) is φαντασία, as it is in the Henry-Schwyzer reading and therefore the claim is that the soul is a kind of matter to the imagination. See Fleet, *On the Impassivity of the Bodiless*, p. 248. Taking into consideration what has been said about the imagination, this seems to be plausible. I therefore support Armstrong, who assumes that the subject of the sentence is ψυχή and digresses from both Henry-Schwyzer and Fleet. The sentence should then be understood as indicating that it is imagination that is the (intelligible) matter to and of the soul.

souls that would have nothing to do with each other, whereas they should be "in tune," harmonized with each other (συμφωνῇ), while the higher rules and defines the lower, "for both have come together into one and the better soul is on top of the other. This other soul, then, sees everything, and takes some things with it which belong to the other when it goes out but rejects others" (*Enn.* IV.3.31.15–8).

In other words, the difference between the two imaginations is established not by the difference of their objects but by their hierarchical and ontological difference in the structure of the whole, which ultimately goes back to the henological difference between the one beyond being and the indefinite dyad as matter. The intermediary status of imagination, then, does not consist in its being located between the intelligible and the sensible but in its being both "here" and "there" as two different, yet not separable imaginations. The imagination is thus inherently double, both with regard to its object (intelligible and sensible) and with regard to the ontological reality with which it is associated (the higher soul and the lower soul).[31] We may then understand *Ennead* IV.3.31 in such a way that the higher imagination, which is the image-making power of the higher soul that belongs to the thinking of intellect, is not different from the primary indefiniteness of thinking as the indefinite dyad. Moreover, if we take into consideration that the imagination is the power of the soul that not only produces but also retains memories and images as a material substrate (see Chapter 5), we may conclude that there is no real difference between intelligible matter and the higher imagination. The dyad and the imagination may then be considered the same because they both represent the same intelligible matter, but they are different only insofar as the objects of the intellect are forms that reside in the intelligible, whereas the objects of the two imaginations are intermediary entities of double and mixed—intelligible and sensible—origin.

But if the two imaginations—the higher and the lower—are not the same yet are not really different, can this also be said about the two matters? In Plotinus, one cannot speak of two different matters. For first, matter is not a definite subject with a number of distinctive predicates that might make it different from another subject. Intelligible matter is not a form because, as dyad, it needs to be defined by the form, and bodily matter is not a mere nothing as a lack of potentiality but can be the source of evil. And, second, before the intelligible cosmos comes to be, there is not even a principle or source of distinction.

---

[31] Blumenthal suggests that the two kinds of imagination corresponding to two different levels of soul are the one between sense-perception and reason and the other subsensitive. See Blumenthal, *Plotinus' Psychology*, pp. 89–95; and H. J. Blumenthal, "Plotinus' Adaptation of Aristotle's Psychology: Sensation, Imagination and Memory," in *The Significance of Neoplatonism*, ed. R. Baine Harris (Norfolk, VA: International Society for Neoplatonic Studies, 1976), pp. 41–58, esp. 51–5. See, however, the convincing criticism by Emilsson, *Plotinus on Sense-Perception*, p. 108.

Therefore, intelligible matter cannot be different from bodily matter at this stage. Perhaps, then, they become distinct later, when the intelligible forms arise? Yet the appearance of τὰ νοητά does not change anything in the nature of matter nor in the relation of the intelligible to the bodily matter. Hence, they cannot be considered different. This is why for Plotinus matter "must not be composite, but simple and one thing in its nature" (*Enn.* II.4.8.13–4), so that matter "keeps [φυλάττει] its own nature" (*Enn.* III.6.18.19; cf. III.6.10.21–2, III.6.11.36–7).

Yet, despite not being different, the two matters cannot be the same either. For, first, in the absence of forms, as it is impossible to judge about difference, it is equally impossible to make a judgment about sameness since there is no principle of sameness either in the not formed matter or in the one that is beyond sameness and otherness. Plotinus speaks about the "nature" (φύσις) of matter, but this nature is the principle (ἀρχή) of becoming that "infects with its own evil that which is not in it but only directs its gaze to it" (*Enn.* I.8.4.20–2; see Chapter 11). The "nature" of matter has no identity and thus cannot be characterized in terms of sameness because, properly speaking, it receives nothing but remains a pure possibility for the form to be expressed in it (*Enn.* III.6.14.29). Matter's identity is in its being always non-identical.

And, second, explaining the non-identity of the two matters, Plotinus argues:

> in the intelligible world the composite being [σύνθετον] is differently constituted, not like bodies, since forming principles are also composite and by their actuality make composite the nature that is active toward the production of a form.... The matter of the things that came into being always receives different forms, but the matter of eternal things is always the same and always has the same form. With matter here, it is rather exactly the other way around. For here it is all things in turn and only one thing at each particular time, so nothing lasts because one thing pushes out another, so it is not the same forever. (*Enn.* II.4.3.5–13)

The two matters may be said to be in a proportion to each other: the relation of intelligible matter as an "*as if*" form of the bodily matter corresponds to the relation (or proportion) of the form to the bodily matter as χώρα. However, intelligible matter is not a form in the proper sense because it is only the potentiality of the forms.

Thus, paradoxically, we cannot consider matter as one, but we cannot consider intelligible and bodily matter as different either. Therefore, matter should be recognized as fundamentally ambiguous. Moreover, ambiguity may be found even in intelligible matter, to the extent that it is represented not only as the indefinite dyad but also as imagination, which, in turn, is double as directed toward both the intelligible and the sensible.

6.5 Matter and Otherness

Matter may thus be characterized in the opposite terms. It may be said to be both the same and not the same, both one (in its nature) and double (as two matters). This appears to violate the law of noncontradiction: τὸ γὰρ αὐτὸ ἅμα ὑπάρχειν τε καὶ μὴ ὑπάρχειν ἀδύνατον τῷ αὐτῷ καὶ κατὰ τὸ αὐτό (Aristotle, *Met.* 1005b20–1). However, this is not really the case because, first, there is no unity of subject (τὸ αὐτό) in matter, since, properly speaking, matter is not a subject. Second, there is no unity of relation (κατὰ τὸ αὐτό) in matter since matter is one and double, same and different in different respects because, again, there is nothing in matter that could be predicated "in one and the same respect." Third, there is not necessarily a unity of "togetherness" (ἅμα): if "at once" is understood in a temporal sense, then matter is not in time, and, if togetherness is understood as simultaneousness by nature,[32] then it also does not apply for the "nature" of matter is to accept opposites (cf. *Enn.* I.8.8.20), while being itself is not anything definite or defined.

In *Ennead* III.6.10.21–2, Plotinus argues that matter is unchangeable. Indeed, there is nothing definite in matter that could be subject to change. And since unalterability does not mean that matter is identically the same, one cannot even claim that matter is unchangeable.

Matter may be described, then, in mutually exclusive terms without violating the principle of contradiction. For Plotinus, "for matter, being is being as matter" (τὸ εἶναι τῇ ὕλῃ ἐστὶ τὸ εἶναι ᾗ ὕλη, *Enn.* III.6.10.25). Yet this "being as matter" is profoundly paradoxical since it means "being different from everything else," even from itself since matter has no sameness or identity. Moreover, being different also means being different and other than being. Hence, "being as matter" is nothing else than "truly not being" (III.6.7.2.11).[33] Because matter's "being" consists in non-being, this non-being should be taken as being, which is, in turn, non-being, and so on. This appears as a kind of reflexivity in matter, an empty mirroring in and by a mirror that does not properly exist, which, however, is not really a reflexivity because, unlike the intellect that is being and reflects itself as being, matter does not turn upon itself since, as said, there is no identical "self" in it.

Hence, paradox is deeply inherent in matter. It is not by chance that matter is repeatedly characterized in paradoxical and mutually exclusive terms: it "appears to be filled, but contains nothing" (*Enn.* III.6.7.26; cf. III.6.1.36),

---

[32] Cf. Paul Vincent Spade, "Quasi-Aristotelianism," in *Infinity and Continuity in Ancient and Medieval Thought*, ed. Norman Kretzmann (Ithaca: Cornell University Press, 1982), pp. 297–307; and Norman Kretzmann, "Continuity, Contrariety, Contradiction, and Change," in *Infinity and Continuity in Ancient and Medieval Thought*, pp. 270–96.

[33] Cf. Fleet, *On the Impassivity of the Bodiless*, pp. 199–200.

"follows... while not really following" (*Enn.* III.6.15.31–2), and is "static without being stable (*Enn.* III.6.7.14). In matter there is "the apparent presence of a kind of image that is not really present" (*Enn.* III.6.12.26–7). Matter may even be said to be both generated and not generated (see Chapter 11). And yet, such paradoxically mutually exclusive descriptions of matter are not meaningless because, as said, the law of noncontradiction does not apply to matter. Therefore, matter always presents opposite appearances (τὰ ἐναντία . . . φανταζόμενον, *Enn.* III.6.7.16–7; cf. VI.3.12.2–6) but is not affected by the opposites because they are not really present in matter. Matter may be described, then, as small and great (μικρὸν καὶ μέγα, *Enn.* III.6.7.16; cf. VI.3.12.3; VI.6.3.29), less and more, deficient and superabundant (see Chapter 2).

Commenting on *Ennead* III.6.10.19, Fleet claims that "matter has no accidental properties."[34] Yet "not having accidental properties" itself is not an accidental property. What, then? It is not an essential property (like that of unlimitedness, inalterability, etc.) because matter is not a subject in the proper sense and thus has no essence. Matter cannot be characterized in terms of accidental/essential properties. In fact, every judgment "misses" matter as its object (as matter itself "misses" its object, first as the dyad when turning back to the one, and then missing the intelligible and bodily things) since matter is not any particular defined object at all. Matter is paradoxical.

Therefore, it is appropriate to speak of matter in terms of otherness: the distinctive characteristic (ἰδιότης) of matter "is not something other than what it is; it is not an addition to it but rather consists in its relationship to other things, its being other than they (πρὸς τὰ ἄλλα, ὅτι ἄλλο αὐτῶν). Other things are not only other (τὰ . . . ἄλλα οὐ μόνον ἄλλα) but each of them is something as form. But this [matter] would appropriately be called nothing but other, or perhaps others (μόνον ἄλλο· τάχα δὲ ἄλλα), so as not to define it as a unity by the term "other" (ἄλλο) but to show its indefiniteness by calling it "others" (ἄλλα, *Enn.* II.4.13.26–32). For this reason, when Plotinus introduces the notion of separateness (τὸ χωρίς) to characterize not the particular individuality of the forms but rather the fact that they are all distinct (which is their common feature), he says that this separateness consists in otherness (ἑτερότης, *Enn.* IV.4.16.10–1). Otherness, then, is nothing else than the indefinite dyad or intelligible matter as the first produced other to the one. The one is not other to itself. Hence, the dyad and imagination as otherness should be present in thinking about the good: "[W]hen what is other than the good [τὸ ἕτερον παρὰ τὸ ἀγαθόν] thinks it, it does so by being 'like the good' [ἀγαθοειδές] and having a resemblance to the good, and it thinks it as the good and as desired by itself, and as if it had a mental image [οἷον φαντασίαν] of the good" (*Enn.* V.6 [24].5.12–5; cf. Plato, *Rep.* 509a).

---

[34] Ibid., p. 199.

In *Ennead* III.6.17.35-7 we find a rather enigmatic phrase: "what is nothing of itself can also become the opposite through something else, and when it has become the opposite is not that either, for if it was it would be static [ἔστη]." Taking into account everything that has just been said, we can understand this claim as suggesting that matter, which is nothing, always and unceasingly becomes, through something other than itself, other to itself, and then again other to that other to itself, and so on, which means that in matter there is no real reflexivity and no sameness, even as the sameness of otherness.

Physical matter is always not the same (οὐ ταὐτὸν ἀεί, *Enn.* II.4.3.13). This obviously contradicts the previously made claim about matter's inalterability. However, if we take into account what has been said about the principle of contradiction as applied to matter, then we can say that being always other to everything and to itself is compatible with the unchangeability of matter. Being-other is matter's mode of overcoming temporality: bodily matter is always not the same. Yet this not being the same is paradoxically itself a kind of sameness. Intelligible matter is always the same and always has the same forms in it. Intelligible matter is always identical but in its identity, as the indefinite dyad, it is the basis of otherness and multiplicity. But since intelligible matter does not know itself, it is non-identical. Therefore, paradoxically, bodily matter is otherness that is always the same to itself, while intelligible matter is sameness that is always other to itself.

Since matter is not a substance and has no proper essence, its "non-essential essence" is to be other to everything else, other to the other, other even to itself since matter is not anything definite. For this reason, matter is always only a relation, or, rather, is *in* relation to everything else that is other than it is. However, matter is not otherness as such, not a principle of otherness but rather is just "the part of otherness which is opposed to the things which in the full and proper sense exist, that is to say rational principles [λόγοι]" (*Enn.* II.4.16.1-3). Even if radically other to everything existent, matter is not anything definite but is defined by the other to itself. As the indefinite dyad before the double act of definition by the other of the one and by the other of the forms, matter is still not yet definite and defined.

Matter is thus paradoxical and elusive in its nature, which can only be described as radical difference, otherness to everything else, as the other nature (ἑτέρα φύσις, *Enn.* III.6.19.25) and the otherness of nature (ἑτερότης τῆς φύσεως, *Enn.* III.6.15.7).

6.6 The Elusive Difference Between Matter and the One

However, since the one is beyond being and as such is different from anything existent before difference, the one can also be considered other to everything that is. Both matter and the one are thus other to everything else, but are they other to each other? What is their difference and can such a difference be thought or established at all? There are a number of features that both the one and matter share in common. Yet, strictly speaking, none has any features, which is why both can be properly characterized only negatively or apophatically. Matter "is" (is not) anything definite or defined (matter: οὔτε ... ψυχὴ οὖσα οὔτε νοῦς οὔτε ζωὴ οὔτε εἶδος οὔτε λόγος οὔτε πέρας, *Enn.* III.6.7.7–8). All of this be also said of the one. Both the one and matter are ἀνείδεον (the one, *Enn.* VI.7.33.21; matter, *Enn.* II.5.4.12); both are ἄπειρον (the one, *Enn.* VI.7.32.15; matter, *Enn.* II.4.15.10); both cannot be said to exist (the one, *Enn.* VI.7.38.11; matter, *Enn.* III.6.15.27–8).

It is remarkable, however, that even when we enter the shaky ground of thinking non-being, we cannot completely fail to distinguish the one and matter. If there is a fundamental difference between them, then it cannot be brought in by matter because, as said, the difference in and of matter is constituted only negatively (to everything else). So it is only the one that may be the cause of such difference because it is the one that ultimately determines the noetic objects when the indefinite thinking of intellect attempts to grasp it.

(1). The difference is already there in terms of difference itself. Matter is different to everything: "Non-being [in matter] does not mean absolute non-being but only something other than being [μὴ ὂν δὲ οὔτι τὸ παντελῶς μὴ ὄν, ἀλλ' ἕτερον μόνον τοῦ ὄντος] ... like an image [εἰκών] of being or something even more non-existent" (*Enn.* I.8.3.6–9). But the one "is not other than itself" (οὐ γάρ ἐστιν ἄλλο αὐτοῦ, *Enn.* V.6.5.11).

(2). The one is the first, whereas intelligible matter is intermediary, and bodily matter is something ultimate and the last (εἶδός τι ἔσχατον, *Enn.* V.8.7.22–3), that after which nothing else may be. Matter is the ultimate non-teleological limit of the procession from the one that is the good: "Since not only the good [is present], there must be the last [τὸ ἔσχατον] in the process of going out past it, or ... going down or going away .... Now it is necessary that what comes after the first should exist, and therefore that the last should exist; and this is matter, which possesses nothing at all of the good" (*Enn.* I.8.7.17–23). Plotinus' argument here is: (I) the one (a) is above being (does not properly exist) and (b) is different from what comes after it; therefore, that which comes after the one should be either (i) being or (ii) somehow participate in being, and thus is said to exist in a way. (II) Matter comes after the one (it is the last and the least after the one as the first); therefore, matter should be existing in certain sense, and yet, it does not properly exist. However, (a) and (b) are equally applicable to matter. The main difference between the one and matter, then, is that matter comes second (as the dyad), but the one does not come or proceed and is thus the first, both logically in the order of procession and as the principle of everything existent.

(3). The one is the good and is the source of light, whereas matter is evil (*Enn.* I.8.7.11–2) and darkness as the privation of light (σκοτεινὴ πᾶσα, *Enn.*

II.4.5.7–9). Matter is the lack of goodness, "a sort of sediment [dregs] of the prior realities, bitter and embittering" (*Enn.* II.3.17.23–4).[35] Matter as evil has to be distinct from the one since there is no evil either in the one as the source of being, nor in being or the intellect. So if evil exists, it exists among the non-existent, in matter as a kind of form of non-existence (εἶδός τι τοῦ μὴ ὄντος, *Enn.* I.8.3.4–5).

(4). Finally, the potentiality of matter is different from the potentiality of the one, even if, again, this difference is established prior to difference and differentiation. The one is the infinite, "unspeakably great" power of everything, δύναμις τῶν πάντων that never becomes everything: it is always absent from anything other than itself (see Chapter 1). Only a certain "trace" of the one is in every thing, as its oneness, uniqueness, or individuality. On the contrary, matter as negative potentiality that by itself is never actualized (*Enn.* II.5.4.3–18) is not power (*Enn.* III.6.7.9) but only a "promise," is always present to everything, to the extent that all things, even the intelligible objects, are associated with matter. The one is thus always absent in its presence, whereas matter is present in its absence.

6.7 Matter and Movement

Finally, otherness is present in intelligible matter in the form of movement. Intelligible matter can be considered as both produced and not produced, although in different respects, which again reflects its inherent paradoxicality. Intelligible matter is produced as coming after the one, as the first yet indefinite being of the thinking that is not yet defined by thinking its objects that it procreates in (re)turning to the unreturnable one. But intelligible matter can also be considered as not produced since it is generated not in time but before time comes to be in the soul (see Chapter 3). Because the intelligible matter is intelligible, the question whether it is eternal (ἀίδιος) amounts to the question of whether the forms are such. And the intelligible objects

> are originated insofar as they have a beginning, but not originated because they have a beginning not in time; they always depend on the other, not as always coming into being, like the universe [ὁ κόσμος], but as always existing, like the universe there [ὁ ἐκεῖ κόσμος]. For otherness there exists always [ἡ ἑτερότης ἡ ἐκεῖ ἀεί], which produces [intelligible] matter; for this is the principle of matter, this and the primary movement [ἡ κίνησις

---

[35] The term Plotinus uses to characterize matter here as "bitter" (πικρά) appears to be a Chaldean reminiscence. See John Dillon, "Plotinus and the Chaldean Oracles," in *Platonism in Late Antiquity*, ed. Stephen Gersh and Charles Kannengiesser (Notre Dame: University of Notre Dame Press, 1992), pp. 131–40, esp. 139–40.

ἡ πρώτη]. For this reason, movement too was called otherness, because movement and otherness sprang forth [ἐξέφυσαν] together.[36] The movement and the otherness that came from the first are indefinite [ἀόριστον], and need the first to define them; and they are defined when they are turned to it [ἐπιστραφῇ]. But before [the turning], matter too was indefinite and the other and not yet good, but unilluminated from the first. For if light comes from the first, then that which receives the light, before it receives it has everlastingly no light; but it has light as other than itself, since the light comes to it from something else. (*Enn.* II.4.5.24–37)

This argument, first, supports the previous discussion of intelligible matter as the indefinite dyad: before turning back to the one, intelligible matter is indefinite and thus is not yet defined. And, second, matter is again portrayed as radical otherness, as other to everything, even to itself, which, however, is not the principle of otherness. At this point, Plotinus brings in another concept into his analysis of matter as otherness, that of primary movement. Plotinus might be referring here to Plato's account of five μέγιστα γένη (being, motion, rest, sameness, and otherness) in the *Sophist* (*Soph.* 254D–257B; see Chapter 3). Otherness and movement represent non-identity and non-rest that stand for the lack of definiteness and stability in matter. However, Plato argues that movement and otherness are mutually irreducible because movement participates both in sameness and otherness (Plato, *Soph.* 255A–B, 256A–B). Indeed, if movement were change in a broader sense, it would have changed otherness into sameness and thus make otherness other to itself. But otherness necessarily presupposes sameness since there is no otherness without sameness and vice versa. Similarly, there is no movement without rest and no rest without movement, but the two mutually presuppose each other.

This reasoning can be applied to matter as well. For when the one produces intelligible matter as the indefinite dyad, it thereby also produces both otherness and sameness as inseparable but not yet defined as sameness and otherness until there is the first "movement" of the intellect's return to the one that is at "rest." Hence, on the one hand, otherness and movement are not identical because, first, there is not yet any sameness before turning back to the one and the production of the noetic cosmos by the indefinite thinking. And, second, otherness and movement express different moments in the relation of intelligible matter to the one: otherness is constituted by πρόοδος, while primary movement is constituted by ἐπιστροφή, although movement is always present in the otherness and otherness is present in movement. On the other hand, otherness and primary movement are not really different because both stand for change into something else, and neither have identity,

---

[36] Cf. Aristotle, *Phys.* 201b16–26.

which—paradoxically—constitutes their non-identical "identity." For this reason, Plotinus turns to both otherness and primary movement to characterize matter.

And yet, in intelligible matter as the potentiality for multiplicity there can be no real separation of otherness/movement from sameness/rest because the one is bound with many in the intelligible matter as imagination without mediation, as one-many, and thus can be imagined as either one or as other (as many). Plotinus provides a remarkable argument in support of this claim: since the first after the one is

> infinite, and infinitely and indefinitely infinite [ἄπειρος καὶ ταῦτα ἀπείρως καὶ ἀορίστως], it could be imagined [φαντασθείη] as either.... But if you approach any of it as one, it will appear many; and if you say that it is many, you will be wrong again: for each [part] of it is not one, all of them cannot be many. And this nature of it according to one and the other of your imaginations [φαντασμάτων] is movement, and, according as imagination [φαντασία] has arrived at it, rest. And the impossibility of seeing it by itself is movement from intellect and slipping away; but that it cannot run away but is held fast from outside and all around and is not able to go on, this would be its rest; so that it is only in motion. (*Enn.* VI.6.3.32–43)

In other words, intelligible matter presupposes motion in the intelligible.[37] Yet because matter is otherness, the primary movement does not "stand still" (*Enn.* VI.6.3.23) but returns to rest, which goes back to movement, and so on. This incessant turning of movement into rest and rest again into movement occurs without mediation and outside of temporality since time does not yet exist.

The primary movement is thus necessarily connected with intelligible matter and imagination.[38] Imagination, then, is capable of originating "movement that starts from imagination of the sensible, or even without imagination [παρ' αὐτοῦ γενομένου τοῦ κινήματος ἐκ τῆς φαντασίας τῆς αἰσθητικῆς ἢ καὶ ἄνευ φαντασίας]" (*Enn.* III.6.4.44–6). In his commentary to this passage, Fleet comes up with a plausible suggestion that ἄνευ φαντασίας "must mean 'without any such (externally produced) impression.'"[39] This means that Plotinus recognizes that both kinds of imaginations—the one dealing with the sensible and the other with the intelligible—are capable of originating

---

[37] Cf. Aristotle, *De an.* 428b11 (ἡ ... φαντασία κίνησίς τις), 429a1–2. See Nikulin, *Matter, Imagination, and Geometry*, pp. 239–45.

[38] Cf.: "All things that change have matter, but different things have different kinds; and of eternal things such as are not generable but are movable by locomotion have matter, matter, however, which admits not of generation, but of motion from one place to another" (Aristotle, *Metaphysics*, trans. Hugh Tredennick [Cambridge, MA: Harvard University Press, 1935], vol. 2, 1069b24–6).

[39] Fleet, *On the Impassivity of the Bodiless*, p. 132.

movement. This implies, once again, that intelligible matter and imagination are closely connected, this time through the primary movement.

For this reason, Plotinus finds it possible to describe the non-physical movement as the movement of the formative principle-λόγος in the imagination-φαντασία:

> The soul that contains the forms of real beings, is itself a form, and contains them all gathered together, and each form is gathered together in itself; and when it sees the forms of things perceived by the senses as it were turning back towards it and approaching it, it does not bear to receive them with their multiplicity, but sees them stripped of bulk; for it cannot become anything else than what it is. . . . that which proceeds from the rational principle in the higher world has already a trace [ἴχνος] of what is going to come into being, for when the rational principle is moved in a sort of picture-making imagination [ἐν φαντασίᾳ εἰκονικῇ κινούμενος ὁ λόγος], either the movement which comes from it is a division [μερισμός], or if it remained the same, it would not be moved but stay as it was; and matter, unlike soul, is not able to harbor all things together; otherwise, it would belong to the intelligible world; it must certainly receive all things, but not receive them undivided [μὴ ἀμερῶς]. (*Enn*. III.6.18.24–37)

Movement in matter makes a thing appear "part by part," in a certain sequential order, which may take place not only in the bodily matter but in the intelligible matter as well. The latter kind of movement takes place not in the physical cosmos but in the intelligible matter in the soul, which moves λόγος that thus becomes imaginable. In the order of the procession from the one, soul is the weaker and more partial representation of the intellect. Hence, in the soul, the whole of the communication (κοινωνία) of the forms in the intellect is broken and becomes fragmented and discursive. The soul has all the forms all together (ὁμοῦ πάντα, *Enn*. III.6.18.25), like the intellect, but needs to trace them discursively and in an order. Since the soul comes after the intellect, which is associated with intelligible matter, the soul, too, is connected with intelligible matter. Therefore, the movement of the rational principle takes place in the imaginary "space" that is imagination as intelligible matter.

The rational principle, then, is moved (κινούμενος) in imagination and by its very movement λόγος brings division (μερισμός) and distinction in the previously undivided and unified thinking of the intellect, in the "space" of imagination in the soul (*Enn*. III.6.18.33–7; see Chapter 8).[40] In the νόησις of the intellect, the form is always what it is. But in the διάνοια of the soul, the

---

[40] In this respect, Plotinus disagrees with Aristotle, who argues that "when we contemplate, we must contemplate [θεωρεῖν] the image [φάντασμα] as one [or: at the same time, ἅμα] because images are like objects of perception except that they lack matter" (Aristotle, *De an*. 432a8–10).

object (e.g., a geometrical figure) can be thought of as a whole, but it may be also considered as produced or constructed by the primary movement in the imagination as the intelligible matter. In this way, the rational principle may be considered as moving and thus tracing or "drawing" its object in the intelligible matter, which allows such imaginary sequential appearance to the extent that matter represents not only sameness but also otherness as non-being (*Enn.* I.8.3.6–9, III.6.7.11).[41]

Plotinus is thus consistent throughout his writings in maintaining that matter is present not only in the physical but also in the noetic, that intelligible matter is connected with the imagination, and that intelligible matter and the imagination presuppose the primary movement that allows for the construction of the objects within the imagination.

---

[41] See Fleet, *On the Impassivity of the Bodiless*, pp. 170–1; and Kalligas, *The Enneads of Plotinus: A Commentary*, vol. 1, p. 228.

PART II

Proclus

7

The Many and the One

Philosophical consideration of the relation of the one to the many constitutes the core of Platonic philosophy. A seemingly simple project that involves only two principles or elements becomes refined and sophisticated in its logical and ontological analysis, resulting in elaborate and sophisticated Neoplatonic philosophical systems (see Chapter 1). Beginning with Plato's *Parmenides*, henological thinking finds its great systematic completion in Proclus' *Platonic Theology*. In what follows, I will first trace the insightful and detailed arguments concerning the relation of the one and the many as presented in the first three chapters of *Theologia Platonica* II (*Theol. Plat.* II 1.3.12–14.16).[1] I will then turn to the discussion of Proclus' implicit presuppositions behind these arguments.

1. Let us assume that only many is, that beings are many (πολλὰ τὰ ὄντα) and not one (ἕν, *Theol. Plat.* II 1.4.8–9.5). Yet, this is impossible for the following reasons.
    1.1. If many exists in some way, everything that constitutes the many is something that should be one. But if one does not exist, every constituent cannot be one and thus the many cannot be as being comprised by its constituents, none of which is one. Hence, in the absence of one the many cannot be (*Theol. Plat.* II 1.4.8–21).
    1.2. In the absence of one, the many will be infinitely infinite (ἀπειράκις ἄπειρα), and as such will be its every constituent. But this is impossible because, first, infinity is ungraspable and unknown (τὸ ἄπειρον ἄληπτόν ἐστι καὶ ἄγνωστον), and, second, the infinity of infinites is more infinite (μᾶλλον ἄπειρον) than a simple infinite (*Theol. Plat.* II 1.4.22–6.2).

---

[1] In what follows, all references to Proclus' *Theologia Platonica* II are to the chapter, page, and line number of the Saffrey and Westerink edition. Numbers in bold refer to the subdivisions of the argument in Proclus' text.

1.3. The law of noncontradiction will be violated because the same beings will both be similar (ὅμοια) and dissimilar (ἀνόμοια) in the same respect. They will be similar insofar as they lack unity due to the absence of the one. But they will be dissimilar to each other insofar as that which lacks unity cannot be considered identical to anything else, especially if that other equally lacks unity. Hence, there is neither a similarity to the other, nor an identity to oneself, in which case everything should be the other to itself (*Theol. Plat.* II 1.6.3–18).

1.4. Similarly, the many will be both identical (ταὐτά) and non-identical (ἕτερα): identical insofar as they lack unity or oneness and non-identical insofar as that which lacks unity cannot be identical either to the other, or to itself (*Theol. Plat.* II 1.6.19–7.7).

1.5. Again, the many will be both moving (κινούμενα) and unmoved (ἀκίνητα). They will be moving because, otherwise, they would have been in the same place or in the same form, thus exemplifying unity, which is impossible by assumption. On the other hand, they also will be stable because, otherwise, a not-one would have changed into a one, which is contrary to the assumption (*Theol. Plat.* II 1.7.8–8.4).

1.6. There will be no number of beings because there will be no number at all since number is constituted by its part (μόριον), by the monad (μονάς), which is one, which is again contrary to the initial assumption (*Theol. Plat.* II 1.8.5–8.14; cf. Aristotle, *Met.* 1001a26–7).

1.7. Finally, there will be neither argument, speech, or account (λόγος), nor knowledge (γνῶσις) of beings because, in order to be complete and to have sense, the former is constituted as one out of many, while the latter presupposes the unity of the knower to the known (and the unity of each of them), which is impossible in the absence of one (*Theol. Plat.* II 1.8.15–9.2).

Therefore, many cannot exist without one or multiplicity cannot be without unity.

2. Let us now assume that there is only one in beings and not many (*Theol. Plat.* II 1.9.5–11.25). But this is also impossible for the following reasons (here Proclus mostly follows the second hypothesis of the *Parmenides* [142B–155E]).

2.1. There will be neither whole (ὅλον), nor parts (μέρη) in all beings (τῶν ἁπάντων) because the whole has parts and parts are many (*Theol. Plat.* II 1.9.5–11).

2.2. There will be neither beginning (ἀρχή), nor middle (μέσον), nor end (τελευτή) of anything because that which has these has parts is thus many and not one, which is impossible by the assumption (*Theol. Plat.* II 1.9.12–5).

2.3. There will be no figure (σχῆμα) in beings because any figure has parts, which is impossible by **2.1** (*Theol. Plat.* II 1.9.16–21).

2.4. A being will be neither in itself (ἐν αὐτῷ), nor in the other (ἐν ἄλλῳ). In the former case, a being should both embrace itself and be embraced by itself, which is already a duality, or many. In the latter case, being in the other presupposes distinction from that other and thus equally a duality, or again, many, which is impossible by the assumption (*Theol. Plat.* II 1.9.22–10.3).

2.5. A being will be neither stable nor moving because, in order to be stable something has to be in itself, which is impossible by **2.4**. And movement is possible only under the assumption of the existence of the other, or of the many, which is impossible by the assumption (*Theol. Plat.* II 1.10.4–13).

2.6. There will be neither the same (ταὐτόν), nor the different (ἕτερον): a being can neither be the same nor different to the other (ἄλλο) since there is no other, for otherwise there would have been many. A being can neither be different from itself because, otherwise, there would have been many; nor can a being be identical to itself because such an identity has to be established as an identity to the other (*Theol. Plat.* II 1.10.14–20).

2.7. There will be neither the similar (ὅμοιον), nor the dissimilar (ἀνόμοιον) because to be similar means being exposed to the same affection (πάθος), while to be dissimilar means being exposed to a different affection, which is impossible by **2.6** (*Theol. Plat.* II 1.10.21–5).

2.8. A being will neither be in touch (ἅπτεσθαι) with another, nor be separate (χωρίς) from another because, in the absence of many, there is no other. But a being cannot touch itself or be separate from itself either because this would have made it two and not one, contrary to the assumption (*Theol. Plat.* II 1.11.1–7).

2.9. Finally, a being will neither be equal (ἴσον), nor unequal (ἄνισον) to the other because there is no other. A being cannot be either equal or unequal to itself because, as equal, it would have measured itself (that is, not as one but as many), and, as unequal, it would have been both greater and smaller, which implies being two and not one, contrary to the assumption (*Theol. Plat.* II 1.11.8–17).

Therefore, one cannot exist without many or unity cannot be without multiplicity.

Hence, since two opposites hypotheses, **1.** and **2.**, are both false, Proclus has to conclude that there should be both many *and* one (πολλὰ καὶ ἕν) in beings (*Theol. Plat.* II 1.12.1). Yet Proclus still needs to clarify the character of their relation. In order to do so, he uses the notion of participation. There can be four different cases of the relation between the one and the many: either the many participates in the one, or the one participates in the many, or the one and the many both participate in each other, or they do not participate in each other at all (*Theol. Plat.* II 1.11.25–14.16; cf. *Elem. theol.* § 5, 4.19–6.21). Eliminating the last three cases by the *reductio ad absurdum*, Proclus concludes that only the first case is tenable: that the many participates in the one, that the one is not mixed with the many, and that there is nothing higher (better) than the one that is the cause of the very being of the many (*Theol. Plat.* II 1.14.8–16).

Proclus' discussion of the one and the many in **1.3–1.5** repeats Plato's *Parmenides* (although in the reverse order, *Parm.* 138B–140B) and the arguments in **2.1–2.9** closely follow those of *Parmenides* 144E–151E. It is important to note a remarkably consistent structure in the arguments of the hypotheses of Plato's *Parmenides*, which are based on the initial positing of only two constituents, the one and the many as the other to the one. Within the logical structure of the *Parmenides*, the one and the many are presented as the opposites, and the very number of hypotheses of their possible mutual relationship—eight (2^3)—refers to their duality.

We may introduce the following notations: E for "positing the one"; ¬E for "negating the one"; e for "the one taken absolutely, in itself"; ¬e for "the one taken relatively, in relation to the not one, or the many"; ε for "drawing conclusions for the one"; and ¬ε for "drawing conclusions for the not one, or for the many."

Then the eight hypotheses of the *Parmenides* may be presented as:

I. E e ε;   II. E ¬e ε;   III. E ¬e ¬ ε;   IV. E e ¬ ε;
V. ¬E ¬e ε; VI. ¬E e ε; VII. ¬E ¬e ¬ε; VIII. ¬E e ¬ε.[2]

The logical symmetry of Plato's discussion of the structure of being comes from the initial logical opposition of the one to the many as not one or the other to the one, as ἕν-ὄν, of the second hypothesis of the *Parmenides*.[3] However, the argument of *Theologia Platonica* II 1.3.12 shows no similar symmetry between hypotheses **1.** and **2.** because Proclus not only refers to the dual opposition of

---

[2] Cf. A. F. Losev, "Analysis of the Composition of the *Parmenides*," in vol. 2 of Plato, *Sobranie sochineniy* (Moscow: Mysl', 1993), pp. 499–501.

[3] The unity of the one is cut (κεκερματισμένον) by being into infinite multiplicity. See Plato, *Parm.* 144E.

the one to the many but also introduces a third element that mediates the other two, which is the plurality of beings (τὰ ὄντα), to which the one and the many are referred (*Theol. Plat.* II 1.4.8, 8.5, 8.15). In other words, Proclus has to *already* assume being in the plurality of beings in order to be able to clarify its structure. Yet this is not a *petitio principii* but an implicit recognition of the impossibility of discussing the presupposition of being(s) as different from either the one or the many. In its multiple unity, being is the third, and thus is not the one-many, ἕν-πολλά, but rather the one-being(s)-many, ἕν-ὄντα-πολλά. In this respect, the unitary yet multiple being in Proclus is more Aristotelian than Platonic, similar to the Aristotelian substrate mediating the opposites, in order to avoid contradiction and the violation of the law of noncontradiction.[4] For this reason, the triad is a pervasive structure in Proclus appearing under many different guises.[5]

A closer look at **1.** shows several kinds of arguments: first, from monadic or numerical unity (μονάς) (**1.1**, **1.6**). Second is the argument from contradiction (**1.3**, **1.4**, **1.5**), which is incomplete since, one might add, following Plato, the consideration of being in itself and in the other, as equal and unequal, and so forth. Third is the argument from infinity (**1.2**), and fourth is the epistemological argument (**1.7**) that establishes the impossibility of knowledge and of the expression of being(s) under the assumption of only the many.

However, one might formulate a number of objections to Proclus. In particular, a counterobjection to the argument from monadic unity might be that the multitude in question should not necessarily be a unity within which one may discern either parts (**1.1**) or units (**1.6**). The whole referred to here is a whole of non-being (of matter) that cannot be conceived as a whole. Hence, **1.1** and **1.6** are sound only under the additional presupposition that the multiplicity already embraces unity or is a unity that consists of discrete, countable parts.

In addition, one might object to the arguments from contradiction that **1.3**, **1.4**, and **1.5** are sound only under the presupposition that the law of noncontradiction is violated if the opposites are predicated of one and the same subject in one and the same respect (κατὰ τὸ αὐτό, *Theol. Plat.* II 1.6.20). Yet nothing suggests the unity of subject or of relation (and in **1.5** also the unity of time), especially under the initial assumption of the non-existence of the one in **1**. An additional postulate of such a unity would contradict this initial presupposition that excludes, together with the one, unity of any kind.

Against the argument from infinity, **1.2**, one might object that the infinity that is infinite an infinite number of times is *not* "more infinite" than the

---

[4] Plato, *Phaedo* 102C–105C; Aristotle, *An. post.* 72a11–4.
[5] See Werner Beierwaltes, *Proklos: Grundzüge seiner Metaphysik* (Frankfurt am Main: Klostermann, 1965), p. 48; and Marije Martijn and Lloyd P. Gerson, "Proclus' System," in *All from One: A Guide to Proclus*, ed. by Pieter d'Hoine and Marije Martijn (Oxford: Oxford University Press, 2017), pp. 45–72.

infinity *simpliciter*. This is the case for both a countable set (e.g., the infinity of numbers, or of discrete entities) and the uncountable set (e.g., the infinity of all points on a line, or the infinity of continuum). For $\aleph_0$, the cardinal number (the number of all the members of a set) of a countable set, the set theory proves that the cardinal number of the infinite sum of the countable set is $\aleph_0 + \aleph_0 + \ldots = \aleph_0$; that is, the resulting set will not be "more infinite" than the initial one. In the case of C, which is the cardinal number of continuum, $C + C + \ldots = C$, so that the resulting set will not be "more infinite" than the initial one either.[6] This implies that Proclus' only intuitively established argument about the infinity of infinites is unsound. Aristotle distinguished two kinds of infinity, in numbers and in continuous magnitudes. Both kinds are potentially, and not actually, infinite: numbers are potentially infinite by increasing or addition, by adding another unit to the current one; and magnitudes are infinite by decreasing or division, by cutting any given magnitude into further parts (see Chapter 8).[7] Yet Proclus does not quite explain what he takes the ἀπειράκις ἄπειρα to be, whether it is a set of all the subsets of a countable set or rather an infinite sum of sets, each one being infinite. In the former case, as said, a new set will be "equally infinite" to the original one or will have the same cardinal number. But, in the latter case, a new set will be "more infinite" than the original one: it will have an (infinitely) greater number, so that the argument from infinity will be unsound. For the cardinal number of the set of all subsets of a countable set is C, proven to be $2^{\aleph_0} = C$, which is (infinitely) "greater" than $\aleph_0$. However, in *Theologia Platonica* II 1.5.3–9, Proclus refers not to subsets of the infinite set but each time takes a "part of a part" (τὸ τοῦ μέρους μέρος, *Theol. Plat.* II 1.5.10). This means that this infinite of the infinite number of parts is the infinite sum of infinite sets, which preserves the cardinal number of the initial set and thus invalidates the argument.

The only argument that appears to stand is epistemological argument **1.7**. Here, Proclus concludes that both the one and the many are present in being(s) and that they are not symmetrical since the many depends on the one by way of participation. The one thus differs from the many in the constitution of being(s).

Participation (μετοχή, μέθεξις) may be taken in the following sense: A participates in B if and only if it is due to B that, first, A *is* and, second, A *is A* (A is such-and-such as having particular properties). In other words, the participating is both existentially and essentially defined or caused by the participated. The concept of participation comes from Plato (cf. *Phaedo* 102B) but is not systematically elaborated by him. This lack of elaboration caused Aristotle to criticize participation, which he took to be just a different name

---

[6] Thomas J. Jech, *Set Theory* (New York: Academic Press, 1978), pp. 42–52.
[7] Aristotle, *Phys.* 206a14–8; cf. Proclus, *In. Tim.* I 453.14–21.

for the Pythagorean imitation (μίμησις, of numbers by sensible things, *Met.* 987b7–13). The distinction between causation and participation is not always explicitly stated by Proclus. At times participation appears to stand for causation: thus, participated may be also considered as a cause (αἴτιον, cf. *Theol. Plat.* II 1.14.10–1, 3.23.15–30.26), although not every cause may be considered as a participated.[8]

One might make two observations about a possible distinction and relation between causation and participation. First, in the case of causation, we should always be able in principle to give an account of the *how*; that is, to describe the kind of a cause (paradigmatic, material, etc.). But, in the case of participation, it suffices to indicate a general ontological and epistemological connection of the participating to the participated, leaving aside the question of *how* it happens: the participating *somehow*, one way or another (πῃ), participates in the participated (*Elem. theol.* § 1, 2.1). And, second, the cause may be transcendent to the caused while the participated, even if considered "higher" than the participating, is still somehow present in the participating. As De Rijk argues, the participated transmits the power (δύναμις) of the transcendent cause while keeping "the shared immanent in the participant."[9]

Along with the concept of participation (μέθεξις, μετοχή), Proclus uses the triad of concepts of unparticipated (ἀμέθεκτον), participated (μετεχόμενον), and participating (μετέχον).[10] Proclus establishes the following relations between the three terms: first, the unparticipated is beyond the participated and the participated is beyond the participating.[11] The notion of the "beyond" ("higher," κρεῖττον) designates the extent of the participation in the good (*Elem. theol.* § 12, 14.15–6).[12] Second, the unparticipated is beyond and transcendent to (ἐξῃρημένον, *Theol. Plat.* II 3.30.23) the participated.[13] The

---

[8] See Werner Beierwaltes, "Primum est dives per se: Meister Eckhart und Der Liber de Causis," in *On Proclus and His Influence in Medieval Philosophy*, ed. E. P. Bos and P. A. Meijer (Leiden: Brill, 1992), pp. 141–69; and L. M. De Rijk, "Causation and Participation in Proclus: The Pivotal Role of 'Scope Distinction' in His Metaphysics," in *On Proclus and His Influence in Medieval Philosophy*, pp. 1–34.

[9] De Rijk, "Causation and Participation in Proclus," p. 12; see also P. A. Meijer, "Participation and Henads and Monads in the 'Theologia Platonica' III, 1–6," in *On Proclus and His Influence in Medieval Philosophy*, pp. 65–87, esp. 65–8.

[10] According to Lloyd, one has to distinguish two types of the participated, the separated henads and the immanent participated. See A. C. Lloyd, "Procession and Division in Proclus," in *Soul and the Structure of Being in Late Neoplatonism: Syrianus, Proclus, and Simplicius: Papers and Discussions of a Colloquium Held at Liverpool, 15–16 April 1982* (Liverpool: Liverpool University Press, 1982), pp. 18–42, esp. 26–8.

[11] Τὸ ἀμέθεκτον τοῦ μεθεκτοῦ κρεῖττον (Proclus, *Theol. Plat.* II 1.23.4–5). Cf. *Elem. theol.* § 24, 28.8–20; *In Tim.* I 298.29–31, II 45.27–46.3, II 105.19–20, III 204.18–21; *In Remp.* I 259.14–7, I 271.20–6, etc.

[12] Cf. Carlos Steel, "L'un et le bien: Les raisons d'une identification dans la tradition platonicienne," *Revue des Sciences Philosophiques et Théologiques* 73 (1989), pp. 69–85.

[13] Cf. Proclus, *Elem. theol.* § 23, 26.26; *In Tim.* I 39.30–40.4; *In Remp.* I 90.22–8.

unparticipated produces the participated without being affected in any way.[14] In turn, the participated strives toward the unparticipated, linked to it by an "upward tension" (ἀνατείνονται, *Elem. theol.* § 23, 26.23–4), which, however, can never be reached, realized, described, or expressed due to the absolute transcendence of the unparticipated.

And third, the participated comes from a higher cause (*Theol. Plat.* II 2.23.3–4). For Proclus, productive causes are sovereign, have power and authority (κύρια) over their effects (*Theol. Plat.* II 2.19.16–20; *Elem. Theol.* § 7, 8.1–28). The participated can be considered the efficient cause (ὑφ' οὗ) for the participating that may also be called its preserving cause (ἐν ᾧ, *Theol. Plat.* II 2.22.25–23.2).[15] Through participation, the participated may define only a few, and not all, participating in what they are (τινὸς . . . καὶ [οὐ] τῶν ὄντων ἁπάντων, *Theol. Plat.* II 2.22.22–3; cf. τινὸς ὂν καὶ οὐ πάντων, *Elem. theol.* §. 24, 28.14; and Syrianus, *In Met.* 109.8–10).

It is important to note that the triad of unparticipated–participated–participating constitutes a vertical heteronomical structure in which the relation between unparticipated and participated differs from that between participated and participating (cf. *Elem. theol.* § 24, 28.8–9). One cannot say that there is a relation between the participated and unparticipated except for a not properly describable production and an "upward tension" since, if there were a relation, it could be described by the concept of participation, and thus the unparticipated would have allowed of participation, contrary to the initial assumption.

Being is constituted by the one and the many, yet the relation between the two is not symmetrical since the many participates in the one and the one is participated by the many. Yet, as Proclus argues, in the absence of the many the one is transcendent to being (*Theol. Plat.* II 2.16.22). And, insofar as the one is transcendent to being, it is the principle of being (*Theol. Plat.* II 2.22.18–9) but not being itself because the many is in being, whereas the one "is" in not being (ἐν μὴ οὐσίᾳ τὸ ἕν, *Theol. Plat.* II 2.21.15–6). These three characteristics—unity, not being, and transcendence to being (or the beyond-being to and from which nothing can be added or removed)—characterize the one as the first principle and the unique cause of being (μία ἀρχή, μὴ οὐσία, ὑπὲρ οὐσίαν, χωριστὸν ἁπάσης οὐσίας, *Theol. Plat.* II 2.23.9–12; cf. 22.5–7).

---

[14] Cf.: "πᾶν τὸ ἀμέθεκτον ὑφίστησιν ἀφ' ἑαυτοῦ τὰ μετεχόμενα" (Proclus, *Elem. theol.* § 23, 26.22).

[15] On the different kinds of causes in Plato and Aristotle as expressed in terms of prepositions that were adopted in Neoplatonism, see Aristotle, *Phys.* 194b16–195a3; Plotinus, *Enn.* VI.6.18.18–9; Proclus, *Theol. Plat.* II 1.60.22–61.9; Porphyry ap. Simplicius, *In Phys.* 10.35–11.3. See also Heinrich Dörrie, "Präpositionen und Metaphysik: Wechselwirkung zweier Prinzipienreihen," *Museum Helveticum* 26:4 (1969), pp. 217–28, esp. 217–8; Willy Theiler, *Die Vorbereitung des Neoplatonismus* (Berlin: Weidmann, 1930), pp. 31–4; and a note of Saffrey and Westerink in Proclus, *Théologie platonicienne: Livre II*, p. 117 n. 4. For Proclus, a participated form is both paradigmatic and efficient cause (*In Parm.* 910.26–34; cf. Lloyd, "Procession and Division in Proclus," p. 28).

Therefore, we have to recognize *two* ones: the one participated by the many, τὸ μετεχόμενον ἕν that defines every particular being in its uniqueness—and the one absolutely transcendent not only to being but also to unity and to participation (παντελῶς ἀμέθεκτος, *Theol. Plat.* II 2.22.21; cf. *In Parm.* 1069.5–9). In Proclus' concise formulation, the unparticipated is to be considered the absolute unity, the unique one beyond and prior to the many (ἓν πρὸ τῶν πολλῶν, *Elem. theol.* § 24, 28.18–9), beyond and outside of every differentiation or determination by the many. The participated is immersed in the many: it is already inseparable from the many, is *both* one and not one (ἓν ἅμα καὶ οὐχ ἕν, *Elem. theol.* § 24, 28.19–20), while the participating is *both* the not one and the one (οὐχ ἓν ἅμα καὶ ἕν, *Elem. theol.* § 24, 28.20). Since there is no third to mediate between the one and the many, we can identify the not one with the many, which is then opposite to the not being, or the one. The participated is then the one-and-many, while the participating is the many-and-one. In other words, the presence of the many is greater and prevails in the participated.

Hence, unity, on the one hand, is necessary for being: without unity nothing can exist since being(s) is (are) constituted by the one and the many (*Theol. Plat.* II 3.25.24). On the other hand, as said, the participated one, the one in being, is connected with the many (ἕν-πολλά), whereas the transcendent one, the one by itself (ἓν καθ' αὑτό, αὐτοέν, ἁπλῶς ἕν, *Theol. Plat.* II 1.9.5, II 1.10.19, II 3.26.3, II 3.30.22–4; cf. Syrianus, *In Met.* 45.18–24), surpasses being and multiplicity.[16] But how can Proclus accept two ones without abandoning the concept of unity? The answer may be provided by recognition of the difference in ontological status of these "two" ones. The one by itself surpasses being and thus can neither be thought nor said to exist nor have a concept and can be presented only negatively (cf. *Theol. Plat.* II 5.37.5–39.5)—but the one in being is participated by the many. Once again, we come across the triadic structure of the not participated one beyond being, of the participated one in being, and of the many in being. Here, the relations of the two ones to the many are not symmetrical but are of a different kind. The relation of the participated one to the many is that of participation; the relation of the unparticipated one to the many is that of production. Due to the radical transcendence of the one by itself to the many, this one cannot have any positively describable relation to anything else, to the other because,

---

[16] The two ones, the first as the principle and the second as produced and subordinated, are already known in middle Platonism. Thus, Moderatus ascribes to Plato the following distinction: "the first one is above being and all essence [ὑπὲρ τὸ εἶναι καὶ πᾶσαν οὐσίαν], while the second one that is the really existent and the object of thought [τὸ ὄντως ὂν καὶ νοητόν] he says is the forms" (Simplicius, *In Phys.* 230.34–231.1). On some accounts, this report should be referred to Porphyry; see John Dillon, *The Middle Platonists: A Study of Platonism, 80 B.C. to A.D. 220* (London: Duckworth, 1977), pp. 346–9. The first and the second one are also traceable in Eudorus; see Horn, *Plotin über Sein, Zahl und Einheit*, p. 335.

first, any description presupposes a multiplicity, and second, the very existence of the other implies plurality. Since actuality pertains to being, it necessarily presupposes plurality. However, since the one beyond being is outside any plurality, it can exercise only an unlimited potency, δύναμις (for there is no intrinsic other to limit it), which first produces the participated one, the one of being, that is then participated by the many. Proclus assumes that the produced always comes after and cannot surpass the first principle (*Theol. Plat.* II 2.22.8–9; 23.6–8), which is the originating δύναμις. It is therefore the participated one that brings the many to unity (ἕνωσις, *Theol. Plat.* II 2.18.2–4) or the union with the participated one in being. Since the transcendent one is not actual, it produces atemporally only through its power as pure potentiality that is not limited yet cannot change either anything in the one itself (for it is beyond being) or be diminished or changed in any way (for it is beyond identity). The first produced is the first in the order of being and is the participated one that makes being actual as one-many. And the producing one is the first principle of being that altogether surpasses being and is thus present only negatively in its absence, by dynamically exercising and extending its power to everything that participates in being.

8

Imagination and Mathematics

8.1 The Intermediate Position of Mathematical Objects

The opening sentence of Proclus' prologue to his commentary on the first book of Euclid's *Elements* runs:

> Mathematical being necessarily belongs neither among the first nor among the last and least simple of the kinds of being, but occupies the middle ground between the realities that are partless, simple, incomposite, and indivisible [ἀμέριστα, ἁπλᾶ, ἀσύνθετα, ἀδιαίρετα] and are divisible things characterized by all kinds of compositions and various divisions. (*In Eucl.* 3.1–7; cf. 52.8)

Mathematical objects are intermediate, "in between" partless simple entities and those that have parts and are complex in their make-up. The former, ἀμέριστα, are identified by Proclus as the plurality of intelligible beings or forms; the latter, μεριστά, with physical things that are subject to change. Mathematical things are then as if "in the vestibule [ἐν προθύροις] of the first forms" (*In Eucl.* 5.2), and thus ontologically follow the forms.[1] Mathematical objects, therefore, are more complex than ideas but more precise than physical things.

That mathematical beings are intermediate can be seen in that, unlike physical things, they are eternal and always identical in their properties, yet unlike intelligible objects, they are divisible and extended and are represented by discursive reasoning (*In Eucl.* 3.7–14). As intermediate, mathematical objects thus share certain features in common with both intelligible and physical things but, at the same time, are also different from each one of them. Hence, the uniqueness of mathematical things consists in their being distinct

---

[1] The "vestibule" allegory comes from Plato's *Philebus* 64C, where Socrates speaks about standing "in the vestibule of the dwelling of the good."

from, yet necessarily connected with, both the intelligible and the physical, being and becoming.[2]

That the being of mathematical objects should be taken as μεταξύ, or intermediate between the intelligible and the physical, is a fundamental insight of Neoplatonic thinkers with respect to mathematics. Proclus ascribes this position directly to Plato, although Plato only suggests that mathematics helps in contemplating (θεάσασθαι) being per se (Plato, *Rep.* 526E). Aristotle's *Metaphysics* A 6, however, suggests that Plato recognized the existence of mathematical entities (τὰ μαθηματικά) as intermediate between (μεταξύ) the forms (τὰ εἴδη) and sensible things (τὰ αἰσθητά). According to Aristotle's testimony, mathematical entities differ from sensible things in being eternal and immovable and from intelligible forms in that every mathematical object can exist in a plurality of similar objects (e.g., circles), whereas each form is one and unique (there is only one form or εἶδος of a circle, Aristotle, *Met.* A 6, 987b14–8; cf. 1059b6–7). Ptolemy already speaks in the *Almagest* (6.3–11) about the middle position of mathematical beings. Later, Iamblichus develops a theory of the intermediateness of geometrical objects that probably became the source for Proclus' discussion of the μεταξύ (Iamblichus, *De comm. math. sci.* 9.4–12.17; 55.1–8; Philoponus, *In Nicom.* 2.56: "τὰ μαθήματα μέσα ἐστί").

Ontology and epistemology are closely tied in (Neo)platonism, in that every kind of being is known in a particular way and through a particular cognitive faculty. Hence, mathematical beings are intermediate both ontologically and epistemologically. Ontologically, as said, they exemplify properties of both intelligible and physical things. At the same time, the ontological order is translated into an epistemological one: every object is studied by a particular discipline that involves its central faculty and its set of criteria for knowledge. The knowledge of the "lower," more complex objects potentially paves the way to an understanding of the "higher," simpler ones. Thus, an imprecise opinion about physical things makes it possible to form an image that may assist in the understanding of a mathematical thing, and an image of a mathematical object might help in knowing the intelligible thing in its simplicity. As Plato argues (*Rep.* 522C–524E), the knowledge of mathematical entities might open a way for understanding the forms and being.

Different classes of objects also correspond to different cognitive faculties: the intelligible objects, νοητά, are known by the non-discursive intellect or νοῦς, which considers them as simple, incomposite, and indivisible in and by an equally simple act of thinking, similar to that of vision. Physical, sensibly perceivable things, αἰσθητά, are conceived in their incompleteness, transience, divisibility, and partiality by opinion or δόξα, which may be correct

---

[2] See Dominic O'Meara, "Mathematics and the Sciences," in *All from One: A Guide to Proclus*, pp. 167–82.

but still is always only an unjustified opinion prone to doubt (Plato, *Meno* 97B–98B; *Soph.* 263D; *Phil.* 64A; Proclus, *In Remp.* I 235.13–21). And intermediate mathematical concepts, λόγοι, are subject to discursive thinking or διάνοια, which is always partial in the thinking and representation of its object, moving step by step from premises in a correct logical order to the conclusion.[3] The νοῦς thus knows its objects directly and with certainty, the διάνοια has to justify its knowledge of intermediate mathematical things by using special logical procedures and deduction, and δόξα may get things right but is never sure about the correctness of its representations and their properties.

It is important to note that Plato does not draw a systematic distinction between these cognitive faculties, even if he uses the term "διάνοια," which refers to thinking in general (*Soph.* 263D–E; *Theaet.* 189E). In the *Republic*, Plato distinguishes between νόησις and διάνοια as higher and lower cognitive faculties within the soul, at the same time stressing the affinity of the διάνοια with geometry (*Rep.* 511D–E; cf. 524B). At times, speaking about reason, Plato also uses the term φρόνησις along with that of νοῦς without making a clear distinction between the two (e.g., *Phil.* 63C). In the simile of the divided line (*Rep.* 511B–E), he distinguishes between four modes of cognition: νόησις, διάνοια, πίστις, and εἰκασία, where only the two first correspond directly to the Neoplatonic triple order of cognitive faculties (cf. Proclus, *In Remp.* I 283.26–284.2). Plato might provide hints at the tripartite distinction between intellection, discursive thinking, and sense perception, or νόησις, διάνοια, and αἴσθησις, but he never explicitly formulates it. This distinction becomes fundamental and commonplace in Neoplatonism, particularly in Syrianus, who, in his commentary to the *Metaphysics*, unambiguously speaks about the difference between the intelligible (noetic, νοητή), discursive (dianoetic, διανοητή), and sensible (aesthetic, αἰσθητή) order of beings (Syrianus, *In Met.* 81.36–82.2).

8.2 Mathematical Objects: Numbers and Geometrical Figures

Speaking about mathematical objects, Proclus usually calls them λόγοι or τὰ τῆς μαθηματικῆς εἴδη or simply τὰ μαθηματικά (*In Eucl.* 4.6–7, 12.3–4, 12.14, 16.22). As was said, by situating mathematical objects "between" intelligibles and physical things, he stresses both the affinity of mathematicals with the two, as well as the distinct identity and properties of mathematical objects. A mathematical object may then be called τὴν μαθηματικὴν οὐσίαν, the mathematical being or substance, which are the opening words of Proclus' commentary on

---

[3] In the *Sophist* (263E), Plato famously calls thinking or διάνοια a (silent) conversation (διάλογος) of the soul with itself. Cf. Proclus, *In Remp.* I 262.25–9.

Euclid (*In Eucl.* 3.1). As such, a mathematical object is not only taken in its Platonic sense as intermediate between being and becoming (τὰ ὄντα καὶ τὰ γινόμενα, *In Eucl.* 62.25–6), but also as a substance (οὐσία) in the Aristotelian sense, which allows for mediation between the contrary opposites, such as partlessness and constructibility, simplicity, and division.

By calling mathematical things λόγοι, Proclus stresses, first, that their properties and structure may become explicit in a discursively developed argument, a λόγος. And, second, mathematical objects are conceived by discursive reason (διάνοια), whose objects are λόγοι, in their connectedness and fullness (πλήρωμα, *In Eucl.* 55.18). For this reason, Proclus also calls mathematical things τὰ διανοητά, objects of discursive reason (*In Eucl.* 4.19, 10.23, 62.24 *et passim*). The precision of mathematical forms (τὰ μαθηματικὰ εἴδη) as λόγοι, as objects of discursive thinking and argumentative reasoning, cannot be explained otherwise than by taking them to be the products (ἔκγονα, *In Eucl.* 13.22) of the soul, which it derives from the intellect or νοῦς but not from physical things by way of abstraction. Otherwise, one would not be able to explain the remarkable precision (ἀκρίβεια, *In Eucl.* 12.14) of mathematical objects since physical things are in a state of constant becoming and thus themselves do not have any precision that they might communicate or bestow on anything that is derived from them, being only subject to opinion-δόξα. Therefore, the discursive reason-διάνοια becomes the ultimate "criterion" (κριτήριον, *In Eucl.* 10.16–7, 11.15) for mathematics as the capacity to judge about the properties and constitution of mathematical things.

Yet Proclus is well aware that mathematical objects are themselves *double* in kind: as numbers and geometrical objects that have different properties (*In Eucl.* 6.7–7.12).[4] Hence, the structure of the tripartite ontological and epistemological division—three ordered layers of being and three distinctive cognitive faculties—needs to be rethought and adjusted, which Proclus does in the second part of the Prologue.

The distinction between arithmetic and geometry is already unambiguously established in Plato. Thus, in the *Republic*, he differentiates between arithmetic and geometry by reference to their distinctive objects, which are numbers and figures, rather than by making a distinction between the corresponding cognitive faculties (Plato, *Rep.* 522C, 525C–526D). Later thinkers and mathematicians, particularly Euclid, consider mathematical investigations to be geometrical par excellence, whereas arithmetic rather becomes a part of a symbolic (Pythagorean) ontology (e.g., in Nicomachus), to the extent that numbers stand for being, or a whole plurality of beings in their distinction yet mutual connection and communication. Aristotle, on the contrary, does not

---

[4] See Dominic O'Meara, *Pythagoras Revived: Mathematics and Philosophy in Late Antiquity* (Oxford: Oxford University Press, 1989), pp. 166–9.

make a clear-cut distinction between arithmetic and geometry within mathematics: when he opposes mathematics to theology (first philosophy) and physics, he suggests that mathematics studies those entities that are immovable (ἀκίνητα) and are not independent (or do not exist separately) but are related to matter (Aristotle, *Met.* 1026a6–19; see Chapter 6).

But what accounts for the distinction between numbers and geometrical figures? Proclus finds at least two reasons for explaining the difference between them: (1) all beings, including intelligible objects and mathematical things, are governed by the same two principles, the limit and the unlimited (τὸ πέρας καὶ τὸ ἄπειρον, *In Eucl.* 5.18; cf. 131.21–132.17).[5] However, the effects of the limit and the unlimited are different at different ontological layers: the stronger presence of the limit, the "closer" an entity is ontologically to these two principles themselves. The limit provides stability and identity to an object. The unlimited, on the contrary, is responsible for otherness, which is already present among the forms as multiplicity. In numbers, the unlimited is present in that number can always can be increased by adding another unit, and, in geometrical figures, in their infinite divisibility. The difference between numbers and geometrical figures is already noticed by Aristotle (*Phys.* 207b1–21), to whom Proclus implicitly refers (*In Eucl.* 6.7–19). In particular, numbers can infinitely (indefinitely) increase but cannot infinitely decrease because their "lower" limit is the unit (μονάς). On the contrary, geometrical figures can be infinitely divided because there is no smallest part in a geometrical figure as a continuous quantity. Yet geometrical figures cannot be increased because, otherwise, they would become another object of the same kind but quantitatively different. In this sense, a particular figure is its own limit from "above." Therefore, arithmetical numbers and geometrical figures behave differently with respect to infinite increase and decrease. This means that the first principles of mathematical being are different for arithmetic and geometry, even though these principles are deducible, or come from (τὸ ἀπ' ἄλλων ἀρχῶν, *In Eucl.* 3.12) the first two principles—the limit and the unlimited—that are present in and at work in all things (cf. *Elem. theol.* §§ 90–3).[6]

In addition, (2) all numbers are commensurable: their common measure is the unit, whereas not all geometrical figures are commensurable but may display irrationality (ἄρρητον, ἄλογον, *In Eucl.* 6.21; cf. Euclid, *Elem.* bk. X, def. 3–4).[7] This means that geometrical objects are connected with matter or materiality and that the measure of precision is different in numbers and figures. In other words, there is a certain inalienable otherness in geometrical

---

[5] Iamblichus, *De comm. math. sci.* 12.18–14.17: "τὸ πεπερασμένον καὶ ἄπειρον."

[6] See the discussion in Gerd Van Riel, "The One, the Henads, and the Principles," in *All from One: A Guide to Proclus*, pp. 73–97.

[7] Cf. Thomas L. Heath, introduction to Euclid, *The Thirteen Books of Euclid's Elements*, 2nd ed., 3 vols. (New York: Dover Publications, 1956), vol. 1, pp. 11–3.

figures that cannot be overcome by the sameness of the limit and that makes geometrical things similar to physical ones. It should be noted that the unit in arithmetic and the point in geometry present a problem in that each one, being indivisible, stands apart from other numbers and geometrical entities and may be considered both as a "generative unit" and as a limit with respect to the objects of its kind (cf. *In Eucl.* 85.1–96.15).

Therefore, the very principles in figures and numbers are generically different (*In Eucl.* 33.5–7; cf. 59.7–8). It is precisely this distinction that underlies Proclus' deduction of the Pythagorean quadrivium, where the difference between τὸ ποσόν and τὸ πηλίκον ("quantity" and "magnitude") matches that between numbers and geometrical figures. The ποσόν–πηλίκον distinction, however, is broader because ποσόν refers to the objects of arithmetic (quantity considered by itself) and music (quantities considered in relation to another), while πηλίκον encompasses those of geometry (unmoving magnitude) and astronomy (magnitude in motion, *In Eucl.* 35.21–36.7; cf. Iamblichus, *De comm. math. sci.* 29.22–31.4).

Thus, both arguments that account for the separation and distinctness of arithmetic and geometry as disciplines refer to the difference in the presence and appearance of otherness as *materiality* and *infinity* in numbers and figures. In particular, unlike numbers, geometrical figures are infinitely divisible and are associated with a kind of matter that allows them to be extended and perceived as extended and visualizable.

8.3 Φαντασία and Geometry

Yet what does it mean that geometrical figures can be visualized or "seen?" Physical things are perceived sensibly and seen as bodies. As such, as Proclus argues, they can never be precise; whereas geometrical figures must be perfect (that is, identical in their properties and representations). Thus, a straight physical line is never straight, and a bodily circle is never round, whereas a geometrical straight line cannot be anything else but straight, and a circle is always perfectly round, which follows from their respective definitions or λόγοι. Therefore, sense perception or αἴσθησις cannot be the faculty responsible for the adequate representation of geometrical figures. On the other hand, discursive reason or διάνοια conceives geometrical objects in their properties that follow from their definitions, which are themselves not extended and do not have the properties they describe (or prescribe) in geometrical figures. This means that there has to be a distinct cognitive faculty capable of representing geometrical objects as *figures*; that is, as both extended *and* perfect. Proclus calls this faculty φαντασία, or imagination, which is not mentioned in his initial discussion of the cognitive faculties but is introduced toward the end of the first part of the Prologue and discussed extensively in the second part

(*In Eucl.* 51.9–56.22, 45.5–15).[8] It should be noted that φαντασία cannot be identified with Plato's εἰκασία from the *Republic*, and sense perception or αἴσθησις cannot be identified with πίστις because, in Plato's order of cognitive modes, πίστις precedes εἰκασία (*Rep.* 533E–534A), whereas in his Euclid commentary Proclus suggests that the order of the cognitive faculties is precisely the reverse.

In this way, φαντασία becomes the *fourth* cognitive faculty in the order of νοῦς–διάνοια–φαντασία–αἴσθησις, intellect–discursive reason–imagination–sense perception (cf. Proclus, *In Remp.* II 277.18–9). By placing imagination between discursive reason and sense perception, Proclus directly follows Aristotle's famous discussion of imagination in his *De anima* III 3.[9] That cognitive faculties follow an order and form a hierarchical succession was a common understanding in Neoplatonism after Plotinus. In particular, the order of discursive reason, imagination, and sense perception (διάνοια, φαντασία, and αἴσθησις) was already established by Themistius in his commentary on Aristotle's *De anima* and was later supported by Simplicius.[10]

In Proclus, the imagination or φαντασία becomes responsible for representing and constructing geometrical forms or figures (τῶν γεωμετρικῶν εἰδῶν, *In Eucl.* 57.5; 285.21) and for submitting them to the consideration and study of discursive reason. For this reason, geometry is preceded by arithmetic, just as, within cognitive faculties, imagination is preceded by discursive reason. The imagination, then, is intermediate between sense perception and discursive reason. With the former, the imagination shares the capacity to represent geometrical figures as extended; with the latter, it shares the capacity to represent its object as unchangeable and identical in its properties.

Nevertheless, geometrical figures are represented in and by each of the four faculties, although differently by each. Therefore, (1) a geometrical figure, for instance a circle, may be considered as both one and fourfold at the same time. As a sensibly perceivable physical image (ἐν τοῖς αἰσθητοῖς), a circle is imperfect, imprecise, and thus is not perfectly circular. But (2) a circle exists as a perfectly circular figure in imagination, ἐν φαντασίᾳ, where it is also infinitely divisible (or can be divided continuously into parts that

---

[8] See Annick Charles, "L'imagination, miroir de l'âme selon Proclus," in *Le Néoplatonisme*, pp. 241–51, esp. 241–8; D. Gregory MacIsaac, "*Phantasia* Between Soul and Body in Proclus' Euclid Commentary," *Dionysius* 19 (2001), pp. 125–36; and Alain Lernoud, "Imagination and Psychic Body: Apparitions of the Divine and Geometric Imagination According to Proclus," in *Gnosticism, Platonism and the Ancient World*, ed. Kevin Corrigan and Tuomas Rasimus (Leiden: Brill, 2013), pp. 595–607, esp. 598–600. However, contra MacIsaac, φαντασία is not a type or mode of διάνοια. Together with discursive reason, imagination is *in* the soul, but Proclus never argues that imagination is contained in, or forms a part of, discursive reason.

[9] "φαντασία γὰρ ἕτερον καὶ αἰσθήσεως καὶ διανοίας" (Aristotle, *De an.* 427b14–5).

[10] See H. J. Blumenthal, "Neoplatonic Interpretations of Aristotle on 'Phantasia,'" *The Review of Metaphysics* 31:2 (1977), pp. 242–57, esp. 253–6.

are themselves divisible), formed, and extended (μεριστὸς ἐσχηματισμένος διάστατος, *In Eucl.* 54.8–9). This is a geometrical figure in the proper sense. In discursive reason, (3) a circle exists as a λόγος or εἶδος τῆς μαθηματικῆς, where it cannot already be visualized; is one, simple, non-extended; and is devoid of magnitude. As a λόγος, it is not circular and is present in thinking without matter, and hence its very magnitude is without magnitude, and its figure is without figure or shape (τὸ μέγεθος ἀμέγεθες, τὸ σχῆμα ἀσχημάτιστον, *In Eucl.* 54.6–8). One may say that a circle as λόγος exists as a definition. An example of this would be "a circle is a plane figure constituted by all the points equidistant from a given point," or "a circle is a plane figure constructed by the motion of a point at a given distance (radius) around a given point (center)." As such, a circle is devoid of matter, shape, and extension even though it has distinct parts that constitute its definition. Such a λόγος is neither extended nor circular but still includes all of the properties of a circle that may be shown or demonstrated in various mutually connected and deducible propositions. Finally, (4) a circle exists as a single, unique, and unified form or εἶδος, which is already not a mathematical εἶδος but a concept. Unlike the image of imagination, this concept is not extended and cannot be visualized; but, unlike the λόγος that still has constituents, it is partless even though it contains all of the circle's properties within a simple act of comprehension by the intellect or νοῦς. The νοῦς has everything about a circle "in concentration" (συνηρημένως), whereas soul contains it in an ordered discursive thinking and obtains it "in separation" (διῃρημένως, *In Eucl.* 16.15–6). At each ontological and cognitive level—sensible, imaginary, dianoetic (discursive), and noetic (intelligible)—a circle remains the same circle, yet is presented differently. One may say that each exemplification of a circle offers itself as a clarification and a *sui generis* illustration of the next one, up to the circle whose form is grasped and thought by the νοῦς. Therefore, the form of a circle is not itself circular; instead, the extended and circular geometrical circle resides in imagination.

8.4 Imagination and Materiality

As λόγος, a circle exists as (1) a definition and (2) a set of discursively structured and logically ordered, mutually connected set of propositions that disclose its intrinsic properties. Again, the λόγος of a circle is not itself circular or is not itself a geometrical figure. The extended and divisible geometrical object that exemplifies its properties without aberration (that is, as properly circular in the case of a circle) is present in imagination as a figure, σχῆμα, which is a visualizable "picture" of its λόγος. The perfect yet extended circle that is conceived or "seen" in and by imagination facilitates discursive logical reasoning about the circle and its properties.

It is important to note that a circle in both sense perception and imagination is represented as multiple. There can be any number of physical and imaginary circles but only one circle in discursive reason and intellect since there is only one λόγος (bound by all of its properties that are already there but need to be discovered and disclosed by discursive logical reasoning) and one εἶδος (concept) of a circle. The difference between the dianoetic, imaginary, and sensible representations of a circle is that, as λόγος, a circle is one; as imaginable, it is not one but rather one and many (οὐχ εἷς μόνον, ἀλλ' εἷς καὶ πολύς, In Eucl. 54.9–10); and, as sensible, it is many, both in number and according to the ways in which the initial unity and simplicity of a circle is distorted.

As multiple and multiplied, and as extended and divisible in parts, a circle should then be conceived as existing in a certain matter (see Chapter 6). Here, one must distinguish between physically embodied, material figures, which are imprecise and only remind us of the properties they bear rather than adequately represent them to discursive reason—and figures in the soul, which are also conceived in and by imagination. It is the imagination that becomes a special "place," τόπος, or a particular matter capable of accommodating extended figures (cf. In Eucl. 15.5–6, 51.13–20).

Therefore, as Proclus argues, one must assume the existence of intelligible or geometrical matter because geometrical figures do not exist either in the physical world (where they are all imprecise) or in discursive thinking as partless and pure λόγοι (λόγοι καθαροί, In Eucl. 49.25). It is thus only in mathematical or geometrical matter (ὕλη τῆς γεωμετρίας) that a geometrical figure has parts, is infinitely divisible, extended, but also is precise and undistorted and has all of its properties open to the "gaze" of discursive reason. Only in geometrical matter (κατὰ τὴν γεωμετρικὴν ὕλην) is the point without parts (In Eucl. 93.18–9) and the circle really circular.

When Proclus distinguishes two matters that contain two classes of things, sensible and geometrical (τὰ μὲν αἰσθητὰ τὰ δὲ ἐν φαντσίᾳ τὴν ὑπόστασιν ἔχοντα, In Eucl. 51.14–6), he follows Aristotle, whom he interprets within the context of a Platonic understanding of mathematics. Aristotle mentions intelligible matter as present in mathematical things (ὕλη νοητή) in opposition to matter in sensible things (ὕλη αἰσθητή).[11] Plato, on the contrary, does not make such a distinction anywhere in his dialogues, nor does he establish any distinct connection between materiality and imagination. At the same time, the concept of φαντασία appears in Plato and is distinguished from διάνοια and δόξα (Soph. 263D), although these cognitive faculties neither refer to nor define the various sciences as they do in Proclus.

---

[11] See Aristotle, Met. 1036a9–12. In the critical apparatus, Jaeger suggests that this sentence appears to have been interpolated at a later time.

To sum up, multiplicity is present in and through a circle's extension, divisibility, and materiality. A specifically geometrical matter, then, accounts for both the extension of geometrical objects and their possible incommensurability with one another (irrationality and inexpressibility through a common measure; see Chapter 6).[12]

8.5 Imagination and Motion

The association of an object with matter means that the object remains forever incomplete, that it never "coincides" with itself as determined by its definition and concept or λόγος and εἶδος. Furthermore, materiality also implies a connection with motion, which Proclus recognizes both in geometrical and physical things. The distinction between the two consist in that geometrical motion is productive, insofar as a geometrical figure may be considered as being produced in and by motion. Because mathematical objects, as said, are subject both to discursive reason and the imagination, motion should somehow be present to both of them. In discursive reason, it is the motion of thinking and reasoning from premises to conclusion, whereby a λόγος of a mathematical thing is completed by being unfolded in a number of steps of reasoning and thus clarified in and by means of a proof. This is a "life-giving" motion (ζωτική) that renders a mathematical object alive in the life of the mind (Proclus, *In Eucl.* 18.20–8). In this respect, imagination is a formative "thinking in motion" (ἡ . . . φαντασία νόησις οὖσα μορφωτική, Proclus, *In Remp.* I 235.18–9) that enables discursive thought to come to a stop and arrive at the "recollection" (ἀνάμνησις) of what it already has: namely, the knowledge of the εἶδος of a (mathematical) thing (*In Eucl.* 46.3–47.6; see Chapter 5).[13]

But motion is also present in imagination. Thus, a circle as an image of imagination may be represented in its entirety as existing all at once and present in a single *act* of imagining. Such an image represents the form of a circle, and yet, unlike the form of a circle, it is not simple because the figure as an image of imagination is extended and infinitely divisible. At the same time, a circle in the imagination may be conceived in the *process* of its construction by the motion of one geometrical object (a point) in imagination that traces the circle, which is thus produced by the continuous (not discrete, as in a number of steps in an argument or proof) "flow" of the point (cf. *In Eucl.* 185.22–187.3).

---

[12] For a more detailed discussion, see Nikulin, *Matter, Imagination, and Geometry*, pp. 183–7.
[13] See also Plato, *Meno* 81B–86C; *Phaedo* 72E–78A; *Phaedr.* 249B–C; *Phil.* 34B–C.

Therefore, motion in imagination is motion that may be taken as producing one geometrical object in and by the motion of another (point, line) in geometrical or intelligible matter (ὕλη νοητή).[14] It is in imagination, then, that such kinematic constructions and divisions take place, facilitating the understanding of the properties of a figure by making them visualizable in imagination. It is in imagination as the locus of the forms of geometrical objects that an imaginable figure is constructed, which then can be thoroughly studied and thus be as if returned back to the non-visualizable simplicity of its λόγος and form (*In Eucl.* 78.18–79.2). Hence, this constructive motion in imagination is a kind of production of a figure, which may also generate a whole plurality of its imaginable representations (e.g., many concentric circles from one single λόγος of a circle), which at the same time fully preserves the properties of the geometrical object.[15] It is here, in the intelligible matter of imagination, that a constructed circle is perfectly circular and the halves of a divided line are identical in length.

8.6 Imagination as Νοῦς Παθητικός

Imagination is thus closely connected to a specific kind of body and materiality and with figure-producing motion,[16] by which it can visualize geometrical figures that then can be studied by discursive reason. This allows Proclus to identify imagination with a "passive intellect," νοῦς παθητικός (*In Eucl.* 52.3–12, 56.17–8). In the famous passage in *De anima*, which has produced many debates and commentaries, Aristotle argues that the hylomorphic structure can be found not only in bodily things but also in the soul, so that one should distinguish an intellect that exists on its own and is pure activity from a "passive intellect," νοῦς παθητικός, that becomes everything that is thought (*De an.* 430a10–25). The identification of the imagination with the passive intellect then becomes widely accepted in the Neoplatonic commentaries on Aristotle, particularly in Asclepius, Simplicius, Stephanus, and Philoponus.[17]

---

[14] See Nikulin, *Matter, Imagination, and Geometry*, pp. 245–54; Orna Harari, "*Methexis* and Geometrical Reasoning in Proclus' Commentary on Euclid's *Elements*," *Oxford Studies in Ancient Philosophy* 30 (2006), pp. 361–89, esp. 383–7; and John Cleary, "Proclus' Philosophy of Mathematics" in *Studies on Plato, Aristotle and Proclus: Collected Essays on Ancient Philosophy of John Cleary*, ed. John Dillon, Brendan O'Byrne, and Fran O'Rourke (Leiden: Brill, 2013), pp 201–20, esp. 214–9.

[15] "εἰς ἐκείνην [scil. νοητὴν ὕλην] οὖν οἱ λόγοι προϊόντες καὶ μορφοῦντες αὐτὴν εἰκότως δήπου ταῖς γενέσεσιν ἐοικέναι λέγονται. τὴν γὰρ τῆς διανοίας ἡμῶν κίνησιν καὶ τὴν προβολὴν τῶν ἐν αὐτῇ λόγων γένεσιν τῶν ἐν φαντασίᾳ σχημάτων εἶναί φαμεν καὶ τῶν περὶ αὐτὰ παθημάτων" (Proclus, *In Eucl.* 78.20–5).

[16] "καὶ γὰρ ἡ φαντασία διά τε τὴν μορφωτικὴν κίνησιν καὶ τὸ μετὰ σώματος καὶ ἐν σώματι τὴν ὑπόστασιν ἔχειν" (Proclus, *In Eucl.* 51.20–2).

[17] See Blumenthal, "Neoplatonic Interpretations of Aristotle," p. 255.

Proclus thus uses two key terms to describe Platonic mathematics that are found in Aristotle but are absent from Plato's writings: imagination is the geometrical or "intelligible" matter of and for geometrical figures that coincides with the passive intellect. At first glance, the very term "passive intellect" appears an oxymoron, for intellect cannot be passive because it is pure activity, an *act* (not a discursive process) of thinking that thinks itself. And yet, imagination can be characterized as νοῦς παθητικός because it can be conceived as both active and passive, although in different respects. Indeed, on the one hand, imagination is active (as νοῦς) because, first, it does not distort that which it represents. Second, imagination is productive of images (οἰστική, *In Eucl.* 52.2). And third, it is "woken up by itself" (ἀνεγείρεται . . . ἀφ᾿ ἑαυτῆς, *In Eucl.* 52.22); that is, is capable of self-motivation and thus of a kind of autonomy. On the other hand, imagination is passive (as παθητικός) because it is associated with materiality or matter, which in Platonism is considered as having nothing of its own, no form or being. Matter is always formed and never forms itself, and thus always needs an active external cause to be formed.

Hence, Proclus chooses to use the term "passive intellect" to describe imagination because, on the one hand, he wants to stress imagination's middle position between becoming and being, sense perception and discursive thinking (*In Eucl.* 52.8–12). On the other hand, since cognitive faculties are defined by their objects, the imagination is the faculty that considers geometrical figures, which have the features of both "passive" physical bodies (as extended and divisible) and of "active" thinkable λόγοι (as unchangeable in their properties), and thus are the objects of the "passive intellect."

8.7 Imagination and Projection: Φαντασία as Screen and Mirror

But what is the importance of imagination for mathematics? The task of a mathematician is to study mathematical forms or λόγοι in their various properties and mutual relations. As was said, discursive reason or διάνοια thinks of its object or λόγος as being always and inevitably partial, and, as such, it is distinct from the intellect or νοῦς that is capable of thinking its object or εἶδος as a whole. This means that discursive thinking is a *weak* form of thinking because, although it already has all of the λόγοι, it is incapable of thinking and "seeing" them in their entirety all at once as "enfolded" (ἀσθενοῦσα . . . συνεπτυγμένως ἰδεῖν, *In Eucl.* 54.27–55.1). Therefore, discursive reason "unfolds" or "unrolls" (ἀνελίττει, *In Eucl.* 55.3) that which is enfolded in each λόγος in order to be able to study it in an orderly manner.

Discursive reason has two ways of overcoming its feebleness: by dialectic and construction in imagination, which, at a certain point, converge because the study of mathematics must lead to the study of dialectic and eventually to the understanding of being.[18] Every λόγος is conceived of in and by a logically structured discursive argument that presupposes a number of closely related dialectical procedures (Proclus distinguishes among analysis, synthesis, definition, and demonstration). Dialectic allows the "unfolding" of a λόγος by showing it in its definition and demonstrating its properties (*In Eucl.* 42.9–43.21). Yet, in dialectical disclosure, λόγος is never given in its entirety but rather only partially at each step and moment of thinking, similarly to a piece of music being heard at each moment only in part.

At the same time, διάνοια is capable of representing the λόγος of a mathematical object all at once. Yet, in this case, the λόγος becomes something alien to and different from itself: it becomes an *image* in imagination (τὸ φανταστόν, *In Eucl.* 51.19), which is an embodiment of an immaterial and invisible λόγος in the geometrical or intelligible matter of imagination. Such an image is a *sui generis* painted picture that is accessible as a whole in all of its detail and components at a glance. Everything that is contained in a mathematical form as latent, hidden, "secret," or concealed (κρυφίως, *In Eucl.* 56.13), becomes visible in and through its image in imagination. Such a picture "unfolds" a λόγος, for instance as an imaginable circle, which is a φανταστόν of the λόγος of a circle (of its definition as "all of the points equidistant from a given point"). This image, again, may be realized either as an *act* (of visualizing a circle in imagination) or a *process* (of tracing a circle by the motion of a point in imagination as geometrical matter). As Proclus explains,

> Every true geometer, should . . . make it his goal to wake himself up and move from imagination to pure discursive reason as it is by itself, thus rescuing himself from the extension and 'passive intellect' for the sake of the dianoetic activity that will enable him to see all things as non-extended and without parts—the circle, diameter, polygons [inscribed] in the circle, all in all and each separately. (*In Eucl.* 55.23–56.4)

Imagination thus facilitates discursive reason's study of a mathematical object, which, as form or εἶδος, is unmoved, not produced, and indivisible (ἀκίνητον, ἀγένητον, ἀδιαίρετον, *In Eucl.* 56.12), but which, in order to be studied, has to be "alienated" from itself by being set into (imaginary) motion, brought into an (imaginable) extension, and placed in (geometrical) matter. A "drawing" or σχῆμα of a mathematical entity, then, is a figure in imagination that helps the geometer to recognize it in a physical drawing and further understand it as λόγος with all of its properties and relations to other geometrical entities (e.g., a circle and a right triangle inscribed into it, *In Eucl.* 142.9–12).

---

[18] Proclus explicitly mentions Plotinus, who, in his treatise *On Dialectic*, implicitly referring to Plato's *Republic* 531C–534E, argues that in following mathematical studies one must turn to dialectic in order to become a complete dialectician (Plotinus, *Enn.* I.3.3.1–10; Proclus, *In Eucl.* 21.21–4; cf. 32.7–20).

It should be noted that, in Plato, both numbers and figures are considered and studied according to their properties by discursive reason or διάνοια. As Aristotle mentions in *Metaphysics* A 6, for Plato, it is the ideal mathematical numbers, and not geometrical figures, that are the primary causes of everything existent (Aristotle, *Met.* 987b24–5). In the *Euthydemus*, however, Plato mentions that the mathematician uses drawings (τὰ διαγράμματα, *Euthyd.* 290B–C; cf. *Meno* 73E), which assist dialectical thinking by making visualizable the properties and demonstrations for which it is searching.

This act or process of picture-like "visualization" of a non-extended and indivisible mathematical object or λόγος as a geometrically extended and divisible figure or φανταστόν may be compared to recollecting a novel or film. Reading and understanding a novel is a discursive activity that involves the attentive gathering of the meaning of what is read and thereby undergone, whereas in film the story is represented as a series of pictures and images projected onto a screen. Similarly, in order to understand itself and its contents, the διάνοια must become a painter: it has to *project* or "throw forward" (προβάλλειν) the λόγος onto the screen of imagination, to observe, understand, and study it and its properties (which, despite the simplicity of mathematical form, may be complex), and then bring the λόγος back to itself into its unity, simplicity, non-extension, and indivisibility. The διάνοια, then, is that which projects (τὸ μὲν προβάλλον ἡ διάνοια); that which is projected is the dianoetic discursive form (τὸ δὲ ἀφ' οὗ προβάλλεται τὸ διανοητὸν εἶδος); and that onto which it is projected is the so-called "passive intellect" (τὸ δὲ ἐν ᾧ τὸ προβαλλόμενον παθητικὸς οὗτος καλούμενος νοῦς, *In Eucl.* 56.15–8; cf. 17.4–6).

Now all of the terms of the geometrical screening are brought together: a geometer must look at the images of the mathematical form that the discursive reason unfolds by painting or projecting it onto the screen of geometrical matter or "passive intellect" of the imagination, make all the necessary divisions and constructions in such an image, discover its properties, and then enfold and bring it back into its mathematical form as being already undivided and only thinkable.

Within this logical sequence of the clarification of λόγος, imagination appears as a plane *mirror* (οἷον ἐπιπέδῳ κατόπτρῳ) into which discursive reason "looks" and recognizes itself as that "to which the λόγοι of the discursive reason send down reflections [ἐμφάσεις] of itself" (*In Eucl.* 121. 4–7). Imagination as a *plane* mirror is a kind of "smooth surface" that, unlike the mirror of bodily matter, does not distort the projections of discursive reason that appear on it as geometrical figures.

> [T]he soul, exercising its capacity to know [τὸ γνωστικὸν ἐνεργοῦσα], projects on the imagination, as on a mirror, the λόγοι of the figures [προβάλλει περὶ τὴν φαντασίαν ὥσπερ εἰς κάτοπτρον τοὺς τῶν σχημάτων

λόγους]; and the imagination, receiving in pictorial form these impressions of λόγοι within the soul, by their means affords the soul an opportunity to turn inward from the pictures [ἀπὸ τῶν εἰδώλων] and attend to itself. It is as if someone looking at oneself in a mirror [ἐν κατόπτρῳ] and marvelling at the power of nature and at one's own appearance should wish to look upon oneself directly and possess such a power as would enable one to become at the same time the seer and the seen [ὁρῶν καὶ ὁρατόν]. (*In Eucl.* 141.4–13)

By making its λόγοι external and reflected in the "mirror" of imagination, discursive reason returns to itself and pure dianoetic activity (πρὸς τὴν διανοητικὴν ἐνέργειαν, *In Eucl.* 56.1) by understanding the fullness of the interconnected λόγοι, which are now presented as separate, pictured and "seen" in the medium of imagination and the extension of geometrical matter. In this way, διάνοια turns back toward itself and thus becomes reflective, although its reflectivity is not immediate, as in the νοῦς, but is obtained through the mathematical or dialectical argument (*In Eucl.* 55.23–56.22).

Being capable of reflectively returning to itself, the discursive thinking moves itself. Or, as Proclus puts it, it is moved by itself toward externality (ἀφ' ἑαυτῆς εἰς τὸ ἔξω κινουμένης, *In Eucl.* 55.12–3) in order to eventually come back to itself.

In the process of externalization of its λόγοι, the discursive thinking is the "projector" (τὸ προβάλλον) of their images in and onto imagination. At the same time, it is also imagination that projects or "throws forward" that which is known (προβάλλει τὸ γνωστόν, *In Eucl.* 52.22) and, in this way, sets what it is looking at into motion. This means that *both* discursive reason and imagination take part in the exteriorization and making visible of the otherwise interior (to thinking) and invisible (only thinkable) mathematical forms or λόγοι. The act of production, of "throwing" of that which becomes known into geometrical matter is thus a *joint action* of διάνοια and φαντασία. The διάνοια thus deploys and unfolds its λόγοι not only *in* but also *with* the help of imagination, which means that imagination is not an altogether passive matter of geometrical objects, but, being geometrical or intelligible matter, also actively contributes to the projection and kinematic production of mathematical forms as precise and perfect geometrical figures.

8.8 Imagination and the Infinite

Once a geometrical figure is constructed in imagination as a projection of a mathematical form, it is conceived as definite and therefore as limited. As I have argued, such a construction is achieved by both discursive reason *and* imagination. In fact, Proclus says that imagination *thinks* (νοεῖ) its object (φάντασμα or φανταστόν), which means that it thinks its (geometrical) object by assigning the object both a form (μορφή) and limit (πέρας) "and in knowing brings to an end its movement [διέξοδον] through the imagined object; it has gone through and comprehends it" (*In Eucl.* 285.7–10). In other words, the constructive motion of imagination is finite because it produces finite objects in imagination as geometrical figures and as such comprehends them.

However, in certain geometrical problems one needs to make a construction that presupposes an *infinite* line. Proclus speaks about infinity in its relation to imagination when commenting on Prop. XII of book I, which is a problem that requires the construction of a perpendicular line on a given infinite line from a given point that does not lie on that line (*In Eucl.* 284.17–286.11). Infinity thus comes up in geometry in construction. That a given line is infinite does not mean that it is already given as infinite or that it is actually infinite—but only that it can always be extended further if needed or that it is potentially infinite. The infinite (τὸ ἄπειρον) is thus that which can always be otherwise (bigger or smaller) than it is, that outside of which one can always take something else (Aristotle, *Phys.* 207a1–2; see Appendix). The infinite is then not a particular object or thing, which is always definite and limited. Rather, the infinite is associated with becoming, which in geometry is present in the construction and production of an object (see Chapter 10). Therefore, the infinite should be linked to *matter*, which is indeterminate.

As indeterminate, matter does not have a proper notion, but rather a vague concept that is referred to as "infinite." As Aristotle says, the infinite as matter is unknowable (ἄγνωστον) because matter has no form (εἶδος γὰρ οὐκ ἔχει ἡ ὕλη, *Phys.* 207a26). In other words, matter is *formless*. Similarly, in the *Timaeus*, Plato argues that matter, as the "receptacle" of things, is indeterminate (*Tim.* 50C–53A). In his own account of matter, Proclus follows both Plato and Aristotle: as the "receptacle" and "seat" of things (ὑποδοχή, ἕδρα, *In Eucl.* 15.12–3), matter cannot be determinate or definite (see Chapter 6). Plato, however, does not recognize a distinct matter or "receptacle" for geometrical things. But for Proclus the infinite in geometry should be associated not with sensible things that are incapable of adequately representing geometrical properties (straightness, circularity, etc.), but with geometrical figures. Hence, the geometrical infinite for Proclus must be linked to imagination because imagination is geometrical matter (ὕλη γεωμετρική) and is the locus of projection and existence of geometrical entities.

Where is the infinite present? As matter, it cannot be said to be or to exist. Rather, it appears as a possibility, particularly as the possibility of a figure to be constructed or a straight line to be extended. As Aristotle argues in the *Physics*, the infinite is matter for the completion of magnitude (τὸ ἄπειρον τῆς τοῦ μεγέθους τελειότητος ὕλη) and in its entirety exists only *potentially*, manifesting itself in the divisibility and the increase of magnitudes (Aristotle, *Phys.* 207a21–5). As Aristotle argues (and Proclus accepts his argument), sensible things cannot be infinite because they are limited in their existence, bodily make-up, power, and motion (Aristotle, *Phys.* 202b30–207a33, esp. 204a8–206a8; see Chapter 10).[19] Yet intelligible things cannot be infinite either because they, too, are limited and definite and, qua forms, are the source of definiteness in geometrical figures and their sensible representations. Therefore, the infinite for Proclus can only be present "in between" the sensible and the intelligible. Hence, again, the infinite has to be associated with imagination as an intermediate faculty that represents entities that are themselves intermediate between sensible bodies and dianoetic λόγοι. As indeterminate, the infinite appears in and as imagination, which, as geometrical matter, can become any figure and can accommodate the further extension of a line without it ever becoming actually infinite.

But the situation with the infinite is even more complex because, on the one hand, the infinite as indefinite potentiality is identical with matter as the indeterminate capacity to become anything that a λόγος or εἶδος makes of it. As such, the infinite is non-being: it is nothing of and by itself. Yet, on the other hand, the infinite as indefinite is one of the two principles, the limit and the unlimited, τὸ πέρας καὶ τὸ ἄπειρον, which are for Proclus the very principles of everything, including mathematical entities (*In Eucl.* 5.18; *Theol. Plat.* III 8.30.15–34.19). Therefore, the infinite appears both as non-being *and* as one of the two intelligible, definite, and thinkable principles of being and of everything existent. Providing an explanation of the relation between these two radically different ways in which the infinite is present in and to all things presents a challenge for Proclus: it is a difficult systematic problem that is never addressed in his consideration of mathematics because it belongs to the discussion of first principles, unity, and multiplicity.[20]

How is the infinite constituted and how is it known? The infinite is not an object: it is not a thing that can be known as a particular object of cognition, which should be limited in order to be known. Proclus' answer is that the infinite is known and constituted in its "what" in a purely negative way. The infinite, then, is that which is not thought but rather is that about which imagination is uncertain, cannot decide what it is, and thus cannot define it. Hence, the infinite is that about which imagination "suspends further thinking, and calls infinite everything that it abandons, as immeasurable and incomprehensible by thought" (ὅσον ἀκαταμέτρητον ἀφίησι καὶ ἀπερίληπτον νοήσει, *In Eucl.* 285.10–3). Whatever imagination "dismisses as something that cannot be gone through, this it calls infinite" (ὃ γὰρ ἀφῆκεν ὡς ἀδιεξίτητον, τοῦτο ἄπειρον λέγει, *In Eucl.* 285.18–9).

---

[19] Cf. Proclus, *Inst. phys.*, props. I 12–3, II 6–15.
[20] Proclus mentions henads (*In Eucl.* 142.5–7) as the source of the multiplicity of figures but does this in passing without elaborating the topic much further. See Proclus, *Theol. Plat.* III 5.17.14–19.30; *Elem. theol.* §§ 113–165, 100.5–144.8.

Consequently, the infinite is constituted purely negatively: it "is" what an object of thinking is not and cannot be. Infinity is thus a "missed subject." The infinite is the unalienable other of a limited (geometrical) object, also appearing in and as imagination. The potentially infinite is a possible "construction" by imagination of that which cannot be constructed. It is the mere possibility of going further, of taking another step in the extension or division of a figure.

Such a possibility of always being otherwise is manifested as imagination's "indivisible power of proceeding incessantly" (*In Eucl.* 285.16–7). The source or "foundation" (ὑπόβαθρα) of the infinite, then, is the very boundlessness of imagination (*In Eucl.* 286.10–1) because thinking is definite. It is the "materiality" of imagination that allows an immaterial mathematical form to become "alienated" or "projected" and thus "materialized" in geometrical matter. Metaphorically, "knowing" the infinite is similar to "seeing" darkness in the dark (see Chapter 6). As an activity, seeing exists and is capable of seeing anything, yet there is nothing to see.

Hence, the imagination thinks the infinite by *not thinking* it (*In Eucl.* 285.15), so that imagination "knows that the infinite exists because it does not know it" (νοεῖ δὲ ὡς ὑποστὰν ὅτι μὴ νοεῖ τὸ ἄπειρον, *In Eucl.* 285.17–8). The infinite is thus a very peculiar "object" that cannot be thought, known, or comprehended because it is not a thing; and yet, it is thought, known, and comprehended as such. The infinite, then, cannot be known by itself: "the infinite is altogether incomprehensible to knowledge" (τὸ γὰρ ἄπειρον ὅλως ἐπιστήμῃ περιληπτὸν οὐκ ἔστιν, *In Eucl.* 285.26–286.1) because there is nothing to be known in the infinite except its very indefiniteness, which is not a thing.

Therefore, the infinite is a *hypothetical* object that comes into being without being from the productive power of imagination. The infinite always is by "being-other." The infinite is not actual because to be *in actu* is to be limited, which the infinite is not. The infinite is potential: it is the mere possibility of a geometrical object being extended, divided, or multiplied. Imagination, then, "assumes the infinite not for the sake of the infinite but for the sake of the finite"; that is, for the sake of demonstration (πρὸς τὴν ἀπόδειξιν, *In Eucl.* 286.1–4), in which an always finite line can be extended as needed.

Imagination is thus indispensable for the constitution of geometrical objects in their being, construction, division, and extension and is the geometrical matter into which mathematical forms are projected and where they are studied as extended by discursive reason with the aid of imagination, which then returns mathematical things to the simplicity of forms.

9

Beauty, Truth, and Being

9.1 Verum, Pulchrum et Bonum Convertuntur

The relation between truth and being can be understood not only ontologically and epistemologically but also aesthetically. In Proclus, beauty appears as truth in knowledge and in various aspects of science.[1] In modern mathematics, as Jacque Hadamard has famously argued, beauty serves as an important heuristic device: beauty arouses the "aesthetic feeling" that both accompanies the process of the search and is an indication of the discovery.[2] And yet, since the system of categories in Proclus is complex and subtly balanced, one might ask whether one single category, such as beauty, univocally describes knowledge in its entirety and exhausts the properties of its objects. While accepting the preceding claim about the relationship between beauty and truth in Proclus, I will argue, mostly with reference to mathematics as the exemplary science, that while beauty is the truth in all we know, both are convertible with regard to the good.

Proclus mentions Plotinus a number of times in his commentaries on Plato (e.g., those on the *Timaeus* and the *Parmenides*) but only once in the commentary on Euclid (*In Eucl.* 21.21), when speaking about the beauty of mathematical objects. Most probably, the reference here is to Plotinus' "On Dialectic," which distinguishes between three philosophical types or dispositions: "musician," "lover," and "philosopher" (*Enn.* I.3 [20].1–3). In the

---

[1] See Marije Martijn, "Why Beauty Is Truth in All We Know: Aesthetics and Mimesis in Neoplatonic Science," *Proceedings of the Boston Area Colloquium in Ancient Philosophy* 25 (2010), pp. 69–108, esp. 69–92.

[2] Jacques Hadamard, *The Mathematician's Mind: The Psychology of Invention in the Mathematical Field* (Princeton: Princeton University Press, 1996), pp. 330–1 ("Esthetics in Invention"). In reference to Poincaré, Hadamard suggests that the sense of beauty plays "its part as an indispensable *means* of finding. We have reached the double conclusion:

  that invention is a choice
  that this choice is imperatively governed by the sense of scientific beauty" (ibid.).

Phaedrus, Plato describes the best human lot as a philosopher who appreciates the beautiful, follows the Muses, and is a lover (φιλοσόφου ἢ φιλοκάλου ἢ μουσικοῦ ... καὶ ἐρωτικοῦ, *Phaedr.* 248D), which Plotinus interprets as various characterizations of one single type of philosopher. The "musician" (μουσικός) is moved and excited by beauty (τὸ καλόν). The "lover" (ἐρωτικός) has a kind of memory of beauty and is thus capable of recognizing it in arts, sciences, and virtues (ἐν τέχναις καὶ ἐν ἐπιστήμαις καὶ ἐν ἀρεταῖς, *Enn.* I.3.2.10–1). And the "philosopher" (φιλόσοφος) progresses from the study of mathematics to dialectic, which leads him to the understanding of the intelligible, at which point he abandons the "literacy" of the discursive logical thinking of syllogistic (and mathematical) proofs and settles in the intellect (*Enn.* I.3.4). Proclus mentions exactly the same three kinds of climbers toward beauty in his commentary on Euclid (*In Eucl.* 21.4–13).

In his very first treatise (*Enn.* I.6 [1], "On Beauty"), Plotinus explicitly speaks about beauty, or the beautiful (τὸ καλόν), which is discussed in reference to Plato's famous hierarchy of beauty in the *Symposium* (210A–212A). Here, Diotima/Socrates/Plato describe(s) the ascent through the orders of beauty: one begins with beautiful bodies (τὰ καλὰ σώματα), then moves on to beautiful customs (τὰ ἐπιτηδεύματα), after which one discovers the beauty of sciences (ἐπιστῆμαι; τὰ καλὰ μαθήματα, *Symp.* 211C), and finally reaches the beautiful by itself, the idea of beauty (καλόν, *Symp.* 211D). For Plotinus, everything beautiful ascends through these same ranks and is beautiful by participation (μετοχῇ) in the ideal beauty (*Enn.* I.6.2.13–5). Moreover, for a Platonist, beauty not only presupposes the erotic, cognitive, and ontological ascension, but also implies an order of cognitive faculties, each of which is defined by its corresponding object (of beauty). Thus, beautiful bodies are known by the senses; (moral) customs are known by the senses and imagination, as well as by memory, which includes the immortal memory of virtue (ἀθάνατον μνήμην ἀρετῆς, Plato, *Symp.* 208D; see Chapter 5). Sciences are known by imagination and discursive reasoning (διάνοια) and the form of the beautiful by non-discursive intellect (νοῦς; see Chapter 8).[3]

Νοῦς is non-propositional, whereas διάνοια is propositional (see Chapter 3). Νοῦς knows immediately that a conclusion is analytically contained in the premises, and all the (true) predicates reside in their subject. It is through the mediation of discursive logical procedures and syllogisms, by mathematical proofs and constructions, that we come to the understanding of non-discursive forms (Plotinus, *Enn.* V.8.7.40–1). For Plato, νοῦς *is* truth (ἀλήθεια) or is most akin to it (*Phil.* 65D). The truth of the forms, including that of beauty, is an immediate attendance to them, and, hence, truth is not a

---

[3] See Dmitri Nikulin, "Memory in Ancient Philosophy," in *Memory: A History*, ed. Dmitri Nikulin (Oxford: Oxford University Press, 2015), pp. 35–84.

correspondence but rather a "touch." As Plotinus argues, "in the intelligible, the truth is not correspondence with something else, but really belongs to each individual thing of which it is the truth" (καὶ ἡ ἀλήθεια δὲ οὐ συμφωνία πρὸς ἄλλο ἐκεῖ, ἀλλ' αὐτοῦ ἑκάστου οὗπερ ἀλήθεια, *Enn.* III.7.4.11–2). Similarly, Plotinus argues that beauty itself resides "there," in the intelligible, and comes from there (ἐκεῖ οὖν κἀκεῖθεν τὸ καλόν, *Enn.* V.8.13.22). Therefore, beauty is not only the way the intelligible things are and are known but is also an existential mode of our very being and (self-)knowledge: we are beautiful when we know, and vice versa.

9.2 The Good and Beauty

The ascension along the path of beauty is defined not only by the participation of one ontological level in another but also by the ultimate goal and purpose of such striving. This goal is the universal object of love and desire, the good (ἐφετὸν μὲν γὰρ ὡς ἀγαθὸν καὶ ἡ ἔφεσις πρὸς τοῦτο, Plotinus, *Enn.* I.6.7.3– 4), which is the one, the ultimate cause of everything existent, including life, intellect, and being (ζωῆς γὰρ αἴτιος καὶ νοῦ καὶ τοῦ εἶναι, *Enn.* I.6.7.11–2; see Chapter 2). The good, then, is the most beautiful and is itself the primary beauty (τοῦτο γὰρ αὐτὸ μάλιστα κάλλος ὂν αὐτὸ καὶ τὸ πρῶτον, *Enn.* I.6.7.28– 9). Yet the problem with this primary beauty is that it is not known in and of itself because the one transcends being, and so it cannot be said to be an object of cognition and science. This beauty by itself "is" above being and can be the source of beauty in the intelligible only by *being desired*.

Proclus closely follows Plato and Plotinus in his understanding of the hierarchy of beauty. In his commentary on the *Parmenides*, Proclus assumes that the beautiful (τὸ καλόν) and the good (τὸ ἀγαθόν) proceeds from the intelligible down to all other entities (*In Parm.* 950.31–951.15). By virtue of the good, things exemplify completeness and perfection (τελειότης), and, by virtue of beauty, they are desirable (ἐράσμιοι). This procession corresponds to, and is reflected in, the arrangement of cognitive faculties: sense-perception (αἴσθησις), opinion (δόξα), discursive reason (διανόησις), thinking with reasoning (νόησις μετὰ λόγου), pure thinking (νόησις), and the "unknowable, completely transcendent on its own, and able to be beheld by its own light alone" (ἄγνωστον, καθ' αὑτὸ παντελῶς ἐξῃρημένον καὶ τῷ ἑαυτοῦ φωτὶ μόνῳ καθορᾶσθαι δυνάμενον, *In Parm.* 951.14–5). The grand procession of the good and the beautiful thus begins with the unknowable and superabundant good and beauty that originate the intelligible beauty, which alone can be known in and of itself. Paradoxically, however, we know the unknowable beauty only negatively, in its unknowability, in the good's and the beautiful's complete removal. To know the beautiful in its transcendence is to know it in self-transcending light, present in its absence from being.

Thus, the good for Proclus is always associated with beauty (cf. Proclus, *In Remp.* I 72.9–13). Among the sciences, mathematics always has the good in itself (τὸ ἐν αὐτῇ μόνῃ τὸ ἀγαθὸν ἔχειν, *In Eucl.* 29.1), to the extent that the good of mathematical λόγοι—definitions, reasonings, proofs, and constructions—is a reflection of the good of the forms. Therefore, "in the realm of the truly real, the complete and indivisible good has primacy over the things that are plural and separated (τοῖς ὄντως οὖσι προηγεῖται τῶν πολλῶν καὶ διῃρημένων τὸ ὅλον καὶ ἀμέριστον ἀγαθόν, *In Eucl.* 131.1–2). In mathematical objects and reasonings, the good is present not only in their mutually shared goodness as seen in the consistency of propositions and coherence of properties, but also, similarly to beauty, the good is present in the reflection of the intelligible good, which in turn reflects the superabundant and inexpressible beauty of the good beyond being (cf. Plato, *Rep.* 509B). For this reason, mathematics as one part of theoretical cognition begins with presuppositions and definitions ("hypotheses," ἐξ ὑποθέσεως), and, accepting them as the starting points for reasoning, moves toward the conclusion, whereas the other part of theoretical cognition does not need such presuppositions (ἀνυπόθετον) but strives in its ascension (ἀναγωγή), as its end and purpose, toward the primary good itself (τὸ ἀγαθόν, *In Eucl.* 31.11–9).

Hence, not only beauty but also the good are present to and constitute the objects of knowledge and science. In the *Philebus*, Socrates argues that the good (τὸ ἀγαθόν) is captured by three ideas—those of beauty (κάλλος), symmetry (συμμετρία), and truth (ἀλήθεια)—which all converge and point toward the good in its different aspects (Plato, *Phil.* 64E–65A). The good and the beautiful always accompany each other so that the good is beautiful (Plato, *Lys.* 216D; *Gorg.* 474D). Proclus explicitly criticizes those who deny beauty and the good to science (*In Eucl.* 25.17). One might add that καλοκἀγαθία is the defining characteristic not only of the moral order and virtues in Plato but also of science and knowledge in its entirety, of everything that is and can be known as beautiful *and* good, considered as different by discursive thinking, yet as identical by non-discursive thought.

In the *Theologia Platonica*, Proclus takes on the task of further clarification of the *Philebus'* triad. Here, he takes the triad to characterize being, which is always a mixture (μικτόν) of the limit and the unlimited (ἐκ πέρατος καὶ ἀπείρου, *Theol. Plat.* III 10.40.12). Following Iamblichus (*Theol. Plat.* III 11.44.2–5), Proclus reorders the triad as beauty (κάλλος, καλόν)–truth (ἀλήθεια, τὸ ἀληθές)–symmetry (συμμετρία), where beauty is necessary for order (τάξις) and intelligible being, truth is necessary for purity (καθαρότης) of thought and being and for real being (τὸ ὄντως εἶναι), and symmetry is necessary for the union and communication of being (ἕνωσις, κοινωνία, *Theol. Plat.* III 11.43.1–44.20). This triad converges on, and is defined by, the good as the limit of all being before being (πρὸ τοῦ ὄντος, *Theol. Plat.* III 11.44.13). All beings, then, remain "in the vestibule of the good" (ἐν προθύροις εἶναι τοῦ ἀγαθοῦ, *Theol. Plat.* III 11.44.9; cf. Plato, *Phil.* 64C), strive toward it, and thus realize their own good in being and thinking, although they never attain to the good itself. The good is the ultimate object of desire (ἐφετόν) of all beings, and, hence, it is the beauty in and by itself and the cause of all beauty (αὐτοκαλόν, τὸ πρῶτον κάλλος, αἴτιον . . . τῶν καλῶν, *Theol. Plat.* III 11.44.14–6; cf. [Plato], *Ep.* II, 312E). As such, the good can be considered the ultimate transcendent *measure* of all things (πάντων χρημάτων μέτρον, Plato, *Legg.* 716C; cf. Protagoras B1 DK), to which they strive and aspire. This measure is the one beyond, above, and before being. Of the three aspects of being—beauty, truth, and symmetry—it is thus beauty that reflects the good as the beautiful in itself, whereas symmetry points toward the good as the transcendent one.

9.3 Order, Symmetry, Definiteness

Mathematics plays a special role in the knowledge of being. For Proclus, the beauty of the objects of science and knowledge (ἐπιστήμη) is exemplified primarily in mathematical objects: the beauty and the order of mathematical λόγοι (τὸ . . . κάλλος καὶ ἡ τάξις τῶν ἐν μαθηματικῇ) bring us in contact with the intelligible (*In Eucl.* 20.27–21.2). In a seminal discussion that establishes the properties of such objects (*In Eucl.* 26.10–27.16), Proclus refers to a passage in Aristotle's *Metaphysics* (1078a31–b5). Here, Aristotle argues that mathematics primarily speaks about the good and the beautiful since it shows, or demonstrates, the ἔργα (properties) and λόγοι (coherent reasonings, proofs, and definitions) of those things that are good and beautiful. The good, then, is mainly present in action (ἐν πράξει), whereas beauty is in immovable objects (ἐν τοῖς ἀκινήτοις, Aristotle, *Met.* 1078a31–2). Following Aristotle, Proclus takes mathematics to confer not only utility (ἡ ὠφέλεια) but also good (τὸ ἀγαθόν) upon those who study it (*In Eucl.* 49.1–4). One might understand Aristotle's claim to be suggesting that the goodness of mathematical things shows itself through the action that demonstrates their mutual relations, dependence, and deducibility as discovered by mathematical (geometrical) proofs and constructions in figures (σχήμασι, *In Eucl.* 21.23). However, the mathematical objects "in action" are neither produced nor created by this activity but are shown and become understandable in their properties as "unfolded" in and through (physical or imaginary) drawings, in a way that is better suited to our cognitive abilities—seeing, imagination, and discursive thinking (see Chapter 8).

Proclus accepts and further elaborates Aristotle's claim that beauty in mathematical knowledge is exemplified in and by order (τάξις), symmetry (συμμετρία), and definiteness (ὡρισμένον, Aristotle, *Met.* 1078a36–1078b2). Proclus accepts these three properties as model characteristics of beauty both in bodies and in souls, but they mostly distinguish the objects of mathematics

(*In Eucl.* 26.10–27.16).[4] In mathematics, τάξις is present and clearly discernible in the "procedure of explaining the derivative and more complex theorems from the primary and simpler ones; for in mathematics later propositions are always dependent on the previous ones, and some are counted as starting-points, others as deductions from the primary hypotheses" (*In Eucl.* 26.23–27.1). Any proposition must be derived from axioms, definitions, or postulates ("hypotheses"), which are distinguished according to their being more or less evident and yet accepted by the student as the starting points for a demonstration (*In Eucl.* 76.4–77.2; see Chapter 10). Συμμετρία appears "in the accord of the demonstrations with one another [ἐν τῇ συμφωνίᾳ τῶν δεικνυμένων πρὸς ἄλληλα]; and in their common reference back to the intellect; for the common measure [μέτρον] of all this science is the intellect [νοῦς], from which it gets its principles and to which it directs the minds of its students" (*In Eucl.* 27.2–6). As was mentioned, συμμετρία is predominantly seen in the communication, coherence, and connection of beings that are expressed in propositions and are known through demonstrations (*Theol. Plat.* III 11.43.13–4). And ὡρισμένον appears "in the fixedness and stability of its mathematical ideas [λόγοις]; for the objects of [mathematical] knowledge do not appear now in one guise and now in another, like the objects of perception or opinion, but always present themselves as the same [ἀεὶ τὰ αὐτά], defined by intelligible forms [ὥρισται τοῖς νοεροῖς εἴδεσιν]" (*In Eucl.* 27.6–10).

In Proclus' account, the three characteristics of beauty have to do with: (1) λόγοι; (2) their mutual relations, which are clarified in a sequence of deductions of properties of mathematical objects; (3) the implicit accord of such properties with each other, which is made explicit by demonstrations; and (4) the definiteness of such λόγοι, which is based in, and reflects, the unity of forms. The beauty of mathematics thus primarily transpires in the mathematical λόγοι and is the beauty of well-ordered relations between them.

These λόγοι appear in propositions that implicitly entail or "communicate" with each other. Thus, symmetry presupposes the communicability of, and communication between, the λόγοι as their mutual yet non-circular "logical" implication (συμμετρία τε καὶ κοινωνία λόγων, *In Eucl.* 7.1–2). This mutual communication of λόγοι, however, is not graspable in and by one singular act of thinking but is revealed only within a process of their deduction, enunciation, and mutual clarification. Λόγοι are objects of discursive thinking and speech.[5] Hence, one needs to do the mathematical "logical" work of making

---

[4] However, in *In Eucl.* 8.4, Proclus mentions only τάξις in relation to beauty. See also *In Remp.* I 72.14–5 and *Theol. Plat.* III 11.43.15, where τάξις is directly subsumed under beauty.

[5] As Martijn argues, in reference to Proclus' commentaries on *Timaeus* and *Cratylus*, discursive thought is also the language (λόγοι) of science, which is the case, however, only when διάνοια thinks its λόγοι as demonstrative, for discursive thinking can also be inconclusive, only rhetorically persuasive, or expressive of no knowledge. See Martijn, "Why Beauty Is Truth in All We Know," pp. 87–9.

them explicit through a system of deductions and propositions by discursive reason helped by imagination (of which Euclid's *Elements* is paradigmatic; see Chapter 10), which brings the λόγοι back to unity and simplicity from dispersion and partiality and thus allows the λόγοι to appear in their beauty.

It should be noted that Proclus does not use the term συμμετρία consistently to describe the beauty of λόγοι throughout his commentary on Euclid. Thus, in one passage (*In Eucl.* 61.2–3), symmetry refers to commensurability within numbers as always having a common measure, in contradistinction to geometrical objects. However, when discussing beauty in *Ennead* I.6, Plotinus argues *against* the (Stoic) thesis that beauty consists in symmetry (*Enn.* I.6.1.20–54). Along with other objections, Plotinus raises the doubt—which goes against Proclus' interpretation—that rational considerations or theorems can be at all meaningfully called "symmetric" or commensurable with each other (θεωρήματα γὰρ σύμμετρα πρὸς ἄλληλα πῶς ἂν εἴη, *Enn.* I.6.1.44–5).

9.4 Different Kinds of Beauty

The soul comes to know a mathematical object by ascending from its representation as a geometrical figure in imagination studied in its properties by discursive thinking, to the unity of its form, by which it is then fascinated (see Chapter 8).

> In the same way, when the soul is looking outside itself at the imagination [εἰς φαντασίαν βλέπουσα], seeing the figures depicted there and being struck by their beauty [τὸ κάλλος] and order [τὴν τάξιν], it is admiring its own λόγοι from which they come; and although it admires their beauty, it dismisses it as something reflected and seeks its own beauty. It wants to arrive at itself to see the circle and the triangle there [in the intelligible, ἐκεῖ], all things without parts and all in one another [πάντα ἀμερῶς καὶ ἐν ἀλλήλοις πάντα], and become one with what it sees and enfold their plurality . . . to uncover the unadorned divine beauty of form [τὴν ἀκαλλώπιστον τῶν θεῶν εὐμορφίαν] and see the circle more partless than any center, the triangle without extension, and every other object of knowledge that has come back to unity [εἰς ἕνωσιν]. (*In Eucl.* 141.13–142.2)

At each ontological and epistemological level, the same mathematical object not only appears differently and is grasped by different cognitive faculties, but it is also associated with a particular kind of beauty within the hierarchical order of the beautiful. Thus, in bodies, beauty is either that of naturally beautiful bodies or is produced in artifacts by art (ἀπὸ τέχνης) "in accordance with the λόγος preexisting in art" (*In Eucl.* 137.4–8). But, in a mathematical object, beauty is present at different levels, according to the way the same object is represented. It is (1) the beauty of the beautiful shape of a sensibly perceivable reproduction of a geometrical figure. In addition, it is (2) the beauty of the imaginable perfect geometrical figure existing in the intelligible matter of the imagination (*In Eucl.* 141.4–6). The role of imagination (φαντασία) is of central importance for the constitution of mathematical objects, the understanding of their properties, and, correspondingly, their beauty (see Chapter 8). The beauty of and within imagination is profoundly erotic and might also be considered autoerotic because the soul is driven by a desire to look at itself and discursively investigate and understand that which is reflected in itself *as* itself. And yet, this is not a narcissistic act on the part of the soul, insofar as the beauty in and of an image in imagination and of a λόγος in discursive thinking is a reflection of the beauty of both the structural arrangement (λόγος) and the eternal imageless paradigm (εἶδος) of a mathematical thing (e.g., a circle). Furthermore, (3) a mathematical object is present in its definition (λόγος) with all its explicit and implicit properties revealed through constructions and in demonstrations. This λόγος is accessible to discursive reasoning (διάνοια), and its beauty is the beauty of reasoning and of the remarkable coherence of properties and mutual relations of mathematical objects. Finally, (4) a mathematical object exists properly as a unique and simple form, to which a discursive mathematical λόγος is brought back through mathematical procedures and, being enfolded, is considered non-discursively by the intellect (νοῦς). The beauty here is the beauty of the simplicity of one single εἶδος that, however, is not isolated but remains in communication (κοινωνία) with other forms.

9.5 Is One Geometrical Figure More Beautiful than Another?

Since there is a whole order of beauty that corresponds to the order of ontological strata and cognitive faculties, the representation of the beautiful and judgment about it may be different for different objects. For this reason, in the prologue to the Euclid commentary, Proclus claims that, on the one hand, (a) making the aesthetic judgment that the circle is more beautiful than the straight line or that the equilateral triangle is more beautiful than the isosceles is not the business of the mathematician (*In Eucl.* 35.3–6). Such a judgment would imply a confusion between the essential and accidental in mathematical λόγοι. But, on the other hand, at a later point Proclus also says (b) that it is "evident to everyone that the equilateral is the most beautiful [κάλλιστον] of all triangles and most akin to the circle, which has all its lines from the center equal and a single simple line bounding it from without" (*In Eucl.* 213.14–8).

Is there a way to reconcile these two apparently contradictory claims? They might be taken to apply to the same geometrical objects—circle and equilateral triangle—yet in *different respects*. In case (a), when the isosceles and equilateral triangles are juxtaposed in their *appearance*, their comparison is up to the aesthetic judgment of sense-perception and imagination. A geometrical figure, then, may also be considered a (beautiful) symbolic sensible and imaginary expression of something that cannot be represented in and by the senses or imagination. Thus, the circle is commonly taken to express the self-contained intellect (Plotinus, *Enn.* VI.8.18.7–30; cf. VI.9.8.1–8; Proclus, *In Tim.* I.28.7–11). The infinite straight line, on the contrary, becomes "the symbol [σύμβολον] of the whole world of becoming in infinite and indeterminate change and of matter itself [αὐτῆς τῆς ὕλης] that possesses neither boundary nor shape" (*In Eucl.* 291.6–10). The imaginary beauty of geometrical figures, which is missing in Plato's hierarchy of beauty, is established in and by imagination as beautiful images accessible to imagination alone and not to sense-perception since sensibly perceivable figures are imprecise imitations of precise geometrical ones. Hence, one can say that the isosceles is more beautiful than other kinds of triangles, although this is a judgment of the senses and the imagination but not of discursive reasoning that operates with the geometrical λόγοι rather than with representations or images.

In case (b), it is up to the rational judgment of διάνοια to claim that the isosceles is more beautiful because now it is taken not as a figure that appeals in its beauty to our senses and/or imagination but as the figure that is related to other figures through mathematical reasonings. Such investigations establish that the isosceles triangle is "most akin" (συγγενεστέραν) to the circle, although not in the isosceles' appearance (its visible or imaginable "look"), but in its *properties*, which have a particular *relation* to the properties of the circle. Only those have the knowledge of triangle, then, who have mathematically (that is, discursively and by construction) proven that a particular property (e.g., that the sum of three angles is equal to two right angles) holds not only for *this* triangle but also for *any* triangle and thus for the *triangle itself* (*In Eucl.* 14.10–5). For this reason, because the circle exemplifies limit (ὅρος) and order (τάξις), it dispenses its beauty (κάλλος), homogeneity (ὁμοιότης), shapeliness (εἰδοποιία), and perfection (τελειότης) to all other things (both mathematical and "down to its humblest beneficiaries") and thus regulates and arranges them for us (*In Eucl.* 150.10–6). Hence, the beauty of the circle is itself "borrowed" from that of λόγοι, which, in turn, reflect the beauty, order, and limit of the forms. Not only beauty but also *precision*, then, is different in different kinds of objects of science (ἐπιστήμη) (*In Eucl.* 34.11–9). One can compare the beauty of various mathematical objects, then, only in relation to other such objects by means of appropriate λόγοι, or relational and discursive reasonings. The beauty of mathematical (geometrical) objects is thus "logical," relative, and relational to the extent that it is mediated by mathematical λόγοι.

9.6 Science

We can now return to the question of why it is science that exemplifies beauty and the good. As ἐπιστήμη, science is the knowledge whose measure (μέτρον) is the intellect (νοῦς, *In Eucl.* 27.3–4) because science brings the knowledge, beauty, and goodness of its objects to completion within the unity of the intellect, where each thing is what it is not in separation and exclusion of other forms but in their communication. Consequently, no science proves its own starting points, or principles (ἀρχαί, *In Eucl.* 75.14–5), which include axioms, definitions, and postulates (cf. *In Eucl.* 76.4–77.2; 178.1–184.29) but borrows them from the non-hypothetical and non-discursive νοῦς, which "illuminates" the science from above (*In Eucl.* 27.13–4).

Within the Platonic hierarchy of beauty that corresponds to the structure of the objects of knowledge and of the cognitive faculties, the non-discursive νοῦς contains and immediately knows the partless forms to which science reduces, or toward which it brings up, its own partial conclusions and cognitions arrived at discursively through διάνοια with the help of the imagination. The exemplary science that provides immediate knowledge through mediated partial knowledge is mathematics, which gives perfection or completion (τελειότης) and order (τάξις) to its λόγοι. As exemplary science, mathematics extends its completion and order even to rhetoric and productive and practical arts whose task and purpose is not to know or prove but rather to produce imitations of the beautiful, good, and useful λόγοι (*In Eucl.* 24.21–7). Mathematics is thus the paradigmatic science (ἐπιστήμη) as the theoretical cognition of the immaterial, whereas other particular sciences borrow from mathematics their λόγοι, reasonings, and conclusions appropriate to the study of their own specific objects (*In Eucl.* 9.11–9).

It should be noted that the knowledge of the forms that is arrived at by discursive, predominantly mathematical, knowledge is *communicable* to others. Knowledge comes with learning about how things really are, and thereby with a transmittance of learning and education, so that knowledge (γνῶσις) *is* education (παίδευσις).[6]

Diotima/Socrates/Plato argue(s) that, in order to be considered knowledge, ἐπιστήμη needs to be supported by λόγος, or reason, explanation, and proof of a claim, which is why knowledge is located between (μεταξύ) wisdom (σοφία) and ignorance (ἀμαθία), neither of which needs an argument or justification (Plato, *Symp.* 202A). Referring to Plato, Proclus defines science as knowledge (γνῶσις) that possesses the λόγος of those things that can be known and of

---

[6] See Proclus, *In Eucl.* 20.10–1, with a wrong reference to Plato's *Timaeus*, which should instead be to *Rep.* 526A–529B. Cf. also the mentioned classification of axioms, definitions, and postulates with reference to the process of learning.

their cause (γνῶσις λόγον ἔχουσα τῶν γνωστικῶν καὶ αἰτίαν, *In Eucl.* 31.2–3). Things that can be known by science are those that can be *proven* by reasoning. By establishing, justifying, and *proving* its conclusions, science brings its reasonings together into one unified system of knowledge, which exemplifies the limit, symmetry, and communication of its λόγοι (*In Eucl.* 7.1–5, 119.4–6). This knowledge is primarily represented as mathematics. But does physics, too, provide knowledge about the world? For Proclus, it does. However, such knowledge is possible only to the extent that the physical cosmos embodies, imitates, and participates in non-physical forms and exemplifies certain mathematical structures. As Proclus shows in his *Elements of Physics*, physics can be structured mathematically in its definitions and propositions in exactly the same way as Euclid's *Elements* (see Chapter 10). Yet the *more geometrico* organization applies only to the *logical* arrangement of physical knowledge, insofar as its propositions are established not as mathematical theorems but rather as logically ordered arguments.

10

The System of Physics

10.1 Contents and Structure of *Institutio physica*

Proclus' treatise Στοιχείωσις Φυσική (*Institutio physica* or *Elements of Physics*) is important for several reasons. The most obvious one is that, although a well-established Greek text with a parallel German translation was published by Albert Ritzenfeld in 1912,[1] there are few works dedicated specifically to a consideration of the *Elements of Physics*.[2] Yet a study of the treatise can shed important light on the ancient understanding of physics in its relation to mathematics. A first look at the content of the treatise shows that, to a great extent, Proclus retells and reinterprets Aristotle. The *Elements of Physics*

---

[1] Proclus, *Procli Diadochi Lycii Institutio physica*, ed. Albert Ritzenfeld (Leipzig: Teubner, 1912). The very first translation into a modern language was that into French in 1565: Proclus, *Deux livres de Proclus du mouvementx*, trans. Pierre Forcadel (Paris: Charles Perier, 1565), followed by Honorat de Meynier, *Paradoxes de Meynier contre les mathematiciens qui abusent la ieunesse: ensemble les definitions, theorems, & maximes d'Euclides, d'Archimedes, de Proclus, de Sacrobosco, & d'Aristotle, utiles a ceux qui se veulent servir proprement des mathematiques & de philosophie: avec un abregé des reigles de la geometrie & des principals maximes & regles des arts, de fortifier & assaillir les places* (Paris: Chez Ivlian Iacquin, 1652). The first Greek edition of the treatise was published in Basel in 1531; the first Latin translation by Martinus Cuneatis in Paris in 1542; the first English translation by Thomas Taylor in 1831. Another Greek edition of the treatise with a medieval Latin translation was published by Helmut Boese, *Die mittelalterliche Ubersetzung der "Stoicheiosis physike" der Proclus: Procli Diadochi Lycii Elementatio physica* (Berlin: Akademie, 1958). For the Arabic version of parts of the *Elements of Physics*, see Shlomo Pines, *Studies in Arabic Versions of Greek Texts and in Medieval Science*, vol. 2 of *The Collected Works of Shlomo Pines* (Jerusalem: Magnes Press, 1986), pp. 287–93. Two translations with fine introductions and commentaries also need to be mentioned: in Italian, Proclus, *I Manuali: Elementi di fisica; Elementi di teologia; I testi magico-teurgici*/Marino di Neapoli, *Vita di Proclo*, trans. and ed. Chiara Faraggiana di Sarzana (Milan: Rusconi, 1985); and, in Russian, Prokl, *Nachala fiziki*, trans. and ed. Svetlana Mesyats (Moscow: Museum Graeco-Latinum, 2001). In what follows, all references are to Ritzenfeld's edition.

[2] O'Meara's discussion of Proclus' appropriation of Aristotle's physics is rather an exception: see O'Meara, *Pythagoras Revived*, pp. 177–9. In most studies of Proclus' thought and of ancient theories of motion, the *Elements of Physics* is hardly mentioned, e.g., Lucas Siorvanes, *Proclus: Neo-Platonic Philosophy and Science* (New Haven: Yale University Press, 1996), p. 298.

consists of two books: in the first book, Propositions 1–31 closely follow book VI of Aristotle's *Physics*. In the second book, Proclus parallels mostly book I of Aristotle's *De caelo* (*Inst. phys.*, props. II.1–15) as well as book I of the *Physics* (*Inst. phys.*, props. II.16–21).[3] Some theorems or propositions of the *Elements of Physics* are at times gathered from various chapters of the same book from Aristotle's *Physics*. In some manuscripts, the *Elements of Physics* also bears the (sub)title Περὶ Κινήσεως (*De motu*, or *On Motion*). Indeed, since nature or φύσις is for Aristotle the source and the principle of motion or change in the broad sense (which includes not only locomotion, but also qualitative and quantitative change), then the science of motion is the science of nature, or at least its central part.[4] Aristotle also considers principles, causes, infinity, time, and place as parts of physics, which, in modern terms, can be characterized as natural philosophy or philosophy of science. At first glance, Proclus' account might appear a rather repetitive compilation of Aristotle's texts on natural philosophy, which might further explain the lack of interest in Proclus' treatise, even from the ancient authors, who do not directly refer to the *Elements of Physics* either.

Let us have a closer look at the organization and structure of the text. The first book of the treatise contains six definitions and thirty-one propositions or theorems, and the second part contains fourteen definitions and twenty-one propositions. In his proofs, Proclus in most cases proceeds by *reductio ad absurdum*, δι' ἀδυνάτου τρόπον (cf. *In Eucl.* 73.21–2). The proof by *reductio ad absurdum* demonstrates the logical impossibility of a thesis opposite to that which is proposed in the formulation of a proposition. Several propositions are proven by syllogisms (e.g., *Inst. phys.*, props. II.16–21), and several proofs are given in a number of different ways (ἄλλως; e.g., *Inst. phys.*, props. I.18, I.31, II.6, and II.15, "No sensibly perceivable body is infinite," is demonstrated in four different ways). A proof is often obtained, as in Aristotle, by going through all of the possible variants and subsequently showing that all of them, except one, are untenable (e.g., *Inst. phys.*, prop. II.15). At times, Proclus provides us with further references to other propositions within one single book (*Inst. phys.*, prop. I.2 refers to I.1; prop. I.11 to I.8 and I.10; prop. II.19 to II.15 and II.18, etc.). In addition, an additional auxiliary proposition (lemma) is sometimes demonstrated within the proof of the proposition. Thus, in prop. II.17, when arguing that circular motion is eternal, Proclus also has to prove in addition that any motion between opposites can be only finite (*Inst. phys.* 54.15–24). Remarkably, there are also cross-references between the two books. Thus, prop. II.6 ("Everything moving in a circle is finite") refers to prop. I.28

---

[3] See the critical apparatus to Ritzenfeld's edition of the treatise.
[4] See Aristotle, *Phys.* 200b12–3: "ἡ φύσις μέν ἐστιν ἀρχὴ κινήσεως καὶ μεταβολῆς." Only motion at an equal speed can be considered in such physics, which has no means to describe accelerated motion.

("If the moved is infinite, it will not cover a finite magnitude in a finite time"), and prop. II.10 ("Infinite heaviness and lightness do not exist") refers to prop. I.17 ("Everything moving moves in time"). Such inner unity makes the treatise a uniquely conceived and consistently presented whole.

The first book begins with definitions of the continuous, of entities touching and following each other, of the first time and place, and of rest. The propositions or theorems following these definitions consider the properties of the indivisible and the divisible, particularly with respect to the motion, infinity, divisibility, and indivisibility of time (the indivisible moment of "now" in reference to time) and magnitude and motion and their mutual relations. In its entirety, book I is dedicated to the consideration of the relation between the continuous and the discrete, as well as of the structure of the continuum, which Proclus, who does not yet recognize the notion of actual infinity in either physics or mathematics (although not denying it in metaphysics), discusses through the quantitative proportionality of continuous magnitudes, in which he closely follows Aristotle.[5] Thus, in proving props. I.12–3, Proclus assumes that any part of the infinite is itself finite since it (wrongly) appears that half of the infinite cannot be infinite.

The second book contains more definitions and less propositions than the first. Here, the definitions introduce movability with respect to place, various kinds of motion, and the distinction between composite and simple bodies (physical elements). The definitions of book II further describe (qualitative) relations between velocities, physical properties of heaviness and lightness (which are proper to all physical bodies that do not move by circular motion; that is, to those moving by rectilinear motion), opposites (important in the characterization of circular motion), time, and single motion. The properties of time, its continuity and divisibility in relation to the indivisible "now," which itself puts limits to the flow of time and allows it to be a number of motion, are already discussed in book I (*Inst. phys.*, props. I.12–8). Proclus returns to the topic of time at a later point in book II when discussing properties of motion, where reference to time (to different times of bodies moving with different velocities) is essential (*Inst. phys.*, def. II.13; props. II.9–13).[6] The primary purpose of the definitions of book II is to provide a foundation for the distinction between simple movements of simple bodies; that is, of the elementary physical constituents of the cosmos, and all other movements. However, the definitions of book II also allow for a further important distinction between elementary rectilinear and circular movements: only the latter can represent

---

[5] For a discussion of the infinite divisibility of the continuum, see Cleary, *Aristotle and Mathematics*, pp. 74–8.

[6] Even when proving, in two different ways, the central theorem on time—namely, that time is continuous and eternal (*Inst. phys.*, prop. II.16)—Proclus does not use the definition of time but only the properties of the continuous in relation to the discrete, which he has already established in book I.

not-coming-to-be and not-passing-away (*Inst. phys.*, prop. II.5) as the eternal motion of the skies. The propositions of book II discuss circular motion, as well as the finite and the infinite in their mutual relation (*Inst. phys.*, props. II.1–13). Circular motion, which does not assume any change, is such because it has no opposite from which it might arise or into which it might dissolve. Circular motion, then, points at a simple (finite) body (since the infinite physical body does not exist, prop. II.15) that moves in identical—circular—motion. Such a motion further displays and implies the necessity of the prime or first mover, τὸ πρῶτον κινοῦν (Aristotle, *Phys.* 267b17–26; *Met.* 1070a1), the proof of the existence of which constitutes the end and the apex of the *Elements of Physics*.[7]

10.2 The Indivisible Unmoved Prime Mover and Self-Movement

If the treatise is indeed not only a systematic arrangement of Aristotle's lectures on physics but also primarily a justification of the existence of the prime mover, then we can better understand the form of the *Elements of Physics*. In particular, it might help to explain why Proclus presents his physics in two books, why he omits the discussion and definitions of a number of Aristotelian physical concepts (such as those of the principle [ἀρχή], cause, void, etc.), and why he does not reference either the other books of the *Physics* or those of *De caelo*. The reason for these omissions might be that the propositions of the two books suffice to prove the existence of the prime mover.

Thus, props. II.14–21, in which Proclus discusses and formulates the properties of simple bodies, of circular movement, and of the prime mover form the core of the entire treatise, which proceeds from establishing the properties of the continuous and the discrete to those of the prime mover as the ultimate first cause of the physical that itself is already not physical. Here, the apex of book I (prop. I.31, its last), parallels the apex of book II (prop. II.21): the *crescendo* of each book is reached at the very end with a final completion of a series of theorems. Prop. I.31 proves the immovability of the quantitatively indivisible, and prop. II.21 establishes the indivisibility of the prime mover, from which it immediately follows (although Proclus does not make this step, leaving it to the reader) that the prime mover is itself unmovable.[8]

By definition, circular motion is the one that continuously returns from the same to the same; that is, comes back to itself (τὸ ἀπὸ τοῦ αὐτοῦ πρὸς τὸ αὐτὸ φερόμενον συνεχῶς, *Inst. phys.*, def. II.10). As such, it has no opposite or

---

[7] See O'Meara, *Pythagoras Revived*, pp. 178–9.
[8] Proclus, however, overlooks that prop. I.31 ("everything indivisible is unmovable") immediately follows from prop. I.19 ("everything movable is divisible," μεριστόν, διαιρετόν).

ἐναντίον (*Inst. phys.*, prop. II.4; τὸ τὴν κυκλοφορίαν μηδὲν ἐναντίον ἔχειν, *In Tim.* II.94.5–6). Rectilinear motion, on the other hand, as well as qualitative and quantitative change, is understood in reference to opposites, going "from the opposite into the opposite" (ἀπὸ τῶν ἐναντίων εἰς τὰ ἐναντία, *Inst. phys.*, def. II.11; cf. Aristotle, *De caelo* 269a14).

Aristotle distinguishes two kinds of opposites, ἀντικείμενον or ἀντίθεσις: the ἐναντίον, contrariety, which allows for the mediation by an opposite-neutral μεταξύ, and the ἀντιφατικόν (or ἀντίφασις), contradiction, which arises when the opposites meet without mediation and thus coincide (Aristotle, *An. post.* 72a11–4). Aristotle argues for the necessity of a mediating and opposition-free (natural) substrate, ὑποκείμενον, or substance because an unmediated interaction of the opposites amounts to a violation of the principle of non-contradiction and is thus impossible (Aristotle, *Met.* 1011b16–8). As such, it has no opposite (Aristotle, *Phys.* 189a32–3; 225b10–1). Plato, on the contrary, considers the immediate interaction of the opposites possible and therefore takes them as contradictories (Plato, *Phaedo* 103C–105C). The view that opposites immediately arise from each other is also ascribed by Aristotle to Anaxagoras and the "physiologists" (Aristotle, *Phys.* 187a31–2). This leads Plato to reject, and Aristotle to accept, the necessity of a third principle.

However, when speaking about physical things, Plato argues in the *Timaeus* that "two things cannot be rightly put together without a third; there must be some bond [δεσμόν] between them" (Plato, *Tim.* 31B–C; cf. Proclus, *In Tim.* II.13.19–16.14). In order that a relation or proportion (ἀναλογία) could arise and exist between two things, there should be (one or two) mediating entities. In proving that of the two simple motions—the circular and the rectilinear—only the latter can have an opposite (ἐναντίον; cf. *Inst. phys.*, defs. II.11–2)—Proclus follows Aristotle and accepts his terminology. Speaking of opposite motions, Proclus does not refer them to a moving body that may move by opposite motions and that may also serve the mediating substrate by assuming such opposites. Rather, he means the motion itself, which is thus considered *without* a substrate, such that a motion is immediately opposite to another one, which is the case with rectilinear motion. But circular motion, which is self-identical and self-contained, constantly returns to itself and thus does not have an opposite. In a sense, it might also be thought as representing the opposites as coinciding without any mediation, which thus excludes any proper relation between them. This provides Proclus with additional support for the idea that the ultimate—prime—unmoved mover is the link that connects (and also separates) the physical and the noetic, physics and metaphysics. It is the prime mover that organizes the world in such a way as to orchestrate the first circular motion, which is the most perfect of all, and which, constantly returning to itself, is eternal (Proclus, *Inst. phys.*, prop. II.17). Depending on interpretation, such perfect self-contained circular motion might be considered as either having no opposite (thus being the Aristotelian substance) or as containing the opposites immediately within itself (thus being the Platonic substance).

But what is the prime mover? Proclus does not explicitly answer this question but rather establishes the properties of the prime mover. In the *Physics* and *Metaphysics*, Aristotle argues that everything that moves is moved by something else (*Phys.* 242a49–55). In addition, one cannot go into infinity (*Phys.* 256a13–9) because the infinite is without a limit and thus cannot be the principle. Therefore, it is necessary to stop (ἀνάγκη στῆναι, *Met.* 1070a4; cf. *Phys.* 242b71–2), and this stop is the beginning both of motion and of reasoning. Therefore, there should be the first indivisible and unmoved mover. For if it is not unmoved and unmovable, it is either moved by something else, in which case we still need to go into infinity, or by itself, in which case we need to stop again. The prime mover for Aristotle, then, is unmovable, indivisible, partless, without magnitude, simple, identical, remaining in itself, and moving by single and simple motion (*Phys.* 256a13–259b1).

Without defining the prime mover, Proclus concludes—in the very last line of the treatise—that the first mover is not a body (ἀσώματον, *Inst phys.* 58.27), but he stops short of identifying it with intellect as the thinking that thinks itself. In *Metaphysics* Λ, Aristotle famously says that it is thinking that thinks itself (ἡ νόησις νοήσεως νόησις, *Met.* 1074b34–5; cf. 1072b18–24), that is the beginning (ἀρχὴ γὰρ ἡ νόησις, *Met.* 1072a30). As such, it thinks itself as its own object of thought without moving, and its thinking is the best and most pleasant (ἡ θεωρία τὸ ἥδιστον καὶ ἄριστον, *Met.* 1072b24). This νοῦς is pure activity and as such is separate from matter. Yet Aristotle does not explicitly identify the prime mover with thinking. At the same time, he argues that the prime mover is the principle of motion (ἀρχή, *Phys.* 259a33), itself unmoved; that is, it moves as the object of desire and thought, which also move without being moved (τὸ ὀρεκτὸν καὶ τὸ νοητόν· κινεῖ οὐ κινούμενα, *Met.* 1072a26–7). Moreover, the prime mover is pure activity; the course of life (διαγωγή) of the prime mover is the best and most pleasant (*Met.* 1072b14) so that its activity is pleasure (ἡδονή, *Met.* 1072b16); and it is an eternal essence (οὐσία) separate from the sensible (κεχωρισμένη τῶν αἰσθητῶν, *Met.* 1073a4–5) and is thus without matter. Therefore, the prime mover and the thinking that thinks itself, being the best and most pleasant, have to be identical. For there cannot be two different objects with these same properties because the principle is the first and the best and, as such, can only be one.

Following Aristotle, Proclus in the *Elements of Physics* establishes the following properties of the prime mover: it is eternal (*Inst. phys.*, prop. II.18), non-corporeal, indivisible (*Inst. phys.*, prop. II.21), and unmovable (*Inst. phys.*, prop. II.19). Moreover, the prime mover has an infinite power (δύναμις), which is demonstrated in the last proposition of the treatise (*Inst. phys.*, prop. II.21). As such, the prime mover is the first principle that orders and moves the cosmos.[9] Being indivisible and unmovable, the prime mover cannot be not physical because every physical thing is divisible. Rather, the prime mover is a necessary link between the physical and the intelligible, both uniting and separating them. It is not by chance, then, that before speaking of the continuous and the divisible, Proclus begins book I with the discussion of the indivisible (*Inst. phys.*, props. I.1–4).

Yet Proclus does not explain *how* the prime mover moves. Following Aristotle, he argues that, on the one hand, everything that is moved has to have a mover, be it either the nature "within" or another body "without," which moves by touch. On the other hand, the unmoved precedes both the moved and the mover (*Inst. phys.*, props. II.19–20; Aristotle, *Phys.* 256a2–3). For Aristotle, the prime mover moves as the intellect that is the object of desire (ὀρεκτόν) of all things, as the final cause of and for the physical world. For Proclus, however, the prime mover also moves as the efficient cause,[10] as the ultimate cause of the eternal circular movement of heaven, although he does not discuss causation in the *Elements of Physics* because it belongs already to metaphysics.

Aristotle accepts three terms for the description of motion: the moving (τὸ κινοῦν), the moved (τὸ κινούμενον), and that into which something is moved (εἰς ὃ κινεῖται, Aristotle, *Phys.* 224a34–224b7). The latter is the end of movement, without which movement would be incomplete and thus indefinite. Ritzenfeld observes that, in the *Institutio physica* (*Inst. phys.*, prop. II.19), Proclus argues that "the unmoved [τὸ ἀκίνητον] precedes the movers [τῶν κινούντων] and the moved [κινουμένων]." However, in the *Elements of Theology*, he takes it that "all that exists is either unmoved or moved; and if it is moved, either by itself or by another; and if by itself, it is self-moving [αὐτοκίνητον]; and if by another, it is moved by another" (ἑτεροκίνητον, *Elem. theol.* § 14)."[11] Proclus then establishes the existence of the self-moving as mediating or a middle (μέσον πως ὄν, *Elem. theol.* 16.25) between the moving and the moved. This middle is then *both* the moving and the moved, thus connecting the unmoved with, and separating it from, that which is moved by another. In Dodds' interpretation, there is no contradiction between the account of the *Elements of Physics*, which is based on the Aristotelian concept of the prime unmoved

---

[9] See Cleary, *Aristotle and Mathematics*, p. 405; and Jan Opsomer, "The Integration of the Aristotelian Physics in a Neoplatonic Context: Proclus on Movers and Divisibility," in *Physics and Philosophy of Nature in Greek Neoplatonism*, ed. Riccardo Chiaradonna and Franco Trabattoni (Leiden: Brill, 2009), pp. 189–229, esp. 193–203.

[10] See Carlos Steel, "Proclus et Aristotle sur la causalité efficiente de l'intellect divin," in *Proclus, lecteur et interprète des anciens: Actes du Colloque international du CNRS, Paris, 2–4 octobre 1985*, ed. Jean Pépin and H. D. Saffrey (Paris: Editions du Centre national de la recherché scientifique, 1987), pp. 213–25; and Alain Lernould, *Physique et théologie: lecture du Timeé de Platon par Proclus* (Villeneuve d'Ascq: Presses Universitaires du Septentrion, 2001), pp. 322–3.

[11] See Albert Ritzenfeld, preface to *Inst. phys.*, p. viii.

mover, and that of the *Elements of Theology*, where the Platonic concept of the self-moving (τὸ αὐτὸ κινοῦν) plays central role (Plato, *Phaedr.* 245C–246A; *Legg.* 894B–895B). For, as Proclus demonstrates in his commentary on the *Timaeus*, the proof of the existence of the unmoved does not necessarily require a reference to the self-moved (Proclus, *In Tim.* III.9.2–15). Moreover, in the *Theologia Platonica*, Proclus suggests an even more complex classification: (1) the moved only (κινούμενα μόνον), which consists of physical bodies; (2) both the moved and the moving (κινούμενα καὶ κινοῦντα), forms in matter (ἔνυλα εἴδη); (3) the self-moving (αὐτοκίνητα), souls; and (4) the unmoved (ἀκίνητα), the intellect, νοῦς (*Theol. Plat.* I 14.60.12–23).[12] Here, Proclus explicitly takes the unmoved mover to be the intellect thinking itself. Following Plato's account of motion in the *Sophist* (251D–259D), he considers the νοῦς to be a kind of unmoved movement when the intellect, thinking itself in the forms of itself, moves as though within them, yet remaining at rest and always returning to itself without ever having left itself since, in the intelligible, everything coexists eternally without detriment or change.[13]

One should disagree with Dodds when he suggests that the eternally moved (τὸ ἀιδίως κινούμενον, *Inst. phys.*, prop. II.18) equally refers to the self-moved, insofar as the self-moved can be taken as a particular case of the moved; namely, that which is moved by itself. Being moved by itself amounts for Aristotle to being moved by nature (φύσις) and thus according to nature (cf. *Inst. phys.*, def. II.6; props. II.2, 3, 6), whereas for Plato being moved by itself means being moved by the soul (Plato, *Tim.* 34B–37C). Yet the eternally moved, contrary to Dodds' suggestion, is neither of the two. In order to reconcile the Aristotelian and the Platonic account about the self-moved, Proclus has to argue in his commentary on the *Timaeus* that, although Plato places the soul above nature, nevertheless his "proper motion" (κίνησις οἰκεία, Plato, *Tim.* 34A) does not differ from motion according to nature (κίνησις κατὰ φύσιν) in Aristotle, which is the motion according to the essence of a thing (Proclus, *In Tim.* II 92.13–95.11).

10.3 The Structure, Form, and Purpose of the *Elements of Physics*

Regarding the structure of the treatise, one might ask why it consists of two books. A plausible explanation might be that the first book discusses the discrete in relation to the continuous, whereas the second book speaks about the movement of simple entities, of the elements. And yet Proclus

---

[12] Proclus, *Théologie platonicienne: Livre I*, trans. and ed. H. D. Saffrey and L. G. Westerink (Paris: Les Belles Lettres, 1968), p. 145 n. 2.

[13] See Stephen Gersh, *ΚΙΝΗΣΙΣ ΑΚΙΝΗΤΟΣ: A Study of Spiritual Motion in the Philosophy of Proclus* (Leiden: Brill, 1973), pp. 103–7.

does not define either the concept of a simple body, or of physical elements, or other concepts central to physics. He argues that the number of simple bodies is finite (*Inst. phys.*, prop. II.14), but never explains what the simple body is, probably assuming that it is already known to the reader. Similarly, Proclus does not explicitly define the concepts of ἐνέργεια and δύναμις, but rather makes them known by using them in the very last proposition, which is central to the whole treatise (*Inst. phys.*, prop. II.21), where he argues that if the prime mover causes eternal motion, its capacity or power to move is itself infinite. And if finite powers have finite activities, and if the activity follows the power, then, if the activity (of eternal motion) is infinite, so should the corresponding power itself be infinite. These terms constitute the very language of philosophy, and their proper use is a precondition for the very possibility of understanding and speaking about (natural) philosophical matters: if one is able to formulate and to understand a proposition, then one is already in command of the basic concepts, which are themselves not further defined.

Similarly, the definitions of the first book contain only a definition of rest (*Inst. phys.*, def. I.6) and not a definition of motion, even if such a definition is explicitly given by Aristotle in the *Physics* (201a27–9). Neither does Proclus define faster and slower motion (introduced in *Inst. phys.*, prop. I.8). Again, the reason for this might be that the two are in fact defined by their being used in the demonstration—and in this way as implicitly defined in reference to other already established propositions. The distinction between faster and slower follows from the very proof of prop. I.8 (the faster covers greater distance in the same time), where the two are introduced in opposition to each other and in reference to proportionally related quantities.

Proclus does not make what would be an otherwise obvious further step in the discussion of the prime mover. Namely, in the demonstration of the last proposition of book II (*Inst. phys.*, prop. II.21), Proclus intends to prove that the prime mover is indivisible (ἀμερές) but in fact proves only that it is non-corporeal or not a physical body. In order to bring the whole treatise to its logical completion, one has yet to demonstrate the thesis of the indivisibility of the prime mover. The conclusion here should be that, since everything divisible is a magnitude, and a physical body is either a magnitude or a collection of magnitudes, each of which is continuous in the sense of def. I.1 (cf. *Inst. phys.*, prop. I.5), then a physical body is divisible. And yet, from the premises that every body is divisible and that the prime mover is not a body, it does not follow that the prime mover is indivisible. Rather, one might restrict the consideration of possible movers to bodies alone. This would exclude both geometrical entities, which are magnitudes but do not belong to the physical, as well as time, which is also a continuous magnitude but is itself unmovable because, by def. II.13, it is a number of motion and therefore "follows" the motion. One might then assume that everything divisible in the realm of physical movers is a body. And since, as demonstrated in prop. II.21, the prime mover is not a body, then, by *modus tollens*, the prime mover is indivisible.

The very form of exposition, presentation, and argument of the treatise is that of "elements." The genre of the στοιχεῖα or στοιχείωσις, paradigmatic of which are the *Elements*, arose initially from an attempt to order a body of knowledge of a certain kind and to provide mutually related elements for the constitution and construction of further knowledge by justifying and establishing related statements and propositions in their mutual consistency. Similarly to other ancient philosophical genres, such as dialectic, the genre of "elements" probably came out of the tradition of oral disputations and of dialectical exercise, in the course of which one interlocutor was trying to show, by means of simple questions, an alleged logical inconsistency of the thesis of the other interlocutor, who thus eventually had to recognize the truth of the opposite thesis.[14] Obviously, the *reductio ad absurdum* proof that is often used in this genre follows exactly the same logical strategy. In its structure, the στοιχείωσις presupposes a number of univocally formulated, clearly stated, self-evident, and thus not themselves demonstrable statements (definitions, later also axioms and postulates), as well as further statements (propositions or theorems) that are deduced from these definitions and that are proved, by using rules of deduction, on the basis of the definitions and the already proven propositions. According to Proclus, the elements, or στοιχεῖα, have a double meaning: on the one hand, they are a means of obtaining something else, which is established on the basis of the elements. And, on the other hand, στοιχεῖα represent simple entities that can be further assembled into a unified and mutually connected composite, and, in this sense, postulates are elements, or principles, for propositions. As such, elements are similar to letters that allow for building and unfolding a complex coherent theory or science (ἐπιστήμη) of a subject matter within a text consisting of a number of mutually related sentences or propositions. The elements, then, are a kind of bricks out of which the whole body of knowledge is constituted. Yet they are equally elementary statements that already contain *in nuce* all other meaningful statements pertaining to a science. It is then very important, but also difficult, to choose the elements and to arrange them in such a way that all deduced knowledge can proceed from (προάγεται) and also can be resolved (ἀναλύεται) into them (Proclus, *In Eucl.* 71.24–73.18).

A discipline, then, is considered logically justified if it is ordered and presented as στοιχεῖα. Such an ideal of justification has a powerful appeal to ancient thinkers, who attempted to provide "elements" for different disciplines, each of which was considered to be a science, such as arithmetic, astronomy,

---

[14] See Michael Frede, "Plato's Arguments and the Dialogue Form," in *Methods of Interpreting Plato and his Dialogues*, supp. vol. of *Oxford Studies in Ancient Philosophy* (1992), pp. 201–19.

and music. Yet the most obvious candidate for being presented in the στοιχεί ωσις form was mathematics, which for Greek antiquity was geometry par excellence, the strictest of the sciences that studied intermediate entities between purely thinkable concepts and physical bodies (see Chapter 8).

Of a number of ancient mathematical Στοιχεῖα, the most well preserved and authoritative is that of Euclid, which the *Elements of Physics* imitate in their form.[15] Proclus was much interested in Euclid's work, leaving an incomplete yet very important commentary on Euclid.[16] In particular, he praises Euclid for having brought together and systematically arranged the previously discovered mathematical theorems, including those of Eudoxus, Theaetetus, and Euclid's own, thus turning mathematics into a perfect science (*In Eucl.* 68.6–10). The structure of the *Elements of Physics*, however, is less sophisticated than that of Euclid's *Elements*, for Proclus uses only definitions and no axioms or postulates, and he makes no distinction between problems and theorems.

The genre and structure of the στοιχεῖα are closely connected with their purpose, σκοπός, which is twofold: on the one hand, it is scientific with regard to the subject matter (κατά τε τὰ πράγματα, περὶ ὦν αἱ ζητήσεις), which is the knowledge of the perfect Platonic ("cosmic") bodies (τῶν κοσμικῶν σχημάτων). On the other hand, the aim of the στοιχεῖα is also pedagogical with regard to the student (κατὰ τὸν μανθάνοντα), providing him with the easily graspable and coherent introduction and arrangement of the science (*In Eucl.* 70.19–71.24). From these, the student should be able to comprehend and study the entire science, which also allows for further independent study as well as for the possibility of the discovery of hitherto unknown propositions. The inseparability of the two aspects of the στοιχείωσις, the scientific and the pedagogical, finds its expression in the very organization of the ancient philosophical school, which, as an institution, effectively combined the functions of both teaching and of scientific research. The contemporary meaning of the "school" preserves this initial inseparable duality remarkably well. The very division in Proclus' *Elements of Physics* into self-evident definitions and demonstrated propositions, then, addresses the dual purpose of the στοιχείωσις, as both pedagogically useful, insofar as it makes learning clearly ordered and easily accessible, and scientifically meaningful,

---

[15] See Heath, introduction to Euclid, *The Thirteen Books of Euclid's Elements*, vol. 1, pp. 114–7. According to Ritzenfeld, the treatise is written "in Euclidis modum" (Ritzenfeld, preface to *Inst. phys.*, p. vii).

[16] Proclus, *In Primum Euclidis Elementorum Librum Commentarii*, ed. Gottfried Freidlein (Leipzig: Teubner, 1873). See also Nicolai Hartmann, *Des Proklus Diadochus philosophische Anfangsgründe der Mathematik: Nach den ersten zwei Büchern des Euklidkommentars dargestellt* (Berlin: De Gruyter, 1909); and Ian Mueller, "Mathematics and Philosophy in Proclus' Commentary on Book I of Euclid's *Elements*," in *Proclus, lecteur et interprète des anciens*, pp. 305–18.

insofar as it shows the consistency and inner coherence of the subject matter. It is also worth noting that in his commentary on Euclid's *Elements*, Proclus explains the difference between axioms and postulates with reference to their relative clarity to the student (*In Eucl.* 76.6–77.2). The studied things, μαθήματα, then, are both the objects of strict demonstrable knowledge and of teaching and learning.

Therefore, the double scientific and educational purpose of the *Elements of Physics* might be considered not only as an ordering of Aristotelian physics for a student in order to make it more accessible, but equally as an attempt to demonstrate and justify the existence of the prime mover, which, as was argued, both connects and separates the physical and the intelligible, and thus the physical and mathematical. In a broader sense, the aim of the treatise may then be considered as the incorporation of Aristotelian physics into systematic philosophy and, at the same time, as a reconciliation of Aristotelian and Platonic physics. For the account of the physical cosmos that Plato presents in the *Timaeus* comes in the form of only a plausible narrative, "fable," or μῦθος, that neither is demonstrated in the *more geometrico* way nor is accompanied by strict proofs. The reason for this is that physics for Plato has to do with the realm of becoming only, in regard to which there can be no strict knowledge but only a justified opinion at best. Perhaps the only exception to this is Plato's explanation of mutual transformation of physical elements or simple bodies, represented by and as regular geometrical "cosmic" bodies. Insofar as these bodies are geometrical, they allow for ἐπιστήμη, although Plato neither explains how the mathematical (geometrical) becomes applicable to and is present in the physical, nor does he describe how geometrical three-dimensional figures, themselves consisting of geometrical triangles of two kinds, can have physical property, such as weight (Plato, *Tim.* 53C–61C).

The *more geometrico* exposition of physics by introducing axioms and definitions and then deducing demonstrable propositions is central to the *Elements of Physics*. However, already in his commentary on the *Timaeus*, Proclus attempts to present the Platonic physics "like geometers" (ὥσπερ οἱ γεωμέτραι, *In Tim.* I.236.15) by laying out definitions and axioms and deducing several propositions about the cosmos on their basis: that it came to be, that it has a cause, that its cause or paradigm is eternal, and so forth (*In Tim.* I.235.32–238.5, I.264.20–265.9, II.93.30–94.15). But the *Elements of Physics* is an ordered presentation of the Aristotelian, and not Platonic, physics. Proclus' intention here appears to be to show that there is no contradiction between the two accounts of the cosmos. Sometimes a contradiction might arise, when, for instance, Plato considers the soul (ψυχή) to be the source of motion in the world, while Aristotle takes it to be nature (φύσις); or when Plato argues that the world has a beginning, although not in time, whereas Aristotle proves its eternity. But in such cases it can be interpreted as only an apparent contradiction when the same subject is considered in different respects, or when an argument is misinterpreted.[17] Aristotelian physics, then, can be a useful propaedeutic to Platonic philosophy, both educationally and systematically, so that the former can eventually be both included into and subsumed under the latter.[18]

10.4 Definitions as First Principles: Requirements for a Definition

As knowledge and science, ἐπιστήμη can be systematically unfolded and brought to completion, which reveals and discloses the already present intelligible paradigm. The *more geometrico* presentation is a particularly useful method and genre for this task since it allows for a deduction of true propositions from first self-evident principles and other already established propositions.[19] Proclus revolutionizes the use of the method, demonstrating that the *more geometrico* genre can be applied not only to mathematics but also to physics and even to philosophy in the *Elements of Theology*. The similarity between the *Elements of Physics* and the *Elements of Theology* is evident at a glance. In addition to the common title, Στοιχείωσις, the two *Elements* are a systematic exposition of the foundations of the respective discipline in a set of mutually related propositions, each of which is accompanied by a strict proof. Yet there is an equally noticeable difference between the two treatises: the latter, unlike the former, contains no definitions.

There should be self-evident, non-provable first principles from which every argument starts because, otherwise, one has to go on into infinity, which makes it impossible for a proof to be completed. Proclus discusses the first principles (ἀρχαί) in his commentary on Euclid. Following Aristotle, Euclid himself distinguishes between definition (ὅρος or ὁρισμός, in Proclus ὑπόθεσις), axiom (or "common notion," ἀξίωμα), postulate (αἴτημα), and the propositions that follow from these first principles. And a proposition can be either a problem (πρόβλημα) or a theorem (θεώρημα).[20] According

---

[17] See the discussion of Proclus' attempt to reconcile Plato and Aristotle in Svetlana Mesyats, introduction to Proclus, *Nachala fiziki*, pp. 22–33.

[18] Referring to the two thinkers, Proclus calls Plato "divine" (ὁ θεῖος), whereas Aristotle is only "genial" (ὁ δαιμόνιος, Proclus, *In Eucl.* 76.8).

[19] Cf. Marije Martijn, "Proclus' Geometrical Method," in *The Routledge Handbook of Neoplatonism*, ed. Pauliina Remes and Svetla Slaveva-Griffin (London: Routledge, 2014), pp. 145–59, who mostly stresses the didactic purpose of the geometrical method.

[20] Book I of Euclid's *Elements* begins with lists of twenty-three definitions, five postulates, and five axioms, followed by forty-eight propositions, some of which (e.g., the very first one) are problems that require construction. Cf. Heath, introduction to Euclid, *The Thirteen Books of Euclid's Elements*, vol. 1, pp. 117–29; and Hartmann, *Des Proklus Diadochus philosophische Anfangsgründe der Mathematik*, pp. 53–7. In general, as Aristotle argues, it is better to take fewer principles (*An. post.* 86a33–5). A proposition may consist of proposition or enunciation (πρότασις), exposition (ἔκθεσις), determination (διορισμός), construction (κατασκευή), demonstration (ἀπόδειξις), and conclusion (συμπέρασμα). The most important of these are proposition, demonstration, and proof, without which no theorem

to Aristotle, a definition presents the properties of an entity, the existence of which is already assumed. In this respect, a definition is closer to an axiom, insofar as both are self-evident and hence acceptable for someone who is to discover or learn something. An axiom, however, must be common to *all* sciences (which is why it is called "common notion" or "common opinion") and must therefore be not hypothetical (ἀνυπόθετον) and the most firmly established of all the first principles (Aristotle, *Met.* 1005b11–7). A definition, on the other hand, is specific and proper to a particular science (hence, different in physics and in mathematics).

In Proclus, a definition is a *hypothesis*, whereas Aristotle makes a distinction between definition and hypothesis: both are *theses*; that is, both are impossible to prove, and yet, unlike the hypothesis that implies the reference to either "is" or "is not," the definition does not presuppose the existence of that whose properties are defined (Aristotle, *An. post.* 72a14–24; Proclus, *In Eucl.* 178.1–184.29). This is the reason why, in Valdanius' Latin translation (*Procli de motu libri duo*) of the *Elements of Physics*, definitions II.1–6 are taken as ὑποθέσεις. For, in order to be able to define and speak about the motion of physical bodies, one has to assume that bodies exist. Aristotle also makes a distinction between hypothesis and postulate, which becomes apparent in the process of learning (which again shows an inseparability between science and education): the hypothesis is assumed to be self-evident and thus is accepted without the consent of the student, whereas the postulate has to be assumed even against the opinion of the learner.

In addition, there is a difference between a postulate and an axiom, which parallels that between a theorem and a problem. As Proclus explains, in a theorem, we have to see what follows from the premises; whereas, in a problem, we are required to do and to find something. A problem, then, is solved by construction (γένεσις), which means that, although still a demonstration, a problem is closer to ποίησις as opposed to the θεωρία of a theorem (*In Eucl.* 79.3–9; cf. 77.7–81.22). As Heath puts it, "an axiom has reference to something known, and a postulate to something done."[21] In this sense, the propositions of Proclus' *Elements of Physics* and those of the *Elements of Theology* are all theorems in the strict sense and therefore do not require a construction. For this reason, in the *Elements of Physics*, propositions often end with a ὅπερ ἔδει δεῖξαι, *quod erat demonstrandum* (cf. props. I.10–1, 13, 20, 22, 25, 27, 29, 31, II.21; it is also the last line of the treatise).

As Heath points out, in his logical treatises, Aristotle presents several requirements for a definition. Thus, (1) each of the different attributes of a

---

can be considered complete, the other three being rather optional and often appearing in problems (Proclus, *In Eucl.* 203.1–205.12).

[21] Heath, introduction to Euclid, *The Thirteen Books of Euclid's Elements*, vol. 1, p. 123.

definition may cover more than the notion defined, although in their entirety they cover exactly the same as the defined (Aristotle, *An. post.* 96a20–97b39).[22] Put otherwise, the intersection of different semantic fields of various attributes has to characterize one particular object in a unique and univocal way. In addition, (2) a definition should be formulated with reference to the things and notions that are prior to the defined and that are either absolutely or relatively better known. For Aristotle, this means referring to the proximate genus and the specific difference, both of which are better known by us than the defined (Aristotle, *Top.* 141a26–142b19). Thus, in definition 1 of book I of Euclid's *Elements*, which states that "a point is that which has no parts [οὗ μέρος οὐθέν]," the notions of part and partlessness are prior to and better known than the notion of point that is being defined. And, finally, (3) for Aristotle, "to know what a thing is [τὸ τί ἐστιν] is the same as to know why it is [διὰ τί ἔστιν]" (Aristotle, *An. post.* 90a31–2). In other words, to know the essence of a thing is to know its cause or the "why" (τὸ διότι), which, however, cannot be known before for Aristotle or until the thing with its "what" (τὸ ὅτι) is already there (Aristotle, *An. post.* 93a16–7). The cause, then, is constitutive of the definition or the "what" of a thing.

Why does Proclus need definitions for his physical theory (every book of the *Elements of Physics* begins with a list of such definitions), yet omits them in the *Elements of Theology*? This might be explained by the fact that Proclus' physics is Aristotelian, whereas his first philosophy and ontology is Platonic. Although Plato does not discuss the problem of definition systematically, he is still very much interested in it because the very task of the elenchic dialogue is to establish the definition of a concept or a thing. However, physics in Proclus depends on and is founded in ontology, which provides the definition for physics, whereas the concepts of first philosophy and ontology are all mutually connected by κοινωνία (see Chapter 3), which is why it is impossible to isolate any given one and give a definition of a single one, for such a definition should imply at the same time every other concept or form (see Chapter 7).

Yet in the discussion of physics definitions are crucial. Aristotle himself provides a number of definitions in his physics, such as those of infinity (*Phys.* 207a1–2), place (*Phys.* 212a6), time (*Phys.* 219b1–2), and continuity (*De caelo* 268a6–7). Aristotle's three requirements for a definition are all present in Proclus' accounts of physics. Thus, (1) a combination of the defining aspects univocally indicates that which is defined. Thus, in *Institutio physica*, definition II.13, "Time is a number of motion of the celestial bodies," the intersection of ranges of the terms "number," "motion," and "celestial body" describes time in a unique and univocal way. Moreover, (2) none of the defining aspects is itself defined (which is why motion is not among the defined), being better known

---

[22] Ibid., pp. 146–50.

both to us and in itself. As was said before, Proclus does not define certain concepts central to his natural philosophy, doing so only for those which he needs for an argument and for the purpose of establishing the existence of the prime mover reigning supreme in the physical cosmos. In addition, Proclus might also omit some definitions because he presupposes them to be either already known to the reader, or self-evident, or provided within the course of a demonstration discussion (e.g., the definition of motion in the demonstration of *Inst. phys.*, prop. II.17), or given by *using* a concept (e.g., that of ἐνέργεια or δύναμις, in the demonstration of *Inst. phys.*, prop. II.21).

The requirement (3) of knowing the cause of a thing that then discloses the essence of the defined is equally fulfilled in the study of physics. Physical bodies, both simple and composite, are not produced either in their existence or in their essence or their "what," but simply are, which allows us to study their properties. Such properties are then systematically ordered and arranged into a sequence of demonstrated and mutually related propositions. If production or construction of a thing with its resulting properties is at all possible, then it belongs not to physics but rather to mathematics, where a mathematical entity (a geometrical figure) is already produced and not produced: it can be constructed kinematically or "drawn" by movement in the imagination according to a rule or λόγος, which itself is already not produced but that refers to the ever-existing and thus equally non-constructible form or concept of the thing (see Chapter 8). As Aristotle observes, the knowledge of the "what" of things is based on sense-perception, whereas the knowledge of their cause comes from science, primarily represented as mathematics (Aristotle, *An. post.* 79a2–3). Proclus (who assigns this claim to Geminus) equally states that it is the mathematician (geometer) who asks about the cause (αἰτία, τὸ αἴτιον, τὸ διὰ τί, *In Eucl.* 202.9–25). But the ultimate cause of all physical things is the prime mover, which is the ultimate cause that can explain the "what" and the "that" (τὸ ὅτι) of a physical thing. The prime mover, however, only causes the motion of all things but not their existence: in its entirety, the world as a whole has no beginning in time and thus is eternal for both Aristotle (*Phys.* 251b19–26) and Proclus (*Inst. phys.*, prop. II.16). Establishing the existence and properties of this ultimate cause is the task not of mathematics but of physics, which then can help with establishing the definition of a particular thing.

10.5 The Mathematization of Physics?

The *more geometrico* form is thus successfully applied by Proclus to physics, which makes it science or ἐπιστήμη. This is a novelty in antiquity since it was used before only in mathematics. But is physics thereby mathematized? The *more geometrico* way of ordering and presenting a discipline is itself logical and not mathematical. In order to be mathematical, physics should be capable of using numerical analysis and calculation in describing differences between various motions as quantitative rather than not qualitative. In other words, physics should be capable of presenting a motion in the very process of change and becoming, and not in its completion. In that case, physics would need to account for motion as a uniform change, but as itself constantly changing. The mathematization of physics also presupposes the possibility of the description of continuous moving magnitude as a pure functional relation between constantly changing distance and time without reference to the moving body. This further implies an ontology that is not based on the notion of substance but rather on the notion of pure relation. For Proclus, however, physics still has to do with real entities, (Aristotelian) substances, whose properties are geometrically ordered only to demonstrate the existence of the (Platonic) substance; that is, being as thinking, the first and ultimate cause of motion in the cosmos. Proclus' geometrization of physics is thus not its mathematization in the modern sense but rather is the introduction of a rational logical order into physics.[23]

The mathematization of physics in antiquity may mean either applying arithmetic to physical things, in which case it is only a *symbolic* ontological Pythagorean expression of their properties, as in Plato's *Timaeus* and its Neoplatonic appropriations. Or it may also mean the *logical* ordering of physics, in which physical bodies are represented through geometrical figures that are intermediate between the intelligible and the sensible, thus both uniting and separating the realms of being and becoming (see Chapter 8). Insofar as geometry is capable of presenting and describing unchangeable properties in its objects, it is capable of presenting being not *in* the cosmos, but rather *for* the cosmos, in which every physical thing depends on an intelligible paradigm and the prime mover as the ultimate cause of motion and change.

This means that one cannot speak about the applicability of mathematics to physics in the modern sense, as a functional mathematical description of physical processes. Rather, mathematics for Proclus contains the same ontological principles as those that are exemplified in and put into the cosmos by the demiurge. Therefore, if the same properties or structures are discovered both in mathematics and physics, then, as O'Meara argues, they arise "not from direct application of mathematics to physics, but rather from the fact that mathematics articulates in a clearer and more accurate way a principle which governs and is expressed in a more imperfect way in the physical structure of the world."[24] There is then only a proportional, *analogical* relation

---

[23] It is not by chance that the peak of interest in Proclus' *Elements of Physics* is in the first half of the sixteenth century, on the eve of the modern mathematization of science, and then it sharply declines with the advent of the new physics.

[24] O'Meara, *Pythagoras Revived*, p. 192.

between mathematical and physical entities.[25] Mathematics clarifies the λόγοι, which themselves are not functions but relations according to which physical things are bound in proportion (ἀναλογία) to each other in the cosmos, where the physical is considered analogically to the mathematical (Proclus, *In Eucl.* 22.17–23.11).[26] In book I of the *Elements of Physics*, Proclus argues at length that continuous magnitudes (such as intervals of distance or time) have various properties in relation to the discrete. Thus, proposition I.23 demonstrates that no continuous motion has a (discrete) beginning, and proposition I.31 that the indivisible (discrete) cannot move. Here, the relation between the continuous and discrete physical in physics is described and established in the same terms as the relation between the continuous interval and the point in geometry.

This, however, does not yet make physics mathematical because the description occurs solely in terms of the proportionality of relations of different and ontologically incommensurable (physical and mathematical) entities. Mathematics and physics are neither mixed nor joined into a single science of the world because they have different objects of study and different principles of describing them. As geometry, mathematics does not prescribe principles to physics, which remains the prerogative of the demiurge alone, although, because of the irreducible otherness of matter, even the demiurge cannot transform the cosmos into a complete and perfect mathematical universe.[27] Rather, mathematics presents and describes these principles, not as specifically physical, but as common to both sciences. It is only in this sense that physics and mathematics can be considered as "woven together" (Proclus, *In Tim.* II 23.13–4), yet the differences between first philosophy, mathematics, and physics remain insurmountable. These differences are distinct within the different kinds of objects: intelligible forms, λόγοι (intermediate), mathematical objects, and physical things. The mathematical description of the physical, then, is neither numerical nor quantitative: in its relation to physics, mathematics does not—and cannot—calculate.

The very proof of a proposition related to physics, both in Aristotle and Proclus, often involes establishing proportional, and not numerical, relations and, in this way, is analogical. This is particularly true of the first thirteen propositions of book II of the *Elements of Physics*, where the properties of moving bodies are established through an analogical relation of entities of

---

[25] See Gerald Bechtle, "Die pythagoreisierende Konzeption der Mathematik bei Iamblichos, Syrianos und Proklos. In Spannungsfeld zwischen pythagoreischer Transposition und platonischer Mittelstellung," in *Proklos: Methode, Seelenlehre, Metaphysik*, ed. Matthias Perkams and Rosa Maria Piccione (Leiden: Brill, 2006), pp. 323–39.

[26] Proportion as ἀναλογία is to be distinguished from the συμμετρία, which, together with the ἀλήθεια and the κάλλος, primarily characterizes being (see Chapter 9). See Joseph Combès, "Les trois monades du *Philèbe* selon Proclus," in *Proclus, lecteur et interprète des anciens*, pp. 177–90.

[27] The insurmountable presence of matter to the physical can be also seen in that the physical point, unlike the geometrical one, is divisible and thus has parts. See Proclus, *In Tim.* I 349.6–350.1.

the same kind, presented in terms of greater and smaller but not in numbers (e.g., when comparing times of motion or distances covered). Only uniform motions can be studied in this way since motion is taken as a whole and in its completion (cf. Proclus, *Inst. phys.*, prop. II.9). And when Aristotle and Proclus designate magnitudes (such as time, distance, or the body as a divisible entity) and discrete entities (indivisible moments of time, "now") by letters, they are representing things symbolically, rather than taking letters to be empty placeholders that could stand for anything whatsoever, as is the case with modern algebra or analysis. And although time is the number of motion, time can only be taken as the number of the motion in its entirety—as the "first time," which is neither greater nor smaller than the motion (*Inst. Phys.*, def. I.4), or as the number of the motion of celestial bodies that do not change (*Inst. phys.*, def. II.13; Aristotle, *De caelo* 279a14–7). Such time is not a function that might describe the position of a body at some future moment of time on the trajectory of a moving, and not already moved, body.

But why is it at all possible to apply logic to physics—that is, to the consideration of bodily things that are in constant flux and change? Proclus uses the logical methods and means (*reductio ad absurdum*, syllogism) in the deduction and organization of the demonstrations of the propositions. In other words, both for Proclus and Aristotle, physics is to be logically ordered. This is the reason why physics is a science or ἐπιστήμη, because it is capable of relating its first principles to justifiable conclusions. The first principles of physics (e.g., *Inst. phys.*, defs. I.1–3) can be used in syllogistic, and, as such, can be applicable not only to physics but also to mathematics, as in Euclid's *Elements*. As O'Meara puts it, "geometry's contribution to physics is then methodological, and this method is essentially that of syllogistic argument."[28] Since there is the true being for Proclus that is comprehended by thinking accompanied by λόγος (ὄντως ὄν ἐστι τὸ νοῆσει μετὰ λόγου περιληπτόν, *In Tim.* I 236.21–2) and reflected in the cosmos, we can align the λόγος of our thought about physical things to the λόγος put into the cosmos by its demiurge as silently uttered in the self-moving cosmos (Plato, *Tim.* 37B), which we can hear and understand, and then present in a systematic account of mutually related, logically consistent, and provable propositions of the science of physics. Physics for Proclus is therefore nether a geometrical nor mathematical, but a logical enterprise.

---

[28] O'Meara, *Pythagoras Revived*, p. 178.

11

Matter and Evil

The intellect thinks determinate objects and defines them in their being and as being by the very act of thinking. Therefore, the intellect always finds it difficult to move in the realm of negativity, where thought is *à bout de souffle*, encountering non-being and stumbling upon the indeterminate. The indefinite is primarily represented as matter but also makes its appearance as evil, which becomes a particularly important topic for Plotinus toward the end of his life. Since Proclus was well aware of Plotinus' discussion of evil, I will begin with an account of Plotinus' views on matter and evil and then turn to Proclus' critical and highly original appropriation of them.

11.1 Matter in Plotinus

For Plotinus, matter stands for radical otherness, negativity, indefiniteness, and non-being. However, negativity is always a problem for a monistic philosophy such as Plotinus'. No wonder, then, that he returns to the problem of matter again and again in the attempt to grasp the ungraspable. In *Ennead* III.6 [26] and II.4 [12], Plotinus uses both Plato's and Aristotle's terminology to describe matter as receptacle and nurse (ὑποδοχὴ καὶ τιθήνη, *Enn.* II.4.6.1, III.6.13.12; cf. Plato, *Tim.* 49A) and the substrate of all things (ὑποκείμενον, *Enn.* III.6.7.1–3, III.6.10.8).[1] Yet, unlike in Plato, matter for Plotinus (1) permeates everything existent and is therefore present even in the intelligible and (2) is produced. And, unlike in Aristotle, matter for Plotinus is the indefinite and unlimited. Since matter is present in everything existent, in *Ennead* II.4 and II.5 [25], Plotinus develops an original interpretation of intelligible matter (ὕλη νοητή),

---

[1] Gary M. Gurtler, "Plotinus: Matter and Otherness, 'On Matter' (II 4[12])," *Epoché: A Journal for the History of Philosophy* 9 (2005), pp. 197–214, argues that Plotinus uses Platonic language to elucidate the Aristotelian concept of matter as indefinite substrate.

which is the matter of the thinkable objects and is itself a kind of form (*Enn.* II.5.3.15; see Chapter 6). This allows him to speak of a "ladder of matters," where the "higher" serves as the form for the "lower" (*Enn.* II.4.3.2–10). In his commentary on the first book of Euclid's *Elements*, Proclus develops his own original interpretation of intelligible matter as geometrical matter. This he takes to be the matter of geometrical objects and a kind of "screen" onto which imagination projects the λόγοι of mathematical objects, thus making them properly geometrical and representable as figures, intermediate between the purely thinkable (the non-discursive forms and discursive concepts-λόγοι) and the physical (*In Eucl.* 49.5, 51.9–20, 53.20–2; see Chapter 8). But here I am primarily interested in the "dark" side of matter, which is translated into the undissolvable connection between matter and evil.

If matter is indefiniteness, how does it come to be? For if matter "is" non-being, it cannot be; yet without matter as otherness, nothing can be either. Therefore, it should be produced. This question has been much discussed in recent years but still cannot be considered ultimately resolved. On the one hand, as O'Brien has argued, there are significant passages in Plotinus—fragmentary and early—that suggest that the lower soul produces something worse than itself (*Enn.* V.1.7.43–8), non-being (τὸ μὴ ὄν) as an image of itself (*Enn.* III.9.3.7–12), or the indefiniteness (ἀοριστία, *Enn.* III.4 [15].1.5–12). These texts, however, never explicitly mention "matter" as produced by the soul. On the other hand, as Narbonne has repeatedly argued, non-being is already present at the very beginning of the sequence of productions of the existent starting with the one. Indeed, matter in Plotinus appears first as intelligible matter, which is the "indefinite dyad" (cf. Aristotle, *Met.* 987b26, 1089a35, 1091a4, with reference to Platonic mathematical ontology; see the Appendix). As the dyad, matter arises as an indefinite thinking of the intellect in its attempt to grasp the ungraspable—its own origin, the one that "is" beyond and prior to being, which is why such a thinking is indefinite until it itself produces intelligible objects as (mis)representations of the first principle beyond being and the productive source of being (*Enn.* V.4.2.1–19). The intelligible and sensible matter are generated at different ontological levels, and the one does not produce the other. Yet it is important to stress that, *qua* indefiniteness, matter is generated right after the one, with the advent of being; and, before matter becomes associated with the lower soul, it is a kind of form or being, and as such is not an utter nothingness, which is the source of evil.[2]

---

[2] See the discussion in Beutler's and Harder's commentary on *Enn.* II.4 [12]: Plotinus, *Die Schriften 1–21 der chronologischen Reihenfolge Anmerkungen*, vol. 1 of *Plotins Schriften*, ed. Rudolf Beutler and Richard Harder (Hamburg: Meiner, 1956), p. 516; see also Schwyzer, "Zu Plotins Deutung der sogenannten platonischen Materie," pp. 266–80; Denis O'Brien, "Plotinus and the Gnostics on the Generation of Matter," in *Neoplatonism and Early Christian Thought: Essays in Honour of A. H. Armstrong*, ed. H. J. Blumenthal and R. A. Markus (London: Variorum Publications, 1981), pp. 108–23,

Matter is characterized by Plotinus mostly in negative terms, which is why the Platonic "receptacle" and the Aristotelian "substrate" need to be rethought and to rather acquire a metaphorical meaning. Primarily, matter "is" non-being, and thus *is* not, and is *not* anything in particular. It "is" the indefinite, the never determined potentiality, the absolute privation and absence of any determination, a lack of being, an unfathomable darkness.

Matter is nothing of itself: it "is" absolute non-being (οὐκ ὄν, *Enn.* II.4.16.26; μὴ ὄν, *Enn.* II.5.4.11, III.6.7.12)—it is the unlimited, infinite, and indefinite (τὸ ἄπειρον καὶ τὸ ἀόριστον, *Enn.* II.4.15.1–2, 10, 17; ἀπειρία, *Enn.* III.6.7.8). The unlimited is present both in the intelligible and in the sensible, where the former is a kind of form or the archetype (ἀρχέτυπον) for the latter as the image (εἴδωλον, *Enn.* II.4.15.22). As Plotinus says, matter is "a kind of unmeasuredness in relation to measure, and unboundedness in relation to limit, and formlessness in relation to creating form, and perpetual neediness in relation to what is self-sufficient; always undefined, nowhere stable, subject to every sort of influence, insatiate, complete need" (*Enn.* I.8.3.12–6). Hence, matter is "not yet stable by itself, and is carried about here and there into every form, and since it is altogether adaptable, becomes many by being brought into everything and becoming everything" (*Enn.* II.4.11.40–2). Matter is that which has nothing of itself, nothing of its own: it neither is nor possesses form, being, rational principle, activity, or actuality. Matter is need or neediness (πενία, *Enn.* I.8.3.16, II.4.16.20, III.6.14.8) that appears in and as everything in potentiality (πάντα δυνάμει, *Enn.* II.5.4.4). Matter is never actualized (*Enn.* II.5.4–5), but is always and only an "announcement" (ἐπαγγελλόμενον, *Enn.* II.5.5.4).[3] Yet the potentiality of matter differs from the potentiality of the one, which is equally beyond being and is ungraspable but is the active power beyond being that *produces* being and matter itself (*Enn.* II.4.15.19–20).

---

esp. 114–5; Kevin Corrigan, "Is There More than One Generation of Matter in the 'Enneads'?," *Phronesis* 31:2 (1986), pp. 167–81; Jean-Marc Narbonne, "Plotin et le problème de la génération de la matière: à propos d'un article recent," *Dionysius* 11 (1987), pp. 3–31; Denis O'Brien, "J.-M. Narbonne on Plotinus and The Generation of Matter: Two Corrections," *Dionysius* 12 (1988), pp. 25–6; *Plotinus on the Origin of Matter*, pp. 47–54; "Le non-être dans la philosophie grecque: Parménide, Platon, Plotin," in *Études sur le Sophiste de Platon*, ed. Michel Narcy (Naples: Bibliopolis, 1991), pp. 318–64; esp. 343–8; Jean-Marc Narbonne, "Le non-être chez Plotin et dans la tradition grecque," *Revue de la philosophie ancienne* 10 (1992), pp. 115–33; *La métaphysique de Plotin*, p. 133; Corrigan, *Plotinus' Theory of Matter-Evil*, pp. 257–63; Nikulin, *Matter, Imagination, and Geometry*, pp. 78–9, 136–9; Jean-Marc Narbonne, "La controverse à propos de la génération de la matière chez Plotin: l'énigme résolue?," *Questio* 7 (2007), pp. 123–63; Simon Fortier, "The Relationship of the Kantian and Proclan Conceptions of Evil," *Dionysius* 26 (2008), pp. 175–92, esp. 185–7; John Phillips, "Plotinus on the Generation of Matter," *International Journal of the Platonic Tradition* 3 (2009), pp. 103–37; and Jean-Marc Narbonne, *Plotinus in Dialogue with the Gnostics* (Leiden: Brill, 2011), pp. 11–47.

[3] See Cinzia Arruzza, "Passive Potentiality in the Physical Realm: Plotinus' Critique of Aristotle in Ennead II.5 [25]," *Archiv für Geschichte der Philosophie* 93 (2011), pp. 24–57.

Hence, matter is other to everything and nothing but other (μόνον ἄλλο; ἄλλα, *Enn.* II.4.13.30–1), yet it is not the same as otherness (ἑτερότης, *Enn.* II.4.16.1–2); that is, not the principle of otherness. Rather, matter is inescapably other, "another being" (ἕτερον ὄν, *Enn.* II.4.16.26; cf. I.8.3.6–9).

Indefinite and infinite, matter "runs away from the idea of limit" (τὸ ἄπειρον φεύγει . . . αὐτὸ τὴν τοῦ πέρατος ἰδέαν) but is captured from outside by the intelligible form (*Enn.* VI.6.3.15–6). Still, matter remains forever unaffected and is inalterable because there is nothing in it that could be subject to change (*Enn.* III.6.10.21–2; cf. III.6.11.15–8). Therefore, since there is no "self," subject, or substance of and to matter, it can only be characterized apophatically, negatively, and privatively: it "is" without qualities, indefinite, impassible, bodiless, and the like. Grammatically, matter is best described by the *alpha privativum*, ἄλφα στερητικόν: it is ἀόριστον, ἄμορφον, ἀπαθής, ἄποιος, ἄποσον, ἄμετρον, ἀμετρία, ἄπειρος, ἀπειρία, ἄνοια, ἀόρατον, ἀμέγεθες, ἀνόλεθρος, ἀνείδεον (*Enn.* II.4.3.1–2, II.4.8.1, II.4.9.4, II.4.12.34–8, II.4.15.17, 33–4, II.4.16.9–10, I.8.3.13–6, I.8.4.27, I.8.6.42, I.8.8.38, I.8.10.1, III.6.18.30).

Because matter has nothing of its own, it has no light and is thus "darkness" (τὸ σκότος, σκοτεινή), inaccessible to the gaze of the intellect and never illuminated by the light of being. However, since there is matter in the intelligible, too, the darkness in the intelligible things differs from the darkness in sensible things (*Enn.* I.8.8.40, II.4.5.6–15).

But how can matter as non-being and darkness be known? Apparently, darkness cannot be seen. Since the intellect thinks the intelligible, which is being, in order to think the non-being or darkness, the intellect must abandon the light and being and therefore itself. Darkness, then, is "thought," or rather *not* thought, by the other in the intellect, οὐ νοῦς (*Enn.* I.8.9.18), "out of one's mind," which is the lower soul (*Enn.* I.8.4.31, I.8.9.14–26). This radical turning away from the light of being to the darkness of matter is sometimes taken to be the moment of the production of the matter of sensible beings, which in fact is the moment of the constitution of the knowledge of the not-knowable, of seeing the not-visible with the eyes of the soul wide shut.

The knowledge of matter is thus necessary but impossible—if knowledge is seeing the intelligible in the light of the intellect's thinking. This knowledge, then, is not-knowledge or is knowledge only by analogy. As "depth" (τὸ βάθος, *Enn.* II.4.5.6–7), matter is unfathomable and cannot be properly thought, and hence it defies and escapes λόγος, any rational detection or argument. As an elusive other to being, matter is a "part" of otherness that opposes any rational considerations (μορίῳ ἑτερότητος ἀντιταττομένῳ πρὸς τὰ ὄντα κυρίως, ἃ δὴ λόγοι, *Enn.* II.4.16.1–3). However, as said, it is not the other properly or the principle of otherness. The knowledge of matter, then, can be gained in its elusiveness by complete removal or abstraction of all positive determinations: as not being, not finite (*Enn.* I.8.9.7). Or, as Plato suggests in the *Timaeus* (52B), matter can be seen in its opaqueness and darkness by non-seeing, by non-thought—but by some kind of "illegitimate consideration" (νόθῳ λογισμῷ, *Enn.* II.4.10.11, II.4.12.33–4; cf. ἐπιβολὴ ἀόριστος, *Enn.* II.4.10.5; see Chapter 6). Strictly speaking, matter does not have a concept, which is why it is always inevitably missed by reasoning. As Plotinus explains, matter as the infinite is *not* a concept (τὸ ... ἄπειρον οὐ λόγος, *Enn.* II.4.15.13; cf. V.8.7.22–3, where matter is called εἶδός τι ἔσχατον)—but the elusive and the ungraspable indefiniteness. This is why in matter, the infinite (τὸ ἄπειρον) and (essentially) being-infinite (ἀπείρῳ εἶναι) are different, since this distinction applies only for those entities for which the concept (λόγος) differs from that of which it is the concept (*Enn.* II.4.15.28–32; cf. Aristotle, *Phys.* 204a23–4). Matter is not the same as the notion of matter, not because the concept differs from its object but because matter does *not* properly have a concept by which it could be grasped.

11.2 Plotinus on Evil

The starting point for Plotinus' reasoning about evil is that it cannot be found among being (and hence, in the intellect and the rational soul) or beyond being (in the one, which is *the* good and the source of being) since these are good. Therefore, evil should be in non-being, as if a "form of non-being" (οἷον εἶδός τι τοῦ μὴ ὄντος, *Enn.* I.8.3.1–6), paradoxically present among the absent, existing among the non-existent. But this is not really a form, but rather "other than being" (ἕτερον μόνον τοῦ ὄντος, *Enn.* I.8.3.7). Since being is defined by being defined, definite and finite, and thus having measure and limit, the other to it is the infinite and indefinite. In Plotinus' own words, evil is "as if unmeasuredness in relation to measure, and unlimited in relation to limit, and formlessness in relation to rational principle, and eternal need in relation to the self-sufficient, always indefinite, nowhere stable, subject to every kind of change, insatiate, complete need; and all this is not accidental to it but as if its essence."[4] Because evil is nothing, unlimited, as non-being, it can only be described metaphorically, always as "*as-if*" (οἷον). For this reason, evil does *not* properly have an essence: "If only there really can be a substance of evil!" (εἴ τις καὶ δύναται κακοῦ οὐσία εἶναι, *Enn.* I.8.3.38), exclaims Plotinus in desperation.

There is nothing to be known in evil as such—it can be known only by abstraction (ἀφαιρέσει, *Enn.* I.8.9.7). And yet we have to try to understand evil, even if there is nothing there to understand. Since evil is the worst, it

---

[4] "οἷον ἀμετρίαν εἶναι πρὸς μέτρον καὶ ἄπειρον πρὸς πέρας καὶ ἀνείδεον πρὸς εἰδοποιητικὸν καὶ ἀεὶ ἐνδεὲς πρὸς αὔταρκες, ἀεὶ ἀόριστον, οὐδαμῇ ἑστώς, παμπαθές, ἀκόρητον, πενία παντελής· καὶ οὐ συμβεβηκότα ταῦτα αὐτῷ, ἀλλ᾽ οἷον οὐσία αὐτοῦ ταῦτα" (*Enn.* I.8.3.13–6).

is that which stands against all things good, true, and beautiful. As such, it violates the ancient Greek ideal of "nothing in excess" (μηδὲν ἄγαν). Evil "is" the *absolute deficiency* (ἔλλειψις, *Enn.* I.8.4.23–4, I.8.5.6–14). Evil is the *unmeasured* (τὸ ἄμετρον κακόν, *Enn.* I.8.8.38; ἀπειρία καὶ ἀμετρία, *Enn.* I.8.6.42, I.8.3.27; ἄπειρον, *Enn.* I.8.9.6). As unmeasured and indeterminate, evil is non-being and "below" anything existent, the unfathomable, the "base base," the depth unreachable to the light and goodness of being. This is evil by itself (αὐτοκακόν, *Enn.* I.8.8.42, I.8.13.9; τὸ κακὸν αὐτό, *Enn.* I.8.13.14), even though there is no "self" to evil since, as indefinite, it cannot be defined—only negatively. The absolute lack of anything that could have a measure or proportion and thus a share in the (or even *a*) good, true, and beautiful—this is evil by itself (κακὸν . . . τὸ αὐτό, I.8.3.24; τὸ ὄντως κακόν, *Enn.* I.8.5.9). Evil is the primary and absolute falsity (πρώτως καὶ ὄντως ψεῦδος, *Enn.* I.8.6.45). It is the lie that does not properly exist yet cannot be extricated from the existent. There is thus something deeply troubling about evil not only practically but also ontologically and epistemologically.

Evil is not a form but rather an "as-if" form, and yet one should distinguish the indistinguishable: absolute or primary and secondary evil. Evil is present in its distortive absence that makes us not only suffer and do improper things but also attempt to think the unthinkable and the negative. Evil for Plotinus resides not in the realm of a shared action that might result in atrocities or mass murder, but rather in the soul, as moral and cognitive evil of vice and ignorance, and in the body, as physical evil of personal misfortune, of being not well, poor, unattractive, and old. "Vice [κακία], which is ignorance and unmeasuredness [ἄγνοια . . . καὶ ἀμετρία], is evil secondarily [δευτέρως], not evil by itself [αὐτοκακόν]" (*Enn.* I.8.8.41–2). The secondary evil is such through "likeness or participation" (ὁμοιώσει ἢ μεταλήψει, *Enn.* I.8.8.39; cf. I.8.3.18–20, I.8.4.1, I.8.8.44) to that which *cannot be participated* because, strictly speaking, evil *is not*. The explanation of particular evils by their "participation" in the primary evil is thus profoundly confusing and should be taken rather as a metaphor. A better way of understanding the secondary evils is through their relation to matter, which, as said, is lack or need. Particular evils, such as illness, ugliness, poverty, are then lack and privation of health, beauty, and wealth. These are *as-if* species (οἷον εἴδη, *Enn.* I.8.5.17) of evil, or "specific" evils. As such, they can be understood as conditioned by deficiency and excess (ἔλλειψις καὶ ὑπερβολή) in relation to matter: "Illness is defect and excess of material bodies which do not keep order and measure; ugliness is matter not mastered by form; poverty is a lack and privation of things which we need because of the matter with which we are coupled, whose very nature is to be in need" (*Enn.* I.8.5.21–6).

This brings us to the question of the relationship between matter and evil. Plotinus describes both in the same terms, as non-being (οὐδὲ γὰρ τὸ εἶναι ἔχει ἡ ὕλη, *Enn.* I.8.5.9–10), darkness (*Enn.* II.4.5.7), need (πενία), deficiency (ἔλλειψις), infinite and indefinite (ἄπειρον), and lacking the good (*Enn.* II.4.16.16–7).[5] Matter and evil, then, are the same since they have the same "properties." Yet, because they "are" non-being, they have no properties at all and thus cannot be the same since "sameness" is not applicable to them. But matter is the *other* (ἄλλο) to everything else, even to itself, which means that in its elusiveness, non-being, need, and deficiency, then, matter paradoxically yet inescapably "*is*" evil (κακὸν ἡ ὕλη, *Enn.* II.4.16.16, VI.7.28.12).

However, in its very description, evil also strangely resembles the one, which is *the* good (ἀγαθόν) and the source of being and everything existent (*Enn.* VI.8.8.9, VI.9.9.1–2), itself beyond being (ἐπέκεινα ὄντος, *Enn.* II.4.16.25; cf. Plato, *Rep.* 509B). Strictly speaking, the one is equally non-being (as beyond being) and infinite. One can say that the distinction between matter/evil and the one/the good lies in the fact that the latter "is" (1) superabundance and not deficiency; (2) it produces in its superabundant potency (*Enn.* V.1.6.38) and is not produced as that which by itself is incapable of production; (3) it is the first and not the last; and (4) it is that to which everything existent aspires (οὗ πάντα τὰ ὄντα ἐφίεται, *Enn.* I.8.2.3; Aristotle, *NE* 1094a3) and does not avoid. Yet, because thinking has to deal with the definite and the existent, it cannot make any statement about that which is beyond and prior to being. This means that all these qualifications are only provisional and the "real" distinction between the one/the good and evil/matter is not properly accessible to thinking because this distinction is inevitable but not "real"; that is, it does not refer to the thinkable and the existent (see Chapter 1).

But since evil is the absolute deficiency, the unlimited and the non-existent, it has no hold on being. This means that intelligible matter, which is a kind of form, cannot be evil; and the intellect and the rational part of the soul cannot be evil either. Therefore, the soul is receptive of evil as unmeasuredness, excess, and defect only in its lower or irrational part (τοῦ ἀλόγου τῆς ψυχῆς, *Enn.* I.8.4.8–9; cf. Plato, *Legg.* 896D–897A: the soul can be the cause of *both* good and evil). Evil takes hold on us when our soul

> is not outside matter but is mixed or by itself. So it is mixed with unmeasuredness and without a share in the form which brings order and reduces to measure, since it is fused with a body which has matter. And then its reasoning part [τὸ λογιζόμενον], if that is damaged, is hindered in its seeing by the passions and by being darkened by matter, and inclined to matter, and altogether by looking towards becoming, not being; and the principle of becoming is the nature of matter, which is so evil that

---

[5] See Rist, "Plotinus on Matter and Evil," pp. 154–66; Arruzza, "Passive Potentiality in the Physical Realm," pp. 25–54; *Les mésaventures de la théodicée: Plotin, Origène, Grégoire de Nysse* (Turnhout: Brepols, 2011), pp. 33–41; and Jean-Marc Narbonne, "Matter and Evil in the Neoplatonic Tradition," in *The Routledge Handbook of Neoplatonism*, pp. 231–44.

it infects with its own evil that which is not in it but only directs its gaze to it. (*Enn.* I.8.4.14–22)[6]

It is in our action that the danger of evil is lurking, when we do not think straight and succumb to vice as the lack of measure, and in our bodily presence, when matter affects and "infects" us, immersing us in becoming and distracting us from being, which is always free of evil.

But even as non-being, evil is *necessary* for Plotinus, which follows from the argument from the order of being: "It is necessary that what comes after the first should exist, and therefore that the last [τὸ ἔσχατον] should exist; and this is matter, which possesses nothing at all of the good. And in this way too evil is necessary" (*Enn.* I.8.7.21–3).[7] But such also is matter: as utter deficiency, it is present in its absence, in the necessity of its existence (τὴν ἀνάγκην τῆς ὑποστάσεως, *Enn.* I.8.15.1–3) because the world cannot exist without matter (*Enn.* I.8.7.2–4; cf. Plato, *Tim.* 47E–49A).

Evil is thus inevitable. It does not appear as an abuse of free choice but is necessary in the order of being. And yet, although evils are perennial and prior to us (πρὸ ἡμῶν, *Enn.* I.8.5.27), we can escape from them by acquiring virtue and by becoming separate from the body and thereby from matter. In this way, we are capable of living the godlike life free from evil, thinking with the intellect and abiding with being (*Enn.* I.8.7.12–6; cf. Plato, *Theaet.* 176B), and even eventually fleeing to the good itself in the "escape in solitude to the solitary" (φυγὴ μόνου πρὸς μόνον, *Enn.* VI.9.11.51).

11.3 Proclus, the Critic of Plotinus

Much of Proclus' discussion of evil appears in his treatise on the existence of evils, *De malorum subsistentia*, as a response to and polemic against Plotinus' consideration of evil in *Ennead* I.8 [51].[8] Proclus summarizes Plotinus'

---

[6] See Christian Schäfer, "Das Dilemma der neuplatonischen Theodizee: Versuch einer Lösung," *Archiv für Geschichte der Philosophie* 82 (2000), pp. 1–35.

[7] See the discussion of the necessity and origin of evil and a careful reconstruction of Plotinus' argument in Christian Schäfer, *Unde malum: Die Frage nach dem Woher des Bösen bei Plotin, Augustinus und Dionysius* (Würzburg: Königshausen & Neumann, 2002), pp. 105–66; and Dominic O'Meara, "The Metaphysics of Evil in Plotinus: Problems and Solutions," in *Agonistes: Essays in Honour of Denis O'Brien*, ed. J. Dillon and M. Dixsaut (Burlington, VT: Ashgate, 2005), pp. 179–85.

[8] Proclus, *Tria opuscula (De providentia, libertate, malo)*, ed. H. Boese (Berlin: De Gruyter, 1960). All Latin quotations of this text follow the translation of William of Moerbeke, while the Greek text follows the paraphrase of Isaak Sebastokrator according to Boese's edition. The English translation is taken from Proclus, *On the Existence of Evils*, trans. Jan Opsomer and Carlos Steel (Ithaca: Cornell University Press, 2003), which also contains an excellent introduction to the text, along with commentaries. See also Proclus, *De l'existence du mal*, vol. 3 of *Trois études sur la Providence*, trans. Daniel Isaac and Carlos Steel (Paris: Les Belles Lettres, 1982).

arguments as follows (without ever naming him): (1) matter is without any qualities, is formless, is a substrate and not *in* a substrate, is simple and not in anything else (*apoios* [*id est sine qualitate*] *et informis est et subiectum, sed non in subiecto, et simplex, sed non aliud in alio* / ἄποιός ἐστι καὶ ἀνείδεος καὶ ὑποκείμενον, ἀλλ᾽ οὐκ ἐν ὑποκειμένῳ, καὶ ἁπλοῦν, ἀλλ᾽ οὐκ ἄλλο ἐν ἄλλῳ, *De mal. subs.* 30.4–6).[9] This all comes to saying that matter is utterly indefinite and practically nothing; that is, nothing definite. However, calling matter "substrate" seems perplexing since the Aristotelian substrate is not formless but is a definite subject (εἶδός τι καὶ τόδε τι), so, in this case, it should rather be the Aristotelian matter as the first substrate of every thing (τὸ πρῶτον ὑποκείμενον ἑκάστῳ, Aristotle, *Phys.* 192a31) or prime matter, which is not anything definite (ὕλη πρώτη οὐ τόδε τι οὖσα, Aristotle, *Met.* 1049a24–36).[10] In other words, according to Proclus, Plotinus does not make a clear distinction between the first substrate and the substrate of concrete things. Since, furthermore, evil is unmeasuredness and utter indefiniteness, matter and evil should be identical, even though such identity cannot be properly grasped because of the utter indefiniteness of the subject-matter. In addition, (2) for Plotinus good and evil are both twofold (*duplex*, διττόν): absolute and particular (a particular good or evil, which is in something else [*in alio*, ἐν ἄλλῳ, *De mal. subs.* 30.14–9]). The absolute good is the first, the proto-Anselmian "that than which nothing can be better," while the absolute evil is the last, "that than which nothing can be worse." Since matter is also the last, it should therefore be identical with evil.

It is noteworthy that Proclus borrows some of Plotinus' major presuppositions regarding evil yet arrives at very different conclusions. Most importantly, Proclus agrees with Plotinus that, first, evil is the weakness in and of the soul (*De mal. subs.* 31.2; cf. *Enn.* I.8.14.49–51) and that evil is unmeasuredness, the absolute infinite, imperfection, and indeterminateness (*immensuratio et autoinfinitum et imperfectum et indeterminatum* / ἀμετρία καὶ αὐτοάπειρον καὶ ἀτελὲς καὶ ἀόριστον, *De mal. subs.* 30.11–2; cf. 29.20–1). Yet Proclus disagrees with Plotinus that these are also the characteristics of matter since Proclus intends to dissolve any connection between matter and evil. For him, if matter can be evil, then it is so only accidentally and not essentially, not evil per se. And, second, Proclus accepts Plotinus' distinction of the good and evil as double (*De mal. subs.* 37.9–10), which, as we will see, he appropriates for a different purpose; namely, to describe evil as a kind of privation. In other words, Proclus understands the elusive nature of evil not

---

[9] On Proclus' criticism of Plotinus' account of matter, see Jan Opsomer, "Proclus vs Plotinus on Matter (*De Mal. Subs.* 30–37)," *Phronesis* 46 (2001), pp. 154–88; "Some Problems with Plotinus' Theory of Matter/Evil: An Ancient Debate Continued," *Quaestio* 7 (2007), pp. 165–89; and Radek Chlup, *Proclus: An Introduction* (Cambridge: Cambridge University Press, 2012), pp. 202–8.

[10] See Happ, *Hyle*, pp. 278–309.

unlike Plotinus, yet in his account of matter he radically disagrees with his predecessor.

Proclus finds several ontological, logical, and hermeneutical flaws in Plotinus' identification of matter and evil. From Proclus' ontological and logical perspective, if matter is evil, then (i) either the good is the cause of evil, or (ii) there are two independent principles of being (cf. *In Remp.* I 37.3–8, with a reference to *De malorum subsistentia* at *In Remp.* I 37.23). But (i) the good cannot be the cause of evil because the effect (the produced) always bears a similarity to, and affinity with, the cause (the producer). Matter for Proclus is produced by the one (*De mal. subs.* 35.8), as matter also is as indefinite dyad for Plotinus. Therefore, because the one is the good, it cannot cause or produce evil (Proclus, *In Parm.* 830.1–7, 831.5–9; cf. Plato, *Tim.* 29E), and matter is not evil. And (ii) the good and evil, or the one and matter, cannot be two independent principles either because there can be no two principles as two firsts (*neque . . . duo prima*, οὔτε . . . δύο τὰ πρῶτα, *De mal. subs.* 31.11) since we would then need to posit another principle for these two, whereas each one is supposed to be the first (*De mal. subs.* 31.5–24). Besides, if matter is disorder and is utterly indeterminate (*De mal. subs.* 29.16–7), it cannot by itself exercise any efficiency, and yet evil for Proclus is efficient in souls and bodies.

From Proclus' exegetical point of view, Plotinus' interpretation does not explain a number of crucial passages, such as Plato's *Philebus* (26C–27C), where the unlimited (matter) is said to be produced from and by the one;[11] the *Republic* (379C), where god (the good) is said not to be the cause of evil; and the *Timaeus* (34B), which claims that the demiurge is blessed and thus good (*De mal. subs.* 32.2; 34.9–14).

11.4 Proclus on Matter

Thus, Proclus' view of matter is much more optimistic. Matter, for him, is *not* evil. This means that both matter and evil play very different roles in Proclus' grand picture of the world, in which everything proceeds from the superessential first good cause and falls into its right place, leaving nothing redundant or obsolete.

For Proclus, (1) matter cannot be evil because, first, it is produced by the good, which cannot cause evil, and, second, matter is that out of which the producer—the good cause—makes the world. In his polemical fervor against Plotinus, Proclus even first concludes that matter is good (*De mal. subs.* 33.29), but later concedes that it is neither good nor evil (*neque . . . bonum*

---

[11] Cf. Gerd Van Riel, "Horizontalism or Verticalism? Proclus vs Plotinus on the Procession of Matter," *Phronesis* 46 (2001), pp. 129–53.

esse materiam neque malum / μήτε ἀγαθὸν εἶναι τὴν ὕλην μήτε κακόν, *De mal. subs.* 36.4). For matter is good to the extent that it has been produced for the sake of a good, the existence of the world, which is good in its entirety; but matter is evil as the "lowest of beings." Yet *by itself* matter is neither good nor evil, insofar as it plays a well-conceived and established role in the divine comedy of the world.

Being neither good nor evil, matter (2) is only *necessary* (*necessarium solum*, ἀναγκαῖον μόνον, *De mal. subs.* 37.2–3; cf. 36.15–6),[12] on which point Proclus agrees with Plotinus (*Enn.* I.8.15.1–3). However, for Plotinus, matter is necessary as absolute negativity and evil, whereas for Proclus it is necessary as the substrate in which the world is generated (cf. Plato, *Tim.* 47E).[13] In the *De malorum subsistentia*, Proclus is silent about *the other* matter, the intelligible matter, which Plotinus discusses explicitly. However, in his commentary on Euclid, Proclus goes to great length to demonstrate the importance of intelligible matter as the matter of geometrical objects, which are intermediate between the intelligible objects (forms and λόγοι as their discursive representations) and physical things. The mathematical objects share with both intelligible and physical entities certain properties, but the mathematicals are also distinct from both to such an extent that they even need their own cognitive faculty (imagination) in order to be constructed and recognized and their own materiality (geometrical matter) in order to exist (see Chapter 8). As we will see, evil for Proclus has the peculiar character of an accidental cause, whereas matter is *not* accidental but necessary. Matter is not nothing but remains as the Aristotelian substrate, when form is present in it, whereas, as it will be demonstrated later, evil is a peculiar kind of privation, which has no being (*esse*) at all (*De mal. subs.* 38.3–5).

Finally, (3) matter, being the last and "lowest," has no being of its own but only dimly participates in being. Therefore, ontologically matter is a perennial "not-yet," that which itself is never entirely good or bad but is the longing or *desire* for the good: "Matter desires the good, strives for it and partakes in it" (*appetere bonum et expetere et transumere, De mal. subs.* 38.5–6; cf. 36.26–7). As such, matter gives forms a chance to be embodied and thus a possibility for the sensible things to come into being, to their being, even if imperfectly and only for a while. Now Proclus can make a proper distinction between evil and matter as unmeasuredness and indefiniteness: matter can be considered

---

[12] For a discussion of necessity in Proclus, see Alessandro Linguiti, "Physis as Heimarmene: On Some Fundamental Principles of the Neoplatonic Philosophy of Nature," in *Physics and Philosophy of Nature in Greek Neoplatonism*, pp. 173–88, esp. 182–3; and Gerd Van Riel, "Proclus on Matter and Physical Necessity," in *Physics and Philosophy of Nature in Greek Neoplatonism*, pp. 231–55.

[13] See Ian Mueller, "What's the Matter? Some Neo-Platonist Answers," in *One Book: The Whole Universe: Plato's* Timaeus *Today*, ed. R. D. Mohr and B. M. Sattler (Las Vegas: Parmenides, 2010), pp. 151–63, esp. 161–3.

disorder (*le inordinatum*) only in the realm of generation, where matter is the absolute absence of measure, indeterminateness, and absolute darkness (*ipsum immensuratio, autoindeterminatio, auto-tenebra, De mal. subs.* 29.17–21). As Opsomer and Steel note, first, all three terms in this description are *hapax legomena* in Proclus, and, second, they replicate the description of matter in Plotinus (ἀοριστία, *Enn.* III.4.1.11–2; τὸ ἀόριστον πάντῃ σκοτεινόν, *Enn.* III.9.3.12–3; ἀμετρία, *Enn.* I.8.3.27; ἀπειρία καὶ ἀμετρία, *Enn.* I.8.6.42).[14] However, for Proclus, matter and evil are unmeasured and indeterminate in different senses. Indeed, following the Prodican and Aristotelian program of the logical distinction of meanings, according to which every concept (primarily, being) is "said in many ways" (*multipliciter dicimus* / πολλαχῶς λέγομεν, *De mal. subs.* 32.10; cf. Aristotle, *Phys.* 185a21 [πολλαχῶς λέγεται τὸ ὄν], 185b6; *Met.* 1003a33), one can discern three senses of the "unmeasured" and "unlimited": as the opposite to measure, as its absence, and as the *need* for measure and limit (*indigens* / τὸ ἐνδεές, *De mal. subs.* 32.17–9; 36.27). Because matter is the desire for the good, it is indefiniteness as the *need* of the good, whereas, as we will see, evil is the *opposite* of measure (cf. Plotinus, *Enn.* I.8.6.43–4).

The conclusion that Proclus draws from his overall very perceptive critique of Plotinus is that evil does not come from matter (*non ex materia malum* / οὐκ ἐκ τῆς ὕλης τὸ κακόν, *De mal. subs.* 35.2). Therefore, matter is *not* the primary evil.

11.5 Proclus on Evil. Privation: Aristotle, Plotinus, and Proclus

Proclus' understanding of evil encompasses three main aspects: the exegesis of Plato, the criticism of Plotinus, and his own systematic interpretation, which, in turn, radically rethinks three main Aristotelian and Platonic concepts of privation, contrariety, and existence.

Let me begin with the first concept, that of privation. Since speaking about evil implies using the language of negativity, Proclus turns to the existing philosophical vocabulary, which, as usual, he reappropriates for his own purposes. In general, Proclus is much more careful with his interpretation of Plato, whom he follows to the word, than he is with Aristotle, from whom he often borrows without paying much attention to the original context in which a concept has been used. For Proclus is convinced that the context of his own debate is the genuine Platonic one, with which the Aristotelian account should be either reconcilable or otherwise ignored.

---

[14] Proclus, *On the Existence of Evils*, p. 119 n. 208.

As we have seen, against Plotinus, Proclus argues that (1) matter is not absolute non-being, (2) matter cannot be the cause of evil, and (3) matter is not identical with (absolute) privation.[15] On this interpretation, negativity resides in privation, rather than in matter, and therefore one needs to look into the category of privation in order to find out whether it can describe what evil is and whether it exists.

When Aristotle discusses the first principles in the *Physics*, he comes to the conclusion that the principles should be opposites, one positively expressing what a thing is, which is its definition (λόγος), and the other negatively denying the λόγος as its lack or privation (στέρησις). However, contrary to Plato, the opposites for Aristotle cannot coexist or interact without mediation since this would amount to the violation of the principle of non-contradiction (Aristotle, *Met.* 1011b16–8). For this reason, nothing is or can be contrary or opposite to substance as either substrate or the subject of predication (Aristotle, *Cat.* 3b24–5; *Phys.* 189a32–3). Therefore, one needs to assume the third, opposite-neutral, principle, which is substrate (ὑποκείμενον), capable of mediating the opposites (Aristotle, *Cat.* 2a12–3, 3a7–8, 4a10–1; *Phys.* 190a36–190b1, 191a12–4). This is why privation differs from negation (ἀφαίρεσις) as a mere absence (ἀπουσία) because privation is always referred to substrate, which can be deprived of something (Aristotle, *Met.* 1004a14–6; cf. 1056a15–6). This might also be considered a distinction between non-being and not-being.

Privation thus becomes a major principle, which in Aristotle has two main features. First, (A) the triad of the principles of substrate, definition, and privation can be rethought as the triad of form, matter, and privation, where the form stands for being and the essence of a thing; whereas matter is non-being, but only accidentally (τὸ ... οὐκ ὄν ... κατὰ συμβεβηκός) because matter is either the first substrate of each thing (and hence, although it is not determinate, it is not nothing)—or it can be formed matter (bronze or wood). Therefore, privation has to assume the role of the *non-being as such* (καθ' αὑτήν, Aristotle, *Phys.* 192a3–5). It is this sense of privation as absolute non-being that Plotinus picks, while denying that matter can be definite in any way.[16]

And second, (B) privation for Aristotle is to be considered as the *opposite* (ἐναντία) either of definition or of being (Aristotle, *Phys.* 229b26). Privation as the opposite of being, as absolute non-being, is not anything that can exist on its own and have active or final causality. Rather, it stands for the indeterminateness of non-being, which is why privation is the being of the infinite or indefinite (Aristotle, *Phys.* 208a1). In the *Physics*, privation comes as the

---

[15] See John Phillips, *Order from Disorder: Proclus' Doctrine of Evil and Its Roots in Ancient Platonism* (Leiden: Brill, 2007), pp. 67–71.

[16] See Christopher Noble, "Plotinus' Unaffectable Matter," *Oxford Studies in Ancient Philosophy* 44 (2013), pp. 233–77.

opposite of matter, as non-being as such, opposite to accidental non-being. However, Aristotle also speaks of the privation of form (εἶδος; the cold is the privation of the form of the warm, *De gen. et corr.* 318b16–7) and of substance (οὐσία, *Met.* 1011b18–9). As such, privation *can be* opposite to substance, although not *qua* substrate or subject of predication, but as the opposite of definition or of genus. (The mole is blind because of the privation of sight in the genus, whereas a person is blind because of the privation of sight in himself, Aristotle, *Met.* 1011b19–20; *Cat.* 12a26–7). Privation as the absence of being is not an active act but a lack, a shadow that happens to "be," or rather not be, there where the light does not penetrate.

Yet everything for Aristotle is said in many ways, and the same category can have various characterizations depending on a particular task he has to address, which also explains why the central category of privation receives a different treatment in different works. In the *Categories*, Aristotle distinguishes the category of the opposite (ἀντικεῖσθαι) into four kinds: relation (τὰ πρός τι), contrarieties (τὰ ἐναντία), privation and having (or disposition, στέρησις καὶ ἕξις), and assertion and negation (κατάφασις καὶ ἀπόφασις, *Cat.* 11b17–23). The paradigmatic examples of these four kinds of opposites are the double and the half, the good and evil, blindness and sight, and "sitting"–"not sitting." Aristotle agrees, then, that evil is the opposite (ἐναντίον) of the good, even if sometimes evil is opposite to another evil (*Cat.* 13b36–14a2). However, privation as not-having appears in a different kind of opposition from that of good and evil and thus, strictly speaking, is not applicable to the description and understanding of evil. In short, privation for Aristotle is opposite to being (as having a disposition to act in a certain way) and not to the good.

Plotinus uses the notion of privation to address the question of evil, although in doing so he has to rethink the concept. Plotinus understands στέρησις in the Aristotelian sense as a "removal," "taking away" (ἄρσις), a lack of quality (ἐρημία ποιότητος, *Enn.* II.4.13.21–3) or of a form that ought to be present (*Enn.* I.8.11.10). As such, privation is opposed to form and does not have an independent existence of itself but is always in something else (στέρησις δὲ ἀεὶ ἐν ἄλλῳ καὶ ἐπ᾽ αὐτῆς οὐχ ὑπόστασις, *Enn.* I.8.11.2–3; cf. II.4.16.4).

However, *contra* Aristotle who distinguishes between the triad of form, matter, and privation, Plotinus explicitly *identifies* matter with privation. For Plotinus, matter is substrate, insofar as both are a mere relation to other things (πρὸς τὰ ἄλλα); and matter is also privation, insofar as both are *indefinite* (τὸ ἀόριστον, *Enn.* II.4.14.24–30; στερήσει ταὐτόν, *Enn.* II.4.16.3).[17] Yet evil, too,

---

[17] Cf.: "Plotinus indeed identifies substrate with privation, thus violating an Aristotelian thesis. Aristotle had defined the substrate as that which persists through a process of change, whereas privation is that which disappears as a result of the change" (Opsomer and Steel, introduction to Proclus, *On the Existence of Evils*, p. 13).

as was said, is characterized as indefiniteness and absolute deficiency (ἄκρατος ἔλλειψις, *Enn.* I.8.4.23–4, I.8.5.5) and as such is privation (*Enn.* I.8.11.3). But of what is evil the privation? Plotinus is quite clear about it: absolute evil is the absolute privation of *the* good (παντελῆ στέρησιν . . . ἀγαθοῦ) and not of *a* good (τινα . . . ἀγαθοῦ, *Enn.* I.8.12.1–5). At the same time, privation is also the privation of form. Therefore, for Plotinus, evil is identical with matter (beyond identity, since either is non-being and indefiniteness) and is privation—both of form (as non-being and indefinite) and of the good (as primary evil). It will be Proclus who makes, partly in criticism of Plotinus, an important and consistent distinction between the privation of the form and the privation of the good.

Proclus appropriates both main features of Aristotle's discussion of privation that were mentioned earlier: first, (A) privation is non-being as such and contrary to being (*le non ens . . . secundum se et contrarium ad ens, De mal. subs.* 38.9). In this respect, for Proclus as for Aristotle, privation differs from matter, which makes Proclus reject Plotinus' understanding of evil as privation and matter.[18] Indeed, with Aristotle, Proclus takes matter to be substrate, which it becomes in the presence of form, whereas privation has no being (*De mal. subs.* 38.3–4). Here again, we need to take into account the foundational Neoplatonic thesis that the one is the good beyond being and thus is not being but the source of being. On this interpretation, if evil is opposite to the good, if non-being is opposite to being, and if privation is non-being, then privation as such is not evil (*De mal. subs.* 38.9–13). Absolute non-being, which is privation as such or absolute privation (*privatio simpliciter*), amounts to the disappearance of evil and the evil nature (*De mal. subs.* 38.13–4). Non-being as privation, then, is sheer negativity that cannot exist in its own right (*De mal. subs.* 7.28) and hence cannot be known or understood from within itself but only as the lack of being or form.

At this point, Proclus makes a crucial distinction: the good is twofold or double (*duplex*)—the primary (*akraton*) good, which is the good itself, which is beyond being and thinking and is their source, and the good mixed with other things (*permixtum*). Evil, then, should be equally twofold—the absolute evil, evil itself (*ipsum*), which, properly speaking, is "below" being and thus does not exist, and evil mixed with the good and present in the multiplicity of things, evil in another and something else (*in alio, De mal. subs.* 9.5–13, 37.9–10; cf. *Theol. Plat.* I 18.86.20–1). This "other" mixed evil does exist; it exists necessarily (*De mal. subs.* 7.1 sqq., 10.12–4; cf. Plato, *Theaet.* 176A), and it exists as a *plurality*, as evil*s*. Evils by necessity are there where plurality is, which inevitably accompanies being and existence. The existent for Proclus participates in the previous orders of being, which break down and display

---

[18] Cf. Proclus, *On the Existence of Evils*, pp. 122–3 n. 274.

an inevitable weakness. Evil, then, as Proclus repeatedly says, is the *weakness* (*debilitas* / ἀσθένεια) of the participants (*De mal. subs.* 18.17, 27.29, 31.2, 46.12, 48.17, 49.15, 51.25; cf. *Theol. Plat.* I 18.85.8, 86.15).

This also means that being is equally twofold: mere being—and being mixed with non-being. Correspondingly, non-being is equally twofold: the non-being that absolutely does not exist and is "below" being—and non-being that always accompanies, and is mixed with, being. If this is the case, then privation has to be twofold, too: one absolute, which does not exist—and the other that is non-being mixed with being, which, with Plato, Proclus calls "otherness" (*De mal. subs.* 8.13–28; cf. ἕτερον τῶν ἄλλων, Plato, *Parm.* 160D). It is this second kind of privation that, as relative non-being, can represent evil.

11.6 Privation of Form Versus Privation of the Good

We also know that, second, (B) privation assumes the role of the opposite. However, Proclus needs to address the problem that privation in Aristotle is opposite to disposition, whereas evil opposes good. Proclus' solution is to introduce the unmediated opposition within each category of good, evil, being, and privation, so that each one is distinguished into the pure and originary as opposed to the participating and mixed. Thus, the good as the unique source of being, itself beyond and before being, does not have an opposite *sensu stricto* (*De mal. subs.* 37.13–5), yet if the good is not being, it can be opposed both to being (*qua* beyond-being) and to evil (*qua* good). Being, too, is opposed to non-being (*qua* being) and to evil (as produced, and thus participating in the goodness of the one).

Privation, then, is distinguished into two: the privation of being (the absolute, Aristotelian privation)—and the privation of the good (the one mixed with being, *De mal. subs.* 51.25–6, 51.34–5, 52.2–3). Proclus' example is that it is better not to exist than to have evil existence (death is better than life in suffering), "as the first case is a privation of being, and the second is a privation of the good" (*melius autem non esse quam male esse: hoc quidem enim est entis, hoc autem boni privatio* / κρεῖττον δὲ τὸ μὴ εἶναι τοῦ κακῶς εἶναι· <τὸ μὲν γάρ ἐστι> τοῦ ὄντος, <τὸ δὲ> τοῦ ἀγαθοῦ στέρησις, *De mal. subs.* 39.39–42). In this way, Proclus also solves Aristotle's dilemma: the privation of being or form is the absolute non-being, which does not exist, is not evil as such (contrary to Plotinus), and is the opposite of disposition as its absence (*De mal. subs.* 7.28–31). But the privation of the good is opposite to the good and, as such, *is* evil that exists necessarily. The complete privation of being (non-existence) is by itself not evil and is thus better than the privation of the good (evil existence), which is evil. The privation of the good, then, is removed from the opposition of privation (of form or being)–disposition (*habitus* / ἕξις, as the lack of being or "having" a form) and is placed into the opposition of good–evil. Plotinus, however, does not make any such distinction, insisting that matter is both absolute privation and non-being—and evil as the privation of the good (*Enn.* II.4.16.14–7). Yet, for Proclus, the distinction between the privation of form and the privation of the good is crucial for solving the problem of evil:

> For being coexistent with the very disposition of which it [evil] is privation, it not only weakens this disposition by its presence, but also derives power and form from it. Hence, whereas privations of forms, being complete privations, are mere absences [*absentie*, ἀπουσίαι] of dispositions, and do not actively oppose them [but are abstract logical oppositions], privations of goods actively oppose [*adversantur*, μάχονται] the corresponding dispositions and are somehow contrary to them. (*De mal. subs.* 52.3–8; cf. 38.25–8)

The absolute privation as non-being thus opposes the disposition as the absence of being; and evil as the privation of a good does actively oppose the corresponding disposition. Thus, blindness as the privation of the form of sight does not actively oppose sight (cf. *Enn.* II.4.13.11, as the privation of quality), but misconception as the privation of the good of knowledge does actively oppose, and it derives its power from knowledge and can be harmful if used wrongly.

A quote from Proclus brings the whole discussion together:

> It is impossible . . . for privation to exist in its own right, nor can privation ever be totally detached from the nature of which it is privation. In a way, privation derives its power from this nature [the good] through its being interwoven with it, and only thus can it establish itself as something contrary to the good. Other privations [of forms or being] are merely absences of dispositions [*privationes absentie solum sunt habituum*], deriving no being from the nature to which they belong. But the good, because of the excellence of its power, gives power even to the very privation of itself. . . . The privation of the good that is interwoven with it gives strength to its own shadowy character through the power of the good. It becomes opposed to the good, yet, by mixing with the good, has the strength to fight against what is close to it. But this privation [of the good] is not in the same situation as the other privations [of forms or being]. (*De mal. subs.* 7.28–42)

At a certain point, however, Proclus makes a rather perplexing statement: in a slip, he claims that evil is the privation of being itself (*ipsius esse privatio*; τοῦ εἶναι στέρησις, *De mal. subs.* 32.5). Here, he argues against Plotinus' understanding of evil as matter that is necessary to the world, which, being good in its entirety and a "blessed god" (*felix deus* / εὐδαίμων θεός; cf. Plato, *Tim.* 34B), cannot exist without matter. Proclus' counterargument points out that necessity is that without which it is impossible to be, whereas evil is *the privation of being itself* and also *differs from the necessary* as such (*aliud enim le malum, et le necessarium aliud* / ἄλλο γὰρ τὸ κακὸν καὶ ἄλλο τὸ ἀναγκαῖον, *De mal. subs.* 32.3–4). This argument might stand against Plotinus, but it definitely contradicts Proclus' own approach, according to which evil is the privation not of being but of the good; and evil is necessary. Since evil is contrary to reason, then, some confusion about its nature seems inevitable.

Proclus further illustrates the distinction between the privation of form or being and the privation of the good with reference to disorder (*inordinatio* / ἀταξία) and unmeasuredness (*immensuratum* / τὸ ἄμετρον). These, too, can be taken in two different ways: either as the lack of measure and order, which is absence (*absentia* / ἀπουσία), deprivation (*ablatio* / ἀφαίρεσις), negation (*negatio* / ἀπόφασις) and the privation of form (which is also removal, *sublatio* / ἄρσις, *De mal. subs.* 32.14)—or as the opposite and contrary (*contraria*) to order and measure, which is the privation of the good (*De mal. subs.* 38.19–25). As was said, matter is unmeasuredness as the need and desire for measure, while evil opposes order and measure. In order to further grammatically (as well as discursively and logically) stress the opposition of the good to evil as the privation of the good, Proclus, similarly to Plotinus, indulges in the use of the *alpha privativum*: evil is ἄμοιρον, ἄπειρον, ἀσθένεια, ἀσυμμετρία, ἀνίδρυτον, ἄστατον, ἀδυναμία, ἄζωϊα, ἀτελές (*De mal. subs.* 51.10–9).

Since privation cannot exist on its own, the privation of the good cannot exist when the good is absent. Therefore, the good gives power to its own privation when the good, not participable by itself, produces the first power, which is the first limit and the first unlimitedness (*In Eucl.* 5.14–7.12; *Elem. theol.* §§ 92, 82.23–35). The absolute good is beyond being and thus not among beings, but the good that is participated by being is mixed with things, which is why it always appears as plural and multiple, as good*s*. For this reason, evil is the privation not of the absolute good, but of goods, each time of a particular good. Therefore, evil always appears in plural: *pluralia tantum*. Evil, then, is not a *privatio boni* but the *privatio bonorum*.

But if evil is necessary and exists in and as a plurality of the negations of goods as privations, how does it obtain its agency and power? As privation, evil is formless, inefficient, weak, impotent, not power but rather the absence of power (*informis et debilis, sed non potentia, magis autem absentia potentie, De mal. subs.* 38.30–31; *est . . . malum inefficax et impotens secundum se* / ἔστιν . . . τὸ κακὸν ἀδρανὲς καὶ ἀδύναμον καθ' αὑτό, *De mal. subs.* 54.1), yet it derives its efficacy from admixture with the plurality of goods. Says Proclus:

> The privation of the good that is interwoven [*complicata* / συμπλεκομένη] with it [evil] gives strength to its own shadowy character through the power of the good. It becomes opposed to the good, yet, by mixing with

the good, has the strength to fight against what is close to it. (*De mal. subs.* 7.34–9)[19]

The "shadowy" and bleak yet inevitable power of evil thus derives from the inevitable yet unintentional abuse of the power of the good that it generously shares with all beings. This is why, using Aristotle's term, Proclus describes privation as "evil-doing" (τὸ κακοποιόν, Aristotle, *Phys.* 192a15; *le malificum*, *De mal. subs.* 38.29; cf. 38.4) whose presence is always felt in everything mixed with being.

11.7 Evil as Subcontrary

As we have seen, Aristotle opposes privation to disposition or having, and evil to good. On such an interpretation, privation has nothing to do with evil, which is why Proclus rethinks Aristotle's distinction by claiming that privation is opposite or contrary to being (*De mal. subs.* 38.9), but not to the good. In order to be applicable to the description of evil, privation itself has to be distinguished by Proclus into the privation of being and the privation of the good. Yet, since the good is beyond being, and as the one is the cause and source of everything existent, privation of the good is a meaningless concept. Hence, it can be only the privation of *a* good or of the good mixed with being. It is, then, the privation of a good that is evil and as such can be opposed to *a* good. However, once we turn to the opposite of the good, a similar problem arises once again, for nothing is opposite to the good. The good as the one is beyond being, and the absolute evil as absolute non-being does not exist and thus cannot be opposed to anything. Thus, strictly speaking, the opposition to the good does not exist.

As was said, it is difficult for Plotinus to establish a real distinction between good and evil. He agrees with Plato (*Rep.* 475E–476A) that virtue is contrary or opposite (ἐναντίον) to vice, and *a* good is opposite to *an* evil. And yet, since *the* good as the one transcends being, how can one speak of the opposite to it (*Enn.* I.8.6.17–21)? For Aristotle, nothing can be opposite or contrary to substance, but this is true only for those contraries that belong to the same species or genus. For Plotinus, however, it is not necessary that if one opposite exists, the other should exist as well. So the non-substance can be considered contrary to substance (τῇ ... οὐσίᾳ ἡ μὴ οὐσία, *Enn.* I.8.6.32), the nature and the principle of the good, to the nature and the principle of evil; the indefiniteness and unmeasuredness, to the definition and measure; and falsity,

---

[19] In this sense, evil as privation of the good is a "non-privative privation." See Narbonne, "Matter and Evil in the Neoplatonic Tradition," pp. 240–1.

to truth since there is nothing in common in them. Therefore, it is not universally true for Plotinus that nothing is contrary to substance (*Enn.* I.8.6.21–48).

Yet, such an account of the opposition of evil to the good presents a problem for Proclus, who will have to introduce (or reuse) a new philosophical notion to address it. For him, "all beings exist because of the good and for the sake of the good" (*omnia . . . entia propter illud et illius gratia sunt* / πάντα . . . τὰ ὄντα δι' ἐκεῖνο καὶ ἐκείνου ἕνεκά ἐστι, *De mal. subs.* 37.14–5; cf. 61.7). Therefore, one needs to conclude that the good of which evil is the contrary does not exist on its own "but exists only in something else and not separately" (*in alio et non separatim* / ἐν ἄλλῳ καὶ οὐ χωρίς, *De mal. subs.* 37.12–3). And since, as said, evil is twofold, "evil itself, and evil in something else" (*hoc quidem ipsum, hoc autem in alio* / τὸ μὲν αὐτό, τὸ δὲ ἐν ἄλλῳ, *De mal. subs.* 37.9–10), it is evil in something else, mixed with being and therefore having some vestige of the good, that is opposed and contrary not to *the* good but only "to those goods that have their being in something else" (*De mal. subs.* 37.11–2). Therefore, evil is opposite to the mixed good, which is *a* good: evil is contrary "to some good, though not to the good in general" (*bono cuidam et non omni* / ἀγαθῷ τινὶ καὶ οὐ παντί, *De mal. subs.* 9.12, 14). It is in this sense that evil is the contrary (*contrarium*) of the good (*De mal. subs.* 61.6). Evil is contrary to particular good*s* and thus, again, comes always in plural, mixed with being and non-being—a confusing mixture of good and non-good that escapes the precise and unambiguous understanding of discursive reason. When we speak and think about evil, nothing seems to work properly, and the familiar concepts turn out to be dim, confused, and unreliable. For this reason (or unreason), Proclus has to reappropriate and recycle well-established philosophical categories, bending their meanings and reinventing their uses.

In his account of opposites, as is common in Neoplatonism, Proclus attempts to reconcile Plato and Aristotle without noticing that he often rethinks and uses their concepts in a different context and for a different purpose. In Aristotle, an opposite (ἀντικείμενον, ἀντίθεσις / *oppositum*) stands either for contrariety (ἐναντίον / *contrarium*), which allows for mediation—or for contradiction (ἀντίφασις / *contradictio*), which does not allow for mediation (Aristotle, *An. post.* 72a11–4; cf. *Phys.* 189a29–189b3). Aristotle himself looks for the mediating third (μεταξύ), which is the opposition-neutral substrate or substance. At the same time, he criticizes Plato for taking the opposites to be unmediated and thus contradictory, which for Aristotle amounts to the violation of the law of non-contradiction and is thus impossible and unthinkable.[20] In other words, unmediated opposites destroy each other. Plato admits that the opposites cannot be present at the same time, yet one always implies

---

[20] See Dmitri Nikulin, *Dialectic and Dialogue* (Stanford: Stanford University Press, 2010), pp. 56–7.

the other without mediation, so that the contradictory opposites should be considered as if coming "from a single summit" (ἐκ μιᾶς κορυφῆς, *Phaedo* 60B; cf. 103B–E).

Proclus agrees with Plato that, first, "contraries are destroyed by each other," that is, are not mediated; and, second, that they are from a single summit (cf. Proclus, *In Parm.* 741.3, speaking about the contraries of likeness and unlikeness). But Proclus also agrees with Aristotle that, third, the opposites belong to the same genus (*De mal. subs.* 37.18).[21] Hence, on the one hand, again, nothing can be opposite to the good because, as the one, the good has no genus of its own but is the source and the ultimate cause of all the subsequent ontological and logical productions and distinctions. Nothing can be "homogeneous" with the good, which literally means "of the same genus" (*homogeneum* / ὁμογενές, *De mal. subs.* 37.19–20). Therefore, neither absolute evil nor mixed evils are contrary to the good, but evils are contraries to particular goods residing in things that exist as a mixture of being and non-being, or in which the participation in being is intermittent and not always the same (*non eodem modo participatio* / μὴ ὡσαύτως ἡ μέθεξις, *De mal. subs.* 37.22–4).

But are (mixed) good and evil mediated as opposites? In other words, are they contrary or contradictory to each other? Contrary to Plato and together with Aristotle, Proclus emphatically stresses that they are mediated in his polemic against Plotinus. The mediating third for Proclus is matter (cf. *De mal. subs.* 53.5), which is therefore close to Aristotle's substrate and is not absolute nothing, as it is in Plotinus. As Proclus says, "the nature of good is one thing, that of evil another, and they are contrary (*contraria* / ἐναντία) to each other. But there is another, a third nature, that is neither simply good nor evil but is necessary, [which is matter]" (*De mal. subs.* 36.13–6). The mediating third between good and evil is thus necessary and is akin to matter in that, as matter, it allows for more or less, or *gradation*: "Every good that admits a difference of more or less is more perfect and is situated closer to its source when leaning to the more" (*De mal. subs.* 6.4–5). Therefore, the surprising conclusion is that *a* good becomes the matter-like mediator that allows for gradation: "When a lesser good increases, it becomes good to a greater degree" (*De mal. subs.* 6.21–2). And yet, although lesser evil is preferable to a greater one (for example, in case of an illness), there is a continuum of goods and evils but *no continuity* between good and evil (*De mal. subs.* 6.19–21). That is, some lesser evil is not

---

[21] According to Aristotle, contraries are "things that stand furthest apart in the same genus" (τὰ γὰρ πλεῖστον ἀλλήλων διεστηκότα τῶν ἐν τῷ αὐτῷ γένει ἐναντία ὁρίζονται, *Cat.* 6a17–9). As Opsomer and Steel note (Proclus, *On the Existence of Evils*, p. 122 n. 269), Plotinus conveniently has left out the last part of Aristotle's definition, "in the same genus," which for Plotinus means that the contraries of being and non-being (as matter) have nothing in common but are contrary in their very nature and thus do *not* belong to the same genus (*Enn.* I.8.6.54–7).

a lesser good because evil *qua* privation of a good is opposite to that good, so that injustice cannot become justice.

Proclus' whole system is based on triads, such as intellect–life–being (*De mal. subs.* 2.16–7) or will–power–activity (*De mal. subs.* 54.3). The concept of triad is paradigmatically represented in the procession–staying–return (πρόοδος–μονή–ἐπιστροφή, cf. *Elem. theol.* §§ 31–9, 34.28–42.7) structure that connects the terms in a triad, in which the middle term does *not* mediate between the other two, nor does it allow for any "sublation" in the Hegelian sense (*Elem. theol.* § 103). That a good for Proclus can be *mediation* (*mesiteia* / μεσιτεία, *De mal. subs.* 9.7, a *hapax legomenon* in Proclus' entire corpus) is a very bold statement. In a sense, it, too, targets Plotinus: if for Plotinus matter is the absolute evil, for Proclus, as said, matter is a relative good. The relative evil is thus opposed to *a* good, and is therefore "among beings, for, because of the mediation of the good, it can no longer remain deprived of being and because of its being it cannot remain deprived of the good" (*De mal. subs.* 9.7–10). In a sense, the relative good is a mediator of itself, insofar as "the greater goods preserve the lesser goods" (*De mal. subs.* 4.31). Hence, a lesser good is *not* contrary to a greater good (*De mal. subs.* 4.34), which means that they do not stand in the relation of contradiction that does not allow for mediation. Greater and lesser goods, lesser and greater evils, and goods and evils, then, oppose each other as opposites mediated by some good; that is, by a particular good of the soul or body.

At the same time, one can say that, since the absolute good and evil do not exist but are "beyond" and "below" being, particular goods and evils, mixed with being and non-being, are in an unmediated opposition to the absolute good and evil. Good strengthens, while evil weakens, although they are always mixed where evil has its hold: in individual and irrational souls and in bodies (*De mal. subs.* 23–9, 55). Therefore, the contrariety of good and evil is of a very peculiar kind: it is not a contradictory opposition but an opposition where a particular good itself becomes a matter-like mediator in the gradation of goods and evils, which are mixed in beings yet are still distinguished from each other. Proclus realizes that such an understanding of the relation between good and evil requires a different philosophical vocabulary. Following Socrates' claim in the *Theaetetus* that evil is neither a privation nor a contrary of the good, Proclus asserts that privation as such is non-being and contrary to being (*De mal. subs.* 38.9), and evil has no power or activity of its own (*De mal. subs.* 54.12–7). Evil is a privation that is the contrary of a disposition taken as a particular good, and thus evil is active and powerful through the reflected power and activity of a good in that disposition of which it is the privation (*De mal. subs.* 52.7–10). Evil, then, is not a contrary of the good properly speaking, but, as Socrates occasionally remarks in the *Theaetetus*, evil is a "subcontrary," *subcontrarium* or ὑπεναντίον, of the good (Plato, *Theaet.* 176A; *De mal. subs.* 54.17–21). For Proclus, evil is not a contrary but a subcontrary, not of *the* good but of *a* good (*De mal. subs.* 9.13–4; cf. *Theol. Plat.* I 18.83.13–6; Syrianus, *In Met.* 184.8–15). As the privation of good, evil is not a real contrary of the corresponding disposition but is *somehow* a contrary (*aliqualiter / πως, De mal. subs.* 52.8).

Evil is never pure or one, but comes in the plural as evils that are a mixture of being and non-being and are mixed with goods (cf. οὐδὲν ἄκρατον κακόν, ἀλλ' ἴχνους ἀγαθοῦ μετείληχεν, *In Remp.* I 38.25–6). As such, evil is only a "somehow-contrary," πως-contrary, or *subcontrary* of the good.

Proclus does not discuss the Aristotelian logical implication of evil as a subcontrary of the good, but it is important to note that in Aristotle the subcontrary applies not to concepts but to propositions. In the traditional square of oppositions, an I-proposition (particular affirmative, "some S is P") and an O-proposition (particular negative, "some S is not P") are subcontrary in that they can both be true but cannot both be false. Although Proclus uses the notion of subcontrary to oppose concepts, the Aristotelian logical scheme still fits well with his own examples of evils of the soul and body. Thus, ignorance is the evil of the soul, so one can have knowledge (which is a particular good) of some things while still being ignorant (which is a particular evil) of some others. Similarly, in illnesses of the body, one part or organ can be sick, while others can be in order and function well (*De mal. subs.* 28).

Proclus' choice of subcontrariety as the way of describing evil's opposition to the good finally unites and establishes a connection between the two Aristotelian pairs of opposites, of privation–disposition and evil–good. Evil is, then, "neither a complete privation nor contrary to the good" (*neque privatio est perfecta, neque contrarium / οὔτε στέρησις ἐστὶ παντελὴς οὔτε ἐναντίον*) but is the privation of the good and a peculiar kind of opposite to the good—subcontrary to the good (*subcontrarium bono / ὑπεναντίον τῷ ἀγαθῷ, De mal. subs.* 54.20–1).

Since evil as mediated by the good is among beings, it is also mixed with the good (*permixtum ad bonum, De mal. subs.* 9.6; cf. 10.8): it is evil in one respect and good in another (ὡδί, *De mal. subs.* 42.7–8; cf. 42.17–8). Evil for Proclus is thus not absolute nothing, which is beyond non-being and thus does not properly exist. And yet, evil is always close to nothing, which is why it is so difficult to think it. In its elusive nature, evil is the unlimited, formless, deficient, and has no activity or power (*De mal. subs.* 51.1–4; cf. 42.10, 48.17–8, 49.15, 50.36–41, 54.5), "for all power is something good, and activity is the extension of some power" (*De mal. subs.* 53.14–5). Yet despite being not active or powerful, as the privation of the good evil is nevertheless efficient since it receives "its capacity for acting and its power from its contrary [*a contrario / παρὰ τοῦ ἐναντίου*].... the good grows weak and ineffectual through its admixture [*propter mixturam / διὰ τὴν ... μίξιν*] with evil, and evil participates in power and activity because of the presence of the good. Both indeed are together in one" (*De mal. subs.* 53.1–4; cf. 52.24–6).

Evil thus draws its efficiency and its dim being from the good, whose power and activity it illegitimately borrows without permission and of which it is a peculiar kind of privation and a contrary—the *subcontrary*, which also gives evil a particular kind of existence. The way evil exists without proper existence further explains the agency of evil.

11.8 The Parypostasis of Evil

When Proclus turns to the clarification of the ontological aspect of evils, he again combines hermeneutical and systematic approaches. In the exegetical part, he follows Plato's *Republic* 379B–C, where Socrates suggests that the good is the cause only of good things, whereas evils have some other multiple causes (cf. Proclus, *In Remp.* I 38.3–9; *Theol. Plat.* I 18.82.8). In his systematic interpretation of this passage, Proclus argues that, because evil is multifaceted and always appears in the plural, as evils between which there is not even a common measure (*De mal. subs.* 47.6), the causes of evils are themselves indeterminate (*De mal. subs.* 47.14; cf. *In Parm.* 829.17–8, with a reference to the *De malorum subsistentia*). On account of this, there cannot be a final, or paradigmatic, or efficient cause of evil (*De mal. subs.* 47–9). For this reason, there can be no intelligible form of evils (*De mal. subs.* 43–4).[22] Moreover, the good, since it is the final cause of all existent things, cannot be the goal of evils (*De mal. subs.* 49.2–9, 50.25–9). Thus, evil has many indeterminate causes, which Proclus even calls non-causes (*non causis*). This means that evil, in a way, is *uncaused*, is not produced, and, strictly speaking, did not come to be since everything that exists comes from a cause that is in accordance with its nature (*De mal. subs.* 50.1–3). And if "we act badly, we do so out of ignorance . . . , despite our desire for the good" (*De mal. subs.* 49.6–7; cf. 48.9–16, 50.11–8). Therefore, since the good is not the cause of evil, evil is *not* produced by and from the principal cause (*ex principali causa* / ἐκ προηγουμένης αἰτίας), is not a definite or determinate cause and did not come to its being (*esse*) according to a particular cause (*De mal. subs.* 50.3–7).[23] In other words, evil exists only accidentally (*secundum accidens* / κατὰ συμβεβηκός, *De mal. subs.* 50.10). Yet, as we remember, evil is also necessary. The "accidental necessity" might appear an oxymoron, yet as Jonathan Barnes has argued, it fits well with both Porphyry's and Aristotle's understanding of accident. For Porphyry, accidents subsist in individuals (*Isag.*

---

[22] See Pieter d'Hoine, "Les arguments de Proclus contre l'existence d'Idées des maux," *Études Platoniciennes* 8 (2011), pp. 75–103, esp. 87–97.
[23] On the influence of Iamblichus on Proclus' understanding of causation and the mode of existence of evil, see Gerald Bechtle, "Das Böse im Platonismus: Überlegungen zur Position Jamblichs," *Bochumer Philosophisches Jahrbuch für Antike und Mittelalter* 4 (1999), pp. 63–82.

10), and, for Aristotle, the notion of accident can be taken in the narrow sense, as contingency, and, in the broad sense, as signifying anything that has happened to an individual that "holds of each thing in its own right but is not in its substance" (Aristotle, *Met.* 1025a30–2; cf. *Top.* 155a28–36).[24] Evil, then, is a necessary accident in the broad sense, as that which happens to individuals but does not belong in the order of causes that ultimately proceed from and to the good.

This means that, despite having a grasp on the world, on our souls and bodies, evil is not a proper cause and is not really caused, and hence does not have a definitive nature: "all evil is outside of substance and is not a substance" (*omne malum extra substantiam et non substantia, De mal. subs.* 45.15). Rather, again, evil is sheer weakness, deficiency, lack, and impotence, the subcontrary of the good and the privation of the good beyond being. Evil is thus "below being." But, if this is the case, what is the mode of the existence of evils? On the one hand, evil is not a substance, not a thing, is formless and thus cannot be known (*De mal. subs.* 51.1–4) and is not any kind of definite cause. On the other hand, evil for Proclus is not nothing because it has efficiency in the world, although, similarly to Plotinus, Proclus holds that evil primarily affects soul and body, while doing evil to others (for example, mass murder) or extreme social inequality are not considered evil. Therefore, one has to recognize that evil has a very peculiar mode of existence. As with privation and contrariety, Proclus has to use a special term to characterize the unbearable idiosyncrasy of evil.

Evil has a very strange kind of existence that Proclus calls *parypostasis* or παρυπόστασις, not only in his treatise on the existence of evils but also consistently elsewhere (*De mal. subs.* 50.2–3, 50.29; cf. *In Remp.* I 38.6, 11, 24; *Theol. Plat.* I 18.85.7, 18.86.17).[25] Since, as was argued, evil exercises its efficiency by (mis)appropriating and (ab)using the power of the good

---

[24] Porphyry, *Introduction*, trans. Jonathan Barnes (Oxford: Clarendon Press, 2003), pp. 15, 220–35.

[25] In the Neoplatonic tradition, *parypostasis* is first used by Porphyry in the sense of dependent subsistence (*Sent.* 42.14) and byproduct (thus, time is the byproduct of the mobility of the soul, whereas eternity is the byproduct of the stability of the intellect, *Sent.* 44.29, 31, 34, 45, 47; cf. 19.9, 43.23). However, it is Iamblichus who is the first to apply the term to the description of the existence of evil. See the commentary to Porphyry, *Sentences*, ed. Luc Brisson (Paris: J. Vrin, 2005), vol. 2, pp. 512–3, 777–82. According to Iamblichus, "ἡ . . . στέρησις ἀδυναμία καὶ παρυπόστασις καὶ παρὰ φύσιν καὶ ἀποτυχία τοῦ εἴδους" (ap. Simplicius, *In Cat.* 418.16–7). For Syrianus, the parypostatic existence of evil means evil's privation of, and falling away from, being and therefore being contrary to nature. See also Syrianus, *In Met.* 107.8–9 (οὔτε γὰρ τῶν κακῶν ἢ αἰσχρῶν [αἱ ἰδέαι], ἐπειδὴ στερήσει μᾶλλον καὶ ἀποστάσει τῶν εἰδῶν ταῦτα παρυφίσταται τῇ φύσει, διὸ καὶ παρὰ φύσιν ἔχειν λέγεται). Cf. Proclus, *In Tim.* I 374.5–375.5, 375.14–8; and Asclepius, *In Met.* 77.2–17. As Lloyd puts it, "'parypostasis' qua 'subcontrarium' means 'existence which is dependent on the existence of that which it is opposed'" (Antony C. Lloyd, "Parhypostasis in Proclus," in *Proclus et son influence*, ed. Gilbert Boss and Gerhard Seel [Zürich: Éditions du Grand Midi, 1987], p. 156).

for itself (*utitur illius potentia ad suum* / χρῆται τῇ ἐκείνου [τοῦ ἀγαθοῦ] δυνάμει πρὸς τὸ οἰκεῖον, *De mal. subs.* 53.10-1), *parypostasis* can be translated as "parasitic existence," as Opsomer and Steel do, as "pseudo-existence," "dependent existence," or "adventitious existence."[26] For evil is not intended, is accidental and contingent, "is defect and indeterminateness and privation" (*defectus est et indeterminatio et privatio* / ἔλλειψίς ἐστι καὶ ἀοριστία καὶ στέρησις, *De mal. subs.* 49.9–10), and yet it exercises a perverse efficacy, which it illegitimately and furtively borrows from the good. As such, evil has a "parasitic" or "vampiric" kind of existence. The mode of existence or *hypostasis* of evils is thus *parypostasis* (*ypostaseos modus . . . parypostasi magis assimilatur*, *De mal. subs.* 49.10–1). In Proclus' own words, *parypostasis* characterizes evil as that which came to be "without end and unintended, uncaused in a way and indefinite" (*imperfectam et ascopon (id est non intentam) et non causatam aliqualiter entem et indeterminatam* / <ἀτελῆ καὶ> ἄσκοπον καὶ ἀναίτιόν πως οὖσαν καὶ ἀόριστον, *De mal. subs.* 50.29–31).

However, if we take into account the literal meaning of the prepositions παρά and ὑπό, we can translate *hypostasis* as that which "stands beneath itself," or supports and underlies itself in its own independent existence according to understandable causes in the order of procession. *Parypostasis*, on the contrary, is that which somehow exists besides that which supports itself. *Parypostasis*, then, is a *misplacement* that accidentally puts a thing in the wrong place. This is misplacement in the way that one might lose track of a set of keys or, in a momentary lack of awareness, misjudge the area of a table-top (the "support" or "hypostasis") while aiming to set down a cup, releasing the cup into the emptiness beside the table only to have it crash down on the ground. Moreover, *parypostasis* can be also taken as a non-intended act of displacement, when the soul happens to be mistaken or has misunderstood something. If we understand evil this way, Proclus' explanation of its murky existence makes perfect sense: "existence [*subsistere* / τὸ . . . ὑφίστασθαι] belongs to those beings that proceed from causes towards a goal, but the 'misplaced' [that is, 'beside'] existence [*paryfistasthe (id est iuxta subsistere)* / τὸ . . . παρυφίστασθαι] to beings that neither appear through causes in accordance with nature nor result in a definitive end" (*De mal. subs.* 50.20–2). Evil is thus an unintended yet necessary misplacement of what should be in the right place in the order and procession of things.

---

[26] See Carlos Steel, "Proclus on the Existence of Evil," *Proceedings of the Boston Area Colloquium in Ancient Philosophy* 14 (1998), pp. 97–8.

Bringing together all three concepts of privation, subcontrariety, and parypostasis that are appropriated by Proclus to characterize the indefinite and indefinable evil, we can finally describe evil in its inescapable deficiency as the privation and subcontrary of the good that exists parypostatically, elusively present in its absence as the misplacement of being and the displacement of the good.

APPENDIX

Indivisible Lines in Ancient Philosophy and Mathematics

The Corpus Aristotelicum includes a well-known short polemical treatise, "On Indivisible Lines" (*De lineis insecabilibus*, Περὶ ἀτόμων γραμμῶν, 968a1–973b25),[1] written against "some" (ἔνιοι) who accept mathematical atomism, in particular, "indivisible lines" (ἄτομοι γραμμαί, *De lin. insecab.* 968a1). In what follows, I will argue that the Aristotelian treatise's polemic primarily targets an inner-Academic debate and makes sense only if we take into consideration the underlying Platonic ontology of mathematical objects.

1 *De lineis insecabilibus*

The treatise "On Indivisible Lines" begins with the exposition of five (on some counts, six) arguments of the proponents of mathematical *minima*, addresses these arguments, and continues with a number of additional arguments (thirty-seven by my count, many of which are formally introduced by ἔτι) against the possibility of indivisible lines. It is commonly accepted in the scholarship that the treatise was not written by Aristotle but comes out of his school and shows a great deal of awareness of the Academic debate about first principles and its

---

[1] Aristotle, "On Indivisible Lines," in *Minor Works*, trans. and ed. W. S. Hett (Cambridge, MA: Harvard University Press, 2000), pp. 413–47. For a discussion, see Michel Federspiel, "Notes exégétiques et critiques sur le Traité Pseudo-Aristotélicien *Des Lignes Insécables*," *Revue des Études Grecques* 94 (1981), pp. 502–13 (textual emendations); Cleary, *Aristotle and Mathematics*, pp. 92–3, 137 n. 114 ("uncuttable lines"), 271; Hellmut Flashar, "Aristoteles," chap. 2 of *Ältere Akademie Aristoteles-Peripatos*, ed. Hellmut Flashar, vol. 3 of *Die Philosophie Der Antike*, ed. Johannes Rohbeck and Helmut Holzhey (Basel: Schwabe, 1983), p. 291.

criticism by Aristotle and the Peripatetics.[2] Whoever the author(s) of the treatise might be, it is clear that the general line of argument against the existence of mathematical atoms falls squarely within Aristotle's discussion of the continuous and the discrete.

In the very opening line of the treatise, the view of the existence of indivisible lines or something indivisible or something "partless" (τι ἀμερές, *De lin. insecab.* 968a2) is ascribed to "some" (ἔνιοι). I accept the established scholarly interpretation that these "some" are Plato, the originator of the view, and Xenocrates, the author of a more elaborate version of "indivisible lines." As a background of the doctrine of the mathematical atoms one should presuppose a critical reaction to Zeno's criticism of the impossibility of the existence of the "many" (cf. Zeno B2–3 DK), as well as Theaetetus' theory of the incommensurability of geometrical magnitudes in book X of Euclid's *Elements*.[3]

2 Arguments for and Against the Existence of Indivisible Lines

2.1 THE ARGUMENT OF GREAT-AND-SMALL

The first argument ascribed to the supporters of indivisible lines is the following:

> If "much" and "big" [τό τε πολὺ καὶ τὸ μέγα] and their opposites "few" and "little" [τό τε ὀλίγον καὶ τὸ μικρόν] are similarly constituted, and that which is commonly taken[4] as having infinite divisions is not small but big, it is evident that "few" and "little" will have a limited number of divisions; if, then, the divisions are limited, there must be some magnitude that has no parts, so that in all magnitudes there will be some indivisible unit, since in all of them there is a "few" and a "little." (*De lin. insecab.* 968a3–9)

According to Dillon,[5] the argument counters Zeno's proof of the impossibility of many (things) because their very existence would prove contradictory: it will have to be *both* "small" (μικρά; that is, infinitely divisible) and "large" (μεγάλα; that is, infinite [ἄπειρα]) by addition (Zeno B1 DK ap.

---

[2] Based on Diogenes Laertius' (*Vitae phil.* V 42) mentioning of one book "On Indivisible Lines" among Theophrastus' writings, Dillon suggests that there is no compelling reason to deny Theophrastus the authorship of the treatise. See John Dillon, *The Heirs of Plato: A Study of the Old Academy* (Oxford: Clarendon Press, 2003), p. 113 n. 9.

[3] See Heath, introduction to Euclid, *The Thirteen Books of Euclid's Elements*, vol. 3, pp. 1–3.

[4] I agree with Dillon that σχεδόν here is important and should be understood as meaning "in the popular perception" (Dillon, *The Heirs of Plato*, p. 113 n. 70).

[5] Ibid., pp. 113–4.

Simplicius, *In Phys.* 140.34–141.8). In order to allow for things such as extended entities to exist, one would need to suppose the existence of indivisible magnitudes.

This interpretation appears to agree with the critical Academic reception of the Eleatic thesis concerning one and many. However, the argument can also be understood as suggesting that the "big" or "large" and the "small" or "little" are opposites (τὰ ἀντικείμενα), and, since it is commonly thought that it is the "big" that allows of infinite divisions (διαιρέσεις), then, as opposite, the "small" allows of *finite* divisions that produce indivisibles. Hence, if both "big" and "small" represent extended continuous magnitudes, the "small" should yield indivisible lines.

This argument appears to refer to the Platonic principle of "great-and-small," which accounts for otherness and thus for a possibility of the infinite. However, Aristotle ascribes *two* different infinities to Plato: one "big," and another "small" (Aristotle, *Phys.* 206b27–33). This, however, runs contrary to other testimony (Alexander, *In Met.* 55.20–56.35; Simplicius, *In Phys.* 453.22–455.14), which suggests that the "great-and-small" was considered by Plato to be *one* principle of otherness and non-identity, opposite to the "one," the other principle of sameness and identity. As he often does, Aristotle reinterprets others' concepts in line with his own theories. For Aristotle, the infinite is only a possibility of taking always "another and another" (ἄλλο καὶ ἄλλο, Aristotle, *Phys.* 206a26–8) or "that outside of which there is always something else" (οὗ ἀεί τι ἔξω ἐστί, Aristotle, *Phys.* 207a1; see Chapters 7 and 8).

The Aristotelian counterargument suggests that the infinite, conceived as a pure possibility of making another step or taking something else outside of a given, is always incomplete and thus can never be actualized. The infinite for Aristotle behaves differently in two mutually irreducible classes of things: the *discrete* numerable entities (number, ἀριθμός), and *continuous* magnitude (μέγεθος).[6] One should note that the two genera are also mutually irreducible for Plato, although the continuous (the geometrical and the physical) is derivable from the discrete (the ideal, which includes ideal numbers). The discrete is finite with respect to division (the unit is the smallest constituent of number) but is potentially infinite with respect to addition, or increasing (any number can be surpassed by adding another unit). On the contrary, the continuous is finite with respect to addition (the magnitude is a unit of itself since, if increased, it becomes a *different* magnitude) but is infinite with respect to division: the continuous for Aristotle can always be divided.

This is the main reason why Aristotle and the author of "On Indivisible Lines" criticize the doctrine of indivisible lines, claiming that it is

---

[6] See Michael J. White, *The Continuous and the Discrete: Ancient Physical Theories from a Contemporary Perspective* (Oxford: Oxford University Press, 1992), pp. 30–1.

inconsistent and that it introduces an impossible, oxymoronic concept. Such a concept does not belong to thinking of the indivisible things that do not admit of falsity (Aristotle, *De an.* 430a26–7).[7] For an Aristotelian, the "indivisible" belongs to the discrete (numbers), whereas the "line" belongs to the continuous (magnitudes), and the difference between the two cannot be bridged.

The treatise suggests a number of counterarguments against the existence of the indivisible (*De lin. insecab.* 968b23–969a17): (a) "little" or "small" allows of infinite divisions (the infinite division of a magnitude). In addition, (b) the argument of great-and-small ignores the properly indivisible, the point (as a privation of the continuous, cf. Aristotle, *De an.* 430b20–1), which can be found within any line and at which any line can be divided (see Chapter 8). Moreover, (c) a line can be divided into segments of *various length* according to a given ratio or λόγος. If (d) the "small" is only finitely divisible, so will be the "great," insofar as it consists of a finite number of "small" divisions. And most importantly, (e) the finite element of number—unit or monad—that is the principle (ἀρχή) of number permits of only finite divisions in number, but the same is not true of magnitudes. Thus, the objections of the author of the Aristotelian treatise are perfectly in line with Aristotle's account of infinity and the distinction between numbers and magnitudes.

2.2 ARGUMENT OF FORM

If there is a form (ἰδέα) of line, it is a whole that is prior to the parts, which are constituents of line; and, if form is indivisible, then this first line should be indivisible (*De lin. insecab.* 968a9–14). This is a logical argument since the form, or idea, of line is indivisible *logically* and *ontologically* but not geometrically or physically. The author of "On Indivisible Lines" dismisses this argument (*De lin. insecab.* 969a17–21), in line with the Aristotelian critique of Plato's concept of the ideal form as ontologically primary to both mathematical and physical things.

2.3 ARGUMENT OF ELEMENTS

If magnitude consists of elements (στοιχεῖα) and the elements are (by definition) indivisible, and if the parts (constituents) are prior to the whole, then the elements of line—indivisible lines—should be indivisible (*De lin. insecab.*

---

[7] See Thomas De Koninck, "La noêsis et l'indivisible selon Aristote," in *La naissance de la raison en Grèce: Actes du Congrès de Nice—Mai 1987*, ed. Jean François Mattéi (Paris: Presses Universitaires de France, 1990), pp. 215–28; and Enrico Berti, "Reconsidérations sur l'intellection des Indivisibles selon Aristote *De anima* III 6," in *Corps et âme: sur le De anima d'Aristote*, ed. Gilbert Romeyer-Dherbey and Cristina Viano (Paris: J. Vrin, 1996), pp. 391–404.

968a14-8). Dillon rightly notes that the doctrine of parts' priority over the whole is quite unorthodox in Platonism but connects it with a fragment of Xenocrates[8] preserved in an Arabic translation of the lost treatise of Alexander of Aphrodisias, *On the Doctrine of Aristotle on the First Principles*.[9] Xenocrates argues that if a part is taken away, the whole is preserved, whereas a part can still exist when the whole no longer does; therefore, parts are antecedent to the whole. Still, for an Aristotelian, it makes no sense to suppose that elements are indivisible for, being bodily, they should be potentially divisible, as any extended magnitude (*De lin. insecab.* 969a21–6).

2.4 ARGUMENT OF THE IMPOSSIBILITY OF INFINITE COUNTING

This argument leans on Zeno in claiming that it is impossible to touch an infinite number of things (and therefore, parts of a magnitude) in a finite time. This is an Aristotelian version of Zeno's argument of dichotomy, which claims that a finite magnitude or line cannot be traversed because, in order to do that, one has to first traverse a half of the magnitude, then a half of this half, *ad infinitum*, which is impossible, even for discursive thought (διάνοια), whose movement is the quickest. But if thought's "touching" a number of things one by one is equivalent to counting them, thought cannot count an infinite number of parts or divisions in a finite time. Therefore, there should exist an indivisible line (*De lin. insecab.* 968a18–968b4; cf. Aristotle, *Phys.* 239b11–4, 263a4–11). The argument follows Aristotle straightforwardly in asserting that any divisible and extended magnitude (of time or length) is both finite (as this magnitude) *and* infinite (as potentially infinitely divisible). Moreover, a finite length and time are divisible exactly in the same way, which establishes a one-to-one correspondence between the two and thus makes possible both an infinite division of a magnitude and time in the same way *and* traversing a finite magnitude in finite time (*De lin. insecab.* 969a26–30; cf. Aristotle, *Phys.* 263a13–5). Moreover, as the author of "On Indivisible Lines" adds, thought's movement of counting (ἀριθμεῖν) goes in discrete steps or leaps from one member to another, which implies stopping or pausing (μετὰ ἐπιστάσεως), whereas the motion in and along a magnitude is continuous (*De lin. insecab.* 969a30–969b3). Again, the supporters of the notion of indivisible lines appear to breach the generic Aristotelian distinction between the discrete (numbers and counting) and the continuous (geometrical and physical magnitudes and the movement along them).

---

[8] Xenocrates fr. 21 IP.
[9] See Dillon, *The Heirs of Plato*, pp. 115–7.

2.5 MATHEMATICAL ARGUMENTS OF COMMENSURATE LINES

2.5.1

The last argument in support of the existence of geometrical minima, ascribed to "mathematicians" (οἱ ἐν τοῖς μαθήμασι λέγουσιν, *De lin. insecab*. 968b4–5), by whom we should understand Platonic thinkers, in particular, Plato and Xenocrates, consists of two closely related arguments. Both presuppose familiarity with the thesis of incommensurability of geometrical entities (lines), knowledge that in some cases (such as 1 and $\sqrt{2}$) there is no common measure or unit that would fit a finite number of times within each line or that there is no relation or λόγος between the two that would be expressible as a relation of two natural numbers, m/n.

First, we are told, if the "'commensurate' lines are measured by the same unit" (σύμμετροί εἰσιν αἱ τῷ αὐτῷ μέτρῳ μετρούμεναι, *De lin. insecab*. 968b6), then these units should be indivisible. For, otherwise, the parts of the units would be new units of the "commensurate" lines, which runs contrary to the premise of their being of the same unit. This argument appears somewhat perplexing since, if one supposes that there is a smallest measure of two lines expressible in whole numbers (say, 5 and 7), nothing prevents dividing this common measure or unit into halves, so that the two lines will be measured by twice the number of units (10 and 14, respectively). Moreover, the argument does not say what happens once there is *no* common measure to the lines (such as 5 and $\sqrt{7}$)" (*De lin. insecab*. 968b4–12).

In order to make sense of this argument, one should presuppose more than the Aristotelian treatise suggests; namely, that a geometrical unit should be considered similar to an arithmetical unit, or monad. But a monad is indivisible: in Platonic and in ancient mathematics, ½ is not a number but a relation of a unit to the number two, whereas the monad is an indivisible basis, or beginning of number, and thus has no parts into which it could be divided.[10] Again, an implicit presupposition in the "mathematical" arguments of commensurate lines seems to be a suggestion that arithmetic and geometry, although still different realms of mathematics, bear important similarities, which include the existence of indivisible units constitutive of their respective objects. Within the Platonic account of mathematically oriented ontology these similarities are explainable, first, by the presupposition that any mathematical object is produced by, and is structured according to, the same principles (of identity and difference), and, second, that both arithmetical numbers and geometrical figures are intermediate between the ideal forms (which also include ideal numbers) and physical things (see Chapter 8).

---

[10] Cf. Euclid, *Elem*. bk. VII, def. 1; Theon, *Expos. rer. math*. 18.22, 19.6–7 (ἀδιαίρετος ... ἡ μονὰς ὡς ἀριθμός), 20.5–7; and Nicomachus, *In. arithm*. 74.5–6.

2.5.2

The second "mathematical" argument uses more technical terms. It suggests that an accepted unit of measurement of geometrical figures will consist equally of indivisible, or "partless," lines. Therefore, such also will be any line, linear as well as planar, measured by this conventional unit because all squares built on rational lines will be commensurable. However, if a measure of a limited line is divided further, it may be neither a rational (ῥητή), nor an irrational (ἄλογος) magnitude, nor apotome (ἀποτομή), nor a line "of two terms" (ἐκ δυοῖν ὀνομάτοιν, or binomial), so that such lines "in themselves [καθ' αὐτάς] have no natural characteristics [φύσεις]" but still "will be rational or irrational in relation to each other [πρὸς ἀλλήλας]" (*De lin. insecab.* 968b12–21). This argument shows a clear familiarity with mathematical terms that were well known in the Academy and became part of the theory of rational and irrational lines worked out by Theaetetus and later included in book X of Euclid's *Elements*. Rational magnitudes are those that are commensurable (σύμμετρα) and are measured by the same measure either in length and in square (e.g., 2 and 4) or in square only (2 and $\sqrt{2}$); hence, as the argument suggests, squares on rational lines are all commensurable (cf. Euclid, *Elem.* bk. X, defs. 1–4). A further classification of irrational lines, established by Theaetetus and Eudemus, includes binomial (e.g., $1 + \sqrt{2}$), apotome ($2 - \sqrt{2}$), and medial ($\sqrt[4]{2}$),[11] which respectively correspond to the three major proportions: arithmetic, harmonic, and geometrical (Philolaus A21 DK; Archytas B2 DK; Pappus, *In Eucl. Elem.* X, I 1–2).[12] Euclid's book X contains a further classification of more complex rational and irrational lines (ἄλογα, ἄρρητα).[13]

Both "mathematical" arguments for the existence of indivisible lines clearly show familiarity with much more sophisticated mathematical analysis of commensurability and incommensurability. In response to the two "mathematical" arguments, the author of "On Indivisible Lines" simply dismisses them as logically flawed and violating the mathematical assumptions, or hypotheses, by which one should understand not only the indefinite divisibility but also the well-established fact of the existence of incommensurable geometrical lines (*De lin. insecab.* 969b6–12). The study of incommensurability originated in the Pythagorean school, and the incommensurability of 1 and $\sqrt{2}$ is well known to Plato (*Meno* 82B–85D; *Theaet.* 147D–148D; cf. *Stat.* 283B–285C)[14] and is

---

[11] However, the text in Hett erroneously suggests that the last two are rational, ὧν δυνάμεις ῥηταί (*De lin. insecab.* 968b20), for their squares are not commensurable, which may be due either to a mistake or to the corruption of the text. See Konrad Gaiser, *Platons ungeschriebene Lehre: Studien zur systematischen und geschichtlichen Begründung der Wissenschaften in der Platonischen Schule* (Stuttgart: Klett, 1963), p. 511 n.

[12] See Árpád Szabó, *The Beginnings of Greek Mathematics* (Dordrecht: Reidel, 1978), pp. 174–7.

[13] For a more detailed classification of rational and irrational lines, see Heath's introductory note in Euclid, *The Thirteen Books of Euclid's Elements*, vol. 3, pp. 3–10.

[14] Theodorus finds square roots of 3 through 17, whereas Theaetetus establishes a general approach to the problem of square roots (Plato, *Theaet.* 147D). Cf. Euclid, *Elem.* bk. X, prop. 2. On the discovery

referred to by Aristotle who knows both the fact of incommensurability *and* its proof (*An. priora* 41a26–7; *De an.* 430a31).

Therefore, Plato and his disciples cannot just ignore the incommensurability of geometrical entities or overcome it by introducing a new concept of indivisible or partless lines. However, since the proponents of indivisible lines do not provide a mathematical or *geometrical* refutation of the thesis of incommensurability, and since of the six arguments only the last one implies some geometrical considerations, this might mean that the notion of indivisible lines is ontological and "pre-geometrical," as it were. That is, it still refers either to the principles of geometrical figures or to ideal entities or numbers, where incommensurability does not *yet* exist, unlike in lines and figures that occupy a middle ground between the purely thinkable and sensible (cf. Iamblichus, *De comm. math. sci.* 9.4–12.17, 55.1–8; Proclus, *In Eucl.* 3.1–7; see Chapter 8).

If this is the case, then the source of incommensurability might lie in the irrationality of matter or materiality, which is necessary for the existence of geometrical and physical things but not for numbers, in which otherness as "great-and-small" is also present, not as incommensurability but as a power of generating or proceeding to the next number. And yet the materiality of geometrical objects differs from that of physical things since incommensurability exists only between *some* geometrical figures, whereas, in a sense, *all* physical things are incommensurable insofar as they are in a constant flux of becoming. The materiality of geometrical things or indefiniteness in them that is responsible for their incommensurability, then, can be ascribed to *imagination* (φαντασία) on Platonic grounds. Just as the realm of geometrical things, imagination is intermediate between thinking and sense-perception and is a medium that allows for mathematical figures to be extended while still keeping their unchanging mathematical properties (Pappus, *In Eucl. Elem.* X, I 13 2; Proclus, *In Eucl.* 52.8–53.5; see Chapter 8).

3 Plato and Xenocrates on Indivisible Lines

Within extant ancient literature, "On Indivisible Lines" is our major source of knowledge about this doctrine, which, however, appears through the lens of a polemic against the theory itself. We have a brief but important testimony from Aristotle who, when speaking about Plato, explicitly mentions the notion of an "indivisible line" (ἄτομος γραμμή) in the famous chapter of the *Metaphysics* A 9 on the inner-Academic doctrines (Aristotle, *Met.* 992a22) and also in book M of the *Metaphysics* ("the first, indivisible line," ἡ πρώτη

---

of incommensurability, see Thomas Heath, *A History of Greek Mathematics* (Oxford: Clarendon Press, 1921), vol. 1, pp. 154–7; and Szabó, *The Beginnings of Greek Mathematics*, pp. 85–91.

γραμμή, <ἡ> ἄτομος, *Met.* 1084b1). Yet in Plato's texts we only find a "plausible story" about the constitution of physical elements out of two elementary triangles, each being a half of either the isosceles or of the square (*Tim.* 53C-D). These two triangles, which can be taken as the "plane figures" mentioned in the second "mathematical argument" (*De lin. insecab.* 968b14–5) are indivisible. But Plato does not explain why this is the case, mentioning in the dialogue that we can only follow reasoning that binds necessity with probability, whereas the "higher," or ontologically prior, principles (ἀρχαί) are known to god and the philosophers, who are friends of god (*Tim.* 53D). There are good reasons to believe that the principles mentioned here are the "one" and the "indefinite dyad," or the "great-and-small," as the principles of the constitution of the mathematical intermediate objects (see Chapters 2 and 6). Aristotle, then, explicitly criticizes Plato for the lack of clarity about how mathematical properties are translated into physical properties (e.g., weight; Aristotle, *De caelo* 298b33–299a6, 307a19–24; *De gen. et corr.* 325b33–4). In particular, the indivisibility of the two primary triangles is not explained by Plato, who seems to imply that they are sufficient to explain the geometrical structure of the four (out of five) regular bodies associated with elements and their mutual geometrical transformations.

For the most part, however, indivisible lines are ascribed to and attested in Xenocrates. Of twenty-five fragments concerning indivisible lines in the collection of Isnardi Parente (frs. 123–47), four come from Aristotle, one from "On Indivisible Lines," and the rest from the scholia in Aristotle's *Physics* and *De caelo* by Alexander of Aphrodisias, who explicitly ascribes the doctrine of indivisible lines not only to Xenocrates but also to Plato (Xenocrates fr. 128 = Alexander, *In Met.* 126.5; cf. frs. 135, 144, which stress the agreement of Plato and Xenocrates), Themistius, and the Neoplatonists, including Porphyry, Syrianus, Proclus, Simplicius, and Philoponus—all of them apparently based on the interpretation of the same Aristotelian texts.

For the most part, Xenocrates' fragments point to the polemic inspired by the Eleatics, primarily Zeno, as the core of the origin of the concept of indivisible lines.[15] In particular, as Zeno has argued, if being has a magnitude, it is divisible; hence, being is many, and there is nothing that is one (that is, one is not); therefore, one does not belong to being or is not among the existent things (Xenocrates fr. 136). This compels Xenocrates to argue, in turn, that if magnitude is to be considered as belonging to the existent (and mathematical magnitudes as intermediate entities exemplify unchangeable properties proper to being) and if, further, many (πολλά) is associated with magnitude, then magnitude cannot be infinitely divisible but should eventually lead to an

---

[15] On the decisive influence of Eleatic philosophy on the development of mathematics in the Academy, see Szabó, *The Beginnings of Greek Mathematics*, p. 304.

indivisible magnitude. Otherwise, one and many will be the same (τὸ αὐτὸ ἓν καὶ πολλὰ ἔσται, Xenocrates fr. 144), which is impossible. Variously exemplified in various objects, such as ideas, numbers, and geometrical objects, being thus should be not just one but also many, a synthetic unity of one and many; in its plurality, being should always exemplify oneness. This is Porphyry's explanation of the reason for Xenocrates' acceptance of indivisible lines (Xenocrates fr. 139 = Porphyry ap. Simplicius, *In Phys.* 140.6–18).

Some of the fragments on indivisible lines mention Democritus as the originator of the doctrine of indivisible magnitudes (Xenocrates frs. 119, 133, 137). We know that Democritus wrote several books on mathematics, including *On Geometry, Geometrica, Numbers*, and *On Irrational Lines and Solids* (Diogenes Laertius, *Vitae phil.* IX 47), of which, however, we do not have any fragments preserved. Yet his indivisibles (ἄτομα) are primarily physical magnitudes, not mathematical partless entities (the "partless bodies" may be a later invention of Diodorus Cronus).[16] It seems likely that Democritus might have thought about mathematical indivisibles or even, in modern language, infinitesimals or magnitudes smaller than any given one (thus, he wrote a book *On a Difference in an Angle, or On Contact with the Circle or the Sphere*; see Diogenes Laertius, *Vitae phil.* IX 47), but again, we have no textual evidence of this. Moreover, since most of the fragments collected under the rubric of "Amere Mathematica" by Lurie in his collection of Democritus' fragments (frs. 106–24)[17] come from Aristotle—who does not quote Democritus when discussing indivisibles specifically in the context of mathematical debate—one should suppose that the context of the polemic was the debate against Plato and Xenocrates, and not Democritus. It is later (mostly, Neoplatonic) interpreters of Aristotle who bring the "Pythagoreans" closer to Democritus in ascribing to them the view that "magnitude consists of indivisibles," even if this statement contradicts geometry (Syrianus, *In Met.* 143.16 = Democritus fr. 127 Lurie). Only when speaking about the constitution of physical things does Aristotle mention a similarity between Leucippus and Plato, saying that the difference between the two consists in the fact that, for Leucippus, atoms are bodies (στερεά), whereas Plato's elements of the physical in the *Timaeus* consist of planes (ἐπίπεδα), which are elementary indivisible triangles (Aristotle, *De gen. et corr.* 325b24–32; cf. Xenocrates fr. 145).[18] But the most important

---

[16] See Democritus, *Teksty, perevod, issledovanija*, trans. S. Ya. Lurie (Leningrad: Nauka, 1970), fr. 124, ap. Aetius, mentioned in Stobaeus.

[17] Drawing parallels between Democritus and Xenocrates belongs to a much later Neoplatonic tradition of commentators; see Democritus fr. 117 Lurie (Aristotle, *De an.* 409a10, and the commentaries of Simplicius and Philoponus *ad loc.*).

[18] Plato uses the term ἄτομον only once (*Soph.* 229D5), when discussing the question of whether education is one indivisible whole or allows of subdivisions. For Plotinus' criticism of atomism, see *Enn.* III.1 [3].1–3; and Erik Eliasson, "Plotinus' Reception of Epicurean Atomism in *On Fate*, tr. 3 (Enn. III 1) 1–3," in *Plotinus and Epicurus: Matter, Perception, Pleasure*, pp. 160–74.

difference between the Atomists and Plato is that for the Atomists the physical atoms constitute ultimate reality, whereas for Plato being is not physical but grounds the physical cosmos in its underlying structures.

4 Further Criticism and Objections

Many later thinkers sympathetic to the Platonic ontological program based on the acceptance of the one and the dyad as the principles of one and many—of sameness and otherness—were, however, critical of the doctrine of indivisible lines. Their criticism is mostly based on two points.

4.1

As was mentioned, the critics, among whom is also Proclus, point out that the concept of geometrical atoms runs contrary to the well-established fact of the incommensurability of geometrical magnitudes (Proclus, *In Remp.* II 27.1–29.4 = Xenocrates fr. 130; cf. *In Eucl.* 3.17).

4.2.1

Another important objection to the acceptance of indivisible lines consists in that a geometrical line is divisible, which means that it is *always divisible* in any of its parts, which, as a scholiast to Aristotle's *Physics* notes, makes the concept of "indivisible lines" imply a contradiction (ἀντίφασις, Xenocrates fr. 144) because (infinite) divisibility is already analytically included in the notion of line. For Aristotle, it is not difficult to refute the teaching of indivisible lines (Aristotle, *Phys.* 206a17–8; 233b16–32) because magnitude (which includes line), as well as time and motion, does not consist of indivisible parts, for, otherwise, a body would be moving through an indivisible part (line) and would have already moved (ἄμα διέρχεται καὶ διελήλυθε, Aristotle, *Phys.* 232a4), and therefore line would not be indivisible. Therefore, as Proclus later suggests, the notion of an indivisible magnitude is paradoxical and absurd (γελοῖον, Proclus, *In Tim.* II 245.23–246.4 = Xenocrates fr. 146).

That any magnitude is always divisible follows from Aristotle's account of continuity in the opening chapters of book VI of the *Physics* (Aristotle, *Phys.* 231a21–b19; cf. Proclus, *Inst. phys.* Prop. I 5; see Chapter 10). Here, Aristotle distinguishes between the continuous (συνεχές), the contiguous or that which touches (ἁπτόμενον), and succession (ἐφεξῆς). Central to his understanding of continuity is, again, the distinction of the discrete within, and in reference to, the continuous as a *sui generis* other of the continuous. On Aristotle's account, the continuous is found both in the physical (bodies, motion, and time) and in the geometrical, and it displays the presence of the infinite flux of becoming, which, unlike in the Platonists, still can be grasped by a proper scientific account, not just a mere opinion. In order to do that, one should *delimit* the continuous by putting proper limits or outer borders (τὰ ἔσχατα) onto it. The continuous is infinite in the sense of being indefinite and is thus indefinitely divisible, whereas the discrete is definite and brings definiteness to the continuous. Such infinity, as Plotinus puts it, "itself runs away from the idea of limit, but is caught by being surrounded externally [ἔξωθεν]" (*Enn.* V.6.3.15–6). In other words, the infinite of the continuum is only defined by the limit(s) or outer borders, which is why that limit is not even thought in the definition of line as such.[19]

The objections to the notion of indivisible lines all follow the notion of divisibility of a continuous magnitude. Referring to Geminus, Proclus says that it is an accepted "common notion" (κοινὴ ἔννοια) or axiom (ἀξίωμα) in geometry that everything that is continuous is divisible (πᾶν συνεχὲς διαιρετόν, Aristotle, *Met.* 1053a24). From here, one can deduce a different claim that the continuous is *infinitely*, or indefinitely, divisible because it can always be divided, again and again (*In Eucl.* 278.10–9).

Metaphorically speaking, inasmuch as it implies infinite divisibility, continuity displays a certain illogical and formless "abyss," an inexhaustible infinity within any magnitude, which corresponds to the materiality of any magnitude, physical in natural bodies and imaginary in geometrical extended objects.[20] The indefinite divisibility of geometrical magnitudes is shown by a *reductio ad absurdum*. Thus, an anonymous (late) scholium to book X of Euclid's *Elements* argues that if one bisects the base of an equilateral triangle, then draws a line by the obtained point parallel to an adjacent side, then forms a new isosceles triangle by drawing a parallel to the original base through the point of intersection, and then continues this process indefinitely, one will not reach the apex lying opposite to the chosen base because otherwise a half of the base at the supposed moment of reaching the apex will be equal to a side of the triangle, and hence two sides will be equal to a third one, which is impossible.[21] We find a similar argument in "On Indivisible Lines," which suggests that "since a triangle can be made from three given straight lines, it will also be made from three indivisible lines. Now in every equilateral triangle the perpendicular from any angle bisects the base and so must divide the indivisible line" (*De lin. insecab.* 970a8–11). This and similar counterexamples, then, show that the very notion of indivisible lines is contrary to mathematical principles and presuppositions (τοῖς ἐν τοῖς μαθήμασιν, *De lin. insecab.* 970a19).

---

[19] "ἐν τῷ λόγῳ τῆς αὐτογραμμῆς οὐκ ἔνι προσνοούμενον πέρας" (*Enn.* VI.6.17.14–5). Cf. Nikulin, *Matter, Imagination, and Geometry*, p. 100.

[20] Cf. (paraphrasing Heraclitus B123 DK) the scholium in Euclid, *Scholia*, vol. 5 of *Opera Omnia*, ed. J. L. Heiburg and H. Menge (Leipzig: Teubner, 1888), p. 417.14–5: "πᾶν τὸ ἄλογον ἐν τῷ παντὶ καὶ ἄλογον καὶ ἀνείδεον κρύπτεσθαι φιλεῖ."

[21] Ibid., pp. 415.7–417.20.

In addition, nothing continuous can be made out of two parts without parts because every continuous magnitude is divisible into many parts. Moreover, any line is divisible into both *equal* and *unequal* parts. Therefore, any line can be cut in half, and, if the line is supposed to consist of an odd number of indivisible lines, then the indivisible line "in the middle" will be bisected, which is impossible by assumption (*De lin. insecab.* 970a23–33). This argument is reproduced (with approval) by Proclus in his commentary on Euclid (Proclus, *In Eucl.* 277.25–278.10).

However, geometrical divisibility needs to be distinguished from logical divisibility. One can assume that indivisible or atomic units can be thought, whereas every geometrical or sensible thing in principle might be always divisible. Therefore, an indivisible line can be taken as geometrically divisible, insofar as it is a line and is extended, but logically and ontologically indivisible, insofar as it is the form of line, and form is indivisible. This is Porphyry's explanation of indivisible lines: they are divisible as magnitudes and materially and thus have parts, but are indivisible and primary in their form (κατὰ μὲν τὸ ποσὸν καὶ τὴν ὕλην τμητὰ καὶ μέρη ἔχοντα, τῷ δὲ εἴδει ἄτομα καὶ πρῶτα, Xenocrates fr. 139, ap. Simplicius, *In Phys.* 140.6–18). Both Gaiser and Dillon also support the argument for the geometrical divisibility of the indivisible lines that does not contradict or exclude their indivisibility in form.[22]

4.2.2

An important principle applied here by Aristotle is that that which is limited and that which limits, or the limited and the limit, are *different* (Aristotle, *Phys.* 231a28–9). Only when a discrete limit—a point—is applied to a physical or geometrical continuous magnitude, can the continuous be known in its structure and for what it is—which is to say, in its purpose. The whole Aristotelian program is aphoristically formulated as "the purpose is the limit" (τὸ δὲ τέλος πέρας, Aristotle, *Phys.* 207a14–5). Thus, something is continuous if its limits are one (ἕν), something is contiguous if its limits are together (ἅμα) but do not coincide, and things are in succession if there is no entity between them of the same kind. From these definitions it immediately follows that the continuous cannot consist of the discrete; in particular, line does not consist of points (Aristotle, *Phys.* 215b19) because the limits of points are not one, for the reason that points have neither limits nor parts and thus cannot touch each other (Aristotle, *Phys.* 231a21–9).[23] In addition, points do not follow each other in a line because, between any two points, there is always something of their own kind—namely, another point. Therefore, every magnitude

---

[22] Gaiser, *Platons ungeschriebene Lehre*, p. 158; Dillon, *The Heirs of Plato*, p. 114.
[23] Contra this position, Eutocius claims that any line can be thought of as consisting of a continuous series of points (τὸ καὶ πᾶσαν γραμμὴν κατὰ συνέχειαν σημείων τὴν ὕπαρξιν ἔχουσαν νοεῖσθαι, Eutocius, *In de sphaera et cyl.* I 12.19–20 = Democritus fr. 125 Lurie).

is continuous, is (always) divisible into magnitudes, and cannot consist of indivisibles (ἐξ ἀτόμων, Aristotle, *Phys.* 232a24). Line, therefore, consists of lines, which means that parts of a line are lines (Aristotle, *De caelo* 299a8). In other words, what is continuous is divisible into what is always divisible (συνεχὲς τὸ διαιρετὸν εἰς αἰεὶ διαιρετά, Aristotle, *Phys.* 232b24–5).

One should note that the notion of indivisible lines does not survive beyond Xenocrates. However, there is a noteworthy parallel to the indivisible lines in Damascius (ap. Simplicius, *In Phys.* 800.10–1), who provides a theory of the constitution of time out of discrete yet extended "leaps" (ἅλμα) of the moments of "now."[24] The similarity between a point and a moment of "now" is a commonplace in Aristotle, for whom "now" is discrete and not a part of time, which is continuous (*Phys.* 218a19–30; cf. 237a5–6). "Now," then, is a limit of time (*Phys.* 223a6) as a measured number of motion, and, as such, "now" is analogous to a point in relation to a line.

Consequently, another—the biggest—set of objections to the doctrine of indivisible lines in "On Indivisible Lines" comes from the doctrine's missing an important point—the geometrical point. The criticism in the treatise intends to show that the theory of continuity based on indivisible lines misses the discrete and indivisible limit of the divisible and continuous, which is a point. However, indivisible line is precisely the discrete and indivisible principle, and the partless limit of the continuous line, which is not a point. The main difference between point and indivisible line is not that the former is not extended and the latter is—the existent fragments do not say anything about the extension of indivisible line—but that the point is of a different genus than the line, whereas the indivisible line is of the same.

Thus, (i) the very notion of indivisible line is contrary to the definition of line or straight line "because it does not lie between points nor has it a middle point" (*De lin. insecab.* 969b31–3). Since (ii) an indivisible line has no parts, one such line added to another indivisible line will not make it any longer (*De lin. insecab.* 970a23–4) and thus cannot count as a line, for a line added to a line extends it. In addition, (iii) anything unlimited has two limits that define a line, yet an indivisible line is not unlimited and therefore should have limits; it will be divisible (into itself and its limit), which is a contradiction in terms (*De lin. insecab.* 970b10–3). However, (iv) if an indivisible line has no point in it (either as its limit or as dividing it), then, since an indivisible line is constitutive of any line, no line will have a point, which is impossible (*De lin. insecab.* 970b14–6). But (v) if there are points (as limits) in any line, then between them there is either nothing or a line (the former is impossible because it runs contrary to the definition of continuity); if there is a line, there is always more

---

[24] See Sambursky and Pines, *The Concept of Time in Late Neoplatonism*, pp. 86–99; and Marie-Claire Galpérine, "Le temps integral selon Damascius," *Les études philosophiques* 3 (1980), pp. 325–41.

than one point in all lines and therefore the line will not be indivisible (*De lin. insecab.* 970b18–20). Importantly, then, (vi), the limit of a line will be a line, for both the limit and indivisible line are extremes (ἔσχατα) of a line; but then there will be no difference between line and point (*De lin. insecab.* 970b23–30). Furthermore, (vii) if one accepts Aristotle's presupposition of limit being different from that of which it is a limit, then, if a point is a beginning and an end of a line, a point cannot be continuous if a line is continuous (but apparently an indivisible line as a beginning and end of a line is continuous) (*De lin. insecab.* 971a7–10). But (viii) if an indivisible line is similar to a point (and if the above argument [ii] is wrong), then one line would be greater than another by a point, which is impossible (*De lin. insecab.* 971a10–6). Therefore, (ix) in accordance with Aristotle's account of continuity, one should conclude that "since what has no parts cannot have dimensions, nothing composed of units without parts can produce a continuous magnitude" (τὸ δ' ἀμερὲς οὐκ ἔχει διάστασιν, ὥστ' οὐκ ἂν εἴη μέγεθος συνεχὲς ἐξ ἀμερῶν); and thus a line cannot be composed of points (*De lin. insecab.* 971b2–3). For (x) any line is a magnitude (and is therefore continuous and extended), but points are not extended and hence no aggregation or combination (σύνθεσις) of points can produce a line (*De lin. insecab.* 971a20–2). Moreover, (xi) points cannot be in contact with each other for they have no parts that could touch each other (whereas indivisible lines should be in contact; that is, be continuous) (*De lin. insecab.* 971b26–31). Therefore, (xii) a line cannot be made by putting points next to each other (*De lin. insecab.* 972a1–6). A line, then, (xiii) does not consist of points, but a point cannot be separated (οὐδ' ἀφαιρεθῆναι) from a line either (which the proponents of indivisible lines do not recognize) (*De lin. insecab.* 972a14–27). A point, then, (xiv) cannot be separated from a line by a "cut" (τομή, *De lin. insecab.* 972a28–30), which is why (xv) a point is not the smallest component (τὸ ἐλάχιστον) in and of a line (*De lin. insecab.* 972a31–2). Consequently, (xvi) line contains nothing but points and lines, and these are not commensurable. In other words, a line cannot be said to be greater than a point, and the smallest is smaller than the entities of which it is the smallest, then such a smallest component cannot be (either a line or) a point (*De lin. insecab.* 972b1–4).

These and other objections of the treatise follow the line of argument that originates in Aristotle's account of continuity. From this perspective, the arguments of those who accept indivisible lines are "feeble" and "false" (ἀσθενεῖς . . . καὶ ψευδεῖς, *De lin. insecab.* 971a4) and their position "absurd" (γελοῖον) in that

> after professing that they are going to demonstrate the mathematicians' own opinions, and to argue from their statements, they merely relapse into contentious [ἐριστικόν] and casuistical [σοφιστικόν] argument, and a weak one at that. For it is weak from many points of view, and in every way

fails to escape both contradictoriness and refutation [καὶ τὰ παράδοξα καὶ τοὺς ἐλέγχους]. (*De lin. insecab.* 969b12–6)

5 Motion and Continuity: Movement of a Point

One possible approach to solving the problem of the continuum and establishing a relation between the discrete (point) and the continuous (line) is the construction of a line not out of points but by a *movement* (κίνησις) of a point that "draws" or "traces" a line within a special medium of the "geometrical matter" of imagination (see Chapter 8).[25] Thus, Aristotle mentions that they say that a line by motion produces a plane, and a point produces a line (φασι κινηθεῖσαν γραμμὴν ἐπίπεδον ποιεῖν, στιγμὴν δὲ γραμμήν, *De an.* 409a4–5). But who are "they" here? For Aristotle himself, a point cannot move because, first, it is not a physical body; second, it does not have a place; and, third, because, as Aristotle argues in book VI of the *Physics*, body, motion (the distance moved), and time are all continuous and hence equally infinitely divisible, whereas point is indivisible and for this reason is incapable of motion. Moreover, construction of a line by the motion of a point is impossible for those who accept indivisible lines, for the reason that an indivisible line cannot be "drawn" insofar as anything that is generated in this way is generated part by part, yet an indivisible line is postulated to be indivisible and thus cannot have parts. The very first independent argument against indivisible lines in "On Indivisible Lines" aims to demonstrate their possibility, for if a straight line (radius) moves in a semicircle, it should touch all the infinite intermediate points of the circumference (*De lin. insecab.* 969b19–25), which cannot happen under the supposition that the diameter is an indivisible line. The argument clearly presupposes a possibility of motion of a geometrical object through another, yet it does not attribute this position to the supporters of indivisible lines.

Although the context of the discussion of the mentioned passage (from Aristotle's *De anima* A 4) is Xenocrates' claim that soul is a self-moving number, the statement that a moving point produces a line (as its "trace") directly contradicts Aristotle's testimony that Plato rejects the point. For this reason, "they" should most probably refer to those Platonists (Speusippus) who accept that a point is a monad that has a position, which comes in the immediately following sentence (*De an.* 409a6).

---

[25] Cf. Proclus, *In Eucl.* 51.20–52.3; 88.2–7 (see Chapter 8). For Plato, there can be no motion within that which is uniform (*Tim.* 57D–58A); hence, there can be no motion within a uniform geometrical materiality. In addition, unlike imagination, Plato's χώρα is a receptacle of all things extended, both physical and geometrical (*Tim.* 52A–D; see Chapter 6).

6 Indivisible Lines and the Inner-Academic Teachings of Plato

The opening arguments of the supporters of the doctrine of indivisible lines as presented in "On Indivisible Lines" intend to show *that* such lines exist. Yet they do not explicitly state or explain *what* these indivisible lines are or might be. As I have argued so far, most of the evidence suggests that the doctrine of indivisible lines originates in Plato and is further developed by Xenocrates. However, Plato speaks about indivisible triangles in the *Timaeus* without explaining their ontological properties, but no passages in his dialogues directly support or clarify the notion of indivisible lines. For the most part, the evidence about Plato's acceptance of indivisible lines comes from Aristotle, who, on the one hand, can be trusted with communicating the facts—in this case, *that* Plato and Xenocrates had a theory of indivisible lines. On the other hand, Aristotle is inclined to interpret and criticize (sometimes, mock and satirize)[26] the views of his opponents *outside* the context of their theories, putting these views within the limits of his own philosophical thought. This, however, should not surprise us for Aristotle accepts only one objective philosophical truth, which is his own.

The extant evidence appears to suggest that Plato and Xenocrates need the notion of indivisible lines not so much for mathematical or geometrical reasons but primarily for *ontological* ones. Therefore, as I have already said, the criticism of the doctrine of indivisible lines, however fair it is within the realm of properly geometrical entities, misses its point, which is primarily ontological and not geometrical.

In particular, in order to explain the constitution and structure of continuous—primarily geometrical—magnitudes, which display a presence of otherness as many exemplified as materiality and incommensurability, Plato and Xenocrates look for something that would account for the same as the "one." Among mathematical objects, in arithmetical numbers this is the monad as the indivisible basis of number. But in geometrical figures, one should equally recognize an indivisible basis or unit for magnitudes, and such is the indivisible line. In other words, indivisible lines are the principles, or beginnings (ἀρχαί) of geometrical lines that account for unity in them.

In order to further situate the notion of indivisible line, I need to provide more of a context for it. I am referring to the Tübingen account of Plato's and Platonic inner-Academic theories, which is based both on Plato's dialogues and the extant testimony. According to this reconstruction, there are two primary ontological principles that are the causes of all things. In establishing the principles, Plato follows the tradition of the Presocratic philosophers of thinking about the ἀρχαί.[27] Plato appears to be particularly influenced here by

---

[26] See Dillon, *The Heirs of Plato*, p. 112.
[27] See Nikulin, "Plato: Testimonia et Fragmenta," pp. 1–38.

the Pythagoreans who also recognize two principles, the limit and the unlimited. Moreover, Plato appears to respond to the ontological positions of both the Eleatic philosophers and the Atomists. Namely, for Parmenides and Zeno, the one (ἕν) is being (ὄν), and the many is non-being; whereas, for Democritus and the Atomists, on the contrary, one (void) is non-being and many (atoms) is (are) being. In contrast to these ontological positions, for Plato the one is opposed to being, for which reason being is a *synthesis* of one and many, is one *and* many (*Parm.* 142B–157B), and thus is the other of the one. In this respect, the one is *beyond* being (cf. Plato, *Rep.* 509B).

In his inner-Academic teachings, Plato begins with an elaboration of the theory of principles or ἀρχαί, which are the one (ἕν) and the indefinite dyad (ἀόριστος δυάς, Aristotle, *Met.* 987b26). The two principles are not subordinated to one another but play a different role in the constitution of things. The one is the principle of *sameness*, whereas the indefinite dyad is the principle of *otherness* (cf. Plato, *Phil.* 16C–D, 26E–31A). The first principle is the formal principle, whereas the second principle is a material principle that appears also as "great-and-small" (τὸ μέγα καὶ τὸ μικρόν, Aristotle, *Met.* 987b20, 988a13–4; *Phys.* 187a17–9; see also Simplicius, *In Phys.* 503.10–8; see Chapter 6). The "great-and-small" accounts for indefiniteness, disorder, and shapelessness (Theophrastus, *Met.* 11b2–7; see also Sextus Empiricus, *Adv. Math.* X 261; TP 49–55). But, as the highest genus of being, the indefinite dyad is represented as the ἕτερον of Plato's *Sophist* (257B–259B) and is not non-being per se (because non-being, properly speaking, *is not*), but an *ideal* principle of otherness and inequality that is further associated with motion (Aristotle, *Phys.* 201b20–1).

The two principles are thus the principles of *all* things, including ideal being(s). The one is responsible for the oneness and unity of each thing. The dyad introduces a difference and differentiation in different kinds of things. Within the ideas, the dyad is responsible for the plurality: there is a whole *multiplicity* of beings or forms. Once again, being has to be considered and thought in its otherness to the one. In numbers, the dyad is responsible for doubling a number and its division into halves. Unity and multiplicity are thus present in things and account for both identity and differentiation in all things, including the ideal forms and numbers. In other words, both unity and multiplicity in and of being come from the first principles.

From these two principles comes a whole order of being: ideal (or "eidetic") numbers and ideas, intermediate entities that are mathematicals (arithmetical numbers and geometrical objects), and physical things (cf. Aristotle, *Met.* 1086a11–2; *De bono*, fr. 2).[28] The ideal numbers are themselves limited in number, and the first number is two (Simplicius, *In Phys.* 454.19–455.14), of which the constitutive "elements" are the one and the great-and-small. The

---

[28] Aristotle, *De bono*, in *Fragmenta Selecta*, ed. W. D. Ross (Oxford: Clarendon, 1955), pp. 113–9.

ideal numbers can also be called "idea-numbers," insofar as they *are* ideal forms (Aristotle, *De an.* 404b24–5). Not all forms are ideal numbers, but the forms are structured in the same way as are numbers, for they are one *and* many. The forms are synthetic unities of the "one" and the "indefinite dyad." The ideal numbers and forms constitute a system of the highest categories of being. Numbers and their constitution from the two principles of one and many, then, are the model pattern for the consideration of the existent of any kind.[29] From ideal numbers, one has to distinguish the arithmetical or mathematical numbers (Aristotle, *Met.* 1076a20), which are derived from, and subordinate to, ideal numbers and forms-ideas. From the ideal numbers come intermediate mathematical objects (τὸ μεταξύ), which are represented by arithmetical numbers and geometrical entities. Finally, after the intermediates come physical material bodies (TP 68–72). There are thus three strata of the existent that are derivable from the first two principles: ideal entities (ideal numbers and ideas), mathematical entities (mathematical numbers and geometrical objects), and physical things.

With these views in mind, one can appreciate Gaiser's suggestion that the acceptance of indivisible lines signifies Plato's ontological preference for the limiting principle over the principle of the unlimited (*De lin. insecab.* 968b4–21).[30] In other words, geometrical objects should exemplify unity as indivisibility, which is ascribed to indivisible lines. However, such unity is not isolated from multiplicity but binds many and one in being. Plato and Xenocrates thus find a viable ontological alterative to both Leucippus and Democritus for whom only many *is* whereas one *is not*, as well as to Parmenides and Zeno for whom only one *is* and many *is not*.

7 One, Two, Three, Four

The very opening sentence of Plato's *Timaeus* runs: "One, two, three, where is the fourth . . . ?" (εἷς, δύο, τρεῖς· ὁ δὲ δὴ τέταρτος . . . ποῦ; Plato, *Tim.* 17A). Here, Socrates is talking about the guests who attended the speech the day

---

[29] As Burnyeat notes, the Platonists agree "that the ultimate principles of explanation are to be derived from reflection on mathematics" (Myles Burnyeat, "Platonism and Mathematics: A Prelude to Discussion," in *Mathematics and Metaphysics in Aristotle / Mathematik und Metaphysik bei Aristoteles*, ed. A. Graeser [Bern: P. Haupt, 1987], pp. 213–40, esp. 216).

[30] See Gaiser, *Platons ungeschriebene Lehre*, pp. 158–63. However, Gaiser notes that the testimony of the treatise can be equally ascribed to Xenocrates. See also Marie-Dominique Richard, *L'enseignement orale de Platon: Une nouvelle interprétation du platonisme* (Paris: Editions du Cerf, 1986 [2nd ed., 2005]), pp. 193–7; and Edward Maziarz and Thomas Greenwood, *Greek Mathematical Philosophy* (New York: Ungar, 1968), pp. 112–5. On Xenocrates' identification of ideal and arithmetical numbers (distinguished in Plato), ascribed to him by Aristotle (*Met.* 1028b24–7, 1083b2–3, 1086a5–14), see Dillon, *The Heirs of Plato*, pp. 108–10.

before, but it might also be taken as a hint to the structure and order of the layers of the existent. Indeed, if ideal numbers are forms, and ideal paradigms are translated into mathematical entities, which are arithmetical numbers and geometrical figures and are also further exemplified in the structures of physical elements and things, then ideal numbers should be present and determine the geometrical realm of being. Moreover, the first four numbers (τετρακτύς) that play an important role in Plato's cosmology might also be present in those entities that are constituted within materiality, particularly in geometrical objects, which, as said, display the presence of a geometrical, "imaginary" matter. Therefore, the first four numbers might be translated into geometrical objects: the first four numbers establish the sequence of geometrical dimensions. As Aristotle says, Plato accepts only a finite number of numbers, up to ten (Aristotle, *Met.* 1084a15, 29, 1084b2; *Phys.* 206b32-3), where one, or monad, is the smallest (*Phys.* 206b31-2). The first (ideal) number that is produced by the two principles is then two, and one, or the monad, is, strictly speaking, not a number but the indivisible basis of number.

One, then, would correspond to point, two to line, three to plane, and four to solid. Such a deduction that begins with a point and ends in a solid is explicitly accepted by Speusippus (Speusippus fr. 4 Lang = fr. 122 IP = fr. 28 Tarán = Iamblichus, *Theolog. arithm.* 84.10-1).[31] In each case, the determining number is the number of points needed as limits to define the corresponding geometrical object. Line is defined by two points as its limits, plane by three, and solid by four (cf. Proclus, *In Eucl.* 85.1-13). And point would correspond to monad since, as Sextus reports, as the monad is the principle, or beginning, in the domain of numbers, so is the point in the domain of lines (Sextus Empiricus, *Adv. Math.* X 278). We might also recall the first seven definitions of book I of Euclid's *Elements*, which begin with the definition of a point (def. 1), move on to define a line and then a straight line (defs. 2, 4), and then a surface and a plane surface (defs. 5, 7).

Moreover, an important testimony comes from Alexander, who says that Plato considered principle (ἀρχή) to be that which is the first and not composite (τὸ πρῶτον . . . καὶ τὸ ἀσύνθετον). On this account, then, planes are primary (πρῶτα) with respect to solids, lines with respect to planes, and points with respect to lines because points are altogether not composite (ἀσύνθετα) and nothing precedes them. But since "mathematicians" (the Platonists who

---

[31] Aristotle reports that Plato associated the first four numbers with various cognitive faculties: one is intellect-νοῦς, two is knowledge-ἐπιστήμη that tends toward one in one way (μοναχῶς γὰρ ἐφ' ἕν) (that is, in one dimension or linearly, so that one might further associate such knowledge with discursive thinking-διάνοια), opinion is a plane number, and sense-perception is a solid number (Aristotle, *De an.* 404b22-4). One might further symbolically associate these cognitive faculties with the point, line, plane, and solid.

support a mathematical ontology) call points monads, the monads, then, are the first of all beings (Aristotle, *De bono*, fr. 2).

8 Monad, Point, Indivisible Line

Several times throughout his writings, when speaking about those who apply the same principles to both the constitution of mathematical objects and being (that is, about Plato and his disciples), Aristotle famously says that they considered the one (ἕν) and the principle (ἀρχή) as a point, for the numerical unit (μονάς), or monad, is a point that has no position, and vice versa: a point is a monad that has position (Aristotle, *De an.* 409a6; *Met.* 1016b24–31, 1084b26–7; see Chapter 2). To whom should we ascribe this position? Aristotle himself does not accept it because there is no difference between a point and the place of a point (*Phys.* 209a11–2), insofar as place is the outer limit of the embracing immovable body (*Phys.* 212a20–1), but a point, being partless, does not have an "outer" and thus has no place. The claim that a point is a monad having position would fit well with Speusippus' mathematical ontology (who, however, rejected the forms and accepted only the existence of mathematical entities—numbers and geometrical objects; Aristotle, *Met.* 1076a21–2, 1080b14–6). Later, Proclus explicitly ascribes this position to the "Pythagoreans" (Proclus, *In Eucl.* 95.21).

The author of "On Indivisible Lines" mentions that the doctrine of indivisible lines misses, or blurs, the notion of point because there is no difference between the indivisible line and the point in that neither one has a property peculiar to it (ἴδιον), except for the *name* (*De lin. insecab.* 970b29–30). There are two terms for "point" in Greek: στιγμή, which is used by Aristotle (and also by the author of "On Indivisible Lines"), and σημεῖον, which is used later (by Euclid, but already in Aristotle's time and occasionally by Aristotle himself [*De gen et corr.* 317a10–2]).[32] According to the first famous definition in Euclid's *Elements* (which is its opening sentence), "A point is that which has no parts" (σημεῖόν ἐστιν, οὗ μέρος οὐθέν, Euclid, *Elem.* bk. I, def. 1). In other words, point is defined negatively or privatively, by reference to constituents or parts, which it does not have. Consequently, a point is not a whole (because a whole has parts) and cannot be defined as something indivisible because divisibility is of a whole. In this case, point can be thought as a limit, πέρας, of a line, which comes in the third definition.[33]

---

[32] See Heath's commentary in Euclid, *The Thirteen Books of Euclid's Elements*, vol. 1, pp. 155–65.
[33] "The extremities of line are points" (γραμμῆς δὲ πέρατα σημεῖα, Euclid, *Elem.* bk. I, def. 3). Aristotle is critical of this kind of definition because, if one defines a point as the limit (πέρας) of a line, line of a plane, and plane of a solid, then one defines the logically prior by the logically posterior (Aristotle, *Top.* 141b19–22). In Euclid's *Elements*, however, point is defined (*Elem.* bk. I, def. 1) prior

The thesis presented by Aristotle is that the numerical unit, the monad (as a representative of the principle of unity, of the one in numbers), corresponds to the point that equally represents the one among those objects that have "position" or θέσις; that is, in geometrical objects. Yet Plato and Xenocrates do *not* accept this thesis since, despite their differences in treating the concept of number (Plato distinguished between ideal and mathematical numbers, whereas Xenocrates identified the two [Aristotle, *Met.* 1076a20–1]), both postulate indivisible lines (Aristotle, *Met.* 1084b1–2). Thus, according to Aristotle, Plato energetically and explicitly *rejected* the point, which he considered a geometrical "dogma," accepting instead the indivisible line (Aristotle, *Met.* 992a19–24). For Plato and Xenocrates, then, what counts as geometrical counterparts of ideal numbers are dimensions, not points: one dimension for line, two for plane, and three for solid, whereas point has no dimensions. This explains the already mentioned sequence in Plato: indivisible line, then two (δυάς), then other numbers. This position is clearly shared by Xenocrates, who takes it that a geometrical magnitude consists of matter and number: from two comes length; from three, plane; from four, solids (Aristotle, *Met.* 1090b21–4).[34] In this sense, geometrical objects *follow* the numbers in the succession of number–line–plane–solid (τὰ μετὰ τοὺς ἀριθμοὺς μήκη τε καὶ ἐπίπεδα καὶ στερεά, Aristotle *Met.* 992b13–4; cf. *Met.* 1080b23–4, 1085a7–9). Yet, in this sequence, point is absent and is not explicitly included among the geometrical objects.

9 Aporias

Despite a relative paucity of textual evidence on indivisible lines, one can say that their acceptance is consistent with the reconstruction of Plato's account of the principles. Because various ontological realms are distinguished in Plato by their variously defined relations to the two principles, which are differently present in each ontological layer, the principle of the one is present, although differently, in different ontological spheres. Moreover, Plato seems to be preoccupied with the preservation of the distinction between the discrete (indivisible, ideal, immaterial) and the continuous (divisible, geometrical or physical, material). This would explain the need for indivisible line, which retains (and embodies) the discrete, whereas line preserves the continuous.

---

to line (*Elem.* bk. I, def. 2, with no mentioning of a point), and then a connection between the two is established (*Elem.* bk. I, def. 3).

[34] To be sure, Aristotle says "from four or other numbers, which does not make any difference" (Aristotle, *Met.* 1090b24). This might mean that among the primary four numbers (the Pythagorean *tetraktys*) only two through four play a role, as ontological patterns, in the constitution of various ontological and geometrical strata.

On this view, as I have argued, an indivisible line (1) is primarily an ontological and not a geometrical, concept. If this is the case, then (2) indivisible line represents the one, the principle of unity, within the geometrical objects. As such, (3) an indivisible line should bear similarity, in its ontological status and function, to the numerical monad, which represents the same principle of the one within numbers, although differently in ideal and in arithmetical numbers.

Here, however, we run into two difficult sets of questions or aporias, the answer to which is not evident on the basis of the extant texts.

9.1 ONE VERSUS ONE AND TWO

If the indivisible line represents the first principle, the one, does line correspond to the second principle, great-and-small? As Alexander suggests in his commentary on the *Metaphysics*, when the second principle, the indefinite dyad, is defined or determined (ὁρισθεῖσαν) by the one, it produces the first number, two (Alexander, *In Met.* 55.20). One might say that when the one determines the great-and-small within the (imaginary) extended (that is, within the geometrical), it produces a line. Similarly, the generation of three and four might parallel the generation of plane and solid. On this view, the indivisible line would be analogous to a unit or monad, and the line to two in the geometrical realm.

On the other hand, if, as Alexander suggests in the commentary on the *Physics* preserved in Simplicius, any number, including the first number two, is constituted by *both* principles of the one and indefinite dyad (Simplicius, *In Phys.* 454.19–455.11, in support of Sextus Empiricus, *Adv. Math.* X 276), then, in the case of geometry, a line should be the first product of the one (indivisible line) and of the great-and-small. But if this is the case, what is this great-and-small within the geometrical? Its role might be played by the pure geometrical extension or the materiality of imagination, but we have no textual ground to be sure.

If a line is a product of the two principles and not a geometrical embodiment of the second principle, of the great-and-small, then one might return to the already mentioned passage from Aristotle's *Metaphysics* A 9, which is one of the crucial testimonies for Plato's acceptance of indivisible line and his rejection of point. Here, Aristotle adds that it is necessary for line to have a limit (πέρας), and, for this reason, if line exists, point exists, too (as the *limit* of a line, Aristotle, *Met.* 992a23–4). This is Aristotle's own critique of Plato's indivisible lines but it could also be taken as suggesting that indivisible line is the *principle* or beginning of line, ἀρχή, whereas *point* is still the limit, πέρας, of a line, as well as of an indivisible line. On this account, the limit is different from the beginning. And yet, as we know, Plato rejected the point because, otherwise, indivisible line would itself be the first geometrical embodiment of *both* the one (represented as point) and the great-and-small (geometrical materiality). In this case, indivisible line would be the first geometrical line proper. But then, first, an indivisible line would not be the indivisible limit of lines but it would have two indivisible limits because the limit is different from that of which it is the limit (τὸ γὰρ πέρας ἄλλο καὶ οὗ πέρας, *De lin. insecab.* 970b12–3). And, second, an indivisible line would bear all the geometrical properties and thus it would be divisible, contrary to its being postulated as indivisible.

9.2 (IN)COMMENSURABILITY

Another difficult problem is that of the commensurability or incommensurability of the indivisible line and the line. Namely, is an indivisible line a constitutive element—or a beginning of a line? In other words, is an indivisible line a unit, μονάς, of a line—or its principle, ἀρχή? A further question is whether there are many indivisible lines (potentially an infinite number of them)—or just one indivisible line as the principle of the continuous in the middle realm of mathematics?

For if an indivisible line is a unit and an element of a line, analogous to the monad in numbers, then we might presuppose a multiplicity of identical indivisible lines that constitute any line. Each indivisible line, then, would be a *limit* (πέρας) of line that is a part of line, unlike the *principle* (ἀρχή) of line that might not be part of line. (A clear parallel to this position is that of Epicurus, for whom the smallest and uncompounded entities are *limits* of all things having length and provide the unit of measurement (τὰ ἐλάχιστα καὶ ἀμιγῆ πέρατα . . . τῶν μηκῶν τὸ καταμέτρημα). However, unlike in Plato, the Epicurean "limits" are bodily, although they can only be thought due to their smallness and invisibility (Diogenes Laertius, *Vitae phil.* X 59).

Moreover, any line would be made up of a number of indivisible lines, and, consequently, all lines would be commensurable. But this is not the case, and, as we know, both Plato and Xenocrates are aware of it. To be sure, the second mathematical argument preserved in "On Indivisible Lines" discussed earlier suggests that all lines are measured by their units, but these units are built up by, or composed of, indivisible lines (ἐξ ἀμερῶν σύγκεινται, *De lin. insecab.* 968b13–4). This does not tell us, however, whether these provisional or conventional units are themselves *measured* by the indivisible lines.

We need to assume, then, that an indivisible line is *not* a unit of line or its element but rather a *principle*; namely, the principle of unity that accounts for the line's being *one* and a *continuous* whole. In this case, there would be only one indivisible line. But then either (1) indivisible line and geometrical line are *not* commensurable, both being lines, or (2) indivisible line is not a line at all but an unextended principle of line. In the first case, in the geometrical, the principle belongs generically to that of which it is the principle, and, in the second case, it does not (which coincides with Aristotle's position in *Phys.* 231a28-9, mentioned earlier). In the second case, all the geometrical arguments against the indivisible lines in the treatise demonstrating, by *reductio ad absurdum*, that indivisible lines should be divisible *qua* lines really miss the point because the principle of the extended might itself not be extended. In this case, the indivisible line is not divisible either geometrically or ontologically. Such is also Proclus' argument (*In Eucl.* 278.2-10): if there were an odd number of indivisible lines within a line, it cannot be divided in halves (whereas from Euclid, *Elem.* bk. I, prop. 10, we know that a straight line can be bisected).

As we know from Aristotle, Plato considered ideal numbers to be incommensurable (ἀσύμβλητοι, Aristotle, *Met.* 1080a15-b4), for although they are constituted by the same principle of unity, they cannot be broken down into commensurable unities: being *forms*, ideal numbers are therefore simple and indivisible. Arithmetical numbers, on the contrary, are commensurable, and their common measure is the monad (arithmetical number three is composed of three, and number four of four indivisible units or monads). All the monads of arithmetical numbers are thus mutually commensurable. In this case, the principle of one or unity is differently exemplified in ideal and arithmetical numbers: in the ideal number, it accounts for the indivisibility and unity of a number, and, in the arithmetical numbers, it stands for the monad, the indivisible basis of divisible number.

But Plato does not accept anything analogous to the distinction between ideal and arithmetical numbers in geometrical magnitudes, which belong to the intermediate realm of mathematical entities. Because of this, a similar reasoning about commensurability and incommensurability of units cannot be applied to indivisible lines.

Finally, if indivisible line and line are incommensurable, then they cannot be in a relation or ratio to each other. In particular, if book V of Euclid's *Elements* indeed belongs to Eudoxus, then its main results and concepts that are formulated in the definitions should have been known to Plato and Xenocrates, as well as to the author of "On Indivisible Lines." Two definitions in book V of the *Elements* run: "a ratio [λόγος] is a sort of relation in respect of size between two magnitudes of the same kind [ὁμογενῶν]" (Euclid, *Elem.* bk. V, def. 3), and "Magnitudes [μεγέθη] are said to have a ratio to one another which are capable, when multiplied, of exceeding each other [ἃ δύναται πολλαπλασιαζόμενα ἀλλήλων ὑπερέχειν]" (Euclid, *Elem.* bk. V, def. 4). Thus, an infinitely large or infinitely small magnitude and a finite magnitude cannot be in proportion to each other. In the case of the indivisible line, if it is not extended but is the principle of extension in lines, the indivisible line and a finite line are then not of the same kind and cannot have a ratio to each other. A parallel in Aristotle would be the claim that geometrical lines are in proportion to each other, and thus one line does not exceed another by a point (Aristotle,

Phys. 215b19),[35] which means that line and point are incommensurable logically, as genera, and not geometrically. If elements are different from that of which they are the elements (e.g., the elements of bodies are not bodies, Sextus Empiricus, *Adv. Math.* X 253), then, again, the indivisible line and line will have no ratio for they would be of different kinds: a principle or element, and that of which it is the principle and element.

Such are the difficulties implied by the concept of indivisible lines. In each case, we face a dilemma to which it is difficult to give a definitive answer because we do not have enough textual evidence to do so. However, from the preceding discussion of the relevant texts, we can say that we have enough textual and systematic grounds to assert that the concept of indivisible line is meaningful in Plato only within a reconstructed system of his inner-Academic theories. "Indivisible line" stands for the principle that provides a basis for the explanation of continuity and unity within the geometrical objects that are intermediate between the ideal entities (forms and ideal numbers) and physical bodies, and thus fits well within Plato's mathematical ontology.

---

[35] See Maurice Caveing, "La proportionnalité des grandeurs dans la doctrine de la nature d'Aristote," *Revue d'histoire des sciences* 47:2 (1994), pp. 163–88.

BIBLIOGRAPHY AND ABBREVIATIONS

Primary

Translations are taken from the following editions, with occasional changes:
Plotinus, *Enneads* from A. H. Armstrong's edition.
Proclus, *A Commentary on the First Book of Euclid's Elements* from Glenn Morrow's edition.

PLOTINUS

Text
Plotini Opera, ed. Paul Henry and Hans-Rudolf Schwyzer, 3 vols. (Brussels: Edition Universalle, 1951–1973).

Translations
Ennead II.5: On What Is Potentially and What Is Actually, trans. and ed. Cinzia Arruzza (Las Vegas: Parmenides, 2015).
Ennead IV.8: On the Descent of the Soul into Bodies, trans. and ed. Barrie Fleet (Las Vegas: Parmenides, 2012).
Ennead V.5: That the Intelligibles Are Not External to the Intellect, and on the Good, trans. and ed. Lloyd P. Gerson (Las Vegas: Parmenides, 2013).
Ennead VI.4 & VI.5: On the Presence of Being, One and the Same, Everywhere as a Whole, trans. and ed. Eyjólfur Emilsson and Steven K. Strange (Las Vegas: Parmenides, 2015).
Enneads, trans. and ed. A. H. Armstrong, 7 vols. (Cambridge, MA: Harvard University Press, 1966–1988).
The Enneads, trans. and George Boys-Stones, John M. Dillon, Lloyd P. Gerson, R. A. H. King, Andrew Smith, and James Wilberding, ed. Lloyd P. Gerson (Cambridge: Cambridge University Press, 2018).
Εννεάς Τετάρτη, ed. Pavlos Kalligas (Athens: Kentron Ereunes tes Hellenikes kai Latinikes Grammateias, 2009).
Plotino sui numeri: Enneade VI 6 [34], trans. and ed. Claudia Maggi (Naples: Università degli Studi Suor Orsola Benincasa, 2009).
Plotins Schriften, trans. Richard Harder and Rudolf Beutler, ed. Willy Theiler, 5 vols. (Hamburg: Meiner, 1956–1967).
Plotinus on Eudaimonia: A Commentary on Ennead I.4, trans. and ed. Kieran McGroarty (Oxford: Oxford University Press, 2006).
Plotinus' Cosmology: A Study of Ennead II.1 (40): Text, Translation and Commentary, trans. and ed. James Wilberding (Oxford: Oxford University Press, 2006).
Traité 12 (II,4), trans. and ed. Eleni Perdikouri (Paris: Cerf, 2014).

Traité sur les nombres: Ennéade VI, 6 [34], ed. Janine Bertier and Luc Brisson (Paris: J. Vrin, 1980).
Traités, trans. and ed. Luc Brisson and J.-F. Pradéau, 9 vols. (Paris: Flammarion, 2002–2010).

PROCLUS

Texts
Procli Diadochi in Platonis rem publicam commentarii, ed. Wilhelm Kroll, 2 vols. (Leipzig: Teubner, 1899–1901).
Procli Diadochi in Platonis Timaeum commentaria, ed. Ernst Diehl, 3 vols. (Leipzig: Teubner, 1903–1906).
Procli Diadochi in primum Euclidis Elementorum librum commentarii, ed. Gottfried Friedlein (Hildesheim: Georg Olms, 1992).
Procli Diadochi Lycii institutio physica, ed. Albert Ritzenfeld (Leipzig: Teubner, 1912).
Procli in Platonis Parmenidem commentaria, ed. Carlos Steel, 3 vols. (Oxford: Oxford University Press, 2007–2009).
Proclus Diadochus in Platonis Cratylum commentaria, ed. Giorgio Pasquali (Leipzig: Teubner, 1908).
Tria opuscula (De providentia, libertate, malo), ed. Helmut Boese (Berlin: De Gruyter, 1960).

Translations
A Commentary on the First Book of Euclid's Elements, trans. and ed. Glenn R. Morrow (Princeton: Princeton University Press, 1992).
Commentary on Plato's Timaeus, trans. and ed. Dirk Baltzly, 6 vols. (Cambridge: Cambridge University Press, 2007–2017).
Deux livres de Proclus du mouvement, trans. Pierre Forcadel (Paris: Charles Perier, 1565).
Die mittelalterliche Übersetzung der "Stoicheiosis physike" der Proclus: Procli Diadochi Lycii Elementatio physica, ed. Helmut Boese (Berlin: Akademie, 1958).
Elementatio Theologica, trans. William of Moerbeke, ed. Helmut Boese (Leuven: Leuven University Press, 1987).
The Elements of Theology, trans. and ed. E. R. Dodds (Oxford: Clarendon, 1933 [2nd ed., 1963]).
I Manuali: Elementi di fisica; Elementi di teologia; I testi magico-teurgici, trans. and ed. Chiara Faraggiana di Sarzana (Milan: Rusconi, 1985).
Nachala fiziki, ed. Svetlana Mesyats (Moscow: Museum Graeco-Latinum, 2001).
On Plato's Cratylus, trans. Brian Duvick (London: Duckworth, 2007).
On Providence, trans. Carlos Steel (London: Duckworth, 2007).
On the Existence of Evils, trans. Jan Opsomer and Carlos Steel (Ithaca: Cornell University Press, 2003).
Proclus' Commentary on the First Alcibiades, trans. and ed. L. G. Westerink and W. O'Neill (Westbury: The Prometheus Trust, 2011).
Sur le premier Alcibiade de Platon, trans. and ed. Alain-Philippe Segonds, 2 vols. (Paris: Les Belles Lettres, 1985–1986).
Ten Doubts Concerning Providence, trans. Jan Opsomer and Carlos Steel (London: Duckworth, 2012).
Théologie platonicienne, trans. and ed. H. D. Saffrey and L. G. Westerink, 6 vols. (Paris: Les Belles Lettres, 1968–1997).

Trois études sur la Providence, trans. Daniel Isaac and Carlos Steel, 3 vols. (Paris: Les Belles Lettres, 1982).

COLLECTIONS

Commentaria in Aristotelem Graeca, ed. Hermann Diels, 23 vols. (Berlin: Reimer, 1882-1909).
Fragmente der Vorsokraitker, ed. Hermann Diels and Walther Kranz (Zurich: Weidmann, 1985).
The Pythagorean Texts of the Hellenistic Period, ed. Holger Thesleff (Åbo: Åbo Akademi, 1965).
Stoicorum Veterum Fragmenta, ed. Hans von Arnim, 4 vols. (Stuttgart: Teubner, 1964).
Testimonia Platonica, in Konrad Gaiser, *Platons ungeschriebene Lehre: Studien zur systematischen und geschichtlichen Begründung der Wissenschaften in der Platonischen Schule* (Stuttgart: Klett, 1963), pp. 441-557.
Testimonia Platonica: Le antiche testimonianze sulle dottrine non scritte di Platone, ed. Konrad Gaiser (Milan: Vita e Pensiero, 1998).

OTHER PRIMARY SOURCES

Alexander of Aphrodisias, *In Aristotelis metaphysica commentaria*, ed. Michael Hayduck, vol. 1 of *Commentaria in Aristotelem Graeca* (Berlin: Reimer, 1891).
Aristotle, *De Bono*, in *Fragmenta Selecta*, ed. W. D. Ross (Oxford: Clarendon, 1955), pp. 113-9.
Aristotle, *On Indivisible Lines*, in *Minor Works*, trans. and ed. W. S. Hett (Cambridge, MA: Harvard University Press, 2000), pp. 413-47.
Aristotle, *Opera*, ed. Immanuel Bekker, 5 vols. (Berlin: G. Reimer, 1831).
Asclepius, *In Aristoteles Metaphysicorum Libros A-Z Commentaria*, ed. Michael Hayduck, pt. 2 in vol. 6 of *Commentaria in Aristotelem Graeca* (Berlin: Reimer, 1888).
Augustine, *Confessiones*, vol. 32 of *Patrologiae Cursus Completus*, ed. J. P. Migne (Paris: Vrayet, 1845).
Boethius, *De consolatione Philosophiae*, ed. C. Moreschini (Leipzig: K. G. Saur, 2005).
Boethius, *The Theological Tractates*, trans. H. F. Stewart, E. K. Rand, and S. J. Tester (Cambridge, MA: Harvard University Press, 1973).
[Cicero], *Rhetorica ad Herennium*, trans. Harry Caplan (Cambridge, MA: Harvard University Press, 1954).
Cicero, *Rhetorica*, ed. A. S. Wilkins, 2 vols. (Oxford: Oxford University Press, 1902-1903).
Damascius, *Damascii successoris dubitationes et solutiones*, ed. Charles-Émile Ruelle (Brussels: Culture et Civilisation, 1964).
Damascius, *Damascius' Problems and Solutions Concerning First Principles*, trans. Sara Ahbel-Rappe (Oxford: Oxford University Press, 2010).
Damascius, *Traité des premiers principes*, trans. J. Combès, ed. L. G. Westerink, 3 vols. (Paris: Les Belles Lettres, 1986-1991).
de Meynier, Honorat, *Paradoxes de Meynier contre les mathematiciens qui abusent la ieunesse: ensemble les definitions, theorems, & maximes d'Euclides, d'Archimedes, de Proclus, de Sacrobosco, & d'Aristotle, vtiles a ceux qui se veulent seruir proprement des mathematiques & de philosophie: avec un abregé des reigles de la geometrie & des principals maximes & regles des arts, de fortifier & assaillir les places* (Paris: Iulian Iacquin, 1652).

Democritus, Тексты, перевод, исследования, составил и перевел, trans. S. Ya. Lurie (Leningrad: Nauka, 1970).
Diogenes Laertius, *Lives of Eminent Philosophers*, trans. R. D. Hicks, 2 vols. (Cambridge, MA: Harvard University Press, 1925).
Euclid, *Elementa*, ed. J. L. Heiberg, 5 vols. (Leipzig: Teubner, 1883–1888).
Euclid, *The Thirteen Books of Euclid's Elements*, trans. and ed. Thomas L. Heath, 3 vols. (New York: Dover Publications, 1956 [2nd rev. ed.]).
Eutocius, *Commentarii in de sphaera et cylindro*, in vol. 3 of Archimedes, *Opera Omnia*, ed. J. L. Heiberg (Leipzig: Teubner, 1881).
Hermias, *In Platonis Phaedrum Scholia*, ed. P. Couvreur (Paris: Librarie Émile Bouillon, 1901).
Hesiod, *Theologonia*, ed. Friedrich Solmsen (Oxford: Oxford University Press, 1970).
[Iamblichus], *Theologumena arithmeticae*, ed. Vittorio de Falco (Leipzig: Teubner, 1922).
Iamblichus, *De communi mathematica scientia*, ed. N. Festa (Stuttgart: Teubner, 1975).
Iamblichus, *De mysteriis*, ed. Edouard Des Place (Paris: Les Belles Lettres, 1966).
Iamblichus, *In Nicomachi arithemeticam introductionem*, ed. Ermenegildo Pistelli (Leipzig: Teubner, 1894).
Longinus, Cassius, *Fragments: Art rhétorique*, ed. Michel Patillon and Luc Brisson (Paris: Les Belles Lettres, 2001).
Nicomachus, *Nikomachou Gerasēnou pythagorikou Arithmētikē eisagōgē = Nicomachi Geraseni Pythagorei Introductionis arithmeticae libri II*, ed. Richard Hoche (Leipzig: Teubner, 1866).
Pappus, *The Commentary of Pappus on Book X of Euclid's* Elements, trans. William Thomson, ed. Gustav Junge and William Thomson (Cambridge, MA: Harvard University Press, 1930).
Philoponus, *Exegesis eis to prōton [-deuteron] tes Nikomachou arithmētikēs eisagōgēs*, ed. Richard Hoche, 3 vols. (Berlin: S. Calvary, 1867).
Plato, *Platonis opera*, ed. John Burnet, 5 vols. (Oxford: Clarendon Press, 1900–1907).
Plutarch, *Isis and Osiris*, trans. Frank Cole Babbit, in vol. 5 of *Moralia*, 16 vols. (Cambridge, MA: Harvard University Press, 1936).
Plutarch, *On the Generation of the Soul in the Timaeus*, trans. Harold Cherniss, in pt. 1 of vol. 13 of *Moralia*, 16 vols. (Cambridge, MA: Harvard University Press, 1976).
Porphyry, *Introduction*, trans. Jonathan Barnes (Oxford: Clarendon Press, 2003).
Porphyry, *Life of Plotinus*, trans. A. H. Armstrong, in vol. 1 of Plotinus, *Enneads*, ed. A. H. Armstrong (Cambridge, MA: Harvard University Press, 1969).
Porphyry, *Porphyrii Philosophi Fragmenta*, ed. Andrew Smith (Stuttgart: Teubner, 1994).
Porphyry, *Sentences*, ed. Luc Brisson, 3 vols. (Paris: J. Vrin, 2005).
Ptolemy, *Claudii Ptolemaei Opera quae extant Omnia*, vol. 1 of *Syntaxis mathematica*, ed. J. L. Heiberg, 2 vols. (Leipzig: B. G. Teubner, 1898–1903).
Quintilian, *The Orator's Education*, trans. Donald A. Russell, 5 vols. (Cambridge, MA: Harvard University Press, 2002).
Sextus Empiricus, *Sextus Empiricus*, ed. Immanuel Bekker (Berlin: Reimer, 1842).
Simplicius, *In Aristotelis Categorias commentarium*, ed. Karl Kalbfleisch, vol. 8 of *Commentaria in Aristotelem Graeca* (Berlin: Reimer, 1907).
Simplicius, *In Aristotelis Physicorum libros commentaria*, ed. Hermann Diels, vols. 9–10 of *Commentaria in Aristotelem Graeca* (Berlin: Reimer, 1882–1895).

Speusippus, *De Speusippi academici scriptis accedunt fragmenta*, ed. Paul Lang (Hildesheim: G. Olms, 1965).
Speusippus, *Speusippus of Athens: A Critical Study with a Collection of the Related Texts and Commentary*, ed. Leonardo Tarán (Leiden: E. J. Brill, 1981).
Stobaeus, Ioannis, *Anthologion*, ed. Thomas Gaisford, 4 vols. (Leipzig: Kuehniano, 1822–1824).
Syrianus, *Syriani in Metaphysica commentaria*, ed. G. Kroll (Berlin: Reimer, 1902).
Syrianus, *The Teachings of Syrianus on Plato's Timaeus and Parmenides*, trans. and ed. Sara Klitenic Wear (Leiden: Brill, 2011).
Themistius, *In libros Aristotelis de anima paraphrasis*, ed. Richard Heinze, vol. 3 of pt. 5 in *Commentaria in Aristotelem Graeca* (Berlin: Reimer, 1899).
Themistius, *Themistius: On Aristotle on the Soul*, trans. Robert B. Todd (London: Bloomsbury, 1996).
Theon of Smyrna, *Theonis Smyrnaei philosophi Platonici expositio rerum mathematicarum ad legendum Platonem utilium*, ed. Eduard Hiller (Leipzig: Teubner, 1995).
Theophrastus, *Metaphysics*, ed. W. D. Ross and F. H. Fobes (Oxford: Clarendon Press, 1929).
Xenocrates, *Darstellung der Lehre und Sammlung der Fragmente*, ed. Richard Heinze (Leipzig: Teubner, 1892).
Xenocrates, *Frammenti*, ed. Isnardi Parente (Naples: Bibliopolis, 1982).

Secondary

COLLECTIONS

Agonistes: Essays in Honour of Denis O'Brien, ed. J. Dillon and M. Dixsaut (Burlington, VT: Ashgate, 2005).
All from One: A Guide to Proclus, ed. Pieter D'Hoine and Marije Martijn (Oxford: Oxford University Press, 2017).
Aristotle in Late Antiquity, ed. Lawrence P. Schrenk (Washington, DC: Catholic University of America Press, 1994).
Aristotle on Mind and the Senses: Proceedings of the Seventh Symposium Aristotelicum, ed. G. E. R. Lloyd and G. E. L. Owen (Cambridge: Cambridge University Press, 1978).
The Cambridge Companion to Plotinus, ed. Lloyd P. Gerson (Cambridge: Cambridge University Press, 1996).
The Concept of Matter in Greek and Medieval Philosophy, ed. Ernan McMullin (Notre Dame, IL: University of Notre Dame Press, 1965).
Corps et âme: sur le De anima d'Aristote, ed. Gilbert Romeyer-Dherbey and Cristina Viano (Paris: J. Vrin, 1996).
Essays on Aristotle's De Anima, ed. Martha Nussbaum and Amélie Oksenberg Rorty (Oxford: Oxford University Press, 1992).
Études sur le Commentaire de Proclus au premier livre des Éléments d'Euclide, ed. Alain Lernould (Villeneuve d'Ascq: Presses Universitaires de Septentrion, 2010).
Études sur le Sophiste de Platon, ed. Michel Narcy (Naples: Bibliopolis, 1991).
Gnosticism, Platonism and the Ancient World, ed. Kevin Corrigan and Tuomas Rasimus (Leiden: Brill, 2013).
Infinity and Continuity in Ancient and Medieval Thought, ed. Norman Kretzmann (Ithaca: Cornell University Press, 1982).

Interpreting Proclus: From Antiquity to the Renaissance, ed. Stephen Gersh (Cambridge: Cambridge University Press, 2014).
Isonomia: Studien zur Gleichheitsvorstellung im Griechischen Denken, ed. Jürgen Mau and Ernst Günther Schmidt (Berlin: Akademie, 1964).
La naissance de la raison en Grèce: Actes du Congrés de Nice—Mai 1987, ed. Jean François Mattéi (Paris: Presses Universitaires de France, 1990).
Le Néoplatonisme, ed. Pierre Maxime Schuhl and Pierre Hadot (Paris: Éditions du Centre national de la recherche scientifique, 1971).
Le Timée de Platon: Contributions à l'histoire de sa reception, ed. Ada Neschke-Hentschke (Leuven: Peeters Publishing, 2000).
Lexicon Plotinianum, ed. J. H. Sleeman and Gilbert Pollet (Leiden: Brill, 1980).
Mathematics and Metaphysics in Aristotle / Mathematik und Metaphysik bei Aristoteles, ed. A. Graeser (Bern: P. Haupt, 1987).
Neoplatonism and Early Christian Thought: Essays in Honour of A. H. Armstrong, ed. H. J. Blumenthal and R. A. Markus (London: Variorum Publications, 1981).
Neoplatonism and the Philosophy of Nature, ed. James Wilberding and Christoph Horn (Oxford: Oxford University Press, 2012).
On Proclus and His Influence in Medieval Philosophy, ed. E. P. Bos and P. A. Meijer (Leiden: Brill, 1992).
One Book, The Whole Universe: Plato's Timaeus *Today*, ed. R. D. Mohr and B. M. Sattler (Las Vegas: Parmenides, 2010).
The Other Plato, ed. Dmitri Nikulin (Albany: SUNY Press, 2012).
Partitioning the Soul: Debates from Plato to Leibniz, ed. Klaus Corcilius and Dominik Perler (Berlin: De Gruyter, 2014).
Paulys Real-Encyclopädie der Classischen Altertumswissenschaft, ed. A. Pauly and G. Wissowa (Stuttgart: J. B. Metzler, 1894–1980).
Physics and Philosophy of Nature in Greek Neoplatonism, ed. Riccardo Chiaradonna and Franco Trabattoni (Leiden: Brill, 2009).
Plato, Aristotle, or Both?: Dialogues Between Platonism and Aristotelianism in Antiquity," ed. Thomas Bénatouïl, Emanuele Maffi, and Franco Trabattoni (Hildesheim: George Olms, 2011).
Platonism in Late Antiquity, ed. Stephen Gersh and Charles Kannengiesser (Notre Dame: University of Notre Dame Press, 1992).
Platons Hermeneutik und Prinzipiendenken im Licht der Dialoge und der antiken Tradition, ed. Ulrike Bruchmüller (Hildesheim: Georg Olms, 2012).
Plato's Meno *in Focus*, ed. Jane M. Day (New York: Routledge, 1994).
Plotinus and Epicurus: Matter, Perception, Pleasure, ed. Angela Longo and Daniela Patrizia Taormina (Cambridge: Cambridge University Press, 2016).
Politische Ordnung und menschliche Existenz: Festgabe für Eric Voegelin, ed. Alois Dempf and Hannah Arendt (Munich: C. H. Beck, 1962).
Proclus et son influence, ed. Gilbert Boss and Gerhard Seel (Zurich: Éditions du Grand Midi, 1987).
Proclus, lecteur et interprète des anciens: Actes du Colloque international du CNRS, Paris, 2–4 octobre 1985, ed. Jean Pépin and H. D. Saffrey (Paris: Editions du Centre national de la recherché scientifique, 1987).
Proklos: Methode, Seelenlehre, Metaphysics, ed. Matthias Perkams and Rosa Maria Piccione (Leiden: Brill, 2006).

Reading Ancient Texts: Essays in Honour of Denis O'Brien, ed. Suzanne Stern-Gillet and Kevin Corrigan, 2 vols. (Leiden: Brill, 2007).
Religious Imagination, ed. James P. Mackey and John McIntyre (Edinburgh: Edinburgh University Press, 1986).
The Routledge Handbook of Neoplatonism, ed. Pauliina Remes and Svetla Slaveva-Griffin (London: Routledge, 2014).
The Significance of Neoplatonism, ed. R. Baine Harris (Norfolk, VA.: International Society for Neoplatonic Studies, 1976).
Soul and the Structure of Being in Late Neoplatonism: Syrianus, Proclus, and Simplicius, ed. H. J. Blumenthal and Antony C. Lloyd (Liverpool: Liverpool University Press, 1982).
The Structure of Being: A Neoplatonic Approach, ed. R. Baine Harris (Norfolk, VA: International Society for Neoplatonic Studies, 1982).
Studi sull'anima in Plotino, ed. Riccardo Chiaradonna (Naples: Bibliopolis, 2005).
Studies on Plato, Aristotle and Proclus: Collected Essays on Ancient Philosophy of John Cleary, ed. John Dillon, Brendan O'Byrne, and Fran O'Rourke (Leiden: Brill, 2013).
Tracce nella mente: Teorie della memoria da Platone ai moderni, ed. Maria Michela Sassi (Pisa: Edizioni della Normale, 2007).

MONOGRAPHS AND ARTICLES

Amado, Éliane, "A propos des nombres nombrés et des nombres nombrants chez Plotin," *Revue Philosophique de la France et de l'Étranger* 143 (1953), pp. 423–5.
Annas, Julia, "Aristotle on Memory and the Self," in *Essays on Aristotle's* De Anima, pp. 297–312.
Armstrong, A. H., *The Architecture of the Intelligible Universe in the Philosophy of Plotinus: An Analytical and Historical Study* (Cambridge: Cambridge University Press, 1940).
Armstrong, A. H., *The Cambridge History of the Later Greek and Early Medieval Philosophy* (Cambridge: Cambridge University Press, 1967).
Armstrong, A. H., "Eternity, Life and Movement in Plotinus' account of Νοῦς," in *Le Néoplatonisme*, pp. 67–74.
Arruzza, Cinzia, *Les mésaventures de la théodicée: Plotin, Origène, Grégoire de Nysse* (Turnhout: Brepols, 2011).
Arruzza, Cinzia, "Passive Potentiality in the Physical Realm: Plotinus' Critique of Aristotle in *Ennead* II.5 [25]," *Archiv für Geschichte der Philosophie* 93 (2011), pp. 24–57.
Ast, Friedrich, *Lexicon Platonicum*, 3 vols. (Leipzig: Libraria Weidmaniana, 1835).
Aubry, Gwenaëlle, *Dieu sans la puissance: Dynamis et energeia chez Aristotle et chez Plotin* (Paris: Vrin, 2006).
Baeumker, Clemens, *Das Problem der Materie in der griechischen Philosophie: eine historisch-kritische Untersuchung* (Frankfurt am Main: Minerva, 1963; orig. pub. 1890).
Baumgarten, Alexander Gottlieb, *Metaphysica* (Hildesheim: Georg Olms, 1963; orig. pub. 1779).
Bechtle, Gerald, "Das Böse im Platonismus: Überlegungen zur Position Jamblichs," *Bochumer Philosophisches Jahrbuch für Antike und Mittelalter* 4 (1999), pp. 63–82.
Bechtle, Gerald, "Die pythagoreisierende Konzeption der Mathematik bei Iamblichos, Syrianos und Proklos: In Spannungsfeld zwischen pythagoreischer Transposition und platonischer Mittelstellung," in *Proklos: Methode, Seelenlehre, Metaphysik*, ed. Matthias Perkams and Rosa Maria Piccione (Leiden: Brill, 2006), pp. 323–39.
Beierwaltes, Werner, *Plotin über Ewigkeit und Zeit* (Frankfurt am Main: Klostermann, 1967).

Beierwaltes, Werner, "Primum est dives per se: Meister Eckhart und Der Liber de Causis," in *On Proclus and His Influence in Medieval Philosophy*, pp. 141–69.
Beierwaltes, Werner, *Proklos: Grundzüge seiner Metaphysik* (Frankfurt am Main: Klostermann, 1965).
Benz, Hubert, *Materie und Wahrnehmung in der Philosophie Plotins* (Würzburg: Königshausen & Neumann, 1990).
Berti, Enrico, "Reconsidérations sur l'intellection des Indivisibles selon Aristote *De anima* III 6," in *Corps et âme: sur le* De anima *d'Aristote*, pp. 391–404.
Bloch, David, *Aristotle on Memory and Recollection: Text, Translation, Interpretation, and Reception in Western Scholasticism* (Leiden: Brill, 2007).
Blumenthal, H. J., "Neoplatonic Interpretations of Aristotle on 'Phantasia,'" *The Review of Metaphysics* 31:2 (1977), pp. 242–57.
Blumenthal, H. J., "Plotinus' Adaptation of Aristotle's Psychology: Sensation, Imagination and Memory," in *The Significance of Neoplatonism*, pp. 41–58.
Blumenthal, H. J., *Plotinus' Psychology: His Doctrines of the Embodied Soul* (The Hague: Martinus Nijhoff, 1971).
Blumenthal, H. J., *Soul and Intellect: Studies in Plotinus and Later Neoplatonism* (Aldershot: Variorum, 1993).
Blumenthal, H. J., *Soul, World-Soul, and Individual Soul in Plotinus* (Paris: Centre national de la recherché scientifique, 1971).
Boethius, *The Theological Tractates*, trans. H. F. Stewart, E. K. Rand, and S. J. Tester (Cambridge, MA: Harvard University Press, 1973; 1st publ. 1918).
Brandwood, Leonard, *A Word Index to Plato* (Leeds: W. S. Maney and Son, 1976).
Bréhier, Emile, *La philosophie de Plotin* (Paris: J. Vrin, 1982; orig. pub. 1928).
Brisson, Luc, "La place de la mémoire dans la psychologie plotinienne," *Études Platoniciennes* 3 (2006), pp. 13–72.
Brisson, Luc, *Le même et l'autre dans la structure ontologique du Timée de Platon: Un commentaire systématique du Timée de Platon* (Paris: l'Université de Paris X Nanterre, 1974).
Burnyeat, Myles, "Platonism and Mathematics: A Prelude to Discussion," in *Mathematics and Metaphysics in Aristotle / Mathematik und Metaphysik bei Aristoteles*, pp. 213–40.
Bussanich, John, *The One and Its Relation to the Intellect in Plotinus* (Leiden: Brill, 1988).
Bussanich, John, "Plotinus' Metaphysics of the One," in *The Cambridge Companion to Plotinus*, pp. 38–65.
Caluori, Damian, *Plotinus on the Soul* (Cambridge: Cambridge University Press, 2015).
Caveing, Maurice, "La proportionnalité des grandeurs dans la doctrine de la nature d'Aristote," *Revue d'histoire des sciences* 47:2 (1994), pp. 163–88.
Charles, Annick, "L'imagination, miroir de l'âme selon Proclus," in *Le Néoplatonisme*, pp. 241–51.
Chiaradonna, Riccardo, *Plotino* (Rome: Carocci editore, 2009).
Chiaradonna, Riccardo, *Sostanza, movimento, analogia: Plotino critico di Aristotele* (Naples: Bibliopolis, 2002).
Chlup, Radek, *Proclus: An Introduction* (Cambridge: Cambridge University Press, 2012).
Cleary, John, *Aristotle and Mathematics: Aporetic Method in Cosmology and Metaphysics* (Leiden: Brill, 1995).

Cleary, John, "Proclus' Philosophy of Mathematics," in *Studies on Plato, Aristotle and Proclus: Collected Essays on Ancient Philosophy of John Cleary*, pp. 201–20.
Collette-Dučić, Bernard, *Plotin et l'ordonnancement de l'être: Étude sur les fondements et les limites de la "détérmination"* (Paris: Vrin, 2007).
Combès, Joseph, "Les trois monades du *Philèbe* selon Proclus," in *Proclus, lecteur et interprète des anciens*, pp. 177–90.
Cornea, Andrei, "*Athroa epibolē*: On an Epicurean Formula in Plotinus' Work," in *Plotinus and Epicurus: Matter, Perception, Pleasure*, pp. 177–88.
Corrigan, Kevin, "Is There More than One Generation of Matter in the 'Enneads'?," *Phronesis* 31:2 (1986), pp. 167–81.
Corrigan, Kevin, *Plotinus' Theory of Matter-Evil and the Question of Substance in Plato, Aristotle, and Alexander of Aphrodisias* (Leuven: Peeters, 1996).
Courtine, Jean-François, *Suarez et le système de la métaphysique* (Paris: Presses universitaires de France, 1990).
D'Ancona, Cristina, "Plotino: memoria di eventi e anamnesis di intelligibili," in *Tracce nella mente: Teorie della memoria da Platone ai moderni*, pp. 67–98.
De Koninck, Thomas, "La noêsis et l'indivisible selon Aristote," in *La naissance de la raison en Grèce*, pp. 215–28.
De Rijk, L. M., "Causation and Participation in Proclus: The Pivotal Role of 'Scope Distinction' in His Metaphysics," in *On Proclus and His Influence in Medieval Philosophy*, pp. 1–34.
D'Hoine, Pieter, "Les arguments de Proclus contre l'existence d'Idées des maux," *Études Platoniciennes* 8 (2011), pp. 75–103.
Dillon, John, *The Heirs of Plato: A Study of the Old Academy* (Oxford: Oxford University Press, 2003).
Dillon, John, *The Middle Platonists: A Study of Platonism, 80 B.C. to A.D. 220* (London: Duckworth, 1977).
Dillon, John, "Plotinus and the Chaldean Oracles," in *Platonism in Late Antiquity*, pp. 131–40.
Dillon, John, "Plotinus and the Transcendental Imagination," in *Religious Imagination*, pp. 55–64.
Dodds, E. R., "The *Parmenides* of Plato and the Origin of the Neoplatonic 'One,'" *Classical Quarterly* 22:3–4 (1928), pp. 129–42.
Dörrie, Heinrich, "Präpositionen und Metaphysik: Wechselwirkung zweier Prinzipienreihen," *Museum Helveticum* 26:4 (1969), pp. 217–28.
Eliasson, Erik, "Plotinus' Reception of Epicurean Atomism in *On Fate*, tr. 3 (Enn. III 1) 1–3," in *Plotinus and Epicurus: Matter, Perception, Pleasure*, pp. 160–74.
Emilsson, Eyjólfur Kjalar, *Plotinus* (London: Routledge, 2017).
Emilsson, Eyjólfur Kjalar, *Plotinus on Intellect* (Oxford: Oxford University Press, 2007).
Emilsson, Eyjólfur Kjalar, *Plotinus on Sense-Perception: A Philosophical Study* (Cambridge: Cambridge University Press, 1988).
Eslick, Leonard J., "The Material Substrate in Plato," in *The Concept of Matter in Greek and Medieval Philosophy*, pp. 55–8.
Fattal, Michel, *Platon et Plotin: Relation, logos, intuition* (Paris: L'Harmattan, 2013).
Federspiel, Michel, "Notes exégétiques et critiques sur le Traité Pseudo-Aristotélicien *Des Lignes Insécables*," *Revue des Études Grecques* 94 (1981), pp. 502–13.

Festugière, André-Jean, "Le sens philosophique du mot aiôn," in *Etudes de philosophie grecque* (Paris: Vrin, 1972).
Flashar, Hellmut, "Aristoteles," chap. 2 of *Ältere Akademie Aristoteles-Peripatos*, ed. Hellmut Flashar, vol. 3 of *Die Philosophie Der Antike*, ed. Helmut Holzhey (Basel: Schwabe, 1983), pp. 167–491.
Fleet, Barrie, *Ennead III.6: On the Impassivity of the Bodiless* (Oxford: Oxford University Press, 1995).
Fortier, Simon, "The Relationship of the Kantian and Proclan Conceptions of Evil," *Dionysius* 26 (2008), pp. 175–92.
Frede, Michael, "Plato's Arguments and the Dialogue Form," in *Methods of Interpreting Plato and his Dialogues*, supp. vol. of *Oxford Studies in Ancient Philosophy* (1992), pp. 201–19.
Frege, Gottlob, *Die Grundlagen der Arithemetik: eine logisch mathematische Untersuchung über den Begriff der Zahl* (Hamburg: Meiner, 1986).
Gadamer, Hans-Georg, "Concerning Empty and Ful-filled Time," *The Southern Journal of Philosophy* 8:4 (1970), pp. 341–53.
Gaiser, Konrad, *Platons ungeschriebene Lehre: Studien zur systematischen und geschichtlichen Begründung der Wissenschaften in der Platonischen Schule* (Stuttgart: Klett, 1963).
Gaiser, Konrad, "Platons Zusammenschau der mathematischen Wissenschaften," *Antike und Abendland* 32 (1986), pp. 89–124 (repr. in Konrad Gaiser, *Gesammelte Schriften* ed. K. Stanzel and Thomas A. Szlezák [Sankt Augustin: Academia, 2004], pp. 137–76).
Galpérine, Marie-Claire, "Le temps intégral selon Damascius," *Les études philosophiques* 3 (1980), pp. 325–41.
Gersh, Stephen, ΚΙΝΗΣΙΣ ΑΚΙΝΗΤΟΣ: *A Study of Spiritual Motion in the Philosophy of Proclus* (Leiden: Brill, 1973).
Gerson, Lloyd P., *Plotinus* (London: Routledge, 1994).
Gloy, Karen, "Die Struktur der Zeit in Plotins Zeittheorie," *Archiv für Geschichte der Philosophie* 71:3 (1989), pp. 303–26.
Gritti, Elena, "La φαντασία plotiniana tra illuminazione intellettiva e impassibilità dell'anima," in *Studi sull'anima in Plotino*, pp. 251–74.
Gritti, Elena, *Proclo: Dialettica, anima, esegesi* (Milan: LED, 2008).
Guitton, Jean, *Le temps et l'éternité chez Plotin et Saint Augustin* (Partis: Vrin, 1959).
Gurtler, Gary M., *Plotinus: The Experience of Unity* (Bern: Peter Lang, 1988).
Gurtler, Gary M., "Plotinus: Matter and Otherness, 'On Matter' (II 4[12])," *Epoché: A Journal for the History of Philosophy* 9 (2005), pp. 197–214.
Hadamard, Jacques, *The Mathematician's Mind: The Psychology of Invention in the Mathematical Field* (Princeton: Princeton University Press, 1996).
Hadot, Pierre, *Être, vie, pensée chez Plotin et avant Plotin* (Geneva: Foundation Hardt, 1960).
Halfwassen, Jens, *Der Aufstief zum Einen: Untersuchungen zu Platon und Plotin* (Stuttgart: Teubner, 1992).
Happ, Heinz, *Hyle: Studien zum Aristotelischen Materie-Bergriff* (Berlin: De Gruyter, 1971).
Harari, Orna, "*Methexis* and Geometrical Reasoning in Proclus' Commentary on Euclid's Elements," *Oxford Studies in Ancient Philosophy* 30 (2006), pp. 361–89.
Hartmann, Nicolai, *Des Proklus Diadochus philosophische Anfangsgründe der Mathematik: Nach den ersten zwei Büchern des Euklidkommentars dargestellt* (Berlin: De Gruyter, 1909).

Heath, Thomas, *A History of Greek Mathematics*, 2 vols. (Oxford: Clarendon Press, 1921).
Helleman-Elgersma, Wypkje, *Soul-Sisters: A Commentary on* Enneads *IV 3 [27], 1-8 of Plotinus* (Amsterdam: Rodopi, 1980).
Hoffmann, Philippe, "Jamblique exégète du pythagoricien Archytas: trois originalités d'une doctrine du temps," *Les études philosophiques* 3 (1980), pp. 307–23.
Horn, Christoph, "The Concept of Will in Plotinus," in *Aristotle and Neoplatonism*, vol. 2 of *Reading Ancient Texts: Essays in Honour of Denis O'Brien*, pp. 153–78.
Horn, Christoph, "Der Platonische *Parmenides* und die Möglichkeit seiner prinzipientheoretischen Interpretation," *Antike und Abendland: Beiträge zum Verständnis der Griechen und Römer und ihres Nachlebens* 41 (1995), pp. 99–113.
Horn, Christoph, *Plotin über Sein, Zahl und Einheit: eine Studie zu den systematischen Grundlagen der Enneaden* (Stuttgart: Teubner, 1995).
Ierodiakonou, Katerina, "The Stoics and the Skeptics on Memory," in *Tracce nella mente: Teorie della memoria da Platone ai moderni*, pp. 47–65.
Jackson, Belford Darrell, "Plotinus and the *Parmenides*," *Journal of the History of Philosophy* 5:4 (1967), pp. 315–27.
Jech, Thomas J., *Set Theory* (New York: Academic Press, 1978).
Jonas, Hans, "Plotin über Zeit und Ewigzeit," in *Politische Ordnung und menschliche Existenz: Festgabe für Eric Voegelin*, pp. 295–319.
Kalligas, Paul, *The Enneads of Plotinus: A Commentary* (Princeton: Princeton University Press, 2014).
Karfík, Filip, "Le temps et l' âme chez Plotin: À propos des *Énneades* VI 5 [23] 11; IV 4 [28] 15–16; III 7 [45] 11," *Elenchos* 33 (2012), pp. 227–57.
Karfík, Filip, "Parts of the Soul in Plotinus," in *Partitioning the Soul: Debates from Plato to Leibniz*, pp. 107–48.
King, R. A. H., *Aristotle and Plotinus on Memory* (Berlin: De Gruyter, 2009).
Krämer, Hans Joachim, *Arete bei Platon und Aristoteles: zum Wesen und zur Geschichte der platonischen Ontologie* (Heidelberg: C. Winter, 1959).
Krämer, Hans Joachim, *Der Ursprung der Geistmetaphysik: Untersuchungen zur Geschichte des Platonismus zwischen Platon und Platin* (Amsterdam: Schippers, 1964).
Kretzmann, Norman, "Continuity, Contrariety, Contradiction, and Change," in *Infinity and Continuity in Ancient and Medieval Thought*, pp. 270–96.
Lang, Helen S., "On Memory: Aristotle's Corrections of Plato," *Journal of the History of Philosophy* 18:4 (1980), pp. 379–93.
Lee, Jonathan Scott, "The Doctrine of Reception According to the Capacity of the Recipient in *Ennead* VI. 4–5. III," *Dionysius* 3 (1979), pp. 79–97.
Lernoud, Alain, "Imagination and Psychic Body: Apparitions of the Divine and Geometric Imagination according to Proclus," in *Gnosticism, Platonism and the Ancient World*, pp. 595–607.
Lernoud, Alain, *Physique et théólogie: Lecture du Timeé de Platon par Proclus* (Villeneuve d'Ascq: Presses Universitaires du Septentrion, 2001).
Linguiti, Alessandro, "Physis as Heimarmene: On Some Fundamental Principles of the Neoplatonic Philosophy of Nature," in *Physics and Philosophy of Nature in Greek Neoplatonism*, pp. 173–88.
Linguiti, Alessandro, "Plotinus and Epicurus on Pleasure and Happiness," in *Plotinus and Epicurus: Matter, Perception, Pleasure*, pp. 189–98.

Lloyd, Antony C., "Parhypostasis in Proclus," in *Proclus et son influence*, pp. 145–57.
Lloyd, Antony C., "Procession and Division in Proclus," in *Soul and the Structure of Being in Late Neoplatonism: Syrianus, Proclus, and Simplicius*, pp. 18–42.
Losev, A. F., "Analysis of the Composition of the *Parmenides*," in vol. 2 of Plato, *Sobranie sochineniy* (Moscow: Mysl', 1993), pp. 499–501.
MacIsaac, D. Gregory, "*Phantasia* Between Soul and Body in Proclus' Euclid Commentary," *Dionysius* 19 (2001), pp. 125–36.
Maggi, Claudia, *Sinfonia matematica: Aporie e soluzioni in Platone, Aristotele, Plotino, Giamblico* (Casoria: Loffredo, 2010).
Manchester, Peter, *The Syntax of Time: The Phenomenology of Time in Greek Physics and Speculative Logic from Iamblichus to Anaximander* (Leiden: Brill, 2005).
Manchester, Peter, "Time and the Soul in Plotinus, III.7 [45], 11," *Dionysius* 2 (1978), pp. 101–36.
Mansfeld, Jaap, *Prolegomena Mathematica from Apollonius of Perga to the Late Neoplatonists: With an Appendix on Pappus and the History of Platonism* (Leiden: Brill, 1998).
Martijn, Marije, *Proclus on Nature: Philosophy of Nature and Its Methods in Proclus' Commentary on Plato's Timaeus* (Leiden: Brill, 2010).
Martijn, Marije, "Proclus' Geometrical Method," in *The Routledge Handbook of Neoplatonism*, pp. 145–59.
Martijn, Marije, "Why Beauty Is Truth in All We Know: Aesthetics and Mimesis in Neoplatonic Science," *Proceedings of the Boston Area Colloquium in Ancient Philosophy* 25 (2010), pp. 69–108.
Martijn, Marije, and Lloyd P. Gerson, "Proclus' System," in *All from One: A Guide to Proclus*, pp. 45–72.
Maziarz, Edward, and Thomas Greenwood, *Greek Mathematical Philosophy* (New York: Ungar, 1968).
McCumber, John, "Anamnesis as Memory of Intelligibles in Plotinus," *Archiv für Geschichte der Philosophie* 60:2 (1978), pp. 160–7.
Meijer, P. A., "Participation and Henads and Monads in the 'Theologia Platonica' III, 1–6," in *On Proclus and His Influence in Medieval Philosophy*, pp. 65–87.
Meiners, Christoph, *Beytrag zur Geschichte der Denkart der ersten Jahrhunderte nach Christi Geburt, in einigen Betrachtungen über die Neu-Platonische Philosophie* (Leipzig: Weidmanns Erben und Reich, 1782).
Merlan, Philip, "Aristotle, Met. A 6,987 b 20–25 and Plotinus, Enn. V 4, 2, 8–9," *Phronesis* 9:1 (1964), pp. 45–7.
Moravcsik, Julius, "Learning as Recollection," in *Plato's* Meno *in Focus*, pp. 112–28.
Moutsopoulos, Evanghelos, "Dynamic Structuralism in the Plotinian Theory of the Imaginary," *Diotima* 4 (1976), pp. 11–22.
Moutsopoulos, Evanghelos, "The Idea of False in Proclus," in *The Structure of Being: A Neoplatonic Approach*, pp. 137–9.
Mueller, Ian, "Iamblichus and Proclus' Euclid Commentary," *Hermes* 115:3 (1987), pp. 334–48.
Mueller, Ian, "Mathematics and philosophy in Proclus' commentary on Book I of Euclid's *Elements*," in *Proclus, lecteur et interprète des anciens*, pp. 305–18.
Mueller, Ian, "What's the Matter? Some Neo-Platonist Answers," in *One Book, The Whole Universe: Plato's* Timaeus *Today*, pp. 151–63.

Narbonne, Jean-Marc, "La controverse à propos de la génération de la matière chez Plotin: l'énigme résolue?," *Questio* 7 (2007), pp. 123–63.
Narbonne, Jean-Marc, *La métaphysique de Plotin* (Paris: J. Vrin, 1994).
Narbonne, Jean-Marc, "Le non-être chez Plotin et dans la tradition grecque," *Revue de la philosophie ancienne* 10 (1992), pp. 115–33.
Narbonne, Jean-Marc, "Matter and Evil in the Neoplatonic Tradition," in *The Routledge Handbook of Neoplatonism*, pp. 231–44.
Narbonne, Jean-Marc, "Plotin et le problème de la génération de la matière: à propos d'un article recent," *Dionysius* 11 (1987), pp. 3–31.
Narbonne, Jean-Marc, *Plotinus in Dialogue with the Gnostics* (Leiden: Brill, 2011).
Nikulin, Dmitri, "Commentary on M. Martin's 'Why Beauty Is Truth in All We Know: Aesthetics and Mimesis in the Neoplatonic Science,'" *Proceedings of the Boston Area Colloquium in Ancient Philosophy* 25 (2009), pp. 93–105.
Nikulin, Dmitri, *Dialectic and Dialogue* (Stanford: Stanford University Press, 2010).
Nikulin, Dmitri, "Foundations of Arithmetic in Plotinus: *Enn*. VI.6 (34) on the Structure and the Constitution of Number," *Méthexis* 11 (1998), pp. 85–102.
Nikulin, Dmitri, "Imagination and Mathematics in Proclus," *Ancient Philosophy* 28:1 (2008), pp. 153–72.
Nikulin, Dmitri, "Indivisible Lines and Plato's Mathematical Ontology," *Platons Hermeneutik und Prinzipiendenken im Licht der Dialoge und der antiken Tradition*, pp. 291–326.
Nikulin, Dmitri, "Intelligible Matter in Plotinus," *Dionysius* 16 (1998), pp. 85–113.
Nikulin, Dmitri, *Matter, Imagination, and Geometry: Ontology, Natural Philosophy, and Mathematics in Plotinus, Proclus, and Descartes* (Burlington, VT: Ashgate, 2002).
Nikulin, Dmitri, "Memory and Recollection in Plotinus," *Archiv für Geschichte der Philosophie* 96 (2014), pp. 183–201.
Nikulin, Dmitri, "Memory in Ancient Philosophy," in *Memory: A History*, ed. Dmitri Nikulin (Oxford: Oxford University Press, 2015), pp. 35–84.
Nikulin, Dmitri, "The One and the Many in Plotinus," *Hermes* 126 (1998), pp. 326–40.
Nikulin, Dmitri, "The One and the Many in the Structure of Being in Proclus' *Theologia Platonica* II 1–3," *Diotima* 28 (2000), pp. 77–87.
Nikulin, Dmitri, "Physica more geometrico demonstrate: Natural Philosophy in Proclus and Aristotle," *Proceedings of the Boston Area Colloquium in Ancient Philosophy* 18 (2003), pp. 183–221.
Nikulin, Dmitri, "Plato: *Testimonia et fragmenta*," in *The Other Plato*, pp. 1–38.
Nikulin, Dmitri, "Plotinus on Eternity," in *Le Timée de Platon: Contributions à l'histoire de sa reception*, pp. 15–38.
Nikulin, Dmitri, "Proclus on Evil," *Proceedings of the Boston Area Colloquium in Ancient Philosophy* 31:1 (2016), pp. 119–46, 156–8.
Nikulin, Dmitri, "Unity and Individuation of the Soul in Plotinus," *Studi sull'anima in Plotino*, pp. 275–304.
Ninci, Marco, "Un Problema Plotiniano: L'identità con l'uno e l'alterità da lui," *Giornale Critico Della Filosofia Italiana* 21:3 (2001), pp. 461–506.
Noble, Christopher, "Plotinus' Unaffectable Matter," *Oxford Studies in Ancient Philosophy* 44 (2013), pp. 233–77.
Nussbaum, Martha, *Aristotle's De Motu Animalium: Text with Translation, Commentary, and Interpretive Essays* (Princeton: Princeton University Press, 1978).

Nussbaum, Martha, "Plotin et le problem de la generation de la matière: à propos d'un article recent," *Dionysius* 11 (1987), pp. 3–31.
Nussbaum, Martha, *Plotin, "Les duex matières": Ennéade II, 4 (12)* (Paris: J. Vrin, 1993).
Nyvlt, Mark J., *Aristotle and Plotinus on the Intellect: Monism and Dualism Revisited* (Lanham, MD: Lexington Books, 2012).
O'Brien, Denis, "J.-M. Narbonne on Plotinus and The Generation of Matter: Two Corrections," *Dionysius* 12 (1988), pp. 25–6.
O'Brien, Denis, "Le non-être dans la philosophie grecque: Parménide, Platon, Plotin," in *Études sur le Sophiste de Platon*, pp. 318–64.
O'Brien, Denis, "Plotinus and the Gnostics on the Generation of Matter," in *Neoplatonism and Early Christian Thought: Essays in Honour of A. H. Armstrong*, pp. 108–23.
O'Brien, Denis, *Plotinus on the Origin of Matter: An Exercise in the Interpretation of the Enneads* (Naples: Bibliopolis, 1991).
O'Meara, Dominic, "Mathematics and the Sciences," in *All from One: A Guide to Proclus*, pp. 167–82.
O'Meara, Dominic, "The Metaphysics of Evil in Plotinus: Problems and Solutions," in *Agonistes: Essays in Honour of Denis O'Brien*, pp. 179–85.
O'Meara, Dominic, *Plotinus: An Introduction to the* Enneads (Oxford: Oxford University Press, 1993).
O'Meara, Dominic, *Pythagoras Revived: Mathematics and Philosophy in Late Antiquity* (Oxford: Oxford University Press, 1989).
O'Meara, Dominic, *Structures hiérarchiques dans la penséee de Plotin: étude historique et interprétative* (Leiden: Brill, 1975).
O'Neill, W., "Time and Eternity in Proclus," *Phronesis* 7:2 (1962), pp. 161–5.
Opsomer, Jan, "The Integration of the Aristotelian Physics in a Neoplatonic Context: Proclus on Movers and Divisibility," in *Physics and Philosophy of Nature in Greek Neoplatonism*, pp. 189–229.
Opsomer, Jan, "Proclus vs Plotinus on Matter (*De Mal. Subs.* 30–37)," *Phronesis* 46 (2001), pp. 154–88.
Opsomer, Jan, "Some Problems with Plotinus' Theory of Matter/Evil: An Ancient Debate Continued," *Quaestio* 7 (2007), pp. 165–89.
Pépin, Jean, "Platonisme et antiplatonisme dans le traité de Plotin (VI.6 [34])," *Phronesis* 24:2 (1979), pp. 179–208.
Perl, Eric D., *Thinking Being: Introduction to Metaphysics in the Classical Tradition* (Leiden: Brill, 2014).
Phillips, John, *Order from Disorder: Proclus' Doctrine of Evil and Its Roots in Ancient Platonism* (Leiden: Brill, 2007).
Phillips, John, "Plotinus on the Generation of Matter," *International Journal of the Platonic Tradition* 3 (2009), pp. 103–37.
Pines, Shlomo, *Studies in Arabic Versions of Greek Texts and in Medieval Science*, vol. 2 of *The Collected Works of Shlomo Pines* (Jerusalem: Magnes Press, 1986).
Rappe, Sara, *Reading Neoplatonism: Non-Discursive Thinking in the Texts of Plotinus, Proclus, and Damascius* (Cambridge: Cambridge University Press, 2000).
Remes, Pauliina, *Plotinus on Self: The Philosophy of the "We"* (Cambridge: Cambridge University Press, 2007).

Richard, Marie-Dominique, *L'enseignement orale de Platon: Une nouvelle interprétation du platonisme* (Paris: Editions du Cerf, 1986 [2nd ed., 2005]).
Rist, John M., "Plotinus on Matter and Evil," *Phronesis* 6:2 (1961), pp. 154–66.
Rist, John M., "The Indefinite Dyad and Intelligible Matter in Plotinus," *Classical Quarterly* 12:1 (1962), pp. 99–107.
Rist, John M., "The Problem of 'Otherness' in the *Enneads*," in *Le Néoplatonisme*, pp. 77–87.
Ross, William David, *Aristotle's Metaphysics* (Oxford: Clarendon Press, 1953).
Sambursky, Samuel, and Schlomo Pines, *The Concept of Time in Late Neoplatonism: Texts with Translation, Introduction and Notes* (Jerusalem: Israel Academy of Sciences and Humanities, 1971).
Schäfer, Christian, "Das Dilemma der neuplatonischen Theodizee: Versuch einer Lösung," *Archiv für Geschichte der Philosophie* 82 (2000), pp. 1–35.
Schäfer, Christian, *Unde malum: Die Frage nach dem Woher des Bösen bei Plotin, Augustinus und Dionysius* (Würzburg: Königshausen & Neumann, 2002).
Schlette, Heinz Robert, *Das Eine und das Andere: Studien zur Problematik des Negativen in der Metaphysik Plotins* (Munich: Hueber, 1966).
Schofield, Malcolm, "Aristotle on the Imagination," in *Aristotle on Mind and the Senses*, pp. 99–140.
Schwyzer, Hans-Rudolf, s.v. "Plotinos," in *RE* 21:1, pp. 471–591.
Schwyzer, Hans-Rudolf, "Zu Plotins Deutung der sogenannten platonischen Materie," in *Zetesis: Festschrift E. de Stryker* (Antwerp: De Nederlandsche Boekhandel, 1973), pp. 266–80.
Scott, Dominic, *Plato's Meno* (Cambridge: Cambridge University Press, 2006), pp. 85–128.
Sedley, David, and Alex Long, introduction to Plato, *Meno and Phaedo*, trans. and ed. David Sedley and Alex Long (Cambridge: Cambridge University Press, 2011), pp. ix–xxxiii.
Siegmann, Georg, *Plotins Philosophie des Guten: eine Interpretation von Enneade VI 7* (Würzburg: Königshausen & Neumann, 1990).
Siorvanes, Lucas, *Proclus: Neo-Platonic Philosophy and Science* (New Haven: Yale University Press, 1996).
Slaveva-Griffin, Svetla, *Plotinus on Number* (Oxford: Oxford University Press, 2009).
Smith, Andrew, "Eternity and Time," in *The Cambridge Companion to Plotinus*, pp. 196–216.
Sorabji, Richard, *Aristotle on Memory* (Chicago: University of Chicago Press, 2006).
Sorabji, Richard, *Time, Creation, and the Continuum: Theories in Antiquity and the Early Middle Ages* (London: Duckworth, 1983).
Spade, Paul Vincent, "Quasi-Aristotelianism," in *Infinity and Continuity in Ancient and Medieval Thought*, pp. 297–307.
Steel, Carlos, "L'un et le bien: Les raisons d'une identification dans la tradition platonicienne," *Revue des Sciences Philosophiques et Théologiques* 73 (1989), pp. 69–85.
Steel, Carlos, "Proclus et Aristotle sur la causalité efficiente de l'intellect divin," in *Proclus, lecteur et interprète des anciens*, pp. 213–25.
Steel, Carlos, "Proclus on the Existence of Evil," *Proceedings of the Boston Area Colloquium in Ancient Philosophy* 14 (1998), pp. 83–102.
Strange, Steven K., "Plotinus on the Nature of Eternity and Time," in *Aristotle in Late Antiquity*, pp. 22–53.
Szabó, Árpád, *The Beginnings of Greek Mathematics* (Dordrecht: Reidel, 1978).

Szlezák, Thomas Alexander, *Platon und Aristoteles in der Nuslehre Plotins* (Basel: Schwabe, 1979).
Szlezák, Thomas Alexander, *Platon und die Schriftlichkeit der Philosophie: Interpretation zu den frühen und mittleren Dialogen* (Berlin: De Gruyter, 1985).
Taormina, Daniela P., "Dalla potenzialità all'attualità: Un' introduzione al problema della memoria in Plotino," in *Plato, Aristotle, or Both?: Dialogues Between Platonism and Aristotelianism in Antiquity*, pp. 139–59.
Tennemann, Wilhelm Gottlieb, *Grundriss der Geschichte der Philosophie für den akademischen Unterricht*, 3rd ed. (Leipzig: Johann Ambrosius Barth, 1820).
Theiler, Willy, *Die Vorbereitung des Neoplatonismus* (Berlin: Weidmann, 1930).
Theiler, Willy, "Einheit und unbegrenzte Zweiheit von Plato bis Plotin," in *Isonomia: Studien zur Gleichheitsvorstellung im Griechischen Denken*, pp. 89–109.
Van Riel, Gerd, "Horizontalism or Verticalism? Proclus vs Plotinus on the Procession of Matter," *Phronesis* 46 (2001), pp. 129–53.
Van Riel, Gerd, "The One, the Henads, and the Principles," in *All from One: A Guide to Proclus*, pp. 73–97.
Van Riel, Gerd, "Proclus on Matter and Physical Necessity," in *Physics and Philosophy of Nature in Greek Neoplatonism*, pp. 231–55.
Vlastos, Gregory, "*Anamnesis* in the *Meno*," in *Plato's Meno in Focus*, pp. 88–111.
Wagner, Michael F., *The Enigmatic Reality of Time: Aristotle, Plotinus, and Today* (Leiden: Brill, 2008).
Wagner, Michael F., "Plotinus' Idealism and the Problem of Matter in *Enneads* VI. 4–5," *Dionysius* 10 (1986), pp. 57–83.
Wagner, Michael F., "Realism and the Foundations of Science in Plotinus," *Ancient Philosophy* 5 (1985), pp. 269–92.
Warren, Edward W., "Imagination in Plotinus," *Classical Quarterly* 16:2 (1966), pp. 277–85.
Warren, Edward W., "Memory in Plotinus," *Classical Quarterly* 15:2 (1965), pp. 252–60.
Watson, Gerard, *Phantasia in Classical Thought* (Galway: Galway University Press, 1988).
Wedin, Michael, *Mind and Imagination in Aristotle* (New Haven: Yale University Press, 1988).
White, Michael J., *The Continuous and the Discrete: Ancient Physical Theories from a Contemporary Perspective* (Oxford: Oxford University Press, 1992).
Zubiri, Xavier, *On Essence* (Washington, DC: Catholic University of America Press, 1980).

Abbreviations

Collections

DK   *Fragmente der Vorsokratiker*
RE   *Paulys Real-Encyclopädie der Classischen Altertumswissenschaft*
SVF   *Stoicorum Veterum Fragmenta*
TP   *Testimonia Platonica (1963)*

Alexander of Aphrodisias

In Met.   *In Aristotelis metaphysica commentaria*

Aristotle

An. post.	*Analytica posterior*
An. priora	*Analytica priora*
Cat.	*Categories*
De an.	*De anima*
De caelo	*De caelo*
De gen. et corr.	*De Generatione et Corruptione*
De lin. insecab.	*De Lineis insecabilibus*
De mem.	*De memoria*
Met.	*Metaphysics*
MM	*Magna Moralia*
NE	*Nicomachean Ethics*
Phys.	*Physics*
Top.	*Topics*

Asclepius

In Met.   *In Metaphysica*

Boethius

De consol.   *De consolatione philosophiae*

Cicero

De ora.   *De oratore*

[Cicero]

Rh. ad Her.   *Rhetorica ad Herennium*

Diogenes Laertius

Vitae phil.   *Vitae philosophorum (Lives of Eminent Philosophers)*

Euclid

Elem.   *Elementa*

Eutocius

In de sphaera et cyl.   *Commentarii in de sphaera et cylindro*

Hermias

In Plat. Phaedr.   *In Platonis Phaedrum scholia*

Hesiod

Theog.   *Theogony*

Iamblichus

De comm. math. sci.   *De communi mathematica scientia*
De myst.   *De mysteriis*
In Nicom. arithm.   *In Nicomachi arithemeticam introductionem*

[Iamblichus]

Theolog. arithm.   *Theologumena arithmeticae*

Nicomachus

In. arithm.   *Introductionis arithmeticae (Arithmētikē eisagōgē)*

Pappus

In Eucl. Elem.   *The Commentary of Pappus on Book X of Euclid's Elements*

Philoponus

In Nicom.   *In Nicomachi arithmeticam introductionem*

Plato

Euthyd.   *Euthydemus*
Gorg.   *Gorgias*
Legg.   *Laws*
Lys.   *Lysis*
Meno   *Meno*
Parm.   *Parmenides*
Phaedo   *Phaedo*
Phaedr.   *Phaedrus*
Phil.   *Philebus*
Prot.   *Protagoras*
Rep.   *Republic*
Soph.   *Sophist*
Stat.   *Statesmen*
Symp.   *Symposium*
Theaet.   *Theaetetus*
Tim.   *Timaeus*

[Plato]

Ep.   *Epistles (Letters)*

Plotinus

Enn.   *Enneads*

Plutarch

De an. procr. in Tim.   *De animae procreatione in Timaeo*
De Is. et Os.   *De Iside et Osiride*

Porphyry

Isag.   *Isagoge*
Sent.   *Sentences*
Vita Plotini   *Vita Plotini*

Proclus

Elem. theol.   *Elementatio theologica*
In Eucl.   *Procli Diadochi in primum Euclidis elementorum librum commentarii*
In Parm.   *Procli in Platonis Parmenidem commentaria*
In Remp.   *Procli Diadochi in Platonis rem publicam commentarii*
In Tim.   *Procli Diadochi in Platonis Timaeum commentaria*
Inst. phys.   *Procli Diodochi Lycii institutio physica*
Theol. Plat.   *Theologia Platonica*

Quintilian

De in. ora.   *De institutione oratoria*

Sextus Empiricus

Adv. Math.   *Adversus Mathematicos*
Hyp. Pyrrh.   *Pyrrhoniae Hypotyposes*

Simplicius

In Cat.   *In Aristotelis categorias*
In Phys.   *In Aristotelis physicorum libros commentaria*

Syrianus

In Met.   *In Metaphysica*

Themistius

In de an.   *In libros Aristotelis de anima*

Theon of Smyrna

Expos. rer. math.   *Expositio rerum mathematicarum*

Theophrastus

Met.   *Metaphysica*

Xenocrates

IP   *Frammenti*
Heinze   *Darstellung der Lehre und Sammlung der Fragmente*

INDEX LOCORUM

Alexander of Aphrodisias
In Met.
55.20: 227
55.20–56.35: 207
56.5–33: 18n14
56.32: 23n26
126.5: 213
510.2–5: 93
562.21: 93
Aristotle
An. post.
71a29–30: 75–6
72a11–4: 162, 196
72a14–24: 171
79a2–3: 173
86a33–5: 170n20
90a31–2: 172
93a16–7: 172
96a20–97b39: 172
An. priora
24b18–20: 76
41a26–7: 211–12
67a21–5: 75–6
Cat.
2a11–4: 19
2a12–3: 189
3a7–8: 189
4a10–11: 189
6a17–9: 197n21
11b17–23: 190
12a26–7: 190
13b36–14a2: 190
De an.
404b22–4: 224n31
404b24–5: 222–3
404b27–8: 21n20
409a4–5: 220
409a6: 27n38, 220, 225
409a10: 214
419a30–1: 86n25
422b34–424a10: 86n25
427b14–5: 135n9
427b14–26: 98
427b14–428a5: 75
428b11: 113n37

429a1–2: 113n37
430a10–25: 139
430a26–7: 208
430a31: 211–12
430b20–1: 208
431a14–7: 75
432a8–10: 114n40
432a8–14: 75
434a22–b9: 47
De caelo
268a6–7: 172
269a14: 162
279a14–7: 176
279a18–28: 51
298b33–299a6: 213
299a8: 218
307a19–24: 213
De gen. et corr.
317a10–2: 225
318b16–7: 190
325b24–32: 214
325b33–4: 213
De lin. insecab.
968a1: 205
968a2: 206
968a3–9: 206
968a9–14: 208
968a14–8: 208–9
968a18–968b4: 209
968b4–5: 210
968b4–12: 210
968b4–21: 223
968b6: 210
968b12–21: 211
968b13–4: 228
968b14–5: 213
968b20: 211
968b23–969a17: 208
969a17–21: 208
969a21–6: 209
969a26–30: 209
969a30–969b3: 209
969b6–12: 211
969b12–6: 219–20
969b19–25: 220

969b31–3: 218
970a8–11: 216
970a19: 216
970a23–4: 218
970a23–33: 217
970b10–3: 218
970b12–3: 228
970b14–6: 218
970b18–20: 218–19
970b23–30: 219
970b29–30: 225
971a4: 219
971a10–6: 219
971a20–2: 219
971b2–3: 219
971b26–31: 219
972a1–6: 219
972a14–27: 219
972a28–30: 219
972a31–2: 219
972b1–4: 219
De mem.
449b6–8: 86
449b24–5: 75
450a12–3: 81
450a29–32: 75
451b1: 76
451b10–452a3: 76
452a1–3: 75
452a17: 76
452b6–7: 83
453a10: 76, 86
453a15: 76
453a28–9: 75
Met.
986a21–6: 18
987b7–13: 124–5
987b14–8: 130
987b20: 222
987b20–3: 56
987b20–988a11: 96
987b24–5: 142
987b26: 21n19, 178, 222
988a13–4: 222
988a14–5: 20n17
992a19–24: 226
992a22: 212
992a23–4: 227
992b13–4: 226
999a1–23: 63
1001a26–7: 120
1003a33: 188
1004a14–6: 189
1004b29: 20n17
1005b11–7: 171
1005b20–1: 107

1011b16–8: 162, 189
1011b19–20: 190
1016b30–1: 27n38
1016b24–6: 27n38
1016b24–31: 225
1020b26–7: 23n28
1024b8–9: 95
1025a30–2: 201
1026a6–19: 133
1029a11–26: 91n4
1035a9–1036a12: 93
1036a8–9: 93
1036a9–12: 12, 137n11
1036a11–2: 93
1036b35–1037a5: 93
1037a4–5: 12, 9
1045a23–4: 92
1045a33–4: 93
1045a33–6: 93
1045b18–9: 92
1049a5: 31
1049a24–36: 185
1052b14–20: 24n29
1053a24: 216
1056a15–6: 189
1059b6–7: 130
1066a7–16: 20n17
1069b21: 37
1069b24–6: 113n38
1070a1: 161
1070a4: 163
1072a26–7: 163
1072a30: 163
1072b14: 163
1072b16: 163
1072b18–24: 163
1072b18–30: 39
1072b24: 163
1073a4–5: 163
1073a19–21: 30n40
1074b34–5: 163
1076a20: 223
1076a20–1: 226
1076a21–2: 225
1078a31–2: 151
1078a31–b5: 151
1078a36–1078b2: 151
1080a–b1: 229
1080a15–b4: 28
1080a30–5: 28
1080b14–6: 225
1080b23–4: 226
1081b14–5: 23n27
1083b23–5: 21n21
1083b36–1084a7: 30n41
1084a12: 30n40

Index Locorum 253

1084a15: 224
1084a12: 30n40
1084a24–5: 30n40
1084a29: 224
1084a35: 20n17
1084b1: 212–13
1084b1–2: 226
1084b5–6: 24
1084b26: 27n38
1084b26–7: 225
1084b29–30: 21n22
1084b36–7: 24n29
1085a6–7: 24n29
1085a7–9: 226
1086a11–2: 222
1088a6–8: 24n29
1088b1: 92
1088b34–5: 15n4
1089a35: 178
1089a35–6: 21n19
1090b21–4: 226
1090b24: 226n34
1090b32–3: 15n4
1091a3–5: 21n19
1091a4: 178
1091b13–6: 20n17
MM
1184b15–7: 75n5
NE
1094a3: 183
Phys.
185a21: 188
185b6: 188
187a17–9: 222
187a31–2: 162
189a29–189b3: 196
189a32–3: 162
190a36–190b1: 189
191a12–4: 189
192a3–5: 189
192a3–6: 91
192a15: 195
192a31: 91n1, 95, 185
194b16–195a3: 126n15
200b12–3: 159n4
200b12–4: 47
201a10–202b29: 44
201a27–9: 166
201b16–26: 112n36
201b20–1: 222
202b30–207a33: 144–5
203a15–6: 21n19
203b23–4: 30n41
204a8–206a8: 144–5
204a23–4: 181
206a14–8: 124n7

206a17–8: 215
206a26–8: 207
206b3–16: 23n27
206b27–33: 207
206b31–2: 224
206b32–3: 30n40, 224
207a1: 207
207a1–2: 144, 172
207a14–5: 217
207a21–5: 144
207a26: 144
207b1–21: 133
208a1: 189
208b30–3: 102n28
209a11–2: 225
212a6: 172
212a20–1: 225
215b19: 217, 229–30
218a19–30: 218
218b1: 35
219b1–2: 172
219b5–9: 30n42
223a6: 218
224a34–224b7: 164
225b10–1: 162
229b26: 189
231a21–9: 217
231a21–b19: 215
231a28–9: 217, 229
232a4: 215
232a24: 217–18
232b24–5: 218
233b16–32: 215
237a5–6: 218
239b11–4: 209
242a49–55: 163
242b71–2: 163
251b19–26: 173
256a2–3: 164
256a13–9: 163
256a13–259b1: 163
259a33: 163
263a4–11: 209
263a13–5: 209
267b17–26: 161
Top.
100a25–7: 76
103b15–6: 67–8
141a26–142b19: 172
141b19–22: 225
143a22–4: 67–8
144a19–22: 67–8
155a28–36: 201
Asclepius
In Met.
77.2–17: 201n25

Augustine
Conf.
XI.13: 33n2
Boethius
De consol.
V.6: 51n23
Cicero
De ora.
II.86.353: 82n15
[Cicero]
Rh. ad Her.
III.23.38-9: 82n15
Diogenes Laertius
Vitae phil.
V.42: 206n2
IX.47: 214
X.31: 22n25
X.59: 228
DK
Anaxagoras B1: 15n5, 50
Archytas B2: 211
Heraclitus B123: 216
Parmenides B7-8: 52
Philolaus A21: 211
Protagoras B1: 151
Zeno B1: 206
Zeno B2-3: 206
Euclid
Elem.
I, def.1: 172, 224, 225, 225n33
I, def. 2: 224, 225-6n33
I, def. 3: 225n33, 226n33
I, def. 4: 224
I, def. 5: 224
I, def. 7: 224
I, 10: 229
V, def. 3: 229
V, def. 4: 229
VII, def. 1: 210n10
X, defs. 1-4: 211
X, defs. 3-4: 133
X, 2: 211n14
Eutocius
In de sphaera et cyl.
I.12.19-20: 217n23
Hermias
In Plat. Phaedr.
102.10-5: 59
Hesiod
Theog.
116: 102n28
Iamblichus
De comm. math. sci.
9.4-12.17: 130, 212

12.18-14.17: 133n5
18.3-4: 26n32
29.22-31.4: 134
55.1-8: 130, 212
In Nicom. arithm.
11.1-26: 19n15
[Iamblichus]
Theolog. arithm.
7.15: 96n17
7.19: 8n8
9.6: 8n8
84.10-1: 224
Longinus
Ars rhet.
314.21: 82n15
Nicomachus
In. arithm.
74.5-6: 210n10
Pappus
In Eucl. Elem.
X, I.1-2: 211
X, I.13.2: 212
Philoponus
In Nicom.
2.56: 130
Plato
Euthyd.
290B-C: 142
Gorg.
448C: 38n6
474D: 150
Legg.
701C: 38n6
716C: 151
894B-895B: 164-5
896D-897A: 183
904A: 38n6
Lys.
216D: 150
Meno
70C-D: 74
72E: 73
73E: 142
80D-E: 73
81B-86C: 138n13
81C-E: 73
82B-85B: 74
82B-85D: 211
97B-98B: 130-1
Parm.
132C-D: 37
137C-142B: 4
138B-140B: 122
142B-155E: 120
142B-157B: 222

142D: 19n15
143A: 15n5, 19n15
144A: 30n41
144B–157B: 4, 23
144D–E: 15n5, 19n15
144E: 36, 122n3
144E–151E: 122
157B–159B: 5
160D: 192
Phaedo
60B: 196–7
72E: 88
72E–78A: 138n13
73C: 73
75E: 73
81A: 74
96E–97B: 23n27
102B: 124
102C–105C: 123n4
103B–E: 196–7
103C–105C: 162
106D: 38n6
Phaedr.
245C: 27n36, 59
245C–246A: 59, 164–5
248D: 148
249B–C: 138n13
249C8–D1: 89
249E: 88
274C–277A: 74
Phil.
14C: 9
15A: 19n15
16C–D: 27, 222
16C–17A: 103
23C–D: 96
24D: 26n34
26C–27C: 186
26E–31A: 222
34B–C: 138n13
56A–57D: 103
63C: 131
64A: 130–1
64C: 129, 151
64E–65A: 150
65D: 148
66A: 38n6
Prot.
345C: 38n6
Rep.
363D: 38n6
379B–C: 200
379C: 186
475E–476A: 195
476A: 10, 36

486D: 74
490C: 74
503C: 74
509A: 108
509B: 4n2, 150, 183, 222
509D–511E: 34n3
510B7: 7
511B–E: 131
511D–E: 131
522C: 132
522C–524E: 130
524B: 131
524B–534B: 73
525A–530D: 103
525C–526D: 132
526A–529B: 156n6
526E: 130
531C–534E: 141
533E–534A: 135
535C: 74
585B–C: 37
611B: 38n6
619E–621B: 66
Soph.
229D5: 214n18
236E–237B: 6
248E–249A: 15n6
249C–D: 77
251D–259D: 165
254B–C: 10, 36
254D–255E: 7n7
254D–257B: 41, 112
254E–255B: 43
255A–B: 47, 112
256A–B: 112
256B: 39, 42
257B–259B: 222
257C–D: 42
259A: 39
263D: 130–1, 137
263D–E: 131
263E: 131n3
Stat.
283B–285C: 211
Symp.
202A: 156
208D: 148
210A–212A: 148
211C: 148
211D: 148
Theaet.
147D: 211n14
147D–148D: 211
176A: 191, 198
176B: 184

189E: 131
191C: 74
191C-E: 74
192A-194D: 74
197C-198A: 74
Tim.
17A: 223
29A-40B: 38
29D: 59
29E: 186
30B-31B: 15n5
30C-D: 16
31B-C: 162
31B-32C: 34n3
34A: 165
34B: 186, 193
34B-37C: 60, 165
35A: 56
37B: 176
37C-38C: 34
37D: 38, 49, 51, 52
37D-E: 43
37D-38C: 37
38B-C: 51
39E: 15n5, 16, 36
47E: 187
47E-49A: 184
49A: 90n1, 98, 177
49A-51B: 11
50C: 90n1
50C-53A: 144
51A: 90n1
52A: 92
52A-D: 90n1, 101, 220n25
52B: 91, 180-1
52B2: 12
53C-D: 213
53C-55C: 103
53C-61C: 169
53D: 213
57D-58A: 220n25
[Plato]
Ep.
II, 312E: 151
Plotinus
Enn.
I.1.13.3-5: 45
I.2.2.20-1: 92
I.3.1-3: 147
I.3.2.10-11: 148
I.3.3.1-10: 141n18
I.3.4: 148
I.3.6.3: 14n2
I.4.1-2: 34
I.4.3.24-8: 48n19

I.4.10.18-9: 100
I.4.10.19-21: 99
I.5.1.3-5: 77
I.5.2.12-3: 50n22
I.5.7.15-6: 51n23
I.5.7.20-2: 77
I.5.7.24-30: 51n24
I.5.8.1-11: 77
I.6: 148
I.6.1.20-54: 153
I.6.1.44-5: 153
I.6.2.13-5: 148
I.6.7.3-4: 149
I.6.7.28-9: 149
I.8: xii, 94, 184
I.8.2.3: 183
I.8.3.1-6: 181
I.8.3.4-5: 111
I.8.3.6-9: 110, 115, 180
I.8.3.7: 181
I.8.3.12-6: 179
I.8.3.13: 92
I.8.3.13-6: 91, 180, 181n4
I.8.3.16: 179
I.8.3.18-20: 182
I.8.3.24: 182
I.8.3.27: 182, 188
I.8.3.38: 181
I.8.4.1: 182
I.8.4.8-9: 183
I.8.4.14-22: 183-4
I.8.4.20-2: 106
I.8.4.23-4: 182, 190-1
I.8.4.27: 180
I.8.4.30-1: 96
I.8.4.31: 91, 180
I.8.5: 91
I.8.5.5: 11, 190-1
I.8.5.6-14: 182
I.8.5.9: 182
I.8.5.9-10: 182
I.8.5.17: 182
I.8.5.21-6: 182
I.8.5.27: 184
I.8.6.17-21: 195
I.8.6.21-48: 196
I.8.6.32: 195
I.8.6.42: 180, 182, 188
I.8.6.43-4: 188
I.8.6.45: 182
I.8.6.54-7: 197n21
I.8.7.2-4: 91, 184
I.8.7.11-2: 110
I.8.7.12-16: 184
I.8.7.17-23: 110

I.8.7.21–3: 184
I.8.8: 65
I.8.8.20: 107
I.8.8.38: 180, 182
I.8.8.39: 182
I.8.8.40: 180
I.8.8.41–2: 182
I.8.8.42: 182
I.8.8.44: 182
I.8.9.6: 182
I.8.9.7: 91, 180, 181
I.8.9.14–26: 180
I.8.9.18: 180
I.8.10.1: 180
I.8.11.1–4: 91
I.8.11.2–3: 190
I.8.11.3: 191
I.8.11.10: 190
I.8.12.1–5: 191
I.8.13.9: 182
I.8.13.14: 182
I.8.14.5: 98
I.8.14.35–6: 12
I.8.14.49–51: 185
I.8.15.1–3: 91, 184, 187
I.8.15.18: 84, 98
I.8.15.28: 88
II.1.1.10–2: 37
II.3.17.23–4: 111
II.4: xii, 21n19, 93n12, 94
II.4.1.1: 90n1
II.4.1.14–8: 93
II.4.2–5: 93
II.4.2.1–2: 94
II.4.3–5: 12
II.4.3.1–2: 180
II.4.3.1–5: 95
II.4.3.2–10: 178
II.4.3.5–13: 106
II.4.3.13: 109
II.4.4.2–7: 94
II.4.4.7–11: 94
II.4.4.8: 10
II.4.4.11–20: 95
II.4.4.14: 95
II.4.4.14–7: 95
II.4.5.6–7: 180
II.4.5.6–15: 180
II.4.5.7: 182
II.4.5.7–9: 110–11
II.4.5.24–37: 111–12
II.4.5.28–30: 26n33
II.4.6.1: 177
II.4.7.7: 39
II.4.8.1: 180

II.4.8.1–3: 92
II.4.8.13–4: 106
II.4.8.23–4: 92
II.4.9.4: 180
II.4.10.5: 181
II.4.10.11: 91, 181
II.4.11.22: 90n1
II.4.11.40–2: 92, 179
II.4.12.33–4: 91, 181
II.4.12.34–7: 92
II.4.13.11: 193
II.4.13.21–3: 190
II.4.13.22–3: 91
II.4.13.26–32: 108
II.4.13.30–1: 180
II.4.13.34–8: 180
II.4.14: 91
II.4.14.24–30: 190
II.4.15: 12
II.4.15.1–2: 179
II.4.15.10: 110, 179
II.4.15.13: 181
II.4.15.17: 92, 179, 189
II.4.15.19–20: 179
II.4.15.22: 179
II.4.15.28–32: 181
II.4.15.33: 92
II.4.15.33–4: 180
II.4.16.1–2: 180
II.4.16.1–3: 109, 180
II.4.16.4: 190
II.4.16.9–10: 92, 189
II.4.16.14–7: 193
II.4.16.16: 183
II.4.16.16–7: 182–3
II.4.16.20: 179
II.4.16.25: 183
II.4.16.26: 179, 180
II.4.16.30: 190
II.5: 94
II.5.3.1–8: 50
II.5.3.15: 177–8
II.5.4: 92
II.5.4–5: 179
II.5.4.3–12: 111
II.5.4.4: 179
II.5.4.11: 179
II.5.4.12: 90, 110
II.5.5.4: 92, 179
II.5.5.9–13: 90
II.9.1.15: 59
II.9.1.34–5: 99
II.9.4.29–31: 36
II.9.7–8: 59
II.9.11.22–3: 97, 99

II.9.12.6–7: 86, 88
II.9.16.43–7: 88
II.9.16.47: 86
III.1.1–3: 214
III.1.3.26: 14n2
III.2.1.30–4: 48n19
III.3.5.17–8: 10
III.4.1.5–12: 178
III.4.1.11–2: 188
III.5.1.32–6: 88
III.5.1.34–5: 86
III.5.6.44: 94
III.5.9.54–5: 92
III.6: 94
III.6.1.36: 107
III.6.2.44: 81
III.6.3.28–30: 79
III.6.4.19–21: 98
III.6.4.44–6: 113
III.6.6.20: 92n10
III.6.7.1–2: 90n1
III.6.7.1–3: 177
III.6.7.3–5: 11
III.6.7.7–8: 110
III.6.7.8: 179
III.6.7.9: 111
III.6.7.11: 107, 115
III.6.7.12: 179
III.6.7.14: 108
III.6.7.16: 108
III.6.7.16–7: 108
III.6.7.21–3: 92
III.6.7.26: 107
III.6.7.30: 92
III.6.8.11–2: 92
III.6.9.34–5: 92
III.6.10.8: 90n1, 177
III.6.10.21–2: 92, 106, 107, 108
III.6.10.25: 107
III.6.11.15–8: 180
III.6.11.18: 92
III.6.11.36–7: 106
III.6.12.26–7: 108
III.6.13.12: 90n1, 177
III.6.13.19: 90n1
III.6.13.46: 91
III.6.14.8: 179
III.6.14.29: 106
III.6.15.7: 109
III.6.15.16–9: 104
III.6.15.17–8: 104n30
III.6.15.18–9: 104n30
III.6.15.27–8: 110
III.6.15.31–2: 108
III.6.17.35–7: 109

III.6.18.19: 106
III.6.18.24–37: 114
III.6.18.25: 114
III.6.18.29–31: 92
III.6.18.30: 180
III.6.18.33–7: 114
III.6.19.14: 92
III.6.19.25: 109
III.7: xi, 33, 34, 34n4, 38n7, 41
III.7.1–6: 77
III.7.1.1: 34n3
III.7.1.1–3: 34
III.7.1.3–9: 33
III.7.1.18–20: 34
III.7.1.20–4: 88
III.7.1.22–3: 86
III.7.2.2: 35
III.7.2.5–9: 35
III.7.2.7–8: 35
III.7.2.9–10: 35
III.7.2.10–5: 37
III.7.2.15–7: 35
III.7.2.17–9: 36
III.7.2.20–36: 40
III.7.2.24–5: 41
III.7.2.25–6: 38
III.7.2.25–9: 37
III.7.2.29: 38
III.7.2.29–31: 41
III.7.2.32–4: 49
III.7.2.34–6: 38
III.7.3.1–4: 37
III.7.3.7–11: 44
III.7.3.7–38: 48
III.7.3.8–11: 7
III.7.3.9–11: 41n11
III.7.3.12–5: 49
III.7.3.15: 49
III.7.3.16–9: 50
III.7.3.17–8: 51n23
III.7.3.19–20: 50
III.7.3.20–1: 49
III.7.3.20–3: 51n23
III.7.3.23: 50
III.7.3.24–5: 50
III.7.3.26–8: 50n22
III.7.3.28–9: 51n23
III.7.3.30: 51n23
III.7.3.34–5: 50
III.7.3.34–8: 52
III.7.3.36: 4
III.7.3.37: 50
III.7.4.2: 49
III.7.4.3–5: 53
III.7.4.8–11: 36

Index Locorum

III.7.4.11–2: 149
III.7.4.12–5: 50
III.7.4.15: 50
III.7.4.17–31: 42
III.7.4.21–2: 42n14
III.7.4.37–43: 52n25
III.7.5.4: 50
III.7.5.9–19: 38n7
III.7.5.11–2: 52
III.7.5.12–8: 38
III.7.5.15–8: 38n8
III.7.5.18: 35
III.7.5.19–23: 51n24
III.7.5.22: 51
III.7.5.22–5: 36
III.7.5.23: 36
III.7.5.23–4: 51
III.7.5.26–7: 52n25
III.7.6.1–4: 49
III.7.6.7–8: 52
III.7.6.12–4: 50
III.7.6.14: 50
III.7.6.29–36: 51
III.7.6.37: 50
III.7.6.37–8: 52n25
III.7.6.49–50: 51
III.7.7–10: 34
III.7.7.3–5: 52
III.7.7.7: 34n3
III.7.7.8: 34n3
III.7.9: 44
III.7.9.1–84: 34
III.7.9.65: 51n23
III.7.10.9: 35
III.7.10.11–2: 34
III.7.11: 26
III.7.11.1–44: 46
III.7.11.2–4: 52n25
III.7.11.4–44: 34
III.7.11.14: 45
III.7.11.15–21: 46
III.7.11.20: 46
III.7.11.36–7: 46
III.7.11.41: 46
III.7.11.43–5: 46
III.7.11.45–6: 45, 47
III.7.11.50: 49
III.7.11.54: 51
III.7.11.55: 50
III.7.11.61–2: 49
III.7.13.23–6: 46
III.7.13.63: 49
III.7.13.68–9: 37
III.7.13.69: 34n3
III.8.4.7–10: 103

III.8.6–7: 9
III.8.9.1–5: 19
III.8.9.3–4: 21n21
III.8.10.1: 9
III.8.10.11: 30
III.8.10.20: 11
III.8.10.28–31: 6
III.8.10.31: 35
III.8.11: 96
III.8.11.36: 10
III.9.1: 17, 36
III.9.1.1–37: 16
III.9.3.7–12: 178
III.9.3.12–3: 188
III.9.4.1–2: 27n35
III.9.5: 95
III.9.6.1–9: 15
IV.2.1.8–9: 55
IV.2.1.12–9: 55
IV.2.1.29–62: 62
IV.2.1.34–8: 66
IV.2.1.41–6: 55
IV.2.1.62–6: 56
IV.2.1.64–6: 62
IV.2.2.10–11: 59
IV.2.2.40–1: 55
IV.2.2.45–7: 56
IV.2.2.52–5: 56
IV.3: xii
IV.3–5: 62
IV.3.2.8–10: 55
IV.3.2.9: 55
IV.3.2.10–24: 62
IV.3.2.50–4: 62
IV.3.2.58: 62
IV.3.2.54–9: 59
IV.3.3.25–6: 56
IV.3.3.29–31: 56
IV.3.5.1–5: 63
IV.3.5.5–6: 55
IV.3.5.9: 68
IV.3.5.9–10: 68
IV.3.5.10–1: 68
IV.3.5.13–4: 58
IV.3.5.14: 69
IV.3.5.17–8: 68
IV.3.6.12: 59
IV.3.6.13: 59
IV.3.6.15–7: 58, 65
IV.3.6.20–3: 60
IV.3.6.25: 55
IV.3.7.22: 64
IV.3.8.2–3: 57
IV.3.8.5–9: 66
IV.3.8.7–9: 66

IV.3.8.12-7: 66
IV.3.8.13: 69
IV.3.8.17-22: 69
IV.3.8.18: 68
IV.3.8.19: 69
IV.3.8.22: 69
IV.3.8.24: 69
IV.3.8.33-4: 51n23
IV.3.8.36-7: 69
IV.3.8.40: 66
IV.3.9.23: 98
IV.3.12: 65
IV.3.12.3: 65-6
IV.3.12.17: 66
IV.3.12.30-5: 65-6
IV.3.12.37-8: 66
IV.3.13.21: 66
IV.3.13.21-2: 51n23
IV.3.13.24: 66
IV.3.15.2: 104
IV.3.20.30: 63
IV.3.20.38-9: 66
IV.3.23.32: 99
IV.3.25-4.12: 72
IV.3.25.14-7: 50
IV.3.25.15: 51n24
IV.3.25.24: 85
IV.3.25.32: 87
IV.3.25.32-3: 85
IV.3.25.33: 85
IV.3.26: 81
IV.3.26.50-4: 81
IV.3.28.16-21: 81
IV.3.29.24: 80
IV.3.30.5-11: 83
IV.3.30.7: 81
IV.3.30.10: 82
IV.3.30.11-6: 83
IV.3.31: 105
IV.3.31.1-20: 104
IV.3.31.2: 83
IV.3.31.6-8: 104
IV.3.31.9-16: 83
IV.3.31.15-8: 105
IV.3.32.6-7: 82
IV.3.32.6-18: 77
IV.3.32.9-18: 89
IV.3.29.16-7: 86
IV.3.29.22-32: 81
IV.3.32.17: 89
IV.4: xii
IV.4.1.1-11: 89
IV.4.1.12: 51n24
IV.4.1.12-4: 77
IV.4.2.1-8: 77

IV.4.3.1-6: 87
IV.4.3.6-8: 83
IV.4.4.1-10: 67
IV.4.4.14-8: 87
IV.4.4.16-7: 79
IV.4.5: 64
IV.4.5-8: 86
IV.4.5.7-8: 85
IV.4.5.11-3: 87
IV.4.5.22-6: 87
IV.4.6.2-3: 77
IV.4.6.8-23: 78
IV.4.12: 86
IV.4.13.13: 78, 82, 99
IV.4.15.2: 77
IV.4.15.2-3: 46
IV.4.15.7: 78
IV.4.15.7-10: 52n25
IV.4.16.10-1: 108
IV.4.17.11-4: 99
IV.4.20.17: 98
IV.4.30.1-2: 78
IV.5.4.22-5: 86n25
IV.5.4.44-5: 86
IV.5.4.45: 86
IV.6: xii, 72, 80, 82n15
IV.6.1.1-3: 79
IV.6.1.3: 80
IV.6.2.1-2: 82
IV.6.2.2-3: 81
IV.6.2.18-9: 79
IV.6.3.5-8: 76
IV.6.3.10: 81
IV.6.3.11-6: 88
IV.6.3.17: 81
IV.6.3.26-35: 91
IV.6.3.27-9: 79
IV.6.3.47-8: 81
IV.6.3.55: 81
IV.6.3.56-7: 79
IV.6.3.58: 81
IV.6.3.59: 86
IV.6.3.63-6: 86
IV.6.3.70-1: 81
IV.6.3.75: 79
IV.7: 78
IV.7.6.37-49: 78
IV.7.6.39-40: 78
IV.7.8.42: 103
IV.7.9.7-9: 48n19
IV.7.9.11: 92
IV.7.10.35: 10
IV.8: 15
IV.8.3.8: 10
IV.8.3.10: 15

Index Locorum

IV.8.3.10–1: 56
IV.8.3.10–3: 60
IV.8.3.12: 66
IV.8.4.25–30: 88
IV.8.6.3–4: 62
IV.8.6.11: 9
IV.9: 57, 60, 62
IV.9.1.5: 56
IV.9.1.10–3: 59
IV.9.1.20: 56
IV.9.2.1–10: 57
IV.9.2.1–12: 64
IV.9.2.20–33: 57
IV.9.2.24–8: 56
IV.9.3.1–4: 57
IV.9.3.10–1: 56
IV.9.3.18: 56
IV.9.3.23–8: 56
IV.9.4: 58
IV.9.4.2–5: 58
IV.9.4.7–8: 58
IV.9.4.9–15: 63
IV.9.4.15–20: 59
IV.9.4.25–6: 55
IV.9.5: 58
IV.9.5.1–3: 58
IV.9.5.4–7: 58
IV.9.5.7–9: 61
IV.9.5.9–12: 64
IV.9.5.16–7: 61
IV.9.5.22–6: 61, 103
IV.9.5.27–8: 61
V.1: 41
V.1.3.22–3: 95
V.1.4.16–35: 41
V.1.4.21: 43
V.1.4.22–4: 42n15
V.1.4.30–4: 15, 41
V.1.4.33–41: 43–4,
V.1.4.35–6: 41n11
V.1.5.13–9: 21n20
V.1.6.6: 9
V.1.6.28: 10
V.1.6.38: 3, 183
V.1.6.53: 20
V.1.7: 96
V.1.7.5–6: 21
V.1.7.10: 9
V.1.7.20: 3
V.1.7.43–8: 178
V.1.10.24–7: 99
V.2.1.8: 10
V.3.2.2–14: 83
V.3.2.9–10: 80
V.3.2.11–4: 88

V.3.3.1–2: 80
V.3.3.5–6: 99
V.3.10.46–7: 5
V.3.10.50–1: 11
V.3.10.51–2: 9
V.3.11: 96
V.3.11.1–16: 9
V.3.13.1: 6
V.3.14.1–3: 6n4
V.3.15.6: 10
V.3.15.7–11: 10
V.3.15.21–2: 50
V.3.15.22: 39
V.3.15.40: 9, 41n11
V.3.16.12–3: 11
V.4.1.5: 4, 40
V.4.1.6: 7
V.4.1.12: 6
V.4.1.36: 9, 30
V.4.2: 96
V.4.2.1–19: 178
V.4.2.3–4: 16
V.4.2.3–5: 5
V.4.2.4–7: 20
V.4.2.7–9: 21, 56
V.4.2.9–12: 10
V.4.2.43–8: 60
V.5.1.17–9: 80
V.5.4.3: 15
V.5.4–5: xi, 14
V.5.4.1: 11
V.5.4.1–19: 18
V.5.4.8–10: 20, 26n34
V.5.4.11: 25
V.5.4.13–4: 30
V.5.4.14–5: 25
V.5.4.16–20: 14
V.5.4.18: 15
V.5.4.20–38: 18
V.5.4.24: 25
V.5.4.24–5: 21n21
V.5.4.27–9: 28
V.5.4.29–33: 24
V.5.4.33–5: 29
V.5.5.2–4: 26n32
V.5.5.11–12: 15
V.5.5.22: 15
V.5.6.17–9: 99
V.5.6.24: 6
V.5.12.11–4: 88n26
V.6.2.7–16: 82
V.6.3.15–6: 216
V.6.5.11: 110
V.6.5.12–5: 108
V.7.1.1–5: 67

V.7.1.7–12: 69
V.7.1.18–21: 70
V.7.1.23: 70
V.7.2.13–4: 64
V.7.2.14–6: 65
V.7.2.16–7: 69
V.7.3: 63
V.7.3.7–13: 70
V.7.3.10–1: 56
V.7.3.13–23: 69
V.7.3.21–2: 69
V.8.1.1: 10
V.8.3.9: 95
V.8.3.11: 42
V.8.4.6–11: 42
V.8.7.22–3: 110, 181
V.8.7.40–1: 148
V.8.13.22: 149
V.9.3: 94
V.9.4.10–2: 95–6
V.9.5.32: 88
V.9.7.6–18: 15
V.9.9.4: 36
V.9.9.7: 10
V.9.10.8–9: 43
V.9.11.24–5: 103
V.9.12.3–4: 67
V.9.12.6: 64
V.9.12.8–11: 64
V.9.12.9–10: 68
V.9.13.4–7: 58
V.9.13.5: 67
V.9.13.6: 67
VI.1–3: 38n7, 41
VI.1.1–30: 34
VI.1.5.15–7: 51n23
VI.1.6.3–4: 23n28
VI.2.6.9–12: 48n19
VI.2.7.4–5: 47
VI.2.7–8: 41
VI.2.7.16–7: 45
VI.2.7.24: 45
VI.2.7.26: 45
VI.2.7.30: 41n11
VI.2.8.8–13: 48
VI.2.8.9–10: 50n22
VI.2.8.14: 45
VI.2.8.20–4: 44
VI.2.8.25–49: 7n7, 44
VI.2.17.25: 5
VI.2.17.25–9: 46
VI.2.18.8–9: 45
VI.2.21.54–5: 52n25
VI.3.7.21–2: 48n19
VI.3.12.2–6: 108

VI.3.12.3: 108
VI.3.12.9–13: 27
VI.3.14.20–6: 104
VI.3.16.14–5: 95, 104
VI.3.16.20–1: 14n2
VI.3.16.20–3: 103
VI.3.18.13: 22
VI.3.18.22–4: 51n23
VI.3.20.42: 40
VI.3.23.1–5: 46
VI.3.28.10–1: 23
VI.4.11.9–10: 20
VI.4.2.30–1: 23
VI.5.4.17–20: 9
VI.5.6.1–4: 9
VI.5.8.15–22: 92
VI.5.11.16–7: 52n25
VI.6: xi, 14, 29
IV.6.1.1–3: 79
VI.6.1.2: 20
VI.6.1.10–1: 20
VI.6.1.10–29: 18
VI.6.1.19–20: 27
VI.6.2: 30n41
VI.6.2–3: 21n23
VI.6.3.3ff: 92
VI.6.3.3–10: 8
VI.6.3.7–9: 21
VI.6.3.15–6: 180
VI.6.3.29: 21, 108
VI.6.3.32: 113
VI.6.3.32–43: 113
VI.6.4: 16
VI.6.4–16: 21n23
VI.6.4.4: 19n15
VI.6.5.4: 23
VI.6.5.6: 19n15
VI.6.5.29–34: 23
VI.6.5.31: 25
VI.6.5.36–8: 19
VI.6.5.37–8: 19n15
VI.6.5.43–6: 24
VI.6.5.49: 24
VI.6.7.4: 15
VI.6.8: 17
VI.6.8.15–22: 15
VI.6.9.13–4: 22n25
VI.6.9.14–24: 16
VI.6.9.27–31: 15
VI.6.9.29: 17n11
VI.6.9.29–31: 16, 22n24
VI.6.9.32–5: 16
VI.6.9.33: 19n15
VI.6.9.34–5: 14
VI.6.9.35–6: 15

Index Locorum **263**

VI.6.9.35–7: 15n3
VI.6.9.35–9: 17n12
VI.6.9.39–40: 17n11
VI.6.10.1–4: 29
VI.6.10.3–4: 19n15
VI.6.10.13: 14n2
VI.6.10.19: 19n15, 108
VI.6.11.6–7: 25
VI.6.11.10–33: 25
VI.6.11.16–24: 19n15
VI.6.11.19: 18
VI.6.11.24–33: 26
VI.6.12.1: 19n15
VI.6.13.9–11: 21
VI.6.13.20: 31
VI.6.13.50–1: 17
VI.6.13.52–3: 19n15
VI.6.14.15–9: 23
VI.6.14.27–8: 24
VI.6.15.2–3: 15
VI.6.15.8–18: 17
VI.6.15.16: 17
VI.6.15.19–20: 20
VI.6.15.24: 24
VI.6.15.29–30: 16n9
VI.6.15.29–35: 27
VI.6.15.34–5: 27n36
VI.6.15.35–6: 30
VI.6.15.37–42: 31
VI.6.16: 9
VI.6.16.18: 31
VI.6.16.25–6: 14
VI.6.16.28–37: 31
VI.6.16.34: 31
VI.6.16.41–2: 24
VI.6.16.45: 21n20
VI.6.16.48: 17
VI.6.16.51: 31
VI.6.17–8: 21n23
VI.6.17–8.6: 30n41
VI.6.17.3: 30
VI.6.17.14–5: 216
VI.6.17.36: 36
VI.6.18.4: 50
VI.6.18.5–6: 30n41
VI.6.18.12–8: 48n19
VI.6.18.17–9: 17n12
VI.6.18.18–9: 26n15
VI.6.18.31–3: 15
VI.7.1.48–57: 50n22
VI.7.8.17–8: 7n6
VI.7.12.18: 7
VI.7.13: 9
VI.7.13.1: 41
VI.7.13.4–8: 45n17

VI.7.13.9: 27
VI.7.13.11–2: 43
VI.7.13.30: 45
VI.7.13.39–57: 45
VI.7.13.44–5: 47
VI.7.13.46–7: 47
VI.7.13.54–5: 43
VI.7.14.11–2: 13
VI.7.14.12: 42
VI.7.15.25: 10
VI.7.16.14: 21
VI.7.16.14–24: 22
VI.7.17.5: 3
VI.7.17.10: 6n5
VI.7.17.14–21: 22
VI.7.17.15–6: 6, 13
VI.7.17.39: 10
VI.7.22.20–1: 4n2
VI.7.23.6–8: 12
VI.7.27.11–2: 11
VI.7.28.11: 12
VI.7.28.12: 183
VI.7.32.15: 110
VI.7.32.31: 9
VI.7.33.21: 110
VI.7.38.11: 110
VI.7.39.4–6: 41n11
VI.7.41.28–9: 7
VI.8.2.17: 99–100
VI.8.4.4–41: 100
VI.8.4.5–7: 7
VI.8.4.6–7: 100
VI.8.6.12–3: 56–7
VI.8.7.35–6: 4
VI.8.8.6: 6
VI.8.8.9: 3, 183
VI.8.9.28: 4n2
VI.8.9.35–50: 6
VI.8.10.26: 7
VI.8.11: 100
VI.8.11.15–22: 100–1
VI.8.13.46–7: 101
VI.8.14.3–4: 39
VI.8.14.30: 6
VI.8.17.14: 10
VI.8.17.27: 9
VI.8.18.7–30: 155
VI.8.20.9–27: 6n5
VI.8.20.14: 6n5
VI.8.20.19: 41n12
VI.8.20.37: 9
VI.8.21.25: 5
VI.8.21.30–3: 4
VI.9.1.4–5: 10
VI.9.2.29–45: 10

264 Index Locorum

VI.9.2.47: 4
VI.9.3.33–4: 9
VI.9.3.37–8: 4
VI.9.3.40: 5
VI.9.5.14: 10
VI.9.5.16: 10
VI.9.5.30: 3
VI.9.5.38: 5
VI.9.6.7–8: 9
VI.9.8.1–8: 155
VI.9.8.25: 13
VI.9.9.1: 183
VI.9.9.1–2: 3
VI.9.9.14–6: 49
VI.9.11.35: 5
VI.9.11.42: 4n2
VI.9.11.51: 3, 184

Plutarch
De an. procr. in Tim.
1012d–f: 47
De Is. et Os.
75: 8n8

Porphyry
Isag.
10: 200–1
Sent.
19.9: 201n25
20: 11
31: 201n25
34: 201n25
42.14: 201n25
43.23: 201n25
44.29: 201n25
45: 201n25
47: 201n25
Vita Plotini
4.45: 93n12
24.46: 93n12

Ptolemy
Almagest
6.3–11: 130

Proclus
De mal. subs.
2.16–7: 198
4.31: 198
4.34: 198
5.14–7.12: 194
6.4–5: 197
6.19–21: 197
6.21–2: 197
7.1 sqq.: 191
7.28: 191
7.28–31: 192
7.28–42: 193
7.34–9: 194–5
8.13–28: 192

9.5–13: 191
9.6: 199
9.7: 198
9.7–10: 198
9.12: 196
9.13–4: 198–9
9.14: 196
10.8: 199
10.12–4: 191
18.17: 192
23–9: 198
27.29: 192
28: 199
29.16–7: 186
29.17–21: 187–8
29.20–1: 185
30.4–6: 185
30.11–2: 185
30.14–9: 185
31.2: 185, 192
31.5–24: 186
31.11: 186
32.2: 186
32.3–4: 194
32.5: 193
32.10: 188
32.14: 194
32.17–9: 188
33.29: 186
34.9–14: 186
35.2: 188
35.8: 185
36.4: 186–7
36.13–6: 197
36.15–6: 187
36.26–7: 187
36.27: 188
37.2–3: 187
37.9–10: 185, 191, 196
37.11–2: 196
37.12–3: 196
37.13–5: 192
37.14–5: 196
37.18: 197
37.19–20: 197
37.22–4: 197
38.3–4: 191
38.3–5: 187
38.4: 195
38.5–6: 187
38.9: 191, 195, 198
38.9–13: 191
38.13–4: 191
38.19–25: 194
38.25–8: 193
38.29: 195

39.39–42: 192
42.7–8: 199
42.17–8: 199
43–4: 200
45.15: 201
46.12: 192
47–9: 200
47.6: 200
47.14: 200
48.9–16: 200
48.17: 192
49.2–9: 200
49.6–7: 200
49.9–10: 202
49.10–1: 202
49.15: 192, 199
50.1–3: 200
50.2–3: 201
50.3–7: 200
50.10: 200
50.11–8: 200
50.20–2: 202
50.25–9: 200
50.29: 201
50.29–31: 202
50.36–41: 199
51.1–4: 201
51.10–9: 194
51.25: 192
51.25–6: 192
51.34–5: 192
52.2–3: 192
52.3–8: 193
52.7–10: 198
52.8: 199
52.24–6: 199
53.1–4: 199
53.5: 197
53.10–1: 201–2
53.14–5: 199
54.1: 194
54.3: 198
54.5: 199
54.12–7: 198
54.17–21: 198
54.20–1: 199
55: 198
61.6: 196
61.7: 196
Elem. theol.
1, 2.1: 125
5, 4.19–6.21: 122
7, 8.1–28: 126
12, 14.15–6: 125
14: 164
16, 25: 164

23, 26.22: 126n14
23, 26.23–4: 126
23, 26.26: 125n13
24, 28.8–9: 126
24, 28.8–20: 125n11
24, 28.14: 126
24, 28.18–9: 127
24, 28.19–20: 127
24, 28.20: 127
31–9, 34.28–42.7: 27n39, 198
90–3: 133
92, 82.23–35: 194
103: 198
113–65, 100.5–44.8: 145n20
In Eucl.
3.1: 131–2
3.1–7: 129, 212
3.7–14: 129
3.12: 133
3.17: 215
4.6–7: 131
4.19: 132
5.2: 129
5.18: 133, 145
6.7–19: 133
6.7–7.12: 132
6.21: 133
7.1–2: 152
7.1–5: 157
8.4: 152n4
9.11–9: 156
10.16–7: 132
10.23: 129
11.15: 132
12.3–4: 131
12.14: 131, 132
13.22: 132
14.10–5: 155
15.5–6: 137
15.12–3: 144
16.15–6: 136
16.22: 131
17.4–6: 142
18.20–8: 138
20.10–1: 156n6
20.27–21.2: 151
21.4–13: 148
21.21: 147
21.21–4: 141
21.23: 151
22.17–23.11: 175
24.21–7: 156
25.17: 150
26.10–27.16: 151, 151–2
26.23–27.1: 152
27.2–6: 152

27.3–4: 156
27.6–10: 152
27.13–4: 156
29.1: 150
31.2–3: 156–7
32.7–20: 141
33.5–7: 134
34.11–9: 155
35.3–6: 154
35.21–36.7: 134
42.9–43.21: 141
45.5–15: 134–5
46.3–47.6: 138
49.1–4: 151
49.5: 178
49.25: 137
51.9–20: 178
51.9–56.22: 134–5
51.13–20: 137
51.14–6: 137
51.19: 141
51.20–2: 139n16
51.20–52.3: 220n25
51.21: 27n37
52.2: 140
52.3–12: 139
52.8: 129
52.8–12: 140
52.8–53.5: 212
52.22: 140, 143
53.20–2: 178
54.6–8: 136
54.8–9: 135–6
54.9–10: 137
54.27–55.1: 140
55.3: 140
55.12–3: 143
55.18: 132
55.23–56.4: 141
55.23–56.22: 143
56.1: 143
56.12: 141
56.13: 141
56.15–8: 142
56.17–8: 139
57.5: 135
59.7–8: 134
61.2–3: 153
62.24: 132
62.25–6: 132
68.6–10: 168
70.19–71.24: 168
71.24–73.18: 167
73.21–2: 159
75.14–5: 156

76.4–77.2: 152, 156
76.6–77.2: 169
76.8: 170n18
77.7–81.22: 171
78.18–79.2: 139
78.20–5: 139n15
79.3–9: 171
85.1–13: 224
85.1–96.15: 134
88.2–7: 220n25
93.18–9: 137
95.21: 225
95.22: 27n38
119.4–6: 157
121.4–7: 142
131.1–2: 150
131.21–132.17: 133
137.4–8: 153
141.2–13: 82n15
141.4–6: 154
141.4–13: 142–3
141.13–142.2: 153
142.5–7: 145
142.9–12: 141
150.10–6: 155
178.1–184.29: 156, 171
185.8–15: 27n37
185.22–187.3: 138
202.9–25: 173
203.1–205.12: 170n20
213.14–8: 154
277.25–278.10: 217
278.2–10: 229
278.10–9: 216
284.17–286.11: 144
285.7–10: 143–4
285.15: 146
285.16–7: 146
285.17–8: 146
285.18–9: 145
285.21: 135
285.26–286.1: 146
286.1–4: 146
286.10–1: 146
291.6–10: 155
In Parm.
741.3: 197
829.17–8: 200
830.1–7: 186
831.5–9: 186
880.22–5: 19n15
910.26–34: 126n15
950.31–951.15: 149
951.14–5: 149
1069.5–9: 127

In Remp.
I.37.3–8: 186
I.37.23: 186
I.38.3–9: 200
I.38.6: 201
I.38.11: 201
I.38.24: 201
I.38.25–6: 199
I.72.9–13: 150
I.72.14–5: 152n4
I.88.11–6: 21n23
I.90.22–8: 125n13
I.140.2: 21n23
I.235.13–21: 130–1
I.235.18–9: 138
I.259.14–7: 125n11
I.262.25–9: 131n3
I.271.20–6: 125n11
I.283.26–284.2: 131
II.27.1–29.4: 215
II.277.18–9: 135 135
In Tim.
I.28.7–11: 155
I.39.30–40.4: 125n13
I.87.28–30: 21n23
I.211.28–212.1: 21n23
I.235.32–238.5: 169
I.236.15: 169
I.236.21–2: 176
I.264.20–265.9: 169
I.274.25–30: 21n23
I.298.29–31: 125n12
I.349.6–350.1: 175n27
I.374.5–375.5: 201n25
I.375.14–8: 201n25
I.427.6–20: 17n10
I.453.14–21: 124n7
II.13.19–16.14: 162
II.23.13–4: 175
II.45.27–46.3: 125n11
II.92.13–95.11: 165
II.93.30–94.15: 169
II.94.5–6: 161–2
II.105.19–20: 125n11
II.215.22–4: 21n23
II.245.23–246.4: 215
III.8.22–4: 33n2
III.9.2–15: 165
III.15.11–16.1: 38n7
III.18.1–2: 21n23
III.204.18–21: 125n11
Inst. phys.
Def.I.1: 166
Def.I.1–3: 176
Def.I.4: 176

Def.I.6: 166
I.1: 159
I.1–4: 164
I.1–31: 159
I.2: 159
I.5: 166, 215
I.8: 159, 166
I.10: 159
I.10–1: 171
I.11: 159
I.12–3: 145n19, 160
I.12–8: 160
I.13: 171
I.17: 160
I.18: 159
I.19: 161n8
I.20: 171
I.22: 171
I.23: 175
I.25: 171
I.27: 171
I.28: 159
I.29: 171
I.31: 159, 161, 161n8, 171, 175
Def.II.1–6: 171
Def.II.6: 165
Def.II.10: 161
Def.II.11: 162
Def.II.11–2: 162
Def.II.13: 160, 166, 172, 176
II.1–13: 161
II.1–15: 159
II.2: 165
II.3: 165
II.4: 161–2
II.5: 160–1
II.6: 159, 165
II.6–15: 145n19
II.9: 176
II.9–13: 160
II.10: 160
II.14: 166
II.14–21: 161
II.15: 159, 161
II.16: 160n6, 173
II.16–21: 159
II.17: 159, 162, 173
II.18: 159, 163, 165
II.19: 159, 163, 164
II.19–20: 164
II.21: 161, 163, 166, 167, 171, 173
58.27: 163
Theol. Plat.
I.14.60.12–23: 165
I.18.82.8: 200

I.18.83.13–6: 199
I.18.85.7: 201
I.18.85.8: 192
I.18.86.15: 192
I.18.86.17: 201
I.18.86.20–1: 191
I.50.18–9: 16n9
II.1–3: xii
II.1.3.12: 122
II.1.3.12–14.16: 119
II.1.4.8: 123
II.1.4.8–9.5: 119
II.1.4.9–21: 119
II.1.4.22–6.2: 119
II.1.5.3–9: 124
II.1.5.10: 124
II.1.6.3–18: 120
II.1.6.19–7.7: 120
II.1.6.20: 123
II.1.6.22–61.9: 126n15
II.1.7.8–8.4: 120
II.1.8.5: 123
II.1.8.5–14: 120
II.1.8.15: 123
II.1.8.15–9.2: 120
II.1.9.5: 127
II.1.9.5–11: 120
II.1.9.5–11.25: 120
II.1.9.12–5: 121
II.1.9.16–21: 121
II.1.9.22–10.3: 121
II.1.10.4–13: 121
II.1.10.14–20: 121
II.1.10.19: 127
II.1.10.21–5: 121
II.1.11.1–7: 121
II.1.11.8–17: 121
II.1.11.25–14.16: 122
II.1.12.1: 122
II.1.14.8–16: 122
II.1.14.10–1: 125
II.1.23.4–5: 125n11
II.2.16.22: 126
II.2.18.2–4: 128
II.2.19.16–20: 126
II.2.21.15–6: 126
II.2.22.5–7: 126
II.2.22.8–9: 128
II.2.22.18–9: 126
II.2.22.21: 127
II.2.22.22–3: 126
II.2.22.25–23.2: 126
II.2.23.3–4: 126
II.2.23.6–8: 128
II.2.23.9–12: 126

II.3.23.15–30.26: 125
II.3.25.24: 127
II.3.26.3: 127
II.3.30.22–4: 127
II.3.30.23: 125
II.5.37.5–39.5: 127
II.60.22–61.9: 17n12
III.5.17.14–19.30: 145n20
III.8.30.15–34.19: 145
III.10.40.12: 150
III.11.43.1–44.20: 150
III.11.43.13–4: 152
III.11.43.15: 152n4
III.11.44.2–5: 150
III.11.44.9: 150–1
III.11.44.13: 150
III.11.44.14–6: 151

Quintilian
De in. ora.
XI.2.21: 82n15
XI.2.29–30: 82n15

Sextus Empiricus
Adv. Math.
X.253: 230
X.261: 21n19, 222
X.274–6: 21n19
X.276: 227
X.278: 224

Simplicius
In Cat.
418.16–7: 201n25
In Phys.
10.35–11.3: 17n2, 126n15
140.6–18: 214, 217
140.34–141.8: 207
225.22–226.16: 91n4
230.34–231.1: 127n16
255.17–256.13: 92n9
454.9–16: 23n26
454.19–455.11: 227
454.19–455.14: 222
454.28: 23n26
503.10–8: 222
800.10–1: 218

Syrianus
In Met.
45.18–24: 127
81.36–82.2: 131
109.8–10: 126
143.16: 214
183.24–5: 19n15
184.8–15: 199
186.30–6: 15n3
453.22–455.14: 207

SVF
I.484: 78n9
II.343: 78n9
Themistius
In de an.
109.18–21: 46
110.5: 51n23
Theon of Smyrna
Expos. rer. math.
18.3: 28
18.22: 210n10
19.6–7: 210n10
20.5–7: 210n10
21.14–6: 19n15
Theophrastus
Met.
11b2–7: 222
TP
49–55: 222
68–72: 223

Xenocrates
Darstellung
IP *Frammenti*
21: 209n8
119: 214
123–47: 213
128: 213
130: 215
133: 214
135: 213
136: 213
137: 214
139: 214, 217
144: 213, 214, 215
145: 214
146: 215
60: 21n20

INDEX

activity, 50, 78
   absence of, 92, 179, 198–9
   of the imagination, 139-43, 146
   in the intellect, 9, 16–17, 31, 41, 43–5, 52, 66
   of the prime mover, 163, 166
addition, 23, 23n27, 31, 108, 124, 133, 206–7
aesthetics, 131, 147–57
affection, 42, 57, 64, 81, 121
Alexander of Aphrodisias, 209, 213. *See also* index locorum
aporia, 16, 86, 226–7
Aristotle, 16, 24, 28, 31, 37, 67, 124, 139, 144–5, 189–92, 195–7, 205–7. *See also* index locorum
   concept of time in, 34, 51n23, 218
   on mathematics, 130, 133, 135, 137, 140, 151, 213
   on matter, 12, 90–4, 107, 177, 185
   on memory and recollection, 75–6, 80–1, 83, 86
   methodology of, 34, 170–2, 188
   physics of, 158–9, 162–5, 169–70, 175–6
arithmetic, 9, 26n34, 132–4, 167, 174, 210–11, 221–4, 229

beauty, 65, 88, 147–57, 182
body, 54–8, 62–4, 66, 81, 88, 100, 182, 184
   and matter, 11, 92, 139
   and motion, 161–4, 166–7, 174, 176, 215, 225

causation, 38–9, 125–6, 140, 156–7, 169, 172–4
   of evil, 183, 186–7, 189, 200–1
   first, 5, 122, 161, 164, 195
commensurability, 31, 133, 138, 153, 175, 206, 210–12, 215, 219, 228–30
complexity, 3–4, 69, 129–30, 152, 167
cosmos
   intelligible, 9–10, 16–17, 22, 35–8, 41, 45, 47, 94, 102, 112
   physical, 58–60, 76, 114, 157, 163–4, 169, 174–6, 215

deficiency, 9–11, 50, 86, 108, 182–4, 199, 201, 203
difference, 50, 105–6, 109–11, 222
   absolute, 7, 11, 109

individual, 63–8, 95
   logical, 70–1
   principle of, 8, 210
   specific, 60, 172
dignity, 35, 67
discursive reason, 85–6, 99, 102, 196
   and mathematical objects, 129, 132, 135–8, 140–3, 153–5
division, 11, 23, 64, 114, 124, 146, 207–9

elements, 10, 119, 160, 165–9, 208–9, 213–14, 224, 230
eternity, 4, 33–53, 77, 111
   and motion, 159, 161–6, 166, 173
Euclid, 61, 132, 153, 157, 168, 170, 206, 211, 224–5, 229. *See also* index locorum
evil, 11–12, 46, 65, 88, 91, 105, 110–11, 177–203

forgetting, 74, 77, 81, 89

Geminus, 173, 216
geometry, 27, 61–2, 66, 93–4, 103–4, 131–46, 168–70, 173–6, 210–15
   beauty in, 153–5

henad, 23–6, 27n38, 28–9, 31, 145n20

Iamblichus, 130, 150, 201n25. *See also* index locorum
identity, 6, 20, 23, 41n12, 58, 120–1, 133, 207, 222
   and matter, 106–7, 109
   and motion, 44–5, 161–2
   self-, 4, 49, 73, 99
imagination, 75, 97–104, 113–15, 153–5, 212
   irrationality of, 84, 97
   and mathematics, 129–46, 178
   and memory, 81–2
   as mirror, 82–4, 98, 142–3
imitation, 43, 58, 69, 88, 94, 125, 155–6
incommensurability. *See* commensurability
indefinite dyad, 13, 20, 96–7, 105, 108–9, 222, 227
infinity, 119, 123–4, 144, 146, 163, 216
   actual and potential, 30, 63, 69, 160
irrationality, 84, 93, 98, 103, 133, 183, 211–12

271

kinematic construction, 26-9, 139, 143, 173

living being, 16-17, 34, 47, 69

magnitude, 124, 134, 136, 144, 166, 174-6, 205-30
mathematical objects, 129-32, 151-2, 155, 178, 187, 223
matter
   and evil, 11-12, 65, 91, 105-6, 110-11, 177-203
   geometrical, 137-8, 141-3, 178, 220
   intelligible, 12, 90-115, 139, 154, 177-8, 187
   as negativity, 12, 91, 177, 187, 189
   physical, 12, 109
memory, 72-89, 102, 148
metaphor, 5, 46, 68, 96, 146, 179, 181-2
motion, 43, 86, 111-15, 172-6, 209, 218, 220
   and imagination, 138-9, 143-4, 159-61
   of the intellect, 21-2, 44-6
   of the prime mover, 161-5
movement. *See* motion

negation, 7, 11-12, 21-2, 91, 92n7, 189
non-contradiction, 6, 57, 62, 162, 189, 196
number, 8-9, 14-32, 63, 120, 124, 131-4, 142, 208-12, 220-30

order of being, 17, 56, 77, 128, 184, 222

paradox, 5-8, 12, 73, 107-9
Parmenides, 52, 222
passive intellect, 139-40, 142
Philoponus, 139, 213. *See also* index locorum
Plato. *See* index locorum
point, 27, 50, 134, 172, 217-20, 225-6
Porphyry, 34n3, 80, 127n16, 200, 201n25, 213-14, 217. *See also* index locorum
predication, 5-6, 23, 35-41, 44, 189-90
prime mover, 161-7, 173
Pythagoreanism, 8, 35, 52, 54, 56, 125, 132, 174, 211, 214, 225

recollection, 72-89, 138
reductio ad absurdum, 159, 167, 176

sense-perception, 57, 74-6, 78-81, 98-9, 134-5, 155
Sextus Empiricus, 78, 224, 227, 230. *See also* index locorum
simplicity, 3-4, 22, 51, 68, 97, 130, 153-4, 165-6
Simplicius, 135, 139, 227.
   See also index locorum
soul, 47-8, 54-71
   higher and lower, 77, 83, 89, 104-5, 178, 180
   individual, 74
   production of, 45-6
   triple movement of, 87-9
   world, 76
subcontrariety, 195-203
symmetry, 122, 150-3
Syrianus, 131, 201n25. *See also* index locorum

Themistius, 135, 213. *See also* index locorum
time, 4, 26, 33-53, 160, 172-3, 176, 218
   and matter, 107, 111
   and memory, 77
triadic structure, 123, 150, 198
   of being-intellect-life, 15-16
   of form-matter-privation, 189-90
   of unparticipated-participated-participating, 125-7

unity
   absolute, 9, 127
   complex, 10, 44
   monadic, 123
   multiple, 40, 49, 123
   synthetic, 11, 15, 22, 54, 95, 214
   the unlimited, 133, 145, 150, 179, 186, 222-3

writing, 74, 79

Xenocrates, 206, 209, 212-15, 220-1, 226, 228-9. *See also* index locorum